Making Sense of Statistics in Psychology

A Second-Level Course

BRIAN S. EVERITT

Professor of Statistics in Behavioural Science,
Institute of Psychiatry, London

Oxford   New York   Tokyo

OXFORD UNIVERSITY PRESS

1996

Oxford University Press, Walton Street, Oxford OX2 6DP
Oxford   New York
Athens   Auckland   Bangkok   Bombay
Calcutta   Cape Town   Dar es Salaam   Delhi
Florence   Hong Kong   Istanbul   Karachi
Kuala Lumpur   Madras   Madrid   Melbourne
Mexico City   Nairobi   Paris   Singapore
Taipei   Tokyo   Toronto
and associated companies in
Berlin   Ibadan

Oxford is a trade mark of Oxford University Press

Published in the United States
by Oxford University Press Inc., New York

A catalogue record for this book is available from the British Library

Library of Congress Cataloging in Publication Data
Everitt, Brian.
Making sense of statistics in psychology: a second-level course/
Brian S. Everitt.
Includes bibliographical references and index.
1. Psychometrics. 2. Psychology—Mathematical models.
3. Psychology—Data processing. I. Title.
BF39.E932   1996   150'. 1'5195— –dc20   96-7622

ISBN 0   19 852366 1 (Hbk)
ISBN 0   19 852365 3 (Pbk)

Typeset by EXPO Holdings, Malaysia
Printed and bound in Great Britain by
Bookcraft (Bath) Ltd., Midsomer Norton, Somerset

Preface

Psychologists (and even those attempting to become psychologists) need little persuasion about the importance of statistics in both the design and analysis of psychological investigations. As a result, almost all undergraduate psychology students are exposed to an introductory statistics course during their first year at college. The topics covered in such a course may vary from place to place, but will almost certainly include **descriptive statistics, correlation, simple regression, elementary significance tests, *P*-values** and **confidence intervals**. In addition, many introductory courses will describe some **non-parametric tests** and begin to explore **analysis of variance**. Laudable and necessary as such courses are, they represent only the first step in equipping students with enough knowledge of statistics to ensure that they have a reasonable chance of progressing to become proficient, creative, influential and even useful psychologists. Consequently, in their second and third years (and possibly in later postgraduate studies), many psychology students will be encouraged to learn more about statistics and, equally importantly, how to apply statistical methods in a sensible fashion. It is to these students that this book is aimed and it is hoped that the following features of the text will help it reach its target:

1. It is **problem** and **data** driven. The central theme is that statistics is about solving problems; data relevant to these problems is collected and analysed to provide useful answers. To this end, the book contains a large number of real data sets arising from real problems. Numerical examples of the type that involve a comparison of the skiing activities of belly dancers and politicians are avoided at all costs.

2. Mathematical details are almost exclusively confined to the displays. For the mathematically challenged, the most difficult of these displays can be regarded as 'black boxes' and largely ignored; attempting to understand the 'input' to and 'output' from the black box will be more important than understanding the minutiae of what takes place within the box. For those students with less anxiety about mathematics, study of the relevant mathematical material (which sometimes includes matrices and vectors) will help in the basic understanding of a technique.

3. Arithmetical details of techniques are noticeable largely by their absence. Although many statistical methods require considerable amounts of arithmetic for their application, the burden of actually performing the necessary calculations has been almost entirely removed by the development of powerful and cheap personal computers and the introduction of statistical software packages. It is assumed that most students will be using such tools for their own analyses. (In the few instances where it is considered that a little arithmetic might be helpful, details will again largely be confined to the appropriate display.)

4. The statistical topics most relevant and important for today's psychologist are covered. The psychology student graduating with an awareness of how to apply the

methods described in this book will be well equipped to deal with most aspects of data analysis encountered in the real world.

5. There are many challenging data sets both in the text and in the exercises provided at the end of each chapter. (Answers, or hints to providing answers, to many of the exercises are given in an Appendix.)

6. A useful glossary is provided to remind students about the most important topics that they will have covered in their introductory course.

7. The aim of the book is to develop a more skilful and realistic approach to data analysis and to overcome an inflexible reliability on P-values.

One of the questions that the author considered long and hard during the preparation of this text was what information should be provided about software. For example, should detailed SPSS or MINITAB codes be included in each chapter, or would a simple appendix listing a variety of packages suffice? However, the final decision was not to include *any* detailed information about software, for the following reasons:

1. Such material quickly becomes dated.

2. The author is probably less computer literate than most of his potential readers.

3. Most computing is now performed in a Windows environment where 'code' as such is largely replaced by using a mouse to click on to menus to provide particular analyses.

Therefore, references to particular pieces of software are largely confined to the more specialized packages needed to apply some of the more exotic methods described in particular chapters.

Another notable absentee from the text is the usual appendix of statistical tables; the necessity for such tables has been largely superseded by the automatic provision of P-values etc. by the statistical software normally used in the analysis of a data set. (Additionally, specialized packages are available that provide access to such information; for example, StaTable produced by the Cytel Software Corporation.)

The book is divided into four parts:

1. **Introduction and initial data analysis** (Chapters 1 and 2): a case is made for a less rigid approach to the favourite statistic of most psychologists, the P-value, and the importance of graphical methods for an initial examination of data is emphasized.

2. **Traditional** (but with many extras) (Chapters 3, 4, 5, 6 and 13): analysis of variance, multiple regression and reliability are covered in these chapters.

3. **Adventurous** (Chapters 7, 8 and 9): modelling of categorical data using log–linear models and logistic regression are covered in Chapter 7; the generalized linear model linking analysis of variance, multiple regression, log–linear models and logistic regression is introduced in Chapter 8; computer-intensive distribution-free methods are described in Chapter 9.

4. **Multivariate** (Chapters 10, 11 and 12); principal components, exploratory and confirmatory factor analysis, discriminant function analysis, cluster analysis and multidimensional scaling are discussed in these chapters.

It is hoped that the text will be useful in a number of different ways including the following:

(1) as the main part of a formal statistics course for advanced undergraduate and postgraduate psychology students;

(2) as a supplement to an existing course;

(3) for self-study;

(4) for quick reference.

The primary aim of this book is that it be used as the main text for second-level statistics courses in psychology. Some further recommended reading is provided at the end of each chapter to aid and stimulate students on such courses to look further afield for other views on a particular topic; these lists should also aid self-study.

London   B.S.E.
November 1995

Contents

1
Data, models and a little history

1.1 Introduction

In an ideal world the stages of a research investigation in psychology (and in other disciplines) would be as follows:

1. Clarify the objectives of the investigation.
2. Collect the data in an appropriate way.
3. Investigate the structure and quality of the data.
4. Carry out an initial examination of the data.
5. Select and carry out the appropriate formal statistical analyses.
6. Interpret and communicate the results.
7. Publish a totally original paper in the most prestigious psychological journal and climb to the top of the citation league table.

However, the world is often far from ideal for research psychologists (and no doubt for psychology students reading this introduction). Each of the steps indicated above can lead to problems and difficulties, and therefore, in practice, few investigations follow such a straightforward pattern. An iterative cycle which will include rethinking, reformulation and reanalysis is more likely. However, it is hoped that this often traumatic procedure will eventually converge to a set of results which, whilst not generally of the 'earth-moving' variety, might become a useful step on the way to understanding a particular phenomenon.

At each stage in this often long and painful process of proceeding from planning to results, a knowledge and understanding of statistics will be essential. Statistical principles will be needed to guide the design of a study and the collection of data. The initial examination of data and their description will involve a variety of informal statistical techniques, and more formal methods of estimation and significance testing may be needed to build a 'model' for the data and assess its fit.

However, most psychologists are not, and have no desire to be, statisticians. Consequently, questions need to be asked about 'what' and 'how much' statistics the average psychologist needs to know. It is generally agreed that psychologists should have some knowledge of statistics, and this is reflected in the almost universal exposure of psychology students to an 'introductory' course in the subject, covering topics such as the following:

(1) descriptive statistics (histograms, means, variances, standard deviations);
(2) elementary probability;
(3) the normal distribution;
(4) inference (t-tests, chi-squared tests, confidence intervals etc.);

(5) correlation and regression;
(6) simple analysis of variance.

Although such a course often provides essential grounding in statistics, it frequently gives the wrong impression of what is and what is not of greatest importance in tackling real-life problems. For example, many psychology students (and their teachers), regard a P-value as the Holy Grail and almost the *raison d' être* of statistics (and providing a P-value is regarded as the chief role of statisticians). Despite the numerous caveats in the literature, many psychologists still seem determined to experience joy on finding a P-value of 0.049 and despair on finding one of 0.051. Again, psychology students may learn how to perform a *t*-test on their introductory course (they may, poor things, even be made to carry out the arithmetic themselves), but will still be ill equipped to answer the question: 'How can I summarize and understand the main features of this set of data?'

The aim of this text is essentially twofold. Firstly, it will introduce the reader to a variety of statistical techniques not usually encountered on an introductory course; secondly, and equally, if not more, importantly, it will attempt to transform the knowledge gained from such a course into a more suitable form for dealing with the complexities of 'real data'. For example, readers will be encouraged to replace the formal use of significance tests and the rigid interpretation of P-values with an approach that regards such tests as giving informal guidance on possible evidence of an interesting effect. They may even be asked to abandon the ubiquitous significance test altogether in favour of, for example, a graphical display which makes the structure in the data apparent without any formal analyses. It is hoped that, by building on and 'reshaping' the statistical knowledge gained in their first-level course, students will be better equipped to overcome the criticisms of much current statistical practice embodied in the following two quotations:

> Most real-life statistical problems have one or more nonstandard features. There are no routine statistical questions; only questionable statistical routines. (Sir David Cox, personal communication).

> Many statistical pitfalls lie in wait for the unwary. Indeed statistics is perhaps more open to misuse than any other subject, particularly by the nonspecialist. The misleading average, the graph with 'fiddled axes', the inappropriate P value and the linear regression fitted to nonlinear data are just four examples of horror stories which are part of statistical folklore. (Christopher Chatfield, 1985)

1.2 Statistics descriptive, statistics inferential and statistical models

In this text we are primarily concerned with the following overlapping components of the statistical analysis of data:

1. The initial examination of the data, with the aim of making any interesting 'patterns' in the data more visible.
2. The estimation of parameters of interest.
3. The testing of hypotheses about parameters.
4. Model formulation, building and assessment.

Most investigations will involve little clear separation between these four components, but for now it will be helpful to try to indicate, in general terms, the unique aspects of each.

1.2.1 *The initial examination of data*

The initial examination of data is a valuable stage in most statistical investigations, not only for scrutinizing and summarizing data, but often also as an aid to later model formulation. The aim is to clarify the general structure of the data, obtain simple descriptive summaries, and perhaps develop ideas for a more sophisticated analysis. At this stage distributional assumptions might be examined (e.g. whether the data are 'normal'), possible 'outliers' identified (i.e. observations very different from the bulk of the data that may be the result of a recording error, for example), relationships between variables examined etc. In some cases the results from this stage may contain such an obvious message that more detailed analysis becomes superfluous (see examples in later chapters). Many of the methods employed in this preliminary analysis of the data are graphical and these are described in Chapter 2.

1.2.2 *Estimation and significance testing*

Although an initial examination of the data will be all that is necessary in some cases, most investigations will proceed to a more formal stage of analysis that involves the estimation of population values of interest and/or testing hypotheses about particular values for these parameters. It is at this point that the beloved significance test (in some form or other) enters the arena. Despite numerous attempts by statisticians to wean psychologists away from such tests (e.g. Gardner and Altman 1986), the P-value retains a powerful hold over the average psychology researcher and psychology student. There are a number of reasons why it should not.

(a) The P-value is poorly understood

Although P-values appear in almost every account of psychological research findings, there is evidence that the general degree of understanding of the true meaning of the term is very low. For example, Oakes (1986) put the following test to 70 academic psychologists;

> Suppose you have a treatment which you suspect may alter performance on a certain task. You compare the means of your control and experimental groups (say 20 subjects in each sample). Further suppose you use a simple independent means t-test and your result is $t = 2.7$, DF = 18, $P = 0.01$. Please mark each of the statements below as true or false:
>
> - You have absolutely disproved the null hypothesis that there is no difference between the population means.
> - You have found the probability of the null hypothesis being true.
> - You have absolutely proved your experimental hypothesis.

Table 1.1 Frequencies and percentages of 'true' responses in test of knowledge of P-values

Statement	f	Percentage
1. The null hypothesis is absolutely disproved	1	1.4
2. The probability of the null hypothesis has been found	25	35.7
3. The experimental hypothesis is absolutely proved	4	5.7
4. The probability of the experimental hypothesis can be deduced	46	65.7
5. The probability that the decision taken is wrong is known	60	85.7
6. A replication has a 0.99 probability of being significant	42	60.0

- You can deduce the probability of the experimental hypothesis being true.
- You know, if you decided to reject the null hypothesis, the probability that you are making the wrong decision.
- You have a reliable experiment in the sense that if, hypothetically, the experiment were repeated a great number of times, you would obtain a significant result on 99% of occasions.

The subjects were all university lecturers, research fellows or postgraduate students. The results presented in Table 1.1 are illuminating. Under a relative frequency view of probability, all six statements are in fact *false*. Only three out of the 70 subjects came to that conclusion. The correct interpretation of the probability associated with the observed *t*-value is:

The probability of obtaining the observed data (or data that represent a more extreme departure from the null hypothesis) if the null hypothesis is true.

Clearly, the number of false statements described as true in this experiment would have been reduced if the true interpretation of a P-value had been included with the six others. Nevertheless the exercise is extremely interesting in highlighting the misguided appreciation of P-values held by a group of research psychologists. (The author realizes, of course, that readers of this text would not so easily have been misled, and would have spotted almost straightaway that all the six original statements about the P-value were false.)

(b) A P-value represents only limited information about the results from a study
Gardner and Altman (1986) make the point that the excessive use of P-values in hypothesis testing simply as a means of rejecting or accepting a particular hypothesis, at the expense of other ways of assessing results, has reached such a degree that levels of significance are often quoted alone in the main text and abstracts of papers with no mention of other more relevant and important quantities. The implications of hypothesis testing—that there can always be a simple 'yes' or 'no' answer as the

fundamental result of a psychological study—is clearly false, and when used in this way hypothesis testing is of limited value.

The most common alternative to presenting results in terms of P-values, in relation to a statistical null hypothesis, is to estimate the magnitude of some parameter of interest together with some interval which includes the population value of the parameter with some specified probability. Such **confidence intervals** can be found relatively simply for many quantities of interest (see Gardner and Altman, 1986, for details), and although the underlying logic of interval estimation is essentially similar to that of significance tests, confidence intervals do not carry with them the pseudoscientific hypothesis-testing language of such tests. Instead, they give a plausible range of values for the unknown parameter. As Oakes (1986) rightly comments:

> The significance test relates to what the population parameter is *not*: the confidence interval gives a plausible range for what the parameter *is*.

So, should the P-value be abandoned completely? Many statisticians would answer 'yes', but a more sensible response would be a resounding 'maybe'. Such values should rarely be used in a purely confirmatory way, but in an exploratory fashion they can give some informal guidance on the possible existence of an interesting effect, even when the required assumptions of whatever test is being used are known to be invalid. It is often possible to assess whether a P-value is likely to be an under- or overestimate, and whether the result is clear one way or the other. In this text both P-values and confidence intervals will be used; purely from a pragmatic point of view, the former are needed by psychology students since they remain central to the bulk of the psychological literature.

1.2.3 *The role of models in the analysis of data*

Models imitate the properties of 'real' objects in a simpler or more convenient form. For example, a road map models part of the Earth's surface, attempting to reproduce the relative positions of towns, roads and other features. Chemists use models of molecules to mimic their theoretical properties, which in turn can be used to predict the behaviour of real objects. A good model follows as accurately as possible the relevant properties of the real object while being convenient to use.

Statistical models allow inferences to be made about an object, activity or process by modelling some associated observable data. Suppose, for example, that a child has scored 20 points on a test of verbal ability and then, after studying a dictionary for some time, scores 24 points on a similar test. If it is believed that studying the dictionary has caused an improvement, a possible model of what is happening is as follows:

$$20 = \{\text{person's initial score}\} \tag{1.1}$$

$$24 = \{\text{person's initial score}\} + \{\text{improvement}\}. \tag{1.2}$$

The improvement can be found by simply subtracting the first score from the second.

Of course, such a model is very naïve, since it assumes that verbal ability can be measured exactly. A more realistic representation of the two scores, which allows for possible measurement error, is:

$$x_1 = \gamma + \epsilon_1 \tag{1.3}$$
$$x_2 = \gamma + \delta + \epsilon_2 \tag{1.4}$$

where x_1 and x_2 represent the two verbal ability scores, γ represents the 'true' initial measure of verbal ability and δ is the improvement score. The terms ϵ_1 and ϵ_2 represent measurement error. Here the improvement score can be *estimated* as $x_1 - x_2$.

A model gives a precise description of what the investigator assumes is occurring in a particular situation. In the case above it states that the improvement δ is considered to be independent of γ and is simply added to it. (An important point that needs to be noted here is that if you do not believe in a model, you should not perform operations and analyses on the data which assume that it is true.)

Suppose now that it is believed that studying the dictionary is more helpful if the child already has a fair degree of verbal ability and that the various random influences which affect the test scores also depend on the true scores. Then an appropriate model would be

$$x_1 = \gamma \epsilon_1 \tag{1.5}$$
$$x_2 = \gamma \delta \epsilon_2. \tag{1.6}$$

Now the parameters are *multiplied* rather than added to give the observed scores x_1 and x_2. Here, δ might be estimated by dividing x_2 by x_1.

A further possibility is that there is a limit λ to improvement, and that studying the dictionary improves performance on the verbal ability test by some proportion $\lambda - \gamma$ of the child's possible improvement. Then a suitable model would be

$$x_1 = \gamma + \epsilon_1 \tag{1.7}$$
$$x_2 = \gamma + (\lambda - \gamma)\delta + \epsilon_2. \tag{1.8}$$

With this model there is no way of estimating δ from the data unless a value of λ is given or assumed.

The choice of an appropriate model should be largely based on the investigator's prior knowledge of an area. However, in many situations, **additive linear models**, such as those given in eqns (1.1) and (1.2), are invoked by default, since such models allow many powerful and informative statistical techniques to be applied to the data. For example, **analysis of variance techniques** (Chapters 3–5) and **regression analysis** (Chapter 6) use such models, and in recent years **generalized linear models** (Chapter 8) have evolved which allow analogous models to be applied to a wide variety of data types.

Formulating an appropriate model can be a difficult problem. The general principles of model formulation are covered in detail in books on scientific method, but include the need to collaborate with appropriate experts, to incorporate as much background theory as possible etc. Apart from models formulated entirely on a priori theoretical grounds, most models are based, to some extent at least, on an initial examination of the data, although completely empirical models are rare. The more usual intermediate case arises when a class of models is entertained a priori, but the initial data analysis is crucial in selecting a subset of models from the class. In regression analysis, for example, the general approach is determined a priori, but a **scatter diagram** (see Chapter 2) will be of crucial importance in indicating the 'shape' of the relationship and in checking assumptions such as normality

The formulation of a preliminary model from an initial examination of the data is the first step in the iterative formulation–criticism cycle of model-building. This can produce some problems since formulating a model and testing it on the same data is not generally considered good scientific practice. It is always preferable to confirm whether a derived model is sensible by testing on new data. However, when data are difficult or expensive to obtain, some model modification and assessment of fit on the original data are almost inevitable. Investigators need to be aware of the possible dangers of such a process.

The most important principle to keep in mind when testing models on data is that of **parsimony**, i.e. the 'best' model is the one that provides an adequate fit to the data with the *fewest* number of parameters. This is often known as **Occam's razor** which, for those with a classical education, is reproduced here in its original form:

entia non stunt multiplicanda praeter necessitatem.

1.3 Types of study

It is said that when Gertrude Stein lay dying, she roused briefly and asked her assembled friends: 'Well, what's the answer?' They remained uncomfortably quiet, at which she sighed: 'In that case, what's the question?'

Research in psychology, and in science in general, is about searching for the answers to particular questions of interest. Do politicians have higher IQs than university lecturers? Do men have faster reaction times than women? Should phobic patients be treated by psychotherapy or by a behavioural treatment such as flooding? Do children who are abused have more problems later in life than children who are not abused? Do children of divorced parents suffer more marital breakdowns than children from more stable family backgrounds?

In more general terms, scientific research involves a sequence of asking and answering questions about the nature of relationships among variables (How does A affect B? Do A and B vary together? Is A significantly different from B?). Scientific research is carried out at many levels which differ in the types of question asked and therefore in the procedures used to answer them. Thus the choice of which methods to use in research is largely determined by the kinds of questions that are asked.

Of the many types of investigation used in psychological research, perhaps the most common are the following:

(1) surveys;
(2) observational studies;
(3) quasi-experiments;
(4) experiments.

Some brief comments about each of these are given below; a more detailed account is available in the papers by Stretch, Raulin and Graziano, and Dane, which all appear in the second volume of the excellent *Companion encyclopedia of psychology* (Colman 1994).

1.3.1 *Surveys*

Survey methods are based on the simple discovery 'that asking questions is a remarkably efficient way to obtain information from and about people' (Schuman and Kalton, 1985, p. 635). Surveys involve an exchange of information between researcher and respondent: the researcher identifies topics of interest, and the respondent provides knowledge or opinion about these topics. Depending upon the length and content of the survey as well as the facilities available, this exchange can be accomplished via written questionnaires, in-person interviews or telephone conversations.

Surveys conducted by psychologists are usually designed to elicit information about the respondents' opinions, beliefs, attitudes and values. Some examples of data collected in surveys and their analysis are given in Chapters 2, 10 and 11.

1.3.2 *Observational studies*

Many observational studies involve recording data on the members of naturally occurring groups, generally over a period of time, and comparing the rate at which a particular event of interest occurs in the different groups (such studies are often referred to as **prospective**). For example, if an investigator was interested in the health effects of a natural disaster such as an earthquake, those who experienced it could be compared with a group of people who did not. Another commonly used type of observational study is the **case–control** investigation. Here a group of people (the **cases**) all having a particular characteristic (a certain disease perhaps) are compared with a group of people who do not have the characteristic (the **controls**), in terms of their past exposure to some event or **risk factor**. A recent example involved comparison of women giving birth to infants with very low birth weight (less than 1500 g) with women having a child of normal birth weight with respect to their past caffeine consumption.

The types of analyses suitable for observational studies are often the same as those used for experimental studies (see Section 1.3.4). Unlike experiments, however, the lack of control over the groups to be compared in an observational study makes the interpretation of any difference between the groups detected in the study open to a variety of interpretations. For example, in an investigation into the relationship between smoking and systolic blood pressure, the researcher cannot allocate subjects to be smokers and non-smokers (as would be required in an experimental approach) for obvious ethical reasons; instead the systolic blood pressures of naturally occurring groups of smokers and non-smokers are compared. In such a study any difference found between the blood pressure of the two groups would be open to three possible explanations.

1. Smoking *causes* a change in systolic blood pressure.
2. The level of blood pressure has a tendency to encourage or discourage smoking.
3. Some unidentified factors play a part in determining both the level of blood pressure and whether or not a person smokes.

1.3.3 *Quasi-experiments*

Quasi-experimental designs resemble experiments proper (see Section 1.3.4), but are less rigorous in some respects. In particular (and like the observational study), the ability to manipulate the groups to be compared is not under the investigator's control. However, unlike the observational study, the quasi-experiment involves the intervention of the investigator in the sense that he or she applies a variety of different 'treatments' to naturally occurring groups. In investigating the effectiveness of three different methods of teaching mathematics to 15-year-olds, for example, a method might be given to *all* the members of a particular class in a school. The three classes that receive the different teaching methods would be selected to be similar to each other on most relevant variables, and the methods would be assigned to classes on a chance basis.

1.3.4 *Experiments*

Experimental studies include most of the work that psychologists carry out on animals and many of the investigations performed on human subjects in laboratories. The essential feature of an experiment is the large degree of control in the hands of the experimenters, in particular the ability to allocate subjects to groups in a way of their choosing. For example, in a comparison of a new treatment with one used previously, the researcher would have control over the scheme for allocating subjects to treatments. The manner in which this control is exercised is of vital importance if the results of the experiment are to be valid. For example, if the subjects who volunteer first are all allocated to the new treatment, the two groups may differ in level of motivation and therefore in performance. Observed treatment differences would be confounded with differences produced by the allocation procedure.

The method most often used to overcome such problems is **random allocation** of subjects to treatments. Whether a subject receives the new or the old treatment is decided, for example, by the toss of a coin. The primary benefit that randomization has is the chance (and therefore impartial) assignment of extraneous influences among the groups to be compared, and it offers this control over such influences whether or not the experimenter knows that they exist. Note that randomization does not claim to render the two samples equal with regard to these influences; however, if the same procedure was applied in repeated samplings, equality would be achieved in the long run. This randomization ensures a lack of bias, whereas other methods of assignment may not.

In a properly conducted experiment (and this is the main advantage of such a study), the interpretation of an observed group difference is largely unambiguous; its *cause* is very likely to be the different treatments or conditions to which the two groups are exposed.

In the majority of cases, the statistical methods most useful for the analysis of data derived from experimental studies are the analysis of variance procedures described in Chapters 3–5.

1.4 Types of data

The foundation of all psychological investigations is the measurements and observations made on a set of subjects. Clearly, not all measurement is the same. Measuring an individual's weight is qualitatively different from measuring his or her response to some treatment on a two-category scale; for example, 'improved' or 'not improved'. Whatever measurements are made, they need to be objective, precise and reproducible for reasons nicely summarized in the following quotation from Fleiss (1986):

> The most elegant design of a study will not overcome the damage caused by unreliable or imprecise measurement. The requirement that one's data be of high quality is at least as important a component of a proper study design as the requirement for randomization, double blinding, controlling where necessary for prognostic factors, and so on. Larger sample sizes than otherwise necessary, biased estimates and even biased samples are some of the untoward consequences of unreliable measurements that can be demonstrated.

Measurement scales are differentiated according to the degree of precision involved. If it is stated that an individual has a high IQ, it is not as precise as the statement that the individual has an IQ of 151. The comment that a woman is tall is not as accurate as specifying that her height is 1.88 m. Certain characteristics of interest are more amenable than others to precise measurement. Given an accurate thermometer, a subject's temperature can be measured very precisely. However, quantifying the level of anxiety or depression of a psychiatric patient or assessing the degree of pain of a migraine sufferer are far more difficult tasks. Measurement scales can be classified into a hierarchy ranging from **categorical**, through **ordinal** to **interval** and finally **ratio scales**. Each of these will now be considered in more detail.

1.4.1 *Nominal or categorical measurements*

Nominal or categorical measurements allow patients to be classified with respect to some characteristic. Examples of such measurements are marital status, sex and blood group.

The properties of a nominal scale are as follows:

1. Data categories are mutually exclusive (an individual can belong to only one category).
2. Data categories have no logical order—numbers can be assigned to categories but merely as convenient labels.

A nominal scale classifies without the categories being ordered.

1.4.2 *Ordinal scales*

The next level in the measurement hierarchy is the ordinal scale. This has one additional property over those of a nominal scale—a logical ordering of the categories. With such measurements the numbers assigned to the categories indicate the **amount** of a characteristic possessed. For example, a psychiatrist may grade patients on an anxiety scale as 'not anxious', 'mildly anxious', 'moderately anxious' or 'severely anxious', and use the numbers 0, 1, 2 and 3 to label the categories, with lower numbers indicating less anxiety. The psychiatrist cannot infer that the difference in anxiety between patients with scores of 0 and 1, say, is the same as that between patients assigned scores 2 and 3. However, the scores on an ordinal scale do allow patients to be **ranked** with respect to the characteristic being assessed. Frequently, measurements on an ordinal scale are described in terms of their mean and standard deviation. This is not appropriate if the steps on the scale are not known to be of equal length. Andersen (1990, Chapter 15) gives a nice illustration of why this is so.

The properties of an ordinal scale are as follows:

1. Data categories are mutually exclusive.
2. Data categories have some logical order.
3. Data categories are scaled according to the amount of a particular characteristic that they possess.

1.4.3 *Interval scales*

The third level in the measurement hierarchy is the interval scale. Such scales possess all the properties of an ordinal scale, plus the additional property that equal differences between category levels, on any part of the scale, reflect equal differences in the characteristic being measured. An example of such a scale is temperature on the Celsius or Fahrenheit scale; the difference between temperatures of 80°F and 90°F is the same as between temperatures of 30°F and 40°F. An important point to make about interval scales is that the zero point is simply another point on the scale; it does not represent the starting point of the scale, nor the total absence of the characteristic being measured. The properties of an interval scale are as follows:

1. Data categories are mutually exclusive.
2. Data categories have a logical order.
3. Data categories are scaled according to the amount of the characteristic that they possess.
4. Equal differences in the characteristic are represented by equal differences in the numbers assigned to the categories.
5. The zero point is completely arbitrary.

1.4.4 *Ratio scales*

The highest level in the hierarchy of measurement scales is the ratio scale. This type of scale has one property in addition to those listed for interval scales, namely a true zero point which represents the absence of the characteristic being measured. Consequently, statements can be made about both differences on the scale *and* the ratio of points on the scale. An example is weight, where not only is the difference between 100 kg and 50 kg the same as between 75 kg and 25 kg, but an object weighing 100 kg can be said to be twice as heavy as one weighing 50 kg. This is not true of, say, temperature on the

Celsius or Fahrenheit scales, where a reading of 100° does not represent twice the warmth of a temperature of 50°. However, if the temperatures were measured on the Kelvin scale, which does have a true zero point, the statement about the ratio could be made.

The properties of a ratio scale are as follows:

1. Data categories are mutually exclusive.
2. Data categories have a logical order.
3. Data categories are scaled according to the amount of the characteristic that they possess.
4. Equal differences in the characteristic are represented by equal differences in the numbers assigned to the categories.
5. The zero point represents an absence of the characteristic being measured.

An awareness of the different types of measurement that may be encountered in psychological studies is important since the appropriate method of statistical analysis will often depend on the type of variable involved, a point which will be taken up again in later chapters.

A further classification of variable types is into **response** or **dependent** variables (also often referred to as **outcome** variables), and **independent** or **explanatory** variables (also occasionally called **predictor** variables). Essentially, the former are the variables measured by the investigator that appear on the left-hand side of the equation defining the proposed model for the data, and the latter are variables which may affect the response variable and appear on the right-hand side of the model. Most studies in psychology are concerned with the relationship between the dependent variable and the so-called independent variables ('independent' variables are often related—see comments and examples in later chapters). In addition, in some contexts, particularly that of analysis of variance (see Chapters 3–5), the independent variables are also often known as **factor variables**, or simply **factors**.

1.5   A little history

The relationship between psychology and statistics is a necessary one (honest!). A widely quoted remark by Galton is 'that until the phenomena of any branch of kowledge have been submitted to measurement and number, it cannot assume the dignity of a science'. Galton was not alone in demanding measurement and numbers as a *sine qua non* for attaining the dignity of a science. Lord Kelvin is quoted as saying that one cannot understand a phenomenon until it is subjected to measurement, and Thorndike has said that whatever exists, exists in some amount, and therefore could eventually be subjected to measurement and counting.

Psychology has long striven to attain 'the dignity of science' by submitting its observations to measurement and quantification. According to Singer (1979), David Hartley (1705–1757), in his major work, *Observations on man* (1749), discussed the relevance of probability theory to the collection of scientific evidence, and argued for the use of mathematical and statistical ideas in the study of psychological processes.

A long-standing tradition in scientific psychology is the application of John Stuart Mill's experimental 'method of difference' to the study of psychological problems.

Groups of subjects are compared who differ with respect to the experimental treatment, but otherwise are the same in all respects. Therefore any difference in outcome can be attributed to the treatment. Control procedures such as randomization or matching on potentially confounding variables help to bolster the assumption that the groups are the same in every way except for the treatment conditions.

The experimental tradition in psychology has long been wedded to a particular statistical technique, namely the analysis of variance. The principles of experimental design and the analysis of variance were developed primarily by Fisher in the 1920s, but took time to be fully appreciated by psychologists who continued to analyse their experimental data using a mixture of graphical and simple statistical methods until well into the 1930s. According to Lovie (1979), the earliest paper that had 'analysis of variance' in its title was by Gaskill and Cox (1937). Other early uses of the technique are reported by Crutchfield (1938) and Crutchfield and Tolman (1940).

Several of these early psychological papers, although paying lip service to the use of Fisher's analysis of variance techniques, relied heavily on more informal strategies of inference in interpreting experimental results. However, in 1940 there was a dramatic increase in the use of analysis of variance in the psychological literature, and by 1943 Garrett and Zubin were able to cite over 40 studies using analysis of variance or covariance in psychology and education. Since then, of course, the analysis of variance in all its guises has become the main technique used in experimental psychology. Examination of two years of issues of the *British Journal of Psychology*, for example, showed that over 50% of the papers contain some application of the analysis of variance.

Whilst the experimental psychologist is most concerned with general principles about human and animal behaviour, other psychologists are most interested in describing and interpreting individual differences, in particular with respect to various dimensions of intellectual ability, personality and psychopathology. (Cronbach, 1957, draws attention to the existence of two relatively separate 'disciplines of scientific psychology'.) This alternative tradition in psychology arises from the early ideas for measures of association of Fechner (1801–1887) and Quetelet (1796–1874), later developed into the **correlation coefficient** by Galton (1822–1911). The introduction of this concept was closely followed by the basic ideas of what is now generally referred to as **factor analysis**. For example, Spearman suggested that the correlation between two variables signified the existence of an underlying common factor. This logic was extended by the psychometric theorists of the 1920s and 1930s, who were interested in investigating individual differences on such general unseen traits as intelligence or various aspects of personality. Whereas the behaviourists and the experimental psychologists tended to see the human mind as a 'black box' and restricted their attention to observable behaviour (such as pressing a button in a learning task), the 'other sort of psychologists' saw the correlation coefficient as a key to the mysteries of personality and mental life. They equated the 'common factors' derived from a matrix of correlations with psychological traits that could be given meaningful names, for example intelligence or personality. (Such labelling or **reification** is often a 'creative' and rather bold pastime.)

In many respects the structure of this text reflects the two traditions of psychological research outlined above. Chapters 3, 4 and 5 deal with analysis of variance, Chapter 6 with regression, and Chapters 10, 11 and 12 with multivariate techniques such as factor analysis. (Chapters 7, 8 and 9 are somewhat 'maverick' chapters for reasons which will become clear in due course.) Chapter 13, although the final chapter of the book, deals with issues of central importance to *all* research psychologists, namely the reliability of their measurements.

1.6   Why can't a psychologist be more like a statistician (and vice versa)?

Over the course of the last 50 years, the psychologist has become a voracious consumer of statistical methods, but the relationship between psychologist and statistician is not always easy, happy or fruitful. Statisticians complain that psychologists put undue faith in significance tests, often use complex methods of analysis when the data merit only a relatively simple approach and in general abuse many statistical techniques. Additionally, many statisticians feel that psychologists have become too easily seduced by user-friendly statistical software. These statisticians are upset (and perhaps even made to feel a little insecure) when their advice to 'plot a few graphs' is ignored in favour of a multivariate analysis of covariance or similar statistical extravagance.

However, if statisticians are at times horrified by the way in which psychologists apply statistical techniques, psychologists are no less horrified by many statisticians' apparent lack of awareness of what stresses psychological research can place on an investigator. A statistician may demand a balanced design with 30 subjects in each cell so as to achieve some appropriate power for the analysis. But it is not the statistician who is faced with the frustration caused by a last-minute telephone call from a subject who cannot take part in an experiment that has taken several hours to arrange. The statistician advising on a longitudinal study may call for more effort in carrying out follow-up interviews, so that no subjects are missed. However, it is the psychologist who must continue to persuade people to talk about potentially distressing aspects of their lives, who must confront possibly dangerous respondents or who arrives at a given (and often remote) address to conduct an interview, only to find that the person is not at home. In general, statisticians do not appear to appreciate the complex stories behind each data point in a psychological study. In addition, it is not unknown for statisticians to perform analyses that are statistically sound but psychologically naïve or even misleading. For example, an accomplished statistician once proposed an interpretation of findings regarding the benefits of nursery education in which all subsequent positive effects could be accounted for in terms of the parents' choice of primary school. For once, it was psychologists who had to suppress a knowing smile; in the country for which the results were obtained, parents typically did not have any opportunity to choose the schools that their children attended!

One way of examining the possible communication problems between psychologist and statistician is for each to know more about the language of the other. It is hoped that this text will help in this process and enable young (and not so young) psychologists to learn more about the way that statisticians approach the difficulties of data analysis, thus making their future consultations with statisticians more productive and less traumatic. (What is missing in this equation is, of course, a suitable text on 'psychology for statisticians'.)

1.7 Computers and statistical software

The development of computing and advances in statistical methodology have gone hand-in-hand since the early 1960s, and the increasing availability, power and low cost of today's personal computers has further revolutionized the way that users of statistics work. It is probably hard for fresh-faced students of today busily 'e-mailing' everybody, exploring the delights of the Internet and in every other way displaying their computer literacy on the current generation of personal computers, to imagine just what life was like for the statistician and the user of statistics in the days of simple electronic or mechanical calculators, or even earlier when large volumes of numerical tables were the only arithmetical aids available. It is a salutary exercise (of the 'young people today hardly know they are born' variety) to illustrate with a little anecdote what things were like in the past.

Godfrey Thomson was an educational psychologist during the 1930s and 1940s. Professor A.E. Maxwell (personal communication) tells the story of Dr Thomson's approach to the arithmetical problems faced when performing a factor analysis by hand. According to Maxwell, early in the evening, Godfrey Thomson and his wife would place themselves on either side of their sitting-room fire, Dr Thomson equipped with several pencils and much paper, and Mrs Thomson with a copy of *Barlow's multiplication tables*. For several hours the conversation would consist of little more than 'What's 613.23 multiplied by 714.62?', '438226.42'; 'What's 904.72 divided by 986.31?', '0.91728', etc.

Nowadays increasingly sophisticated and comprehensive **statistics packages** are available that allow investigators easy access to an enormous variety of statistical techniques. This is not without considerable potential for performing very poor and often misleading analyses (a potential that many psychologists have grasped with apparent enthusiasm), but it would be foolish to underestimate the advantages of statistical software to users of statistics such as psychologists. In this text it will be assumed that readers will be carrying out their own analyses using one or other of the many statistical packages now available. One major benefit of this assumption is that details of the arithmetic behind the methods will only rarely need to be given; consequently, descriptions of arithmetical calculations will be noticeable largely by their absence, although some displays *will* contain a little arithmetic. Some displays will also contain a little mathematical nomenclature and, occasionally, even some equations, which in a number of places will use vectors and matrices. Readers who find this too upsetting even to contemplate should pass speedily by the offending material, regarding it merely as a 'black box' and taking heart that, in most cases, understanding its 'input' and 'output' will be sufficient to undertake the corresponding analyses and to understand their results.

1.8 Summary

1. Statistical principles are central to most aspects of a psychological investigation.
2. Data and their associated statistical analyses form the evidential parts of psychological arguments.
3. Significance testing is far from the be all and end all of statistical analyses, but it does

still matter because evidence that can be discounted as an artefact of sampling will not be particularly persuasive. However, *P*-values should not be taken too seriously; confidence intervals are often more informative.

4. Good statistical analysis should highlight those aspects of the data that are relevant to the psychological arguments, do so clearly and fairly, and be resistant to criticisms.
5. Experiments lead to the clearest conclusions about causal relationships.
6. The type of variable often determines the most appropriate method of analysis.

Exercises

1.1 A well-known professor of experimental psychology once told the author: 'If psychologists carry out their experiments properly, they rarely need statistics or statisticians.'

1. Guess the professor!
2. Comment on his or her remark.

1.2 The Pepsi-Cola Company carried out research to determine whether people tended to prefer Pepsi-Cola to Coca-Cola. Participants were asked to taste two glasses of cola and then state which they preferred. The two glasses were not labelled Pepsi or Coke for obvious reasons. Instead, the Coke glass was labelled Q and the Pepsi glass was labelled M. The results showed that 'more than half choose Pepsi over Coke' (Huck and Sandler, 1979, p. 11). Are there any alternative explanations for the observed difference, other than the taste of the two drinks? Explain how you would carry out a study to assess any alternative explanation that you think possible.

1.3 Suppose that you develop a headache while working for hours at your computer (this is probably a purely hypothetical possibility, but use your imagination). You stop, go into another room and take two aspirins. After about 15 minutes your headache has gone and you return to work. Can you infer a definite causal relationship between taking the aspirin and curing the headache?

1.4 Attribute the following quotations about statistics and/or statisticians:

1. To understand God's thoughts we must study statistics, for these are a measure of His purpose.
2. You cannot feed the hungry on statistics.
3. A single death is a tragedy, a million deaths is a statistic.
4. Thou shalt not sit with statisticians nor commit a Social Science.
5. Facts speak louder than statistics.
6. I am one of the unpraised, unrewarded millions without whom statistics would be a bankrupt science. It is we who are born, marry and who die in constant ratios.

Further reading

Brook, R.J., Arnold, G.C., Hassard, T.H. and Pringle, R.M. (ed.) (1986). *The fascination of statistics*. Marcel Dekker, New York.

Colman, A.M. (ed.) (1995). *Psychological research methods and statistics*. Longman, London.

Everitt, B.S. and Hay, D. (1992). *Talking about statistics*. Edward Arnold, London.

Lovie, S. (1993). A short history of statistics in twentieth century psychology. In *New developments in statistics for psychologists and the social sciences*, (ed. P. Lovie and A.D. Lovie), Vol. 2. BPS Books and Routledge, London.

2
Graphical methods of displaying data

2.1 Introduction

According to Chambers *et al.* (1983), 'there is no statistical tool that is as powerful as a well-chosen graph'. Now this may be a trifle exaggerated, but it **is** true that there is considerable evidence that there are patterns in data, and relationships between variables, that are easier to identify and understand from graphical displays than from the results produced by other data analysis methods. For this reason, researchers are often encouraged by statisticians both to make a preliminary graphical examination of their data and to use a variety of plots and diagrams as aids in the interpretation of the results from more formal analyses. The possible advantages of graphical presentation methods have been summarized by Schmid (1954) as follows:

1. In comparison with other types of presentation, well-designed charts are more effective in creating interest and in appealing to the attention of the reader.
2. Visual relationships as portrayed by charts and graphs are more easily grasped and more easily remembered.
3. The use of charts and graphs saves time, since the essential meaning of large measures of statistical data can be visualized at a glance (like Chambers and his colleagues, Schmid may perhaps be accused of being prone to a little exaggeration here).
4. Charts and graphs provide a comprehensive picture of a problem that makes for a more complete and better balanced understanding than could be derived from tabular or textual forms of presentation.
5. Charts and graphs can bring out hidden facts and relationships and can stimulate, as well as aid, analytical thinking and investigation.

During the last two decades, a wide variety of new methods for displaying data have been developed with the aim of making this particular aspect of the examination of data as informative as possible. Graphical techniques have evolved that will hunt for special effects in data, indicate outliers, identify patterns, diagnose models and generally search for novel and unexpected phenomena. Large numbers of graphs may be required and computers will generally be needed to draw them for the same reasons that they are used for numerical analysis, namely that they are fast and accurate.

In this chapter we are largely concerned with the graphical methods most relevant in the initial phase of data analysis. Graphical techniques useful for diagnosing models and interpreting results will be dealt with in later chapters.

2.2 Pop charts

Newspapers, television and the media in general are very fond of two very simple graphical displays, namely the **pie chart** and the **bar chart**. Both can be illustrated using the data shown in Table 2.1 which were obtained by asking a sample of female teenagers about health problems that caused them concern. In the pie chart, the percentages of teenagers with each particular problem are simply represented by the sectors of a circle with areas proportional to the observed percentages. Figure 2.1 shows the pie charts for both age groups in Table 2.1.

In a bar chart, percentages are represented by rectangles of appropriate size placed along a horizontal axis (Fig. 2.2). Alternatively, the corresponding rectangles for each age group could be placed alongside one another as shown in Fig. 2.3.

Despite their widespread popularity, both the general and scientific use of pie charts and bar charts have been severely criticized. For example, Tufte (1983) comments that 'tables are preferable to graphics for many small data sets. A table is nearly always

Table 2.1 Reported health problems among female teenagers

Problem	Percentage	
	12–15 years	16–17 years
Sex/reproduction	9	14
Menstrual problems	4	16
How healthy I am	19	20
Nothing	71	62

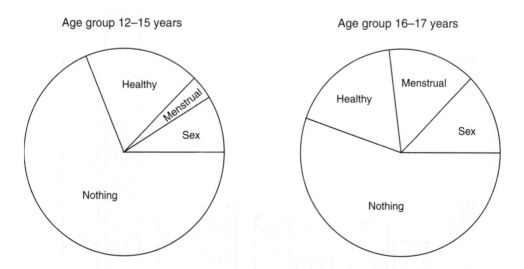

Fig. 2.1 Pie charts for the health problems of female teenagers.

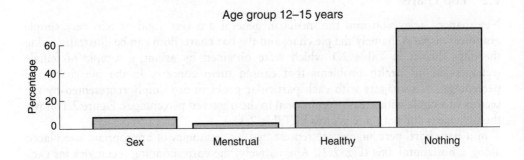

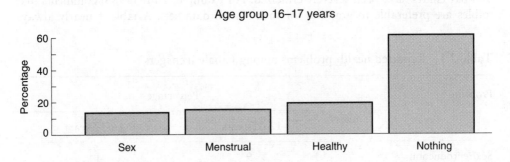

Fig. 2.2 Bar charts for the health problems of female teenagers.

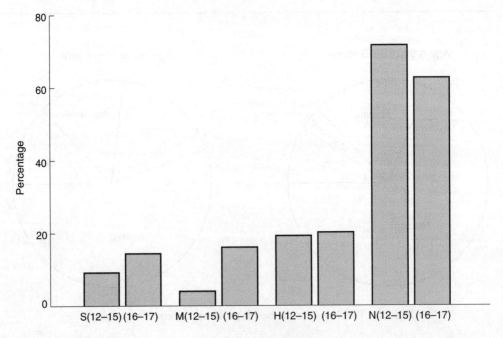

Fig. 2.3 Side-by-side bar chart for the health problems of female teenagers: S, sex; M, menstrual;
H, healthy; N, nothing.

better than a dumb pie chart; the only worse design than a pie chart is several of them . . . pie charts should never be used'. A similar lack of affection is shown by Bertin (1981), who declares that 'pie charts are completely useless'. The standard model bar chart encountered in many publications is also criticized by Tufte, who demonstrates a number of ways in which it could be made more helpful.

Two examples will help to illustrate the reasons behind the critical comments on pie charts and bar charts quoted above; both are taken from Cleveland (1994).

Example 2.1 Figure 2.4 shows a pie chart of 10 percentages. Figure 2.5 shows an alternative representation of the same set of percentages using what is generally known as a **dot plot**. Pattern perception is far more efficient for the latter than for the pie chart. In the dot plot it is far easier to see a number of properties of the data that are either not apparent at all in the pie chart or only barely noticeable. First, the percentages have a **bimodal distribution**: odd-numbered bands cluster about the value 8% and even-

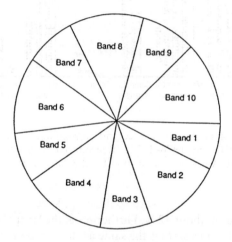

Fig. 2.4 Pie chart for 10 percentages. (Reproduced with permission from Cleveland, 1994.)

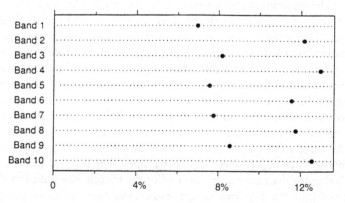

Fig. 2.5 Dot plot for 10 percentages. (Reproduced with permission from Cleveland, 1994.)

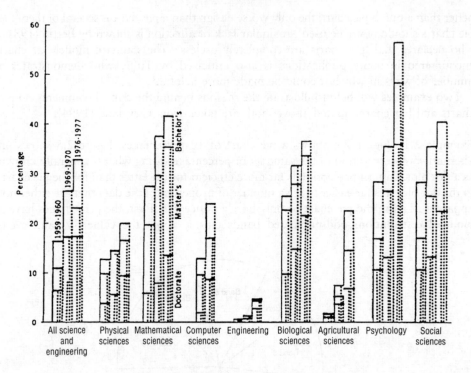

Fig. 2.6 Proportion of degrees in science and engineering earned by women in the periods 1959–1960, 1969–1970 and 1976–1977. (Reproduced with permission from Vetter, 1980, © 1980 American Association for the Advancement of Science.)

numbered bands cluster about 12%. Furthermore, the 'shape' of the pattern for the odd values as band number increases is the same as the shape for the even values; each even value is shifted with respect to the preceding odd value by about 4%.

Example 2.2 The diagram in Fig. 2.6 originally appeared in Vetter (1980); its aim is to display the percentages of degrees awarded to women in several disciplines of science and technology during three time periods. At first glance the labels suggest that the graph is a standard divided bar chart with the length of the bottom division of each bar showing the percentage for doctorates, the length of the middle division showing the percentage for master's degrees and the top division showing the percentage for bachelor's degree. In fact, a little reflection shows that this is *not* correct, since it would imply that in most cases the percentage of bachelor's degrees given to women is generally lower than the percentage of doctorates. Closer examination of the diagram reveals that the three values of the data for each discipline during each time period are determined by the three adjacent vertical dotted lines. The top end of the left-hand line indicates the value for doctorates, the top end of the middle line indicates the value for master's degrees and the top end of the right-hand line indicates the position for bachelor's degrees.

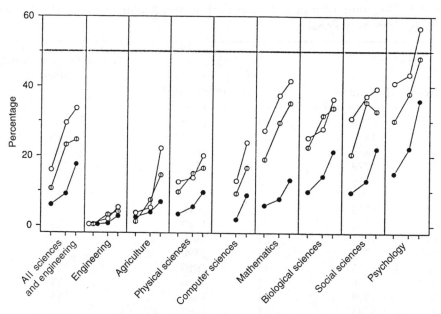

Fig. 2.7 Percentage of degrees earned by women for three degrees (o bachelor's degree; ⊕ master's degree; • doctorate), three time periods and nine disciplines. The three points for each discipline and degree indicate the periods 1959–1960, 1969–1970, 1976–1977. (Reproduced with permission from Cleveland, 1994.)

Cleveland (1994) discusses other problems with the diagram in Fig. 2.6, and also points out that its manner of construction makes it hard to connect visually the three values of a particular type of degree for a particular discipline, i.e. to see change through time. Fig. 2.7 shows the same data as in Fig. 2.6 replotted by Cleveland in a bid to achieve greater clarity. It is now clear how the data are represented, and the design allows viewers to see easily the values corresponding to each degree in each discipline through time. Finally, the figure caption explains the graphs in a comprehensive and clear fashion. All in all Cleveland appears to have produced a plot that would satisfy even that doyen of graphical presentation, Edward R. Tufte, in his demand that 'excellence in statistical graphics consists of complex ideas communicated with clarity, precision and efficiency'.

2.3 Histograms, stem-and-leaf plots and box plots

The data given in Table 2.2 show the heights of both husbands and wives in a random sample of 169 married couples in the UK. (Various ages are also given in Table 2.2; these are for use in Exercise 2.1.) It is extremely difficult to assess even general features of the height data tabulated in this way and almost impossible to identify any potentially interesting patterns. The usual first step in dealing with such data would be to construct separate **frequency distribution tables** (Table 2.3) and then **histograms**

Table 2.2 Data on husbands and wives (Taken with permission from Marsh, 1988, Cambridge University Press)

Husband		Wife		Husband's age at marriage (years)
Age (years)	Height (mm)	Age (years)	Height (mm)	
49	1809	43	1590	25
25	1841	28	1560	19
40	1659	30	1620	38
52	1779	57	1540	26
58	1616	52	1420	30
32	1695	27	1660	23
43	1730	52	1610	33
47	1740	43	1580	26
31	1685	23	1610	26
26	1735	25	1590	23
40	1713	39	1610	23
35	1736	32	1700	31
35	1799	35	1680	19
35	1785	33	1680	24
47	1758	43	1630	24
38	1729	35	1570	27
33	1720	32	1720	28
32	1810	30	1740	22
38	1725	40	1600	31
29	1683	29	1600	25
59	1585	55	1550	23
26	1684	25	1540	18
50	1674	45	1640	25
49	1724	44	1640	27
42	1630	40	1630	28
33	1855	31	1560	22
27	1700	25	1580	21
57	1765	51	1570	32
34	1700	31	1590	28
28	1721	25	1650	23
37	1829	35	1670	22
56	1710	55	1600	44
27	1745	23	1610	25
36	1698	35	1610	22
31	1853	28	1670	20
57	1610	52	1510	25
55	1680	53	1520	21
47	1809	43	1620	25
64	1580	61	1530	21
31	1585	23	1570	28
35	1705	35	1580	25
36	1675	35	1590	22
40	1735	39	1670	23

Table 2.2 Data on husbands and wives – *cont'd*

Husband		Wife		Husband's age at marriage (years)
Age (years)	Height (mm)	Age (years)	Height (mm)	
30	1686	24	1630	27
32	1768	29	1510	21
20	1754	21	1660	19
45	1739	39	1610	25
59	1699	52	1440	27
43	1825	52	1570	25
29	1740	26	1670	24
47	1731	48	1730	21
43	1755	42	1590	20
54	1713	50	1600	23
61	1723	64	1490	26
27	1783	26	1660	20
27	1749	32	1580	24
32	1710	31	1500	31
54	1724	53	1640	20
37	1620	39	1650	21
55	1764	45	1620	29
36	1791	33	1550	30
32	1795	32	1640	25
57	1738	55	1560	24
51	1666	52	1570	24
50	1745	50	1550	22
32	1775	32	1600	20
54	1669	54	1660	20
34	1700	32	1640	22
45	1804	41	1670	27
64	1700	61	1560	24
55	1664	43	1760	31
27	1753	28	1640	23
55	1788	51	1600	26
41	1680	41	1550	22
44	1715	41	1570	24
22	1755	21	1590	21
30	1764	28	1650	29
53	1793	47	1690	31
42	1731	37	1580	23
31	1713	28	1590	28
36	1725	35	1510	26
56	1828	55	1600	30
46	1735	45	1660	22
34	1760	34	1700	23
55	1685	51	1530	34
44	1685	39	1490	27

Table 2.2　Data on husbands and wives – *cont'd*

Husband		Wife		Husband's age at marriage (years)
Age (years)	Height (mm)	Age (years)	Height (mm)	
45	1559	35	1580	34
48	1705	45	1500	28
44	1723	44	1600	41
59	1700	47	1570	39
64	1660	57	1620	32
34	1681	33	1410	22
37	1803	38	1560	23
54	1866	59	1590	49
49	1884	46	1710	25
63	1705	60	1580	27
48	1780	47	1690	22
64	1801	55	1610	37
33	1795	45	1660	17
52	1669	47	1610	23
27	1708	24	1590	26
33	1691	32	1530	21
46	1825	47	1690	23
54	1760	57	1600	23
54	1905	46	1670	32
49	1739	42	1600	28
62	1736	63	1570	22
34	1845	32	1700	24
23	1868	24	1740	19
36	1765	32	1540	27
59	1720	56	1530	24
53	1871	50	1690	25
55	1720	55	1590	21
62	1629	58	1610	23
42	1624	38	1670	22
50	1653	44	1690	35
37	1786	35	1550	21
51	1620	44	1650	30
25	1695	25	1540	19
54	1674	43	1660	35
34	1864	31	1620	23
43	1643	35	1630	29
43	1705	41	1610	22
58	1736	50	1540	32
28	1691	23	1610	23
45	1753	43	1630	21
47	1680	49	1530	20
57	1724	59	1520	24
34	1638	38	1570	33

Table 2.2 Data on husbands and wives – *cont'd*

Husband		Wife		Husband's age at marriage (years)
Age (years)	Height (mm)	Age (years)	Height (mm)	
57	1725	42	1580	52
27	1725	21	1550	24
48	1774	42	1580	30
37	1771	35	1630	28
25	1815	26	1650	20
57	1575	57	1640	20
40	1729	34	1650	26
61	1749	63	1520	21
25	1705	23	1620	24
24	1774	23	1680	22
47	1658	46	1670	24
44	1790	40	1620	24
52	1798	53	1570	25
45	1824	40	1660	23
20	1796	22	1550	19
60	1725	60	1590	21
36	1685	32	1620	25
25	1769	24	1560	18
25	1749	28	1670	21
35	1716	40	1650	17
49	1773	48	1470	21
33	1760	33	1580	20
50	1725	49	1670	23
63	1645	64	1520	28
57	1694	55	1620	24
41	1851	41	1710	23
38	1691	38	1530	20
30	1880	31	1630	22
52	1835	52	1720	30
51	1730	43	1570	22
46	1644	51	1560	27
50	1723	47	1650	25
52	1718	32	1590	25
30	1723	33	1590	22
20	1786	18	1590	19
51	1675	45	1550	25
64	1641	64	1570	30
44	1743	43	1560	25
40	1823	39	1630	23
59	1720	56	1530	24

Table 2.3 Frequency distribution tables for heights of husbands and wives

Class interval	Frequency
Husbands	
1550–1599	5
1600–1649	12
1650–1699	36
1700–1749	55
1750–1799	35
1800–1849	16
1850–1899	9
1900–1949	1
Wives	
1400–1449	3
1450–1499	5
1500–1549	27
1550–1599	54
1600–1649	43
1650–1699	29
1700–1749	7
1750–1799	1

(Fig. 2.8) of the heights of both husbands and wives; here each histogram indicates that the height distributions are symmetric and relatively 'normal'.

A convenient method of displaying the heights of husbands and wives on the same diagram, thus making comparison of their distributions simpler, is the **frequency polygon** which consists of a plot of the midpoint of each class in the frequency distribution table against class frequency, with the points joined by a series of straight lines. Such a diagram for the heights of married couples is shown in Fig. 2.9. As expected, the heights of wives have a lower mean than the heights of husbands; however, the spread of each distribution appears to be very similar.

The histogram is generally used for two purposes: counting and displaying the distribution of a variable. However, according to Wilkinson (1992), 'it is effective for neither'. Histograms can often be misleading for displaying distributions because of their dependence on the number of classes chosen. Simple tallies of the observations are usually preferable for counting, particularly when shown in the form of a **stem-and-leaf plot** as described in Display 2.1. Such a plot has the advantage of showing the 'shape' of a frequency distribution, whilst retaining the values of individual observations. Stem-and-leaf plots of the heights of husbands and wives are shown in Fig. 2.10.

A further, often very useful, graphical display can be obtained from what is known as the **five-number summary** of a data set. The five numbers in question are the **minimum, lower quartile, the median, the upper quartile** and **the maximum**. The median is a measure of the centre, or **location**, of a distribution which, unlike the mean, is not affected by departures from symmetry. The distance between the upper and lower

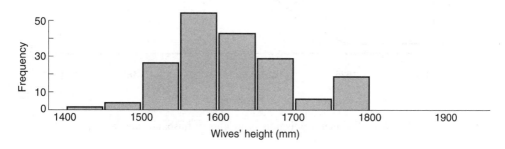

Fig. 2.8 Histograms of heights of husbands and wives.

Display 2.1 Stem-and-leaf plots

To construct the simplest form of stem-and-leaf display of a set of observations, begin by choosing a suitable pair of adjacent digits in the heights data, the tens digit and the units digit. Next 'split' each data value between the two digits. For example, the value 98 would be split as follows:

Data value	Split	stem	and	leaf
98	9/8	9	and	8

Then a separate line in the display is allocated for each possible string of leading digits (the **stems**). Finally, the trailing digit (the **leaf**) of each data value is written down on the line corresponding to its leading digit.

quartiles, or the **interquartile range**, is a measure of the **spread** of a distribution. The relative distances of the upper and lower quartiles from the median give information about the **shape** of a distribution; for example, if one distance is much greater than the other, the distribution is **skewed**. In addition, the median and the upper and lower quartiles can be used to define the rather arbitrary, but often useful, limits L and U to help identify possible outliers in the data. The two limits are defined as follows:

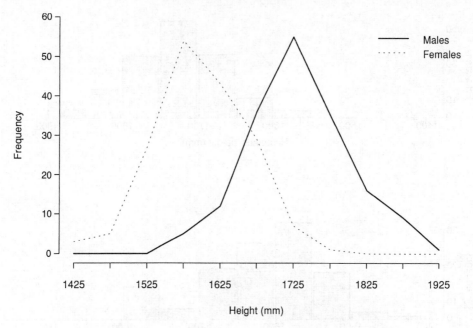

Fig. 2.9 Frequency polygons of heights of husbands and wives.

$$U = UQ + 1.5\,IQR \qquad (2.1)$$
$$L = LQ - 1.5\,IQR \qquad (2.2)$$

where UQ is the upper-quartile value, LQ is the lower-quartile value and IQR is the interquartile range, i.e. simply UQ − LQ. Observations outside the limits L and U are those to be regarded as potential outliers (they are sometimes referred to specifically as **outside** observations). Such observations may merit particular attention before further analyses of a data set are undertaken, since they can often considerably influence the results obtained.

The graphical display resulting from the five-number summary is the **box-and-whisker plot** or, more usually, simply the **box plot**. Its construction is described in Fig. 2.11, and box plots for the heights of husbands and wives are shown in Fig. 2.12. The plots indicate the symmetry of the height distributions (the median in each case is near the centre of the 'box' and the observations show similar spread above and below the median). Wives clearly tend to be shorter than husbands (not very surprising), and a number of outside observations are indicated corresponding to one rather tall and one rather short husband and two relatively short wives.

2.4 The simple scatter plot and related graphical displays

The small set of data in Table 2.4 shows the average vocabulary size of children at various ages. Clearly there is a relationship between the two variables, but is it entirely

```
N = 169  Median = 1725
Quartiles = 1691, 1774
```

Decimal point is two places to the right of the colon

```
15 : 67
15 : 888
16 : 1
16 : 222233
16 : 444445
16 : 66667777777
16 : 88888888889999999
17 : 0000000000001111111
17 : 222222222222222222333333333
17 : 444444444455555555
17 : 666666667777777
17 : 888899999999
18 : 0000001111
18 : 2222333
18 : 44555
18 : 6777
18 : 88
19 : 0
```

```
N = 169   Median = 1600
Quartiles = 1560, 1650
```

Decimal point is two places to the right of the colon

```
14 : 1
14 : 2
14 : 4
14 : 7
14 : 99
15 : 00111
15 : 22223333333
15 : 4444455555555
15 : 666666667777777777
15 : 88888888889999999999999
16 : 000000000011111111111
16 : 22222222233333333
16 : 444444455555555
16 : 666666667777777777
16 : 88899999
17 : 00011
17 : 223
17 : 44
17 : 6
```

Fig. 2.10   Stem-and-leaf plots of heights of husbands and wives.

linear and is there any evidence of an outlier? A rather more substantial data set appears in Table 2.5, namely crime rates for seven different crimes in the 50 states of the USA plus the District of Columbia. Assessing relationships between the rates for different crimes by simply examining the tabulated values is extremely difficult, if not impossible.

The basic graphical tool for examining the relationships between variables in data sets such as those in Tables 2.4 and 2.5 is the **scatter plot,** i.e. a simple $x-y$ plot of the values of two variables for a sample of subjects or objects of interest. Fig. 2.13 shows such a plot for the vocabulary size data. There does appear to be some departure from linearity, and in addition the value for children aged 6 appears to be somewhat out of line with the remaining observations. (These data will be examined again in Chapter 6.)

To construct a box plot, a 'box' with ends at the lower and upper quartiles is first drawn. A horizontal line (or some other feature) is used to indicate the position of the median in the box. Next, lines are drawn from each end of the box to the most remote observations that, however, are *not* outside observations as defined in the text. The resulting diagram schematically represents the body of the data *minus* the extreme observations. Finally, the outside observations are incorporated into the final diagram by representing them individually in some way (lines, stars etc.)

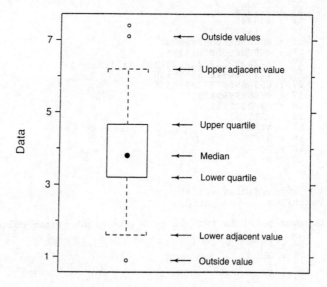

Fig. 2.11   Constructing a box plot.

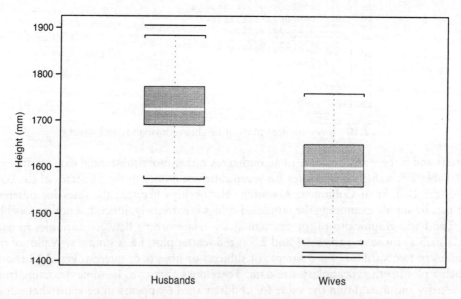

Fig. 2.12   Box plots for heights of husbands and wives.

Table 2.4 The average oral vocabulary size of children at various ages

Age (years)	Number of words
1.0	3
1.5	22
2.0	272
2.5	446
3.0	896
3.5	1222
4.0	1540
4.5	1870
5.0	2072
6.0	2562

Twenty-one scatter plots, each corresponding to the rates for a particular pair of crimes, can be drawn from the state crime data. However, simply plotting the 21 graphs of each rate against the others, without any coordination, is likely to result in a confusing collection of graphs that are hard to integrate, both visually and cognitively. Therefore how should such a large number of diagrams be presented to make them as useful and informative as possible? One particularly helpful method is to arrange the

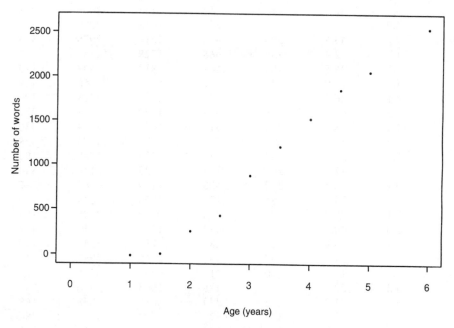

Fig. 2.13 Scatter plot of vocabulary size of children of different ages.

Table 2.5 Crime rates in the USA (numbers of offences known to the police per 100 000 residents of the 50 states of the USA plus the District of Columbia for the year 1986)

State	Murder	Rape	Robbery	Assault	Burglary	Theft	Car theft
ME	2	14.8	28	102	803	2347	164
NH	2.2	21.5	24	92	755	2208	228
VT	2	21.8	22	103	949	2697	181
MA	3.6	29.7	193	331	1071	2189	906
RI	3.5	21.4	119	192	1294	2568	705
CT	4.6	23.8	192	205	1198	2758	447
NY	10.7	30.5	514	431	1221	2924	637
NJ	5.2	33.2	269	265	1071	2822	776
PA	5.5	25.1	152	176	735	1654	354
OH	5.5	38.6	142	235	988	2574	376
IN	6	25.9	90	186	887	2333	328
IL	8.9	32.4	325	434	1180	2938	628
MI	11.3	67.4	301	424	1509	3378	800
WI	3.1	20.1	73	162	783	2802	254
MN	2.5	31.8	102	148	1004	2785	288
IA	1.8	12.5	42	179	956	2801	158
MO	9.2	29.2	170	370	1136	2500	439
ND	1	11.6	7	32	385	2049	120
SD	4	17.7	16	87	554	1939	99
NE	3.1	24.6	51	184	748	2677	168
KS	4.4	32.9	80	252	1188	3008	258
DE	4.9	56.9	124	241	1042	3090	272
MD	9	43.6	304	476	1296	2978	545
DC	31	52.4	754	668	1728	4131	975
VA	7.1	26.5	106	167	813	2522	219
WV	5.9	18.9	41	99	625	1358	169
NC	8.1	26.4	88	254	1225	2423	208
SC	8.6	41.3	99	525	1340	2846	277
GA	11.2	43.9	214	319	1453	2984	430
FL	11.7	52.7	367	605	2221	4373	598
KY	6.7	23.1	83	222	824	1740	193
TN	10.4	47	208	274	1325	2126	544
AL	10.1	28.4	112	408	1159	2304	267
MS	11.2	25.8	65	172	1076	1845	150
AR	8.1	28.9	80	278	1030	2305	195
LA	12.8	40.1	224	482	1461	3417	442
OK	8.1	36.4	107	285	1787	3142	649
TX	13.5	51.6	240	354	2049	3987	714
MT	2.9	17.3	20	118	783	3314	215
ID	3.2	20	21	178	1003	2800	181
WY	5.3	21.9	22	243	817	3078	169
CO	7	42.3	145	329	1792	4231	486
NM	11.5	46.9	130	536	1845	3712	343
AZ	9.3	43	169	437	1908	4337	419

Table 2.5 Crime rates in the USA (numbers of offences known to the police per 100 000 residents of 50 states of the USA plus the District of Columbia for the year 1986) – *cont'd*

State	Murder	Rape	Robbery	Assault	Burglary	Theft	Car theft
UT	3.2	25.3	59	180	915	4074	223
NV	12.6	64.9	287	354	1604	3489	478
WA	5	53.4	135	244	1861	4267	315
OR	6.6	51.1	206	286	1967	4163	402
CA	11.3	44.9	343	521	1696	3384	762
AK	8.6	72.7	88	401	1162	3910	604
HI	4.8	31	106	103	1339	3759	328

plots into a grid or matrix with shared scales as shown in Fig. 2.14. This type of arrangement is often known as a **draughtsman's plot** or simply as a **scatter-plot matrix**. Each panel of the matrix is a scatter plot of one crime rate against another. For example, in the six graphs in the bottom row of Fig. 2.14 the vertical scale is the car theft rate and the six horizontal scales are the murder, rape, robbery, assault, burglary and theft rates. The upper left-hand triangle of the scatter-plot matrix contains all 21 pairs of scatter plots, and so does the lower right-hand triangle. The reasons for including both the upper and lower triangles in the matrix, despite the seeming redundancy, is that it enables a row and a column to be visually scanned to see one variable against all others, with the scales for the one variable lined up along the horizontal or the vertical.

The scatter-plot matrix for the city crime data shows that overall the rates corresponding to different crimes are positively correlated. The rates for murder and rape and for theft and robbery are particularly strongly related. The panels involving murder show one state (District of Columbia) with a very high murder rate, and several other panels give evidence of other possible outliers. More detailed interpretation of Fig. 2.14 is left as an exercise for the reader.

It is often possible to include information about additional variables on a scatter plot, although this may not always lead to a particularly helpful graph if the number of observations is large. Some examples will serve to illustrate the possibilities.

Example 2.3 Bickel *et al.* (1975) analysed the relationship between admission rate and the proportion of women applying to the various academic departments at the University of California at Berkeley. The scatter plot of percentage women applicants against percentage applicants admitted is shown in Fig. 2.15; the plot is enhanced by 'boxes', the sizes of which indicate the relative number of applicants. The negative correlation indicated by the scatter plot is due almost exclusively to a trend for the large departments. If only a simple scatter plot had been used here, vital information about the relationship would have been lost.

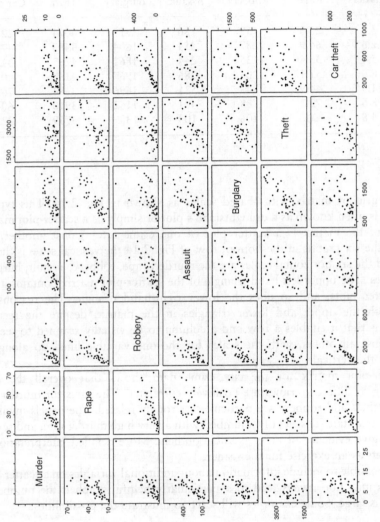

Fig. 2.14 Scatter-plot matrix for crime data in Table 2.5.

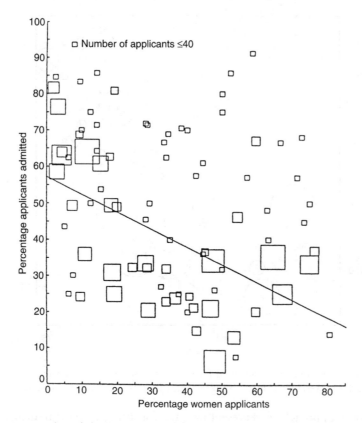

Fig. 2.15 Scatter-plot of the percentage of female applicants versus percentage of applicants admitted for 85 departments at the University of California at Berkeley. (Reproduced with permission from Bickel *et al.*, 1975.)

Example 2.4 As a further example of the enhancement of scatter plots, Fig. 2.16 shows a plot of the height and weight of a sample of individuals with their gender indicated. Also included in the diagram are circles centred on each plotted point; the radii of these circles represent the value of the change in the pulse rate of the subject after running on the spot for 1 min. Therefore, in essence, Fig. 2.16 records the values of four variables for each individual: height, weight, change in pulse rate and gender. Information was also available on whether or not each person in the sample smoked, and this extra information is included in Fig. 2.17, as described in the caption. Fig. 2.17 is very useful for obtaining an overall picture of the data. The increase in pulse rate after exercise is clearly greater for men than for women, but appears to be unrelated to whether or not an individual smokes. There is perhaps a relatively weak indication of a larger increase in pulse rate amongst heavier women, but no such relationship is apparent for men. Two men in the sample, one a smoker and one a non-smoker, show a decrease in pulse rate after exercise.

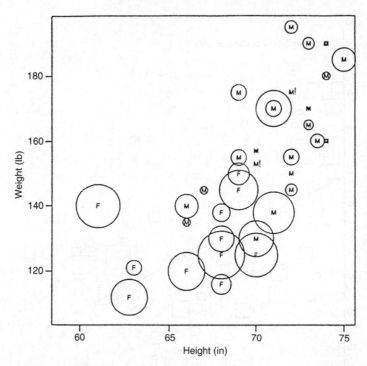

Fig. 2.16   Scatter plot of height and weight for male (M) and female (F) participants: the radii of the circles represent a change in pulse rate, ! indicates a decrease in pulse rate.

An alternative approach to representing data consisting of measurements on three variables for each individual is the **conditioning plot** or, more simply, the **coplot,** a method suggested by Cleveland (1994). The technique provides a graphical display that allows the relationship between two of the variables, *conditional* on values of the third, to be studied. The data given in Table 2.6 will be used to illustrate the application of the coplot. These data show, for each of 36 occupations in the USA, a measure of occupational prestige, the male suicide rate (amongst males aged 20–64), the median income in dollars and the median years of education (the latter will not be considered here but will be used in later chapters). A coplot corresponding to the first three variables in these data is shown in Fig. 2.18. The panel at the top of the figure is known as the **given panel**; the panels below are the **dependence panels**. Each rectangle in the given panel specifies an interval of values of income. On a corresponding dependence panel, prestige score is plotted against suicide rate for those observations whose income values lie in a particular interval. To match income intervals to dependence panels, the latter are examined from left to right in the bottom row and then again from left to right in subsequent rows.

Figure 2.18 highlights a number of interesting features of the data in Table 2.6. The dependence panel corresponding to the lowest income band indicates very clearly the presence of an outlier. The corresponds to the occupation clergyman, which has low income, a relatively high prestige rating and a low suicide rate (vicars and the like are clearly poor but happy). Similarly the dependence panel corresponding to the highest

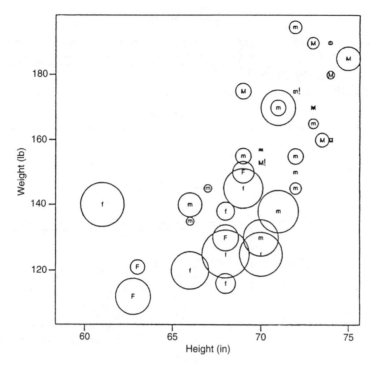

Fig. 2.17 Scatter plot of height and weight with additional information about sex, smoking status and change in pulse rate: M, male smoker; F, female smoker; m, male non-smoker; f, female non-smoker; ! indicates a decrease in pulse rate.

incomes contains a point relatively widely separated from the others in the panel. This point corresponds to managers, officials and proprietors, manufacturing. The coplot further suggests that the relationship between suicide rate and prestige rating may not be the same at all income levels.

Finally, we give an example of a particularly creative way of enhancing a scatter plot to illustrate a specific point. Fig. 2.19 (Zeeman, 1976) shows the effect of two variables interacting by the changing faces on the plotting area.

2.5   Representing multivariate data by cartoon faces

Data consisting of observations on more than a single variable for each subject or object in a study are generally referred to as **multivariate** (for example, most of the data sets used in previous sections are multivariate). The analysis of multivariate data is taken up in detail in Chapters 10, 11 and 12; a graphical method of displaying such data is described here.

Chernoff (1973) suggested representing a multivariate observation by a cartoon face, the features of which (e.g. its shape, the curve of the mouth, and the position and shape of the eyes) are governed by the observation's variable values. Thus a collection of multivariate observations is represented by a collection of cartoon faces, and these can be examined to assess patterns of differences and similarities between the observations.

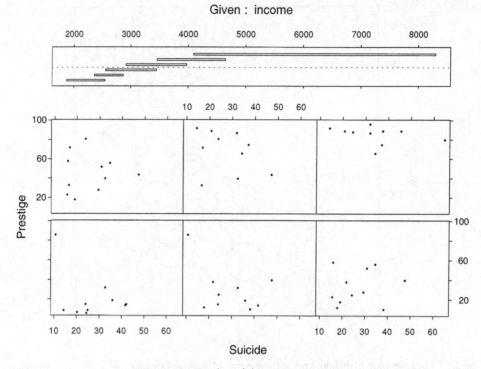

Fig. 2.18 Coplot of data on occupations.

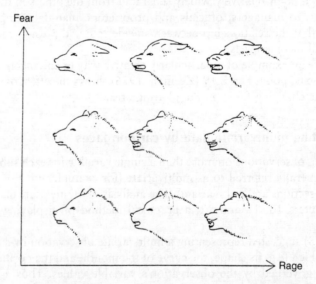

Fig. 2.19 Scatter plot showing interaction between two variables. (Reproduced with permission from Zeeman, 1976, © 1976 by *Scientific American* Inc.)

Table 2.6 Prestige, income, education, and suicide rates for 36 occupations (reproduced from Labovitz, 1970, with permission of the American Sociological Association)

Occupation	Prestige rating	Male suicide rate	Median income by 1949 ($)	Median number of years of education completed
Accountants	82	23.8	3977	14.4
Architects	90	37.5	5509	16
Authors	76	37.0	4303	15.6
Chemists	90	20.7	4091	16
Clergymen	87	10.6	2410	16
Professors	93	14.2	4366	16
Dentists	90	45.6	6448	16
Civil engineers	88	31.9	4590	16
Lawyers	89	24.3	6284	16
Physicians	97	31.9	8302	16
Social workers	59	16.0	3176	15.8
Teachers	73	16.8	3456	16
Managers manufacturing (self employed)	81	64.8	4700	12.2
Managers retail (self employed)	45	47.3	3806	11.6
Book-keepers	39	21.9	2828	12.7
Mail-carriers	34	16.5	3480	12.2
Insurance agents	41	32.4	3771	12.7
Salesmen	16	24.1	2543	12.1
Carpenters	33	32.7	2450	8.7
Electricians	53	30.8	3447	11.1
Locomotive engineers	67	34.2	4648	8.8
Machinists	57	34.5	3303	9.6
Mechanics	26	24.4	2693	9.4
Plumbers	29	29.4	3353	9.3
Parking attendants	10	14.4	1898	10.3
Mine operatives	15	41.7	2410	8.2
Motormen	19	19.2	3424	9.2
Taxi driver	10	24.9	2213	8.9
Truck driver	13	17.9	2590	9.6
Operatives	24	15.7	2915	9.6
Barbers	20	36.0	2357	8.8
Waiters	7	24.4	1942	9.8
Cooks	16	42.2	2249	8.7
Guards	11	38.2	2551	8.5
Janitors	8	20.3	1866	8.2
Policemen	41	47.6	2866	10.6

Table 2.7 What do people in the UK think about themselves and their partners in the European Community[a]

Country	Characteristic[b]												
	1	2	3	4	5	6	7	8	9	10	11	12	13
French	37	29	21	19	10	10	8	8	6	6	5	2	1
Spanish	7	14	8	9	27	7	3	7	3	23	12	1	3
Italian	30	12	19	10	20	7	12	6	5	13	10	1	2
British	9	14	4	6	27	12	2	13	26	16	29	6	25
Irish	1	7	1	16	30	3	10	9	5	11	22	2	27
Dutch	5	4	2	2	15	2	0	13	24	1	28	4	6
German	4	48	1	12	3	9	2	11	41	1	38	8	8

[a] Entries in the table give the percentages of respondents agreeing that the nationals of a particular country possess a particular characteristic.
[b] 1, stylish; 2, arrogant; 3, sexy; 4, devious; 5, easy-going; 6, greedy; 7, cowardly; 8, boring; 9, efficient; 10, lazy; 11, hard working; 12, clever; 13, courageous.

The faces approach to representing multivariate data graphically has never been popular with statisticians (who, on the whole, are rather a conservative bunch), despite its use in a variety of applications (Pike, 1974; McDonald and Ayers, 1978; Wang and Lake, 1978). Perhaps the use of the technique might be more acceptable (or at least forgivable) in situations where the data involve observations on human subjects, or where the face can be used to indicate some type of 'judgement' about a particular set of

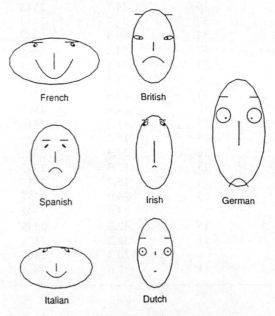

Fig. 2.20 Faces representation of data in Table 2.7.

variable values. The data in Table 2.7 will be used as an illustration. These data were obtained by asking a large number of people in the UK questions about various characteristics that might or might not be associated with the UK's partners in the European Community. A faces representation of each county's profile is shown in Fig. 2.20. Judicious assignment of characteristics to facial features leads to faces which reflect, at least in the author's opinion, the probable satisfaction of the nationals of each country with respect to their perceived stereotypes.

2.6   Graphical deception

In general, graphical displays of the kind described in previous sections are extremely useful in the examination of data; indeed, they are almost essential both in the initial phase of data exploration and in the interpretation of the results from more formal statistical procedures, as will be seen in later chapters. Unfortunately, it is relatively easy to mislead the unwary with graphical material, and not all graphical displays are as honest as they should be! For example, consider the plot of the death rate per million from cancer of the breast, for several periods over the last three decades, shown in Fig. 2.21. The rate appears to show a rather alarming increase. However, when the data are replotted with the vertical scale beginning at zero, as shown in Fig. 2.22, the increase in the breast cancer death rate is altogether less startling. This example illustrates that undue exaggeration or compression of the scales is best avoided when drawing graphs (unless, of course, you are actually in the business of deceiving your audience).

A very common distortion introduced into the graphics most popular with newspapers, television and the media in general, is when *both* dimensions of a *two-dimensional figure* or **icon** are varied simultaneously in response to changes in a *single* variable. The examples shown in Fig. 2.23, both taken from Tufte (1983), illustrate this point. Tufte quantifies the distortion with what he calls the **lie factor** of a graphical display, which is defined as

$$\text{lie factor} = \frac{\text{size of effect shown in graphic}}{\text{size of effect in data}}.\qquad(2.3)$$

Lie factor values close to unity show that the graphic is probably representing the underlying numbers reasonably accurately. The lie factor for the 'oil barrels' is 9.4 since a 454% increase is depicted as 4280%. The lie factor for the 'shrinking doctors' is 2.8.

A further example given by Cleveland (1994), and reproduced in Fig. 2.24, demonstrates that even the manner in which a simple scatter plot is drawn can lead to misperceptions about data. The example concerns the way in which judgement about the correlation of two variables made on the basis of looking at their scatter plot can be distorted by enlarging the area in which the points are plotted. The coefficient of correlation in the lower diagram in Fig. 2.24 appears greater.

Being misled by graphical displays is usually a sobering but not a life-threatening experience. However, Cleveland (1994) gives an example where using the wrong graph contributed to a major disaster in the American space programme, namely the explosion of the *Challenger* space shuttle and the deaths of the seven people on board. To assess the suggestion that low temperature might affect the performance of the

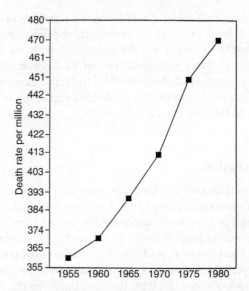

Fig. 2.21 Death rates from cancer of the breast where the *y* axis does not include the origin.

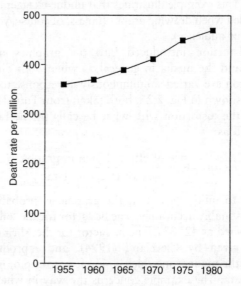

Fig. 2.22 Death rates from cancer of the breast where the *y* axis does include the origin.

O-rings that sealed the joints of the rocket motor, engineers studied the graph of the data shown in Fig. 2.25. Each data point was from a shuttle flight in which the O-rings had experienced thermal distress. The horizontal axis shows the O-ring temperature, and the vertical scale shows the number of O-rings that had experienced thermal distress. On the basis of these data, *Challenger* was allowed to take off when the temperature was 31°F, with tragic consequences.

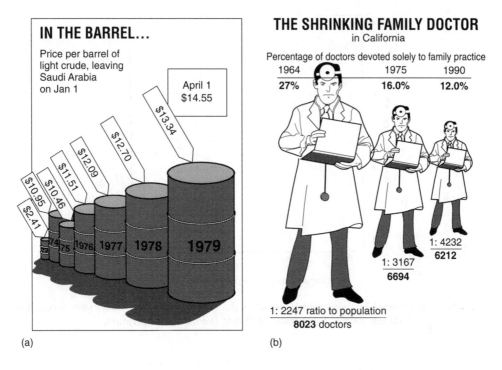

(a)   (b)

Fig. 2.23 Graphics exhibiting lie factors of (a) 9.4 and (b) 2.8.

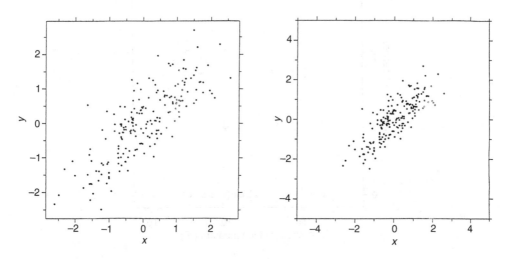

Fig. 2.24 Misjudgement of size of correlation caused by enlarging the plotting area.

The data for 'no failures' are not plotted in Fig. 2.25. The engineers involved believed that these data were irrelevant to the issue of dependence. They were mistaken, as

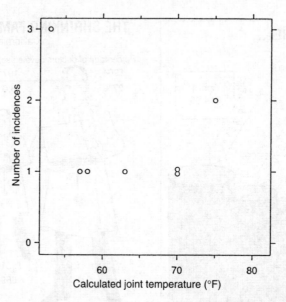

Fig. 2.25 Data plotted by space shuttle engineers the evening before the *Challenger* accident to determine the dependence of O-ring failure on temperature.

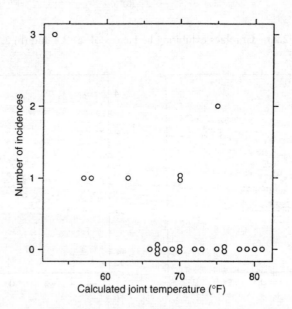

Fig. 2.26 The complete set of O-ring data.

shown by the plot in Fig. 2.26 which includes *all* the data. Here a pattern *does* emerge and a dependence of failure on temperature is revealed.

Fig. 2.27 Misperception and miscommunication are sometimes a way of life! (Drawing by Charles E. Martin; © 1961, 1989, *The New Yorker Magazine*, Inc. Used with permission.)

To end on a less sombre note, and to show that misperception and miscommunication are certainly not confined to statistical graphics, see Fig. 2.27!

2.7 Summary

1. Graphical displays are an essential feature in the analysis of empirical data.
2. In some case a graphical 'analysis' may be all that is required (or merited).
3. Stem-and-leaf plots are usually more informative than histograms for displaying frequency distributions.
4. Box plots display much more information about data sets and are very useful for comparing groups. In addition, they are useful for identifying possible outliers.
5. Scatter plots are the fundamental tool for examining relationships between variables. They can be enhanced in a variety of ways to provide extra information.
6. Beware graphical deception!
7. Some of the graphics used in this chapter are not available in standard statistical packages such as SPSS, SAS and MINITAB, although this is likely to change in the near future. Most of the graphs in this chapter were produced using S-PLUS, a powerful programming language described by Everitt (1994) and by Venables and Ripley (1994).

Exercises

2.1 To investigate in more detail the relationship between the heights of husbands and wives and their ages, produce and examine the following plots:

(1) height of husband against height of wife;

(2) height of husband against height of wife, with age difference of husband and wife
     represented by circles of appropriate size;
(3) height of husband against height of wife, with age of husband at marriage
     represented by circles of appropriate size.

What, if anything, do the graphs reveal about these data?

2.2 Figure 2.28 shows a plot of traffic deaths in a particular area before and after
stricter enforcement of the speed limit by the police. Does the graph convince you that
the efforts of the police have had the desired effect? If not, why not?

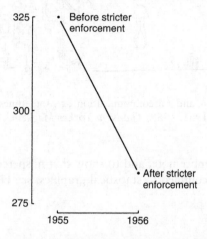

Fig. 2.28 Traffic deaths before and after introduction of stricter enforcement of speed limit.

Table 2.8 Data on 10 states of the USA

State	Variable[a]						
	1	2	3	4	5	6	7
Alabama	3615	3624	2.1	69.05	15.1	41.3	20
California	21198	5114	1.1	71.71	10.3	62.6	20
Iowa	2861	4628	0.5	72.56	2.3	59.0	140
Mississippi	2341	3098	2.4	68.09	12.5	41.0	50
New Hampshire	812	4281	0.7	71.23	3.3	57.6	174
Ohio	10735	4561	0.8	70.82	7.4	53.2	124
Oregon	2284	4660	0.6	72.13	4.2	60.0	44
Pennsylvania	11860	4449	1.0	70.43	6.1	50.2	126
South Dakota	681	4167	0.5	72.08	1.7	52.3	172
Vermont	472	3907	0.6	71.64	5.5	57.1	168

[a] 1, Population (×1000); 2, average per capita income ($); 3, illiteracy rate (% population); 4, life expectancy (years);
5, homicide rate (per 1000); 6, percentage of high school graduates; 7, average number of days per year below freezing

Table 2.9 Mortality rates (rates per 100 000) from suicide for males, 1971

Country	25–34	35–44	45–54	55–64	65–74
Canada	22	27	31	34	24
Israel	9	19	10	14	27
Japan	22	19	21	31	49
Austria	29	40	52	53	69
France	16	25	36	47	56
Germany	28	35	41	49	52
Hungary	48	65	84	81	107
Italy	7	8	11	18	27
Netherlands	8	11	18	20	28
Poland	26	29	36	32	28
Spain	4	7	10	16	22
Sweden	28	41	46	51	35
Switzerland	22	34	41	50	51
UK	10	13	15	17	22
USA	20	22	28	33	37

2.3   Table 2.8 gives the values of a number of variables for 10 states in the USA.

1. Construct a scatter-plot matrix of the data, labelling the points in each panel with the appropriate state name.
2. If possible, construct a faces representation of the data, assigning features to variables in a bid to identify the 'worst' state to live in (worst in this context should be taken to imply certain things about particular variables, such as more days below freezing, greater homicide rate etc.).

2.4   Table 2.9 shows the mortality rates per 100 000 from male suicides for a number of age groups and a number of countries. Construct side-by-side box plots for the data in the different age groups.

Further reading

Cleveland, W.S. and McGill, M.E. (ed.) (1988). *Dynamic graphics for statistics*. Wadsworth, Belmont, CA.

Flury, B. and Riedwyl, H. (1981). Graphical representation of multivariate data by means of asymmetrical faces. *Journal of the American Statistical Association*, **76**, 757–65.

Everitt, B.S. (1994). Exploring multivariate data graphically: a brief review with examples. *Journal of Applied Statistics*, **21**, 63–94.

Wainer, H. and Thissen, D. (1993). Graphical data analysis. In *A handbook for data analysis in the behavioural sciences* (ed. G. Keren and C. Lewis). Lawrence Erlbaum, Hillsdale, NJ.

3

Analysis of variance: the one-way design

3.1 Introduction

In an experiment to compare different methods of teaching arithmetic (Wetherill, 1982), 45 students were divided randomly into five groups of equal size. Two groups were taught by the current method and three by one of three new methods. At the end of the investigation, all pupils took a standard test with the results shown in Table 3.1. What conclusions can be drawn about differences between teaching methods?

This study is an example of what is generally known as a **one-way design**; the effect of a single independent factor variable (teaching method) on a response variable (test score) is of interest. The question posed in such a design is: 'Do the populations corresponding to the different levels of the independent variable have different means?' What statistical technique(s) can be used to answer this question?

3.2 Student's *t*-tests

Most readers will recall Student's *t*-test from their introductory statistics course (those that do not should return at once to their notes or to the appropriate definition in the glossary in Appendix A). One form of this test is used to assess whether the means of two populations differ. Since interest in the data on teaching methods also involves the question of mean differences, is it possible that the straightforward application of *t*-tests to each pair of group means in the teaching study would provide the required answer to

Table 3.1   Data on teaching methods

A	B	C	D	E
17	21	28	19	21
14	23	30	28	14
24	13	29	26	13
20	19	24	26	19
24	13	27	19	15
23	19	30	24	15
16	20	28	24	10
15	21	28	23	18
24	16	23	22	20

A, current method; B, current method; C, praised; D, reproved; E, ignored.

Display 3.1   The problem with multiple *t*-tests for testing the equality of a set of k means, $\mu_1, \mu_2, \ldots, \mu_k$

- The null hypothesis H_0 of interest is

$$H_0 : \mu_1 = \mu_2 = \ldots = \mu_k.$$

- Suppose that the hypothesis is tested by a series of *t*-tests, one for each pair of means.
- The total number of *t*-tests needed is $N = k(k-1)/2$.
- Suppose that each *t*-test is performed at significance level α, so that for each of the tests

  $P(\text{rejecting the equality of the two means given they are equal}) = \alpha,$

  where P represents probability.

- Consequently,

  $P(\text{accepting the equality of the two means when they are equal}) = 1 - \alpha.$

- Therefore

  $P(\text{accepting equality for all } N, \; t\text{-tests performed}) = (1-\alpha)^N.$

- Hence, finally,

  $P(\text{rejecting the equality of } at\; least\; one\; pair\; of\; means \text{ when } H_0 \text{ is true})$
  $= 1 - (1-\alpha)^N.$

- For particular values of k and $\alpha = 0.05$ this leads to the following:

k	N	P
2	1	$1 - (0.95)^1 = 0.05$
3	3	$1 - (0.95)^3 = 0.14$
4	6	$1 - (0.95)^6 = 0.26$
10	45	$1 - (0.95)^{45} = 0.90$

- The probability of falsely rejecting the null hypothesis quickly increases above the nominal significance level of 0.05. It is clear that such an approach is very likely to lead to misleading conclusions. Investigators unwise enough to apply the procedure would be led to claim more statistically significant results than were justified by their data.

whether the teaching methods differ? Sadly, this is an example of where putting two and two together arrives at the wrong answer. To explain why requires a little simple probability and algebra, and so the details are confined to Display 3.1. Clearly, however, the consequence of applying a series of simple t-tests to a one-way design with even a moderate number of groups is very likely to be the claim that there is a significant difference amongst the means, even when no such difference actually exists. The chances of such a misleading conclusion increases with the number of levels of the independent variable. The message is clear: avoid multiple t-tests like the plague!

The appropriate 'formal' method for the analysis of data derived from one-way design is the **one-way analysis of variance**. (No doubt, many readers will have already covered this topic in their introductory statistics course. If so, feel free to move on to Chapter 4, although, of course, you may miss something to your advantage.) However, before launching into the standard analysis of the data on teaching methods using an analysis of variance model, it should be examined by more informal techniques in the spirit of the discussion in Chapter 1.

3.3   Initial examination of the data on teaching methods

Table 3.2 shows the means and standard deviations of the test scores given by each of the five teaching methods. The roughly similar within-group variation supports the assumption of **homogeneity of variance** required by the usual analysis of variance tests (see next section). The differences in sample means look high when compared with the average within-group standard deviation. These differences are highlighted when the data are displayed as a series of box plots as shown in Fig. 3.1. There is no overlap between the observations of teaching methods C and E, whilst B and C only just 'touch'. Figure 3.1 provides convincing evidence that there really are differences between the teaching methods. Since the evidence from the box plots is so clear, it might be argued that no formal analysis is required; in particular the calculation of the ubiquitous P value is largely unnecessary. In theory, this is an argument with which the author would have much sympathy (although, unfortunately, editors of most psychological journals would probably disagree). However, in the context of this book stopping here would make the chapter far too short and so consideration will now be given to the formal analysis of the data on teaching methods.

Table 3.2   Means and standard deviations for the data on teaching methods

	A	B	C	D	E
Mean	19.67	18.33	27.44	23.44	16.11
SD	4.21	3.57	2.45	3.09	3.62

A, B, C, D and E are as defined as Table 3.1.

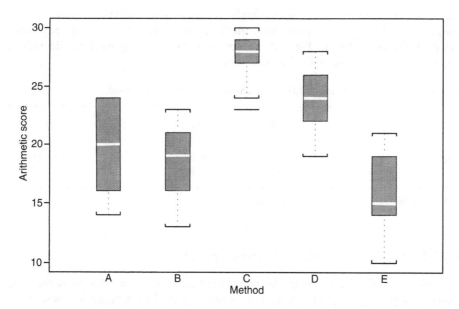

Fig. 3.1 Box plots for the data on teaching methods given in Table 3.1: A, current method; B, current method; C, praised; D, reproved; E, ignored.

3.4 One-way analysis of variance

The phrase 'analysis of variance' was coined by arguably the most famous statistician of the twentieth century, Sir Ronald Aylmer Fisher, who defined it as 'the separation of variance ascribable to one group of causes from the variance ascribable to the other groups'. Stated another way, the analysis of variance (ANOVA) is a partitioning of the total variance in a set of data into a number of component parts. How does this separation or partitioning of **variance** help in assessing differences between *means*?

For the one-way design the answer to this question can be found by considering two sample variances, of which one measures variation between the observations within the groups, and the other measures the variation between the group means. If the populations corresponding to the various levels of the independent variable have the same mean for the response variable, both the sample variances described estimate the *same* population value. However, if the population means differ, variation between the sample means will be greater than that between observations within groups, and therefore the two sample variances will be estimating *different* population values. Consequently testing for the equality of the group means requires a test of the equality of the two variances. The appropriate procedure is an **F-test**. (This explanation of how an F-test for the equality of two variances leads to a test of the equality of a set of means is not specific to the one-way design; it applies to *all* analysis of variance designs, which should be remembered in later chapters where the explanation is not repeated in detail.)

A more formal account of the model and measures of variation behind the F-test in a one-way analysis of variance is given in Display 3.2. The results of applying the procedure to the data on teaching methods are shown in Table 3.3. The *P*-value associated with the *F*-test is extremely small, confirming what has already been suggested by the box plots in Fig. 3.1, namely that the teaching methods do indeed differ in their effects on the arithmetic test scores.

Table 3.3 Analysis of variance table for the data on teaching methods

Source	SS	DF	MS	F	P
Teaching methods	722.67	4	180.67	15.27	< 0.0001
Error	473.33	40	11.83		

SS, sum of squares; DF, degrees of freedom; MS, mean square.

Display 3.2 The one-way analysis of variance model

- In a general sense, the usual model considered for a one-way design is that the subjects in a particular group all have the same **expected** or **average** response, with differences between subjects within a group being accounted for by some type of random variation. Consequently the model can be written as

    observed response = expected response + error.

- The expected response in a group is modelled as the sum of the overall mean of the response plus the effect of the group, so that the model above can be rewritten as

    observed response = mean + group effect + error.

- More specifically, let y_{ij} represent the *j*th observation in the *i*th group. The **linear model** assumed for the observations is

$$y_{ij} = \mu + \alpha_i + \epsilon_{ij}$$

    where μ represents the overall mean, α_i is the effect on an observation of being in the *i*th group $(i = 1, 2, \ldots, k)$ and ϵ_{ij} is a random error term, assumed to be normally distributed with zero mean and variance σ^2.

- When written in this way, the model is said to be **overparameterized**, since $k + 1$ parameters are used to describe only k group means. This feature of analysis of variance models is discussed in detail by Maxwell and Delaney (1990), and also briefly in Chapter 8 of this text . One way of overcoming the difficulty is to introduce the constraint that $\sum_{i=1}^{k} \alpha_i = 0$, so that one of the α_i parameters can be expressed as the negative of the sum of the others. The number of parameters is thus reduced by one. (Other possible constraints are discussed in the exercises in Chapter 8.)

- If this model is assumed, the hypothesis of the equality of group means (see Display 3.1) can be rewritten in terms of the parameters α_i as

$$H_0 : \alpha_1 = \alpha_2 = \ldots = \alpha_k = 0.$$

- The total variation in the observations is partitioned into that due to differences in the group means and that due to differences amongst observations within groups. Under the hypothesis of the equality of group means, both the between-group and the within-group variances are estimates of σ^2. Consequently, an F-test of the equality of the two variances provides a test of H_0.
- The necessary terms for the F-test are usually arranged in an **analysis of variance table** as follows (N is the total number of observations):

Source	DF	SS	MS	MSR(F)
Between groups	$k-1$	BGSS	BGSS/$(k-1)$	MSBG/MSWG
Within groups (error)	$N-k$	WGSS	WGSS/$(N-k)$	
Total	$N-1$			

DF, degrees of freedom; SS, sum of squares; MS, mean square; BGSS, between-group sum of squares; WGSS, within-group sum of squares.

- If H_0 is true (and the assumptions discussed in the text are valid), the MSR has an F-distribution with $k-1$ and $N-k$ degrees of freedom.

The data collected from a one-way design need to satisfy the following assumptions to make the F-test involved strictly valid:

1. The observations in each group come from a normal distribution.
2. The population variances of each group are the same.
3. The observations are independent of one another.

An informal assessment of these assumptions is often provided by the methods used in an initial examination of the data. For example, the box plots given in Fig. 3.1 for the data on teaching methods show no obvious departures from the homogeneity of variance assumption. These plots also indicate that, apart perhaps from teaching method E, the observations have a symmetric distribution within each group and suggest that the normality assumption is unlikely to be too far from the truth. (The independence assumption will become of more relevance in the designs to be considered in Chapter 5.)

More formal methods for checking the assumptions of both normality and homogeneity of variance are available, for example the Shapiro–Wilk test for normality (Shapiro and Wilk, 1965) and Bartlett's test for homogeneity of variance (Bartlett, 1950). However, such tests are of very limited practical relevance since the good news is that even when the group variances are a little unequal and the observations are a little non-normal, the usual F-test is unlikely to mislead. This is because the F-test is what is known as **robust** against departures from both normality and homogeneity of variance, particularly when the numbers of observations in each group are equal or approximately equal. The consequence is that departures from normality and homogeneity will not, in general, lead to greatly distorted P-values or, consequently, inappropriate conclusions. Only if the departures from either or both assumptions are extreme will there be cause for concern; and such gross departures are usually clearly indicated by the initial graphical displays of the data without the need for more formal analyses. If the departures from the assumptions above are deemed to be too extreme to rely on normal-based analysis of variance, there are at least three alternative approaches:

1. **Transform** the raw data to make it more suitable for analysis, i.e, perform the required analysis not on the raw data, but on the values obtained after applying some suitable mathematical function. For example, if the data are skewed, a logarithm transformation may help. Transformations are discussed in detail by Howell (1992) and are also involved in some of the exercises in this chapter and in Chapter 4. Transforming the data is sometimes felt to be a 'trick' used by statisticians, a belief that is based on the idea that the natural scale of measurement is sacrosanct in some way. This is not really the case, and indeed some measurements (e.g. pH values) are effectively already logarithmically transformed values. However, it is almost always preferable to present results in the original scale of measurement.
2. Use **distribution-free methods** (see Chapter 9).
3. Use a model that explicitly specifies more realistic assumptions than normality and homogeneity of variance (see Chapter 8).

Returning to the specific example of the teaching methods, it is clear from the analysis of variance F-test reported in Table 3.3 that the hypothesis that the means of the five methods are equal must be rejected. Of course, this does not imply that each mean differs from all the others; for example, the equality hypothesis might be rejected because the mean of one of the methods is different from those of the other four, which are all equal. Discovering more about mean differences in a one-way design often requires the use of what are known as **multiple comparison techniques**.

3.5 Multiple comparison techniques

When a significant result has been obtained from the one-way analysis of variance, further analysis may be required to find out just which means differ. One possibility is to compare each pair of means in turn, or perhaps just those pairs of particular interest (see later), by using a t-test. However, is this not the very process dismissed as hopelessly misleading in Section 3.2? Well, yes and no is the somewhat unhelpful answer. Clearly some more explanation is needed.

1. The series of t-tests contemplated here is carried out only after finding a significant F-value in the one-way analysis of variance.
2. Each t-test in this series uses the pooled estimate of variance obtained from all groups rather than from just the two whose means are being tested. In other words the within-groups mean square (more commonly referred to as the **error mean square**) obtained from the analysis of variance is used in the calculation of each t-test.
3. The problem of inflating the type I error, as discussed in Section 3.2, is tackled by judging the P-value from each t-test against a significance level of α/m, where m is

the number of t-tests performed and α is the size of the type I error that the investigator wishes to maintain in the testing process. (This is known as the **Bonferonni correction.**)

The practical consequence of using this procedure is that each t-test applied will need to result in a more extreme value than usual for a significant difference to be claimed. In this way the overall type I error rate will be kept close to the desired value α. The disadvantage of this approach is that it may be highly conservative if a large number of comparisons are involved, i.e. some 'significant' differences may be missed. (Contemplating a 'large' number of comparisons may, of course, reflect a poorly designed study.) However, this procedure can be recommended for a small number of comparisons, and the results of its application to the data on teaching methods are shown in Display 3.3. The conclusions to be drawn from these results are that the mean of method B differs from those of methods C and D, and that the mean of method E also differs from those of methods C and D. This matches the informal assessment of the means that can be made from the box plots in Fig. 3.1.

There are many alternatives to the Bonferonni correction procedure for investigating differences between a set of means following a significant F-test, most of which are based on the t-statistic given in Display 3.3. The methods differ in the choice of critical values with which the t-statistic is compared. One alternative which is particularly useful when a large number of comparisons is involved is Scheffé's procedure, which is described in Display 3.4. Using this procedure on the data on teaching methods gives the results also shown in Display 3.4. Note first that all the confidence intervals are wider than the corresponding intervals in Display 3.3. This indicates that, in this example at least, Scheffé's procedure is more conservative than the Bonferonni method. This may not always be the case since, as remarked earlier, the latter is highly conservative if a large number of comparisons are contemplated. Although the conclusions are largely similar to those obtained using the Bonferonni approach, with Scheffé's method the confidence interval for teaching methods B and D now contains the value zero and so strictly no difference between those methods can be claimed. However, most people, including the author, would be inclined to interpret the confidence interval limits as suggesting that method D leads to a somewhat higher mean on the arithmetic test than method C.

One general point to make about multiple comparison tests is that, on the whole, they all err on the side of safety (non-significance). Consequently, it is quite possible (although always disconcerting) to find that, although the F-test in the analysis of variance is statistically significant, no pair of means is judged by the multiple comparison procedure to be significantly different. One further point is that a host of such tests are available, often with exotic sounding names. Statisticians are usually very wary of an over-reliance on such tests (the author is no exception), and readers need to avoid being seduced by the ease with which multiple comparison tests can be applied in most statistical software packages.

3.6 Planned comparisons

Most analyses of one-way designs performed in psychological research involve the approach described in the previous two sections, namely a one-way analysis of variance in which finding a signficant F-value is followed by the application of some type of multiple comparison test. But there is another way! Consider, for example, the data shown in Table 3.4, which were obtained from an investigation into the effect of the

Display 3.3 Bonferonni t-tests for the data on teaching methods

- The t-statistic used is

$$t = \frac{\text{mean difference}}{s(1/n_1 + 1/n_2)^{1/2}}$$

  where s^2 is the error mean square and n_1 and n_2 are the number of observations in the two groups being compared.
- Each observed t-statistic is compared with the value from the t-distribution with $N - k$ degrees of freedom corresponding to a significance level of α/m rather than α, where m is the number of comparisons made.
- Alternatively (and preferably) a confidence interval can be constructed as

$$\text{mean difference} \pm t_{N-k}(\alpha/m) \times s\left(\frac{1}{n_1} + \frac{1}{n_2}\right)^{1/2}$$

  where $t_{N-k}(\alpha/m)$ is the t value with $N - k$ degrees of freedom, corresponding to significance level α/m. (These confidence intervals are available from most statistical software packages.)
- In the teaching methods example $N - k = 40$, and $n_1 = n_2 = 9$ for all pairs of groups. Ten comparisons can be made between the pairs of means of the five methods, so that the relevant t-value is that corresponding to 40 degrees of freedom and $\alpha/10$; for $\alpha = 0.05$ the value is 2.97. Finally, $s^2 = 11.83$ (see Table 3.3).
- The constructed confidence intervals are as follows:

M1	M2	MD	Confidence interval
A	B	1.33	$1.33 \pm 2.97 \times 1.62 = 1.33 \pm 4.82 = (-3.48, 6.14)$
A	C	-7.78	$(-12.59, -2.96)^*$
A	D	-3.78	$(-8.60, 1.04)$
A	E	3.56	$(-1.26, 8.38)$
B	C	-9.11	$(-13.93, -4.29)^*$
B	D	-5.11	$(-9.93, -0.29)^*$
B	E	2.22	$(-2.60, 7.04)$
C	D	4.00	$(-0.82, 8.82)$
C	E	11.33	$(6.51, 16.15)^*$
D	E	7.33	$(2.51, 12.15)^*$

M1, method 1, M2, method 2, MD, mean difference.
* Interval does not include zero.

Display 3.4 Scheffé's multiple comparison procedure

- The test statistic used here is once again the t-statistic used in the Bonferroni procedure and described in Display 3.3, but in this case each observed test statistic is compared with $[(k-1)F_{k-1,N-k}(\alpha)]^{1/2}$, where $F_{k-1,N-k}(\alpha)$ is the F-value with $k-1$, $N-k$ degrees of freedom, corresponding to significance level α. (Details are given by Maxwell and Delaney, 1990.)
- For the teaching methods example the required critical value is $[4F_{4,40}(\alpha)]^{1/2}$. Choosing $\alpha = 0.05$ leads to a value of 3.23.
- The method can again be used to construct a confidence interval for two means as

$$\text{mean difference} \pm \text{critical value} \times s\left(\frac{1}{n_1} + \frac{1}{n_2}\right)^{1/2}.$$

- The only difference from the confidence intervals in Display 3.3 involves the 'critical values' for the two procedures. In the Bonferroni procedure this was 2.97; with the Scheffé procedure it is 3.23. Consequently, the Scheffé confidence intervals will be wider. They are as follows:

M1	M2	MD	Confidence interval
A	B	1.33	$1.33 \pm 3.23 \times 1.62 = (-3.90, 6.56)$
A	C	-7.78	$(-13.01, -2.55)^a$
A	D	-3.78	$(-9.01, 1.45)$
A	E	-3.56	$(-1.67, 8.79)$
B	C	-9.11	$(-14.34, -3.88)^a$
B	D	-5.11	$(-10.34, 0.12)$
B	E	2.22	$(-3.01, 7.45)$
C	D	4.00	$(-1.23, 9.23)$
C	E	11.33	$(6.10, 16.56)^a$
D	E	7.33	$(2.10, 12.56)^a$

* Interval does not include zero.

stimulant caffeine on the performance of a simple physical task. Forty male students were trained in finger tapping. They were then divided at random into four groups of 10 and the groups received different doses of caffeine (0, 100, 200 and 300 ml). Two hours after treatment, each man was required to carry out finger tapping and the number of taps per minute was recorded. Here, since the question of interest is whether caffeine affects performance on the finger-tapping task, the investigator may be interested a priori in the specific hypothesis that the mean of the three groups treated with caffeine differs from the mean of the untreated group, rather than in the general hypothesis of equality of means that is usually tested in a one-way analysis of variance. Such a priori

Table 3.4　Caffeine and finger-tapping data[a]

0 ml	100 ml	200 ml	300 ml
242	248	246	248
245	246	248	250
244	245	250	251
248	247	252	251
247	248	248	248
248	250	250	251
242	247	252	252
244	246	248	249
246	243	245	253
242	244	250	251

[a] The response variable is the number of taps per minute.

planned comparisons are generally more powerful, i.e. more likely to reject the null hypothesis when it is false, than the usual 'catch-all' F-test. The relevant test statistic for the specific hypothesis of interest can be constructed relatively simply (see Display 3.5). As also shown in Display 3.5, appropriate confidence intervals can be constructed for the comparison of interest. In the caffeine example the interval constructed indicates that it is very likely that there is a difference in finger-tapping performance between the 'no caffeine' and 'caffeine' conditions. More finger tapping takes place when subjects are given the stimulant.

Display 3.5　Planned comparisons

- The hypothesis of particular interest in the finger-tapping experiment is

$$H_0 : \mu_0 = \tfrac{1}{3}[\mu_{100} + \mu_{200} + \mu_{300}]$$

where μ_0, μ_{100}, μ_{200}, and μ_{300} are the population means of the 0 ml, 100 ml, 200 ml and 300 ml groups respectively.
- The hypothesis can be tested using the following t-statistic:

$$t = \frac{\bar{x}_0 - \tfrac{1}{3}(\bar{x}_{100} + \bar{x}_{200} + \bar{x}_{300})}{s\left(\tfrac{1}{10} + \tfrac{1}{30}\right)^{1/2}}$$

where $\bar{x}_0$, $\bar{x}_{100}$, $\bar{x}_{200}$, and $\bar{x}_{300}$ are the sample means of the four groups, and s^2 is once again the error mean square from the one-way analysis of variance.
- The values of the four means are $\bar{x}_0 = 244.8$, $\bar{x}_{100} = 246.4$, $\bar{x}_{200} = 248.3$ and $\bar{x}_{300} = 250.4$, and $s^2 = 4.40$.
- The t-statistic takes the value -4.6566. This is tested as a Student's t with 36 degrees of freedom (the degrees of freedom of the error mean square). The associated P-value is very small ($P = 0.000043$), and the conclusion is that the mean of the groups given caffeine does differ from the mean of the group not given the stimulant.

- A corresponding 95% confidence interval can be constructed in the usual way to give the interval $(-5.098, -2.035)$.
- An equivalent method of looking at planned comparisons is first to put the hypothesis of interest in a slightly different form from that given above, namely

$$H_0 : \mu_0 - \tfrac{1}{3}\mu_{100} - \tfrac{1}{3}\mu_{200} - \tfrac{1}{3}\mu_{300} = 0.$$

- The estimate of this comparison of the four population means (called a **contrast** since the defining constants sum to zero) obtained from the sample means is;

$$\bar{x}_0 - \tfrac{1}{3}\bar{x}_{100} - \tfrac{1}{3}\bar{x}_{200} - \tfrac{1}{3}\bar{x}_{300} = -3.5667.$$

- The sum of squares (and the mean square, since only a single degree of freedom is involved) corresponding to the comparison is found simply as

$$\frac{(-3.5667)^2}{\tfrac{1}{10}[1 + \tfrac{1^2}{3} + \tfrac{1^2}{3} + \tfrac{1^2}{3}]} = 95.410.$$

(For details and the general case, see Rosenthal and Rosnow, 1985.)

- This mean square is tested as usual against the error mean square as an F with 1 and ν degrees of freedom where ν is the number of degrees of freedom of the error mean square, i.e.

$$F = 95.410/4.40 = 21.684$$

which, with 1 and 36 degrees of freedom, gives an associated P-value agreeing with that from the t-test described earlier.
- The two approaches outlined above are exactly equivalent, since the calculated F-statistic is actually the square of the calculated t-statistic: i.e. $21.684 = (-4.6566)^2$. The second version of assessing a contrast is given here since it helps in the explanation of constructing the sums of squares corresponding to orthogonal polynomials to be described in Display 3.6.

The essential difference between planned and unplanned comparisons (i.e. those discussed in the previous section) is that the former can be assessed using conventional significance levels whilst the latter require rather stringent significance levels. An additional difference is that when a planned comparison approach is used, ominibus analysis of variance is not required. The investigator moves straight to the comparisons of most interest. However, there is one caveat: planned comparisons need to be just that, and not the result of hindsight after inspection of the sample means!

3.7 The use of orthogonal polynomials: trend analysis

In a one-way design where the independent variable is nominal, as in the teaching methods example, the data analysis is usually limited to testing the overall null hypothesis of the equality of the group means and subsequent *post hoc* comparisons using some type of multiple comparison procedure. However, if the independent variable has levels which form an ordered scale, it is often possible to extend the analysis to examine the relationship of these levels to the group means of the dependent variable. An example is provided by the caffeine data in Table 3.4, where the levels of

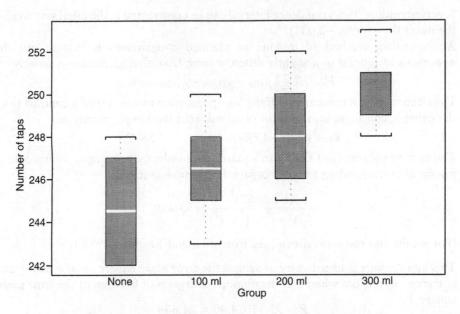

Fig. 3.2   Box plots of the finger-tapping data in Table 3.8.

the independent variable take the values 0 ml, 100 ml, 200 ml and 300 ml. For such data most interest will centre on the presence of **trends** of particular types, i.e. increases or decreases in the means of the dependent variable over the ordered levels of the independent variable. Such trends can be assessed relatively simply using what are known as **orthogonal polynomials**. These correspond to particular comparisons amongst the levels of the independent variable, with the coefficients defining the required comparisons depending on the number of levels of this variable. How these coefficients arise is not of great importance (and anyway is outside the level of this book), but how they are used *is* of interest and this is explained in Display 3.6. (Comprehensive tables of orthogonal polynomial coefficients corresponding to a number of different levels of the factor in a one-way design can be found in Howell, 1992.) Using these coefficients enables the between-groups sum of squares to be partitioned into a number of single-degree-of-freedom terms, each of which represents the sum of squares corresponding to a particular trend component. (The arithmetic involved is similar to that described for planned comparisons in Display 3.5.) The particular results for the caffeine example are also shown in Display 3.6 and indicate that there is a very strong linear trend in the finger-tapping means over the four levels of caffeine. A box plot of the data demonstrates the effect very clearly (Fig. 3.2).

3.8   Analysis of covariance

In the teaching methods example it is very likely that some of the variation between the students' arithmetic test scores is due to differences in initial arithmetic ability, which could have been assessed before the experiment began. Could these initial scores be usefully introduced into the analysis of the data? The answer, of course, is that they

Display 3.6 The use of orthogonal polynomials

- When the levels of the independent variable form a series of ordered steps, it is often of interest to examine the relationship between the levels and the means of the response variable. In particular the following questions would be of interest.

  (a) Do the means of the treatment groups increase in a linear fashion with an increase in the level of the independent variable?
  (b) Is the trend just linear or is there any evidence of non-linearity?
  (c) If the trend is non-linear what degree equation (polynomial) is required?

- The simplest way to approach these and similar questions is by the use of **orthogonal polynomial contrasts**. Essentially, these correspond to particular comparisons amongst the means, representing linear trend, quadratic trend etc. They are defined by a series of coefficients specific for the particular number of levels of the independent variable. The coefficients are available from most statistical tables. A small part of such a table is shown below.

Coefficients of orthogonal polynomials

k	Trend	Level				
		1	2	3	4	5
3	Linear	−1	0	1		
	Quadratic	1	−2	1		
4	Linear	−3	−1	1	3	
	Quadratic	1	−1	−1	1	
	Cubic	−1	3	−3	1	
5	Linear	−2	−1	0	1	2
	Quadratic	2	−1	−2	−1	2
	Cubic	−1	2	0	−2	1
	Quartic	1	−4	6	−4	1

(Note that these coefficients are only appropriate for equally spaced levels of the independent variable.)

- These coefficients can be used to produce a partition of the between-groups sums of squares into single-degree-of-freedom sums of squares corresponding to the trend components. These sums of squares are found using the approach described for planned comparisons in Display 3.5. For example, the sum of squares corresponding to the linear trend for the caffeine data is found as follows:

$$\text{SS linear} = \frac{[-3 \times 244.8 + (-1) \times 246.4 + 1 \times 248.3 + 3 \times 250.4]^2}{\frac{1}{10}[(-3)^2 + (-1)^2 + (1)^2 + (3)^2]} = 174.83.$$

- The resulting analysis of variance table for the finger-tapping example is as follows:

Source	DF	SS	MS	F	P
Caffeine levels	3	175.47	58.49	13.29	< 0.0001
Linear	1	174.83	174.83	39.71	< 0.0001
Quadratic	1	0.62	0.62	0.14	0.71
Cubic	1	0.00	0.00	0.00	0.97
Within	36	158.50	4.40		

- Note that the sum of squares of linear, quadratic and cubic effects add to the between-groups sum of squares.
- Note also that in this example the difference in the means of the four ordered caffeine levels is dominated by the *linear effect*; departures from linearity have a sum of squares of only $(0.62 + 0.00) = 0.62$.

---

could and *should* be included as what is generally termed a **covariate** or **concomitant variable**, using the technique known as **analysis of covariance**. By using this method the precision of an experiment can be increased, leading to a more powerful test of the equality of the group means of the response variable.

The analysis of covariance essentially 'adjusts' the response variable for the influence of the covariate and then tests for differences between the adjusted means in the usual manner. The covariate variable itself is not of experimental interest but it can lead to increased precision by decreasing the estimate of experimental error, i.e. the within-group mean square. In its simplest form the procedure assumes a *linear* relationship between the response variable and the covariate; the details of the model used are given in Display 3.7. An important point to note about this model is that the slopes of the regression lines relating response variable and covariate are assumed to be the same in each group.

Display 3.7 The analysis of covariance model

- In general terms the model is

    observation = mean + group effect + covariate effect + error.

- More specifically, if y_{ij} is used to denote the value of the response variable for the jth individual in the ith group and x_{ij} is the value of the covariate for this individual, then the model assumed is

$$y_{ij} = \mu + \alpha_i + \beta(x_{ij} - \bar{x}) + \epsilon_{ij}$$

where β is the regression coefficient linking response variable and covariate and $\bar{x}$ is the grand mean of the covariate values. (The remaining terms in the equation are as in the model defined in Display 3.2.)

- NB The regression coefficient is assumed to be the same in each group.
- The means of the response variable adjusted for the covariate are obtained simply as

adjusted group mean = group mean

$$+ \hat{\beta}(\text{grand mean of covariate} - \text{group mean of covariate})$$

where $\hat{\beta}$ is the estimate of the regression coefficient in the model above.

To illustrate the application of the analysis of covariance, suppose that the initial arithmetic test scores corresponding to the post-teaching values in Table 3.1 are as shown in Table 3.5. The results of applying analysis of covariance to the data are shown in Table 3.6. The estimated regression coefficient and the adjusted means of each group are also shown in Table 3.6.

Before discussing the results in Table 3.6, some attempt must be made to assess the validity of the assumption that the slopes of the regression equations linking initial and final arithmetic test scores in each group are the same. An informal check on the assumption can be made by drawing a scatter plot of the data, identifying the observations from each group and showing the estimated regression lines. This diagram is shown in Fig. 3.3. It must to be confessed that this graphical display does not appear to be particularly informative or helpful! There seems to be considerable variation in the slopes of the five regression lines, but it must be remembered that each is based on only nine observations. In fact a formal test of the equality-of-slopes assumption (usually known as the **parallelism** assumption), the details of which need not concern us, indicates that there is no evidence for departure from the assumption.

The analysis of variance table in Table 3.6 includes an extra line additional to those given in Table 3.3; this gives a test of the hypothesis that the slope of the regression equation linking the response variable and the covariate is significantly different from

Table 3.5   Initial arithmetic test scores

A	B	C	D	E
12	17	20	14	20
11	16	16	16	14
14	12	17	14	15
12	17	14	17	14
15	13	15	18	12
17	14	18	14	15
16	14	12	17	13
16	17	13	14	14
19	15	14	16	13
14.67	15.00	15.44	15.55	14.44

A, B, C, D and E are as defined in Table 3.1.
The grand mean of the observations is 15.02.

Table 3.6 Analysis of covariance of teaching methods examples

Source	SS	DF	MS	F	P
Between-groups	620.96	4	155.24	15.62	< 0.0001
Covariate	85.80	1	85.80	8.63	0.0055
Error	387.54	39	9.94		

Estimated regression coefficient 0.66
Adjusted group means
A: 19.90 (found from $19.67 + 0.66 \times (15.02 - 14.67)$)
B: 18.35
C: 27.17
D: 23.09
E: 16.49

A, B, C, D and E are as defined in Table 3.1.

zero. For the teaching methods example there is clearly strong evidence of a non-zero slope, implying a relationship between the initial and final scores. One other difference between the analysis of variance tables in Tables 3.3 and 3.6 is that the error sum of squares in the latter has one less degree of freedom. This difference arises because of the presence of an extra parameter β in the analysis of covariance model. (Note also that

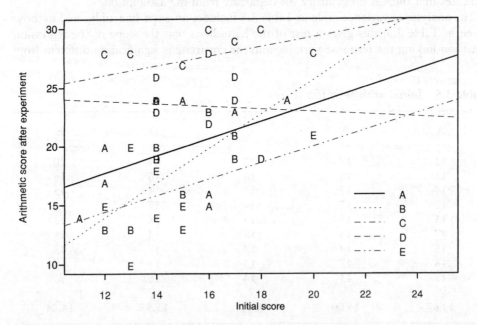

Fig. 3.3 Regression lines for the final arithmetic score on the initial score for the five teaching methods given in Tables 3.1 and 3.5.

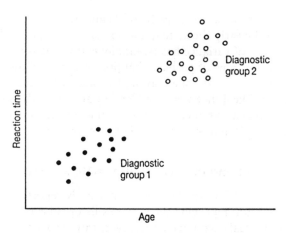

Fig. 3.4 Plot of reaction time against age for two groups of psychiatric patients.

the error mean square in the analysis of covariance is *less* than that in the corresponding analysis of variance.) In Table 3.16, the mean square ratio now corresponds to a test for the equality of the *adjusted* means. Clearly, the evidence against equality is very strong.

More examples of the analysis of covariance will be presented in later chapters, but one point about the method which should be made here concerns its use with naturally occurring or intact groups, rather than groups formed by random allocation.

The analysis of covariance was first introduced by Fisher (1935) and was originally intended to be employed in investigations where randomization had been used to assign patients to treatment groups. Experimental precision could be increased by removing from the error term in the analysis of variance that part of the residual variability in the response that was linearly predictable from the covariate. Gradually, however, the technique became more widely used to test hypotheses which are generally stated in such terms as 'the mean group differences on the response are zero when the group means on the covariate are made equal', or 'the group means on the response after adjustment for mean differences on the covariate are equal'. Indeed, some authors (e.g. McNemar, 1962) have suggested that 'if there is only a small chance difference between the groups on the covariate, the use of covariance adjustment may not be worth the effort'. Such a comment rules out the very situation for which the analysis of covariance was originally intended, since in the case of groups formed by randomization, any group differences on the covariate are necessarily the result of chance! Such advice is clearly unsound because more powerful tests of group differences result from the decrease in experimental error achieved when analysis of covariance is used in association with random allocation.

In fact, it is the use of analysis of covariance in an attempt to undo built-in differences amongst intact groups that causes concern. For example, Fig. 3.4 shows a plot of reaction time and age for psychiatric patients belonging to two distinct diagnostic groups. An analysis of covariance with reaction time as response and age as covariate might lead to the conclusion that reaction time does not differ in the two groups. In other words, given that two patients, one from each group, are of approximately the same age, their reaction times are also likely to be similar. Is such a conclusion sensible? Examination of Fig. 3.4 clearly shows that it is not, since the ages of the two groups do not overlap and analysis of variance has essentially extrapolated into a region with no data. Presumably, it is this type of problem that provoked the following somewhat acid comment from Anderson (1963): 'one may well wonder what exactly it means to ask what the data would be like if they were not like they are!'. Clearly, some thought needs to be given to the use of analysis of covariance on intact groups and readers are referred to Fleiss and Tanur (1972) and Stevens (1992) for more details.

3.9   Hotelling's T^2-test and one-way multivariate analysis of variance

The data shown in Table 3.7 were obtained from a study reported by Novince (1977) which was concerned with improving the social skills of college females and reducing their anxiety in heterosexual encounters. There were three groups in the study: a control group, a behavioural rehearsal group and a behavioural rehearsal plus cognitive restructuring group. The values of the following four dependent variables were recorded for each subject in the study:

(1) anxiety–physiological anxiety in a series of heterosexual encounters;
(2) measure of social skills in social interactions;
(3) appropriateness;
(4) assertiveness.

Between-group differences in this example could be assessed by separate one-way analyses of variance on each of the four dependent variables. An alternative and, in many situations involving multiple dependent variables, a preferable procedure is to consider the four dependent variables simultaneously. This is particularly sensible if the variables are correlated and believed to share a common conceptual meaning. In other words, the dependent variables considered together 'make sense' as a group. Consequently, the real question of interest is: 'Does the set of variables as a whole indicate any between-group differences?' To answer this question requires the use of a relatively complex technique known as **multivariate analysis of variance** or MANOVA. The ideas behind this approach are introduced most simply by considering first the two-group situation and the multivariate analogue of Student's t-test for testing the equality of two means, namely **Hotelling's T^2-test**. The test is described in Display 3.8 (the little adventure in matrix algebra is unavoidable, I'm afraid), and its application to the two experimental groups in Table 3.7, is detailed in Display 3.9. The conclusion to be drawn from the T^2-test is that the mean vectors of the two experimental groups do not differ.

It might be thought that the results from Hotelling's T^2-test would simply reflect those of a series of univariate t-tests, in the sense that if no differences are found by the separate t-tests, then Hotelling's T^2-test will also lead to the conclusion that the population multivariate mean vectors do not differ, whereas if any significant difference is found for the separate variables, the T^2-statistic will also be significant. In fact, this is not necessarily the case (if it was, the T^2-test would be a waste of time); it is possible to have no significant differences for each variable tested separately but a significant T^2-value, and vice versa. Both situations are illustrated most simply by considering just two variables and drawing suitable diagrams (Fig. 3.5).

Table 3.7 Data from Novince (1977)

Anxiety	Social skills	Appropriateness	Assertiveness
Behavioural rehearsal			
5	3	3	3
5	4	4	3
4	5	4	4
4	5	5	4
3	5	5	5
4	5	4	4
4	5	5	5
4	4	4	4
5	4	4	3
5	4	4	3
4	4	4	4
Control group			
6	2	1	1
6	2	2	2
5	2	3	3
6	2	2	2
4	4	4	4
7	1	1	1
5	4	3	3
5	2	3	3
5	3	3	3
5	4	3	3
6	2	3	3
Behavioural rehearsal + cognitive restucturing			
4	4	4	4
4	3	4	3
4	4	4	4
4	5	5	5
4	5	5	5
4	4	4	4
4	5	4	4
4	6	6	5
4	4	4	4
5	3	3	3
4	4	4	4

Display 3.8 Hotelling's T^2-test

- If there are p dependent variables, the null hypothesis is that the p means of the first population equal the corresponding means of the second population.
- By introducing some vector and matrix nomenclature the null hypothesis can be

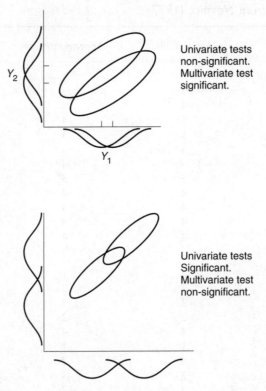

Y_2

Univariate tests
non-significant.
Multivariate test
significant.

Y_1

Univariate tests
Significant.
Multivariate test
non-significant.

Fig. 3.5 Diagrams showing how significant multivariate and non-significant univariate effects, and vice versa, can arise.

written as

$$H_0 : \boldsymbol{\mu}_1 = \boldsymbol{\mu}_2$$

where $\boldsymbol{\mu}_1$ and $\boldsymbol{\mu}_2$ contain the population means of the dependent variables in the two groups, i.e. they are the population **mean vectors**.

• The test statistic is

$$T^2 = \frac{n_1 n_2 D^2}{n_1 + n_2}$$

where n_1 and n_2 are the numbers of observations in the two groups and D^2 is defined as

$$D^2 = (\bar{x}_1 - \bar{x}_2)' S^{-1} (\bar{x}_1 - \bar{x}_2),$$

where $\bar{x}_1$ and $\bar{x}_2$ are the sample mean vectors in the two groups and S is the estimate of the assumed common covariance matrix calculated as

$$S = \frac{(n_1 - 1)S_1 + (n_2 - 1)S_2}{n_1 + n_2 - 2},$$

where S_1 and S_2 are the sample covariance matrices in each group. (If you are a little shaky on 'covariances', see Chapter 10.)

- Note that the form of the multivariate test statistic is very similar to that of the univariate independent sample t-test of your introductory course; it involves a difference between the 'means' (here the means are vectors and the difference between them takes into account the covariances of the variables) and an assumed common 'variance' (here the variance becomes a matrix).
- Under H_0 (and when the assumptions listed below are true), the statistic F given by

$$F = \frac{(n_1 + n_2 - p - 1)T^2}{(n_1 + n_2 - 2)p}$$

has a Fisher F-distribution with p and $n_1 + n_2 - p - 1$ degrees of freedom.
- The assumptions of the test are completely analogous to those of an independent samples t test. They are as follows:

(a) The data in each population are from a multivariate normal distribution.
(b) The populations have the same covariance matrix.
(c) The observation are independent.

Display 3.9 Calculation of Hotelling's T^2 for the data in Table 3.7

- The two sample mean vectors are given by
$$\boldsymbol{\mu}_1' = [4.27, 4.36, 4.18, 3.82] \quad \boldsymbol{\mu}_2' = [4.09, 4.27, 4.27, 4.09].$$

- The sample covariance matrices of the two groups are

$$S_1 = \begin{pmatrix} 0.42 & -0.31 & -0.25 & -0.44 \\ -0.31 & 0.45 & 0.33 & 0.37 \\ -0.25 & 0.33 & 0.36 & 0.34 \\ -0.44 & 0.37 & 0.34 & 0.56 \end{pmatrix}$$

$$S_2 = \begin{pmatrix} 0.09 & -0.13 & -0.13 & -0.11 \\ -0.13 & 0.82 & 0.62 & 0.57 \\ -0.13 & 0.62 & 0.62 & 0.47 \\ -0.11 & 0.57 & 0.47 & 0.49 \end{pmatrix}.$$

- The combined covariance matrix is

$$S = \begin{pmatrix} 0.28 & -0.24 & -0.21 & -0.31 \\ -0.24 & 0.71 & 0.52 & 0.52 \\ -0.21 & 0.52 & 0.54 & 0.45 \\ -0.31 & 0.52 & 0.45 & 0.59 \end{pmatrix}.$$

- Consequently $D^2 = 0.6956$ and $T^2 = 3.826$.
- The resulting F-value is 0.8130 with 4 and 17 degrees of freedom. The corresponding P-value is 0.53.

Table 3.8 Multivariate tests for the data in Table 3.7

Test name	Value	Corresponding F-value	DF1	DF2	P
Pillai	0.67980	3.60443	8.00	56.00	0.002
Hotelling	1.57723	5.12600	8.00	52.00	< 0.001
Wilk	0.36906	4.36109	8.00	54.00	< 0.001

When a set of dependent variables is to be compared in more than two groups, the multivariate analogue of the one-way analysis of variance is used. Without delving into the technical details, what the procedure attempts to do is to combine the dependent variables in some optimal way, taking into consideration the correlations between them and deciding what *unique* information each variable provides. A number of such composite variables giving maximum separation between groups are derived, and these form the basis of the comparisons made. Unfortunately, in the multivariate situation, when there are more than two groups to be compared, no single test statistic can be derived which is always the most powerful for detecting *all* types of departures from the null hypothesis of the equality of the mean vectors of the groups. A number of different test statistics have been suggested which may give different results when used on the same set of data, although the resulting conclusion from each is often the same. (When only two groups are involved, all the proposed test statistics are equivalent to Hotelling's T^2.) Details and formulae for the most commonly used MANOVA test statistics are given in Stevens (1992), for example, and in the glossary in Appendix A. (The various test statistics are eventually transformed into F-statistics to enable P-values to be calculated.) Only the results of applying the tests to the data in Table 3.7 will be discussed here (the results are given in Table 3.8). Each test indicates that the three groups are significantly different on the set of four variables. Combined with the earlier T^2-test on the two experimental groups, this result seems to imply that it is the control group which gives rise to the difference. This conclusion could be checked by using the multivariate equivalent of the multiple comparison tests described in Section 3.5 (see Stevens, 1992, for details). (The multivariate test statistics are based on analogous assumptions to those of the F-tests in a univariate one-way analysis of variance, i.e. the data are assumed to come from a **multivariate normal distribution** and each population is assumed to have the same covariance matrix. For more details see Stevens, 1992, and the glossary in Appendix A.)

In situations where the dependent variables of interest can genuinely be regarded as a set, there are a number of advantages in using a multivariate approach rather than a series of separate univariate analyses.

1. The use of a series of univariate tests leads to a greatly inflated type I error rate; the problem is analogous to the multiple *t*-test problem described in Section 3.2.
2. The univariate tests ignore important information, namely the correlations amongst the dependent variables. The multivariate tests take this information into account.
3. Although the groups may not be significantly different on any of the variables individually, *jointly* the set of variables may reliably differentiate the groups, i.e.

small differences on several variables may combine to produce a reliable overall difference. Thus the multivariate test will be more powerful in this case.

However, it should be remembered that these advantages are genuine only if the dependent variables can honestly be regarded as a set sharing a conceptual meaning. Multivariate analysis of variance on a number of dependent variables where there is no strong rationale for regarding them simultaneously, is *not* to be recommended.

3.10 Summary

1. A one-way analysis of variance is used to compare the means of k different populations.
2. The null and alternative hypothesis are

$$H_0 : \mu_1 = \mu_2 \cdots = \mu_k$$
$$H_1 : \text{not all the means are equal.}$$

3. The test of the null hypothesis involves an F-test for the equality of two variances.
4. A significant F-value should be followed by one or other multiple comparison test to assess which particular means differ, although care is needed in the application of such tests.
5. When the levels of the independent variable form an ordered scale, the use of orthogonal polynomial contrasts is often informative.
6. Including variables which are (linearly) related to the response variable as covariates increases the precision of the study in the sense of leading to a more powerful F-test for the equality of means hypothesis.
7. The examples considered in this chapter have all involved the same number of subjects in each group. This is not a necessary condition for a one-way analysis of variance, although it is helpful since it makes departures from the assumptions of normality and homogeneity of variance even less critical than usual. Some of the formulae given in displays need minor amendments for unequal group sizes.
8. In the one-way analysis of variance model considered in this chapter the levels of the independent variable are considered as **fixed**, i.e. the levels used are those of specific interest. An alternative model in which the levels are considered as a **random sample** from some population of possible levels might also have been considered. However, such models are of greater interest in the case of more complex designs and therefore will be described more fully in later chapters.
9. Several dependent variables can be treated simultaneously by MANOVA; this approach is only sensible if the variables can truly be regarded, in some sense, as a set.

Exercises

3.1   Reproduce all the results given in this chapter using a piece of statistical software of which you are particularly fond. (This exercise should be repeated in subsequent chapters.)

Table 3.9   The effect of knee-joint angle on the efficiency of cycling: total distance covered (km)

50°	70°	90°
8.4	10.6	3.2
7.0	7.5	4.2
3.0	5.1	3.1
8.0	5.6	6.9
7.8	10.2	7.2
3.3	11.0	3.5
4.3	6.8	3.1
3.6	9.4	4.5
8.0	10.4	3.8
6.8	8.8	3.6

The data in Table 3.9 were collected in an investigation described by Kapor (1981), in which the effect of knee-joint angle on the efficiency of cycling was studied. Efficiency was measured in terms of the distance pedalled on an ergocycle until exhaustion. The experimenter selected three knee-joint angles: 50°, 70° and 90°. Thirty subjects were available for the experiment and 10 subjects were randomly allocated to each angle. The drag of the ergocyle was kept constant at 14.7 N and subjects were instructed to pedal at a constant speed of 20 km/h until exhaustion.

1. Carry out an initial data analysis to assess whether there are any aspects of the data that might be a cause for concern in later analyses.
2. Calculate the appropriate analysis of variance table for the data.
3. What technique would you use to explore differences amongst the means of the three groups in more detail? What are the results of applying your chosen method?

3.3   Suggest sensible estimates for the parameters μ and α_i in the one-way analysis of variance model given in Display 3.2. Use your suggestion to estimate the parameters for the data on teaching methods.

3.4   Test the following planned comparisons for the teaching methods example:

(1) A + B versus C + D + E (control vs. others);
(2) D versus E.

3.5   The data in Table 3.10 show the anxiety scores, both before and after the operation, for patients undergoing wisdom tooth extraction by one of three methods. The ages of the patients (who were all women) were also recorded. Patients were randomly assigned to the three methods.

1. Carry out a one-way analysis of variance on the anxiety scores on discharge.

Table 3.10 Anxiety scores for patients having wisdom teeth extracted

Method of extraction	Age (years)	Initial anxiety	Final anxiety
Method 1	27	30.2	32.0
	32	35.3	34.8
	23	32.4	36.0
	28	31.9	34.2
	30	28.4	30.3
	35	30.5	33.2
	32	34.8	35.0
	21	32.5	34.0
	26	33.0	34.2
	27	29.9	31.1
Method 2	29	32.6	31.5
	29	33.0	32.9
	31	31.7	34.3
	36	34.0	32.8
	23	29.9	32.5
	26	32.2	32.9
	22	31.0	33.1
	20	32.0	30.4
	28	33.0	32.6
	32	31.1	32.8
Method 3	33	29.9	34.1
	35	30.0	34.1
	21	29.0	33.2
	28	30.0	33.0
	27	30.0	34.1
	23	29.6	31.0
	25	32.0	34.0
	26	31.0	34.0
	27	30.1	35.0
	29	31.0	36.0

2. Carry out a one-way analysis of variance on the difference between anxiety scores on discharge and those prior to the operation.
3. Carry out an analysis of covariance on the anxiety scores on discharge using the initial anxiety score as covariate.
4. Comment on any differences found between the above three analyses.
5. Suggest a suitable model which would allow both initial anxiety and age to be used as covariates, and carry out the corresponding analysis.

3.6 Apply Hotelling's T^2-test to each pair of groups in the data in Table 3.7. Use the three T^2-values and the Bonferonni correction procedure to assess which groups differ.

Further reading

Keren, G. and Lewis, C. (ed.) (1993). *A handbook for data analysis in the behavioural sciences: statistical issues*. Lawrence Erlbaum, Hillsdale, NJ.

Klockars, A.J. and Sax, G. (1986). *Multiple comparisons*. Sage, Beverly Hills, California.

Timm, N.M. (1993). MANOVA or MANCOVA: an overview. In *A handbook for data analysis in the behavioural sciences: statistical issues*. (ed. G. Keren and C. Lewis). Lawrence Erlbaum, Hillsdale, NJ.

4
Analysis of variance: factorial designs

4.1 Introduction

Many experiments in psychology involve the simultaneous study of two or more independent factor variables. Such an arrangement is usually referred to as a **factorial design**. Consider, for example, the data shown in Table 4.1 which were obtained from a study in which the effects of three different poisons and four different treatments on the survival times of rats were investigated. As in the previous chapter, questions of interest about these data would concern the equality of the mean survival time for the different poisons and similarly for the different treatments. Consequently, the reader may enquire why we do not simply apply a one-way analysis of variance separately to the poison and treatment factors and proceed quickly to the next topic. The answer is that such analyses would omit an aspect of factorial design which is often very important. The problem is illustrated in the next section.

4.2 Interactions in a factorial design

Consider the data set shown in Table 4.2 (Lindman, 1974), giving the improvement scores made by patients in two psychiatric categories under three different tranquillizer

Table 4.1 Survival times of rats

Poison	Treatment			
	A	B	C	D
1	0.31	0.82	0.43	0.45
	0.45	1.10	0.45	0.71
	0.46	0.88	0.63	0.66
	0.43	0.72	0.76	0.62
2	0.36	0.92	0.44	0.56
	0.29	0.61	0.35	1.02
	0.40	0.49	0.31	0.71
	0.23	1.24	0.40	0.38
3	0.22	0.30	0.23	0.30
	0.21	0.37	0.25	0.36
	0.18	0.38	0.24	0.31
	0.23	0.29	0.22	0.33

drugs. The results of a one-way analysis of variance of (1) psychiatric categories only, (2) tranquillizer drugs only and (3) all six groups of observations are shown in Table 4.3. At first sight the results appear a little curious. The F-test for the equality of psychiatric category means is not significant, and neither is that for tranquillizer drug means. Nevertheless, the F-test for the six groups together *is* significant, indicating a difference between the six means that has not been detected by the separate one-way analyses of variance. A clue to the cause of the problem is provided by considering the degrees of freedom associated with each of the three between-groups sums of squares. That corresponding to psychiatric categories has a single degree of freedom and that for drugs has two degrees of freedom, making a total of three degrees of freedom for the separate analyses. However, the between-groups sum of squares for the six groups combined has five degrees of freedom. The separate one-way analyses of variance appear to have omitted some aspect of the variation in the data. What has been left out is the effect of the combination of factor levels that is not predictable from the effects of the two factors separately, an effect usually known as the **interaction** between the factors. Both the model and the analysis of a factorial design need to allow for such interaction effects.

Table 4.2 Improvement scores for two psychiatric categories (A1 and A2) and three tranquillizer drugs (B1, B2 and B3)

Category	Drug		
	B1	B2	B3
A1	8	8	4
	4	10	6
	0	6	8
A2	10	0	15
	6	4	9
	14	2	12

Table 4.3 Analysis of variance of improvement scores in Table 4.2

Source	SS	DF	MS	F	P
Psychiatric categories only					
Diagnosis	20.05	1	20.05	1.07	0.31
Error	298.9	16	18.68		
Drugs only					
Drug	44.11	2	22.05	1.20	0.33
Error	274.83	15	18.32		
All six groups					
Groups	212.28	5	42.45	4.78	0.01
Error	106.67	12	8.89		

4.3   Two-way designs

Many aspects of the modelling and analysis of factorial designs can be conveniently illustrated using examples with only two factors. Such **two-way designs** are considered in this section. More complex examples with more than two factors will be described later in the chapter.

Initially, a suitable model must be formulated, and details are given in Display 4.1. Notice that this model contains a term to represent the possible interaction between factors. The total variation in the observations can be partitioned into parts due to each factor and a part due to their interaction, and these can be arranged into an analysis of variance table as shown in general terms in Table 4.4 and, specifically for the data in Table 4.1, in Table 4.5.

Table 4.4   Analysis of variance table for a general two-way design with factors A (a levels), B (b levels) and n subjects per cell

Source	SS	DF	MS	F
A	ASS	$a - 1$	$ASS/(a - 1)$	MSA/error MS
B	BSS	$b - 1$	$BSS/(b - 1)$	MSB/error MS
AB	ABSS	$(a - 1)(b - 1)$	$ABSS/(a - 1)(b - 1)$	MSAB/error MS
Within cell (error)	WCSS	$ab(n - 1)$	$WCSS/ab(n - 1)$	

Table 4.5   Analysis of variance for survival times in Table 4.1

Analysis of variance table

Source	SS	DF	MS	F	P
Poison (P)	1.03	2	0.52	23.22	< 0.0001
Treatment (T)	0.92	3	0.31	13.81	< 0.0001
P × T	0.25	6	0.04	1.87	0.11
Error	0.80	36	0.02		

Means and standard deviations

	A	B	C	D
Poison 1				
Mean	0.41	0.88	0.57	0.61
SD	0.07	0.16	0.16	0.11
Poison 2				
Mean	0.32	0.81	0.37	0.67
SD	0.07	0.34	0.06	0.27
Poison 3				
Mean	0.21	0.33	0.23	0.32
SD	0.02	0.05	0.01	0.03

Display 4.1 Model for a two-way design with factors A and B

- The observed value of the response variable for a subject is assumed to be of the form
  observed response = expected response + error.
- The expected value of the response variable for a subject is made up of the effect of the level of factor A under which the subject is observed, the corresponding term for factor B and the AB interaction effect for the respective levels. Consequently, the model above can be rewritten as
  observed response = mean + factor A effect + factor B effect
  + AB interaction + error.
- More specifically, let y_{ijk} represent the kth observation in the jth level of factor B (with b levels) and the ith level of factor A (with a levels). Assume n subjects in each of the ab cells of the design. The levels of both A and B are assumed to be of particular interest, and so both factors are considered to have fixed effects (see Section 4.5). The model assumed for the observations is

$$y_{ijk} = \mu + \alpha_i + \beta_j + \gamma_{ij} + \epsilon_{ijk}$$

where μ represents the overall mean, α_i is the effect on an observation of being in the ith level of factor A, β_j is the corresponding effect for the jth level of factor B, γ_{ij} represents the interaction effect and ϵ_{ijk} is a random error term which is assumed to be normally distributed with zero mean and variance σ^2.
- Without some constraints on the parameters, the model is again overparameterized (see Chapter 3). The most common method of overcoming this difficulty is to require that the parameters in this fixed-effects model are such that $\sum_{i=1}^{a} \alpha_i = \sum_{j=1}^{b} \beta_j = \sum_{i=1}^{a} \gamma_{ij} = \sum_{j=1}^{b} \gamma_{ij} = 0$. For details see Maxwell and Delaney (1990).
- The hypotheses of interest can be written in terms of the parameters in the model as

$$H_0^{(1)} : \alpha_1 = \alpha_2 = \ldots = \alpha_a = 0$$

$$H_0^{(2)} : \beta_1 = \beta_2 = \ldots = \beta_b = 0$$

$$H_0^{(3)} : \gamma_{11} = \gamma_{12} = \ldots = \gamma_{ab} = 0.$$

- The total variation in the observations is partitioned into that due to differences between the means of the levels of factor A, that due to differences between the means of the levels of factor B, that due to the interaction of A and B, and that due to differences amongst observations in the same cell. Under the hypotheses above, factor A, factor B and the interaction mean squares are all estimates of σ^2. The error mean square is an estimate of σ^2 whether or not any of the three hypotheses are true. Consequently, the corresponding F-tests (see Table 4.4) provide tests of each hypothesis.
- The F-tests are valid under the following assumptions:
  (a) normality;
  (b) homogeneity of variance;
  (c) independence of the observations.

- The F-tests are relatively robust against departures from normality and homogeneity, although in extreme cases, where departures are clear, a transformation of the data prior to analysis may be in order.

The appropriate F-tests in Table 4.5 indicate very clearly that the poison means differ as do the treatment means. However, the F-test for the interaction effect is not significant. It appears that what is generally known as a **main effects model** provides an adequate description of these data. In other words, poison effects and treatment effects (the **main effects**) act independently on survival time. (Multiple comparison tests could now be applied to both poison means and treatment means to identify more specifically where differences occur; this is left as an exercise for the reader.)

When the interaction effect is non-significant, the interaction mean square becomes a further estimate of the error variance σ^2. Consequently, there is the possibility of **pooling** the error sum of squares and interaction sum of squares to provide an 'improved' error mean square based on a larger number of degrees of freedom. In some cases use of a pooled error mean square will provide more powerful tests of the main effects. The results of applying this procedure to the survival time data are shown in Table 4.6. Here the results are very similar to those given in Table 4.5.

Although pooling is often recommended, it can be dangerous for a number of reasons. In particular, cases may arise where the test for interaction is non-significant, but where there is in fact an interaction. As a result the pooled mean square may be larger than the original error mean square, and the difference may be large enough for the increase in degrees of freedom to be more than offset. The net result is that the experimenter *loses* rather than gains power. (This appears to happen in the example above.) Pooling is really only acceptable when there are good a priori reasons for assuming no interaction and the decision to use a pooled error term is based on considerations that are independent of the observed data.

As a further example of a two-way design consider the data shown in Table 4.7. These data arise from an investigation into types of slimming regime. In this case the two factor variables are treatment with two levels, namely whether or not a woman was advised to use a slimming manual based on psychological behaviourist theory as an addition to the regular package offered by the clinic, and status, also with two levels, i.e. 'novice' and 'experienced' slimmer. The dependent variable recorded was a measure of weight change over three months with negative values indicating a decrease in weight.

Table 4.6 Pooling error and interaction terms in the analysis of variance of survival times

Source	SS	DF	MS	F	P
Poison	1.03	2	0.52	20.8	< 0.0001
Treatment	0.92	3	0.31	12.4	< 0.0001
Pooled error	1.05	42	0.025		

Table 4.7 Slimming data

	Weight change	
	Novice	Experienced
No manual	−2.85	−2.42
	−1.98	0.00
	−2.12	−2.74
	0.00	−0.84
Manual	−4.44	0.00
	−8.11	−1.64
	−9.40	−2.40
	−3.50	−2.15

The analysis of variance table and the means and standard deviations for these data are shown in Table 4.8. Here the main effects of treatment and status are significant; in addition there is a significant interaction between treatment and status. The presence of a significant interaction means that some care is needed in arriving at a sensible interpretation of the results. Firstly, a plot of the four cell means as shown in Fig. 4.1 is helpful in drawing conclusions about the significant interaction effect between the two

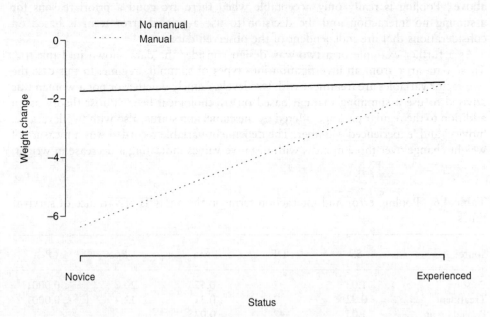

Fig. 4.1 Plot of cell means for slimming data.

Table 4.8 Analysis of variance of slimming data

Analysis of variance table

Source	SS	DF	MS	F	P
Condition (C)	21.83	1	21.83	7.04	0.021
Status (S)	25.53	1	25.53	8.24	0.014
C × S	20.95	1	20.95	6.76	0.023
Error	37.19	12	3.10		

Means and standard deviations

	Novice	Experienced
No manual		
Mean	−1.74	−1.50
SD	1.22	1.30
Manual		
Mean	−6.36	−1.55
SD	2.84	1.08

factors. Examining the plot it is clear that the decrease in weight produced by giving novice slimmers access to the slimming manual is far greater than that achieved with experienced slimmers, where the reduction is negligible. Formal significance tests of the differences between experienced and novice slimmers for each treatment level could be performed—they are usually referred to as tests of **simple effects**—but in general they are unnecessary since the interpretation of a significant interaction is usually clear from a plot of cell means. It is never wise to perform more significance tests than are absolutely essential. The significant main effects might be interpreted as indicating differences in the average weight change for novice compared with experienced slimmers, and for slimmers having access to the manual compared with those who do not; however, in the presence of the large interaction such an interpretation is not at all helpful. The clear message from these results is as follows:

1. No manual—no difference in weight change of novice and experienced slimmers.
2. Manual—novice slimmers win!

(It might be useful to construct a confidence interval for the difference in the weight change of novice and experienced slimmers when both have access to the manual; see Exercise 4.3.)

One final point to note about the two-way design is that when there is only a single observation available in each cell, the error mean square has zero degrees of freedom. In such cases it is generally assumed that the factors do not interact so that the interaction mean square can be used as 'error' to provide F-tests for the main effects. Some examples will be given in Chapter 13.

4.4 Higher-order factorial designs

Maxwell and Delaney (1990) and Boniface (1995) give details of an experiment in which the effects of three treatments on blood pressure were investigated. The three treatments were as follows:

(1) **drug**, with three levels, drug X, drug Y and drug Z;
(2) **biofeed**, in which biofeedback is either present or absent;
(3) **diet**, in which a special diet is either given or not.

Seventy-two subjects were used in the experiment, with six being randomly allocated to each of the 12 treatment combinations. The data are shown in Table 4.9. A suitable model for a three-factor design is shown in Display 4.2 together with the corresponding analysis of variance table. The specific analysis of variance table for the blood pressure data is shown in Table 4.10.

Table 4.9 Blood pressure data

	Biofeedback present			Biofeedback absent		
	Drug X	Drug Y	Drug Z	Drug X	Drug Y	Drug Z
Diet absent						
	170	186	180	173	189	202
	175	194	187	194	194	228
	165	201	199	197	217	190
	180	215	170	190	206	206
	160	219	204	176	199	224
	158	209	194	198	195	204
Diet present						
	161	164	162	164	171	205
	173	166	184	190	173	199
	157	159	183	169	196	170
	152	182	156	164	199	160
	181	187	180	176	180	179
	190	174	173	175	203	179

The first thing to note about the analysis of variance table in Table 4.10 is the significant diet × biofeed × drug interaction; an interaction between three factors is known as a **second-order interaction**. (Interactions between two factors are sometimes termed **first-order**, but most often are referred to simply as interactions.) Just what does such an effect imply? Essentially the result means that the first-order interactions between any two of the factors differ either in form or in magnitude at the different levels of the third factor. Once again the simplest method of reaching a greater

Display 4.2 Model and analysis of variance table for a three-factor design with factors A, B and C

- In general terms the model is

  observation = mean + factor A effect + factor B effect + factor C effect

  + AB interaction + AC interaction + BC interaction

  + ABC interaction + error.

- More specifically, let y_{ijkl} represent the lth observation in the kth level of factor C (with c levels), the jth level of factor B (with b levels) and the ith level of factor A (with a levels). Assume n subjects per cell, and assume that the factor levels are of particular interest so that A, B and C have fixed effects (see Section 4.5).

- The linear model for the observations is

  $$y_{ijkl} = \mu + \alpha_i + \beta_j + \gamma_k + \delta_{ij} + \tau_{ik} + \omega_{jk} + \theta_{ijk} + \epsilon_{ijkl}$$

  where α_i, β_j and γ_k represent main effects, δ_{ij}, τ_{ik} and ω_{jk} represent first-order interactions, θ_{ijk} represents the second-order interaction and ϵ_{ijkl} are random error terms assumed to be normally distributed with zero mean and variance σ^2. (Once again the parameters have to be constrained in some way; for details see Maxwell and Delaney, 1990.)

- The hypotheses of interest can be written in terms of the parameters in the model as:

  $$H_0^{(1)} : \alpha_1 = \alpha_2 = \ldots = \alpha_a = 0$$
  $$H_0^{(2)} : \beta_1 = \beta_2 = \ldots = \beta_b = 0$$
  $$H_0^{(3)} : \gamma_1 = \gamma_2 = \ldots = \gamma_c = 0$$
  $$H_0^{(4)} : \delta_{11} = \delta_{12} = \ldots = \delta_{ab} = 0$$
  $$H_0^{(5)} : \tau_{11} = \tau_{12} = \ldots = \tau_{ac} = 0$$
  $$H_0^{(6)} : \omega_{11} = \omega_{12} = \ldots = \omega_{bc} = 0$$
  $$H_0^{(7)} : \theta_{111} = \theta_{112} = \ldots = \theta_{abc} = 0.$$

- The analysis of variance table is as follows:

Source	SS	DF	MS	F
A	ASS	$a-1$	ASS/$(a-1)$	MSA/ErrorMS
B	BSS	$b-1$	BSS/$(b-1)$	MSB/ErrorMS
C	CSS	$c-1$	CSS/$(c-1)$	MSC/ErrorMS
A × B	ABSS	$(a-1)(b-1)$	ABSS/$(a-1)(b-1)$	MSAB/ErrorMS
A × C	ACSS	$(a-1)(c-1)$	ACSS/$(a-1)(c-1)$	MSAC/ErrorMS
B × C	BCSS	$(b-1)(c-1)$	BCSS/$(b-1)(c-1)$	MSBC/ErrorMS
A × B × C	ABCSS	$(a-1)(b-1)(c-1)$	ABCSS/$(a-1)(b-1)(c-1)$	MSABC/ErrorMS
Within cell (error)	WCSS	$abc(n-1)$	WCSS/$abc(n-1)$	

Table 4.10 Analysis of variance for blood pressure data

Source	SS	DF	MS	F	P
Diet	5202	1	5202.0	33.20	< 0.0001
Biofeed	2048	1	2048.0	13.07	0.0006
Drug	3675	2	1837.5	11.73	< 0.0001
Diet × biofeed	32	1	32	0.20	0.6563
Diet × drug	903	2	451.5	2.88	0.0639
Biofeed × drug	259	2	129.5	0.83	0.4410
Diet × biofeed × drug	1075	2	537.5	3.43	0.0389
Error	9400	60	156.67		

understanding of this finding is to produce a diagram, in this case a series of interaction plots for two factors for each level of the third factor. Figure 4.2 shows the interaction plots for diet and biofeed for each of the three drugs used in the study. For drug X, the plot indicates that diet has a negligible effect when biofeedback is given, but has the effect of substantially reducing blood pressure when biofeedback is not received. For drug Y, the situation is essentially the reverse of that for drug X. For drug Z, diet and biofeed do not interact, and receiving the diet leads to lower blood pressure whether or not biofeedback is used.

Because of the presence of the significant second-order interactions there is little point in proceeding to discuss the significant main effects or non-significant first-order interactions, although the interpretation of the data might be simplified by carrying out separate two-way analyses of variance within each drug (see Exercise 4.6).

Clearly, factorial designs will become increasingly complex as the number of factors is increased. A further problem is that the number of subjects required for a complete factorial design quickly becomes prohibitively large. Consequently, alternative designs have to be considered which are more economical in terms of subjects. Perhaps the most common of these is the **latin square** (described in detail by Maxwell and Delaney, 1990). In such a design, economy in number of subjects required is achieved by assuming a priori that there are no interactions between the factors.

4.5 Random effects and fixed effects models

In the summary of Chapter 3 a passing reference was made to *random* and *fixed* effects factors. It is now time to consider these terms in a little more detail, beginning with some formal definitions.

1. A factor is random if its levels consist of a random sample of levels from a population of all possible levels.
2. A factor is fixed if its levels are selected by a non-random process or its levels consist of the entire population of possible levels.

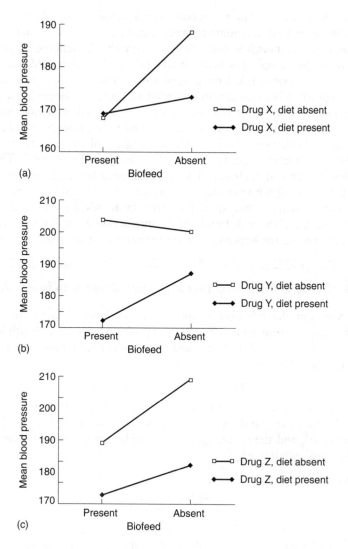

Fig. 4.2 Interaction plots for diet × drug × biofeed: (a) diet × biofeed for drug X; (b) diet × biofeed for drug Y; (c) diet × biofeed for drug Z.

Three basic types of models can be constructed depending on what types of factors are involved.

1. A model is called a **fixed effects model** if all the factors in the design have fixed effects.
2. A model is called a **random effects model** if all the factors in the design have random effects.
3. A model is called a **mixed effects model** if some of the factors in the design have fixed effects and some have random effects.

No doubt readers will not find this wildly exciting until some explanation is at hand as to why it is necessary to differentiate between factors in this way. In fact the philosophy behind random effects models is quite different from that behind the use of fixed effects models both in the sampling scheme used and in the parameters of interest. The difference can be described relatively simply using a two-way design; a suitable model for such a design when both factors are regarded as random is shown in Display 4.3. The important point to note about this model when compared with that for fixed effect factors (see Display 4.1), is that the terms α_i, β_j and γ_{ij} are now assumed to be **random variables** with particular distributions. The parameters of interest are the **variances** of these distributions, and they can be estimated as shown in Display 4.3. The analysis of variance table, also shown in Display 4.3, is calculated as for the fixed effects model, but the F-tests for assessing whether the 'main effect' variances are zero now involve the interaction mean square rather than the error mean square. However, the test for whether the variance of the distribution of the interaction parameters is zero is the same as that used for testing the hypothesis of no interaction in the fixed effects model.

Display 4.3   Random effects model for a two-way design with factors A and B

- Let y_{ijk} represent the kth observation in the jth level of factor B (with b levels randomly sampled from some population of possible levels) and the ith level of factor A (with a levels also randomly sampled from some population of possible levels).
- The linear model for the observations is

$$y_{ijk} = \mu + \alpha_i + \beta_j + \gamma_{ij} + \epsilon_{ijk}$$

where the α_i are random variables from a normal distribution with mean zero and variance σ_a^2, the β_j are random variables from a normal distribution with mean zero and variance σ_b^2 and the γ_{ij} are random variables from a normal distribution with mean zero and variance σ_{ab}^2.

- The hypotheses of interest are now

$$H_0^{(1)} : \sigma_a^2 = 0$$
$$H_0^{(2)} : \sigma_b^2 = 0$$
$$H_0^{(3)} : \sigma_{ab}^2 = 0.$$

The calculation of sums of squares and mean squares is the same as in the fixed effects model. Now, however, the various mean squares are estimators of combinations of the variance terms in the model, i.e.:

- (a) A mean square: estimator of $\sigma^2 + n\sigma_{ab}^2 + nb\sigma_a^2$;
- (b) B mean square: estimator of $\sigma^2 + n\sigma_{ab}^2 + na\sigma_b^2$;
- (c) AB mean square: estimator of $\sigma^2 + n\sigma_{ab}^2$;
- (d) error mean square: estimator of σ^2.
- When $H_0^{(3)}$ is true, the AB mean square and error mean square are both estimators of σ^2.
- When $H_0^{(1)}$ is true the A mean square and the AB interaction mean square are both estimators of $\sigma^2 + n\sigma_{ab}^2$.

- When $H_0^{(2)}$ is true the B mean square and the AB interaction mean square are both estimators of $\sigma^2 + n\sigma_{ab}^2$.
- Consequently the AB interaction mean square is tested against the error mean square and the A and B mean squares are tested against the AB interaction mean square.
- Estimators of the variances σ_a^2, σ_b^2 and σ_{ab}^2 are obtained as follows:

$$\hat{\sigma}_a^2 = \frac{\text{MSA} - \text{MSAB}}{nb}$$

$$\hat{\sigma}_b^2 = \frac{\text{MSB} - \text{MSAB}}{na}$$

$$\hat{\sigma}_{ab}^2 = \frac{\text{MSAB} - \text{ErrorMS}}{n}.$$

To illustrate the application of a random effects model the data in Table 4.1 will again be employed, making the unrealistic assumption that both the particular treatments and the particular poisons used are a random sample from a large population of possible treatments and poisons. The resulting analysis is shown in Table 4.11. The F-tests indicate that the variances of both the poison and treatment parameter distributions are not zero; however, the hypothesis that $\sigma_{ab}^2 = 0$ is not rejected.

The main differences between using fixed effects and random effects models are as follows:

1. Since the levels of a random effects factor have been chosen randomly, the experimenter is not interested in the means of the particular levels observed. In particular, planned or *post hoc* comparisons are no longer relevant.
2. In a random effects model interest lies in the estimation and testing of variance parameters.

Table 4.11 Analysis of survival times using a random effects model

Source	SS	DF	MS	F	P
Poisons (P)	1.03	2	0.52	13.0	0.006
Treatments (T)	0.92	3	0.31	7.75	0.017
P × T	0.25	6	0.04	1.87	0.11
Error	0.80	36	0.02		

The estimates of the three variance terms are

$$\hat{\sigma}_a^2 = \frac{\text{MSA} - \text{MSAB}}{nb} = 0.0300$$

$$\hat{\sigma}_b^2 = \frac{\text{MSB} - \text{MSAB}}{na} = 0.0225$$

$$\hat{\sigma}_{ab}^2 = \frac{\text{MSAB} - \text{ErrorMS}}{n} = 0.005$$

Table 4.12   Improvement scores (I) and severity of illness (S)

Diagnostic category	Drug B1		Drug B2		Drug B3	
	I	S	I	S	I	S
A1	8	5	8	7	5	3
	4	3	10	7	4	6
	0	4	6	4	8	6
A2	10	5	0	2	15	8
	6	6	4	7	9	3
	14	7	2	6	12	7

3.   An advantage of a random effects model is that it allows the experimenter to generalize beyond the levels of factors actually observed.

It must be emphasized that generalizations to a population of levels from the tests of significance for a random effects factor are warranted *only* when the levels of the factor are actually selected at random from a population of levels. It seems unlikely that such a situation will hold in most psychological experiments employing factorial designs and, consequently, fixed effects models are those most generally used (although see Chapter 5).

4.6   Analysis of covariance in factorial designs

Analysis of covariance for a one-way design was introduced in Chapter 3. The technique can be generalized to factorial designs, and in this section an example of its use in a two-way design will be described using data reported by Lindman (1974). The data are given in Table 4.12. (The data are those previously considered in Section 4.2 with the addition of a severity of illness rating for each patient.) The appropriate model for the analysis of covariance of a two-way design is shown in Display 4.4 together with the results of applying the method to the data in Table 4.12. (The analysis of variance table for these data also appears in Display 4.4.) Once again the validity of the analysis of covariance depends on the parallelism assumption; in this case that the slope of regression of the dependent variable on the covariate is the same in each cell of the two-way design. Checking this assumption is difficult since there are only three observations per cell. If we assume that parallelism is valid, the results of the analysis of covariance indicate that there is a significant interaction between the two factors. The adjusted cell means (see Display 4.5) can be plotted as an aid to explaining the interaction (Fig. 4.3). The most striking feature of this plot is that for drug B2, diagnostic category A2 has a lower mean than for category A1; for the other two drugs, category A1 has a higher mean than category A2.

Display 4.4 Analysis of covariance model for a two-way design with factors A and B, and the analysis of covariance of improvement and severity of illness data

- In general terms the model is

    observation = mean + factor A effect + factor B effect + AB interaction

    + covariate effect + error.

- More specifically, the analysis of covariance model for a two-way design is

$$y_{ijk} = \mu + \alpha_i + \theta_j + \gamma_{ij} + \beta(x_{ijk} - \bar{x}) + \epsilon_{ijk}$$

    where x_{ijk} is the value of the covariate for observation k in the jth level of factor B and the ith level of factor A, $\bar{x}$ is the grand mean of the covariate values and β is the regression coefficient linking dependent variable and covariate. The other terms are as in the model for the two-way design described in Display 4.1.

- The analysis of variance table for improvement scores is as follows.

Source	SS	DF	MS	F	P
Diagnosis (D)	20.06	1	20.06	2.26	0.1589
Treatment (T)	44.11	2	22.06	2.48	0.1254
D × T	148.11	2	74.06	8.33	0.0054
Error	106.67	12	8.89		

- The analysis of covariance table for improvement scores with severity of illness as covariate is as follows.

Source	SS	DF	MS	F	P
Diagnosis (D)	9.55	1	9.55	1.54	0.24
Treatment (T)	45.26	2	22.63	3.64	0.06
D×T	87.01	2	43.50	6.99	0.01
Covariate	38.20	1	38.20	6.14	0.03
Error	68.46	11	6.22		

- The estimated regression coefficient = 0.9318.

Display 4.5 Calculation of adjusted means from the analysis of covariance of improvement and severity of illness data

- The 'adjusted' value of an observation is given by

    adjusted value = observed value of response + estimated regression coefficient

    × (grand mean of covariate − covariate value).

- For example, the adjusted values for the first cell of Table 4.12 are calculated as

$$8 + 0.9318(5.33 - 5) = 8.3075$$
$$4 + 0.9318(5.33 - 3) = 6.1711$$
$$0 + 0.9318(5.33 - 4) = 1.2392.$$

- Consequently, the adjusted mean of the cell is

$$\frac{8.3075 + 6.1711 + 1.2392}{3} = 5.24.$$

(The grand mean of the severity scores is 5.33.)

- The adjusted means for all cells are as follows:

	B1	B2	B3
A1	5.24	7.38	5.98
A2	9.38	2.31	11.38

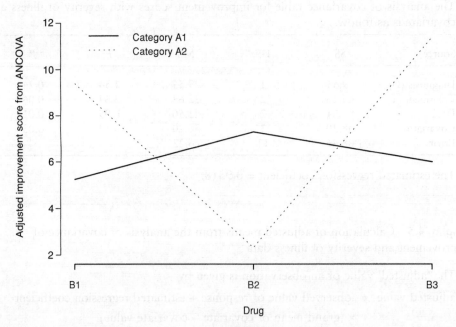

Fig. 4.3   Interaction plot of adjusted means from analysis of covariance (ANCOVA) of the data in Table 4.12.

4.7   Factorial designs with unequal numbers of observations in each cell

More observant readers will have noticed that all the examples discussed in the previous sections of this chapter have had the same number of observations in each cell. In most laboratory-type experiments this will be the usual situation (or at least the usual aim— the death of an animal or the failure of a subject to attend an experimental session, for example, may mean that it is not always achieved). However, in studies which lack the control of a randomized experiment, such equality of cell size may no longer be the norm. As an example, consider the data in Table 4.13, which were obtained from an investigation into the effect of the mother's post-natal depression on child development. Mothers who gave birth to their first-born child in a major teaching hospital in London were divided into two groups, depressed and not depressed, on the basis on their mental state 3 months after the birth. The children's fathers were also divided into two groups, namely those who had a history of psychiatric illness and those who did not. The dependent variable in the study was the child's IQ at age 4 years. (The other variables shown in Table 4.13 will be used later in the chapter.)

So why do unbalanced factorial designs merit special consideration? Why is the usual analysis of variance for balanced designs now not applicable? The answers to both these questions lie in recognizing that in factorial designs with unequal numbers of observations in each cell, the so-called independent variables are no longer independent. (Recall the comment in Chapter 1 that the label 'independent', although widely used, was in many cases a misnomer.) For example, the 2×2 table of counts of children of depressed and non-depressed mothers and 'well' and 'ill' fathers is as follows:

Father	Mother		
	Not depressed	Depressed	Total
Well	75(70)	9(14)	84
Ill	4(8)	6(2)	10
Total	79	15	94

The numbers in parentheses show the 'expected' number of observations under the hypothesis that the mother's state is independent of the father's state (rounded to the nearest whole number). Clearly, there are more depressed mothers whose partners are psychiatrically ill than expected under independence. (Review the coverage of the chi-squared test given in your introductory course and in Chapter 7 for details of how expected values are calculated.)

The result of this dependence is that it is no longer possible to partition the total variation in the data into **non-overlapping** or **orthogonal** sums of squares representing main effects and interactions. For example, in a unbalanced two-way design there is a proportion of the variance of the response variable that can be attributed to (explained by) either factor A or factor B. A consequence is that A and B together explain less of the variation of the dependent variable than the sum of what each explains alone. The result is that the sum of squares corresponding to a factor depends on which other

Table 4.13 Data obtained in a study of the effect of post-natal depression of the mother on the child's cognitive development

			Variable[a]			
1	2	3	4	5	6	7
1	1	103	56	50	42	0
1	1	124	65	64	61	0
1	1	124	67	61	63	0
1	2	104	52	55	44	0
2	2	96	46	52	46	0
1	1	92	46	43	43	0
1	2	124	58	68	65	0
1	2	99	55	46	50	0
1	1	92	46	41	55	0
1	1	116	61	58	51	0
1	1	99	58	45	50	0
2	2	22	22	50	22	1
2	2	81	47	38	41	1
1	2	117	68	53	63	0
2	2	100	54	47	53	1
1	2	89	48	41	46	0
1	2	125	64	66	67	0
1	1	127	64	68	71	1
1	2	112	50	57	64	0
1	2	48	23	20	25	0
1	1	139	68	75	64	0
1	2	118	58	64	61	0
2	2	107	45	58	58	1
1	1	106	46	57	53	0
2	1	129	63	70	67	0
1	1	117	43	71	63	0
1	1	123	64	64	61	1
1	2	118	64	56	60	0
2	1	84	47	37	43	1
1	1	117	66	64	61	0
2	2	102	48	52	52	0
1	1	141	66	76	69	0
1	1	124	60	77	58	0
1	1	110	50	61	52	0
1	1	98	54	47	48	0
1	1	109	64	48	50	0
1	1	120	71	53	63	0
1	1	127	67	68	59	0
1	2	103	55	52	48	0
1	1	118	65	57	61	0
1	1	117	60	64	48	0
1	1	115	52	67	55	0
1	1	119	63	62	58	0

Table 4.13   Data obtained in a study of the effect of post-natal depression of the mother on the child's cognitive development – *cont'd*

| | | | Variable[a] | | | |
1	2	3	4	5	6	7
1	1	117	63	56	59	0
1	1	92	45	42	55	0
1	2	101	53	48	52	0
1	1	119	59	65	59	0
1	1	144	78	67	65	0
1	1	119	66	54	62	0
1	1	127	67	63	67	0
1	2	113	61	54	58	0
1	1	127	60	59	68	0
1	1	103	57	50	48	0
1	2	128	70	65	60	0
1	2	86	45	45	28	0
1	1	112	62	51	60	0
1	2	115	59	58	59	0
1	2	117	48	68	62	0
1	2	99	58	48	41	0
1	2	110	54	61	47	0
2	2	139	70	72	66	0
1	2	117	64	57	51	0
1	1	96	52	45	47	0
2	1	111	54	60	50	0
1	1	118	58	62	62	0
1	1	126	66	64	67	0
1	2	126	69	66	55	0
1	2	89	49	36	36	0
1	1	102	56	49	50	0
1	1	134	74	68	59	0
1	1	93	47	46	45	0
1	1	115	55	61	60	0
2	2	99	50	48	54	1
1	2	99	58	44	47	0
1	2	122	55	64	74	0
1	2	106	49	54	59	1
1	2	124	66	58	68	0
1	1	100	43	56	48	0
1	1	114	61	56	55	0
1	1	121	64	66	50	0
1	1	119	63	61	60	0
1	1	108	48	60	50	0
1	1	110	66	56	48	0
1	1	127	62	71	61	0
1	2	118	66	56	58	0
1	2	107	53	54	52	0

Table 4.13 Data obtained in a study of the effect of post-natal depression of the mother on the child's cognitive development – *cont'd*

1	2	3	Variable[a] 4	5	6	7
2	2	123	62	68	59	0
2	2	102	48	52	58	0
1	2	110	65	47	55	1
1	1	114	64	56	47	0
1	2	118	58	63	52	0
2	1	101	44	56	47	0
2	1	121	64	62	62	0
1	2	114	50	65	51	0

[a] 1, Depression of mother at 3 months (1 = yes; 2 = no); 2, sex of child (1 = boy; 2 = girl); 3, IQ score; 4, perceptual score; 5, verbal score; 6, quantitative score; 7, husband's psychiatric history (0 = no previous history; 1 = has previous psychiatric history).

factors are currently in the model for the observations; in other words, the sums of squares depend on the order in which the factors are considered. (This point will be taken up again in more detail in the discussion of regression analysis in Chapter 6.)

The dependence between the so-called independent variables in an unbalanced factorial design, and the consequent problems of partitioning the sums of squares, has led to a great deal of confusion about the appropriate analysis of such designs. The issues are not completely straightforward and even statisticians (yes, even statisticians!) are not agreed on the most suitable method of analysis for all situations, as witnessed by the discussion following the papers of Nelder (1977) and Aitkin (1978). However, the method of analysis favoured by Aitkin has much to recommend it, and it is this procedure which will be illustrated here; it involves considering factors in different orders and calculating what are known as **sequential sums of squares** (again, more details will be given in Chapter 6). For a two-factor design, *two* analyses of variance tables are now needed to establish a suitable model for the data. The sums of squares in these two tables are as follows:

Table 1	Table 2
Sum of squares for A	Sum of squares for B
Sum of squares for B|A	Sum of squares for A|B
Sum of squares for AB|A,B	Sum of squares for AB|A,B

The sum of squares in the first line of each table will contain a part which could also be attributed to the second factor. The sum of squares in the second line represents the sum of squares contributed by a factor, *over and above* that contributed by the other factor. Finally the third line (which will be the same in each table) represents the sum of squares due to the interaction term, above that due to both main effects.

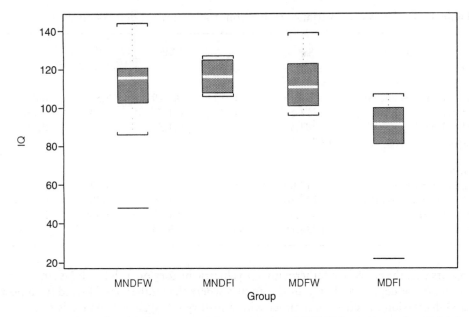

Fig. 4.4 Box plots of IQ for the post-natal depression data: MNDFW, mother no depression and father well; MNDFI, mother no depression and father ill; MDFW, mother depression and father well; MDFI, mother depression and father ill.

Before applying such an analysis to the data in Table 4.13, one important point needs to be stressed: the recommended procedure never uses sums of squares of main effects adjusted for interaction (however defined) for both logical and practical reasons which are detailed in the papers of Nelder (1977) and Aitkin (1978), to where interested readers are referred for the detailed arguments. (NB Both papers require technical expertise well above that required by this text.)

As always, some initial examination of the data is in order before launching into a formal analysis of variance, and Fig. 4.4 shows the box plots of the observations in the four cells of the data in Table 4.13. The most notable feature of this diagram is the two clear outliers, corresponding to two children with very low IQs. One of these children suffered from autism and the other had suffered brain damage at birth. Consequently, they will not be included in further analyses.

The two analysis of variance tables, corresponding to the two orders for the main effects for the data in Table 4.13, are shown in Table 4.14. In order 2, for example, the sum of squares for depression should actually be regarded as explaining the effect of the mother's depression while controlling for the father's psychiatric condition. In other words, it addresses the question, 'Is there a maternal depression effect over and above anything arising solely due to the psychiatric condition of the father and the inequitable distribution of well and ill fathers in the two depression groups?' The results in this display demonstrate how the significance of effects can change depending on which other terms are already in the model. However, the most critical result is that there is strong evidence of an interaction. A plot of the cell means is shown in Fig. 4.5. It

Table 4.14 Analysis of variance of IQ from the post-natal depression data

Source	SS	DF	MS	F	P
Order 1					
Mother depression (M)	565.29	1	565.29	3.54	0.0631
Father history (F)|M	371.57	1	371.57	2.33	0.1305
M × F|M,F	881.57	1	881.57	5.53	0.0210
Error	14 036.18	88	159.50		
Order 2					
Father history (F)	713.00	1	713.00	4.47	0.0373
Mother depression (M)|F	223.86	1	223.86	1.40	0.2393
M × F|M,F	881.57	1	881.57	5.53	0.0210
Error	14 036.18	88	159.50		

appears that the effect of a father with a psychiatric history on a child's IQ is small if the mother is not depressed, but in those families where the mother has suffered from post-natal depression the effect of a father with a history of psychiatric illness is to lower a child's IQ dramatically.

4.8 Multivariate analysis of variance

In the study of the effect of mother's postnatal depression on child development, a number of cognitive variables in addition to IQ were recorded for each child, as shown in Table 4.13. Separate analyses of variance of the type described in the previous section for IQ could be carried out on each variable, but in this case the investigator may be more interested in answering questions about the variables regarded in some way as a **unit**. In other words, comparisons of group differences of the variables treated **simultaneously** are of most concern. Such an approach might be sensible if, for example, the variables were regarded as **indicators** of a single underlying concept that could not be measured directly (see Chapters 10 and 11). The required analysis is now a multivariate analysis of variance as described in the previous chapter. The results of applying the procedure to the perceptual, verbal and quantitative variables in Table 4.13 are shown in Table 4.15. These results suggest that there is no strong evidence of either main effects or interaction for the three variables considered simultaneously. (However, see Exercise 4.7.)

4.9 Summary

1. Factorial designs allow interactions between factors to be studied.
2. The factors in factorial designs can be assumed to have random or fixed effects. The latter are generally more applicable to psychological experiments.
3. Planned comparison and multiple comparison tests can be applied to factorial designs in a similar way to that described for a one-way design in Chapter 3.

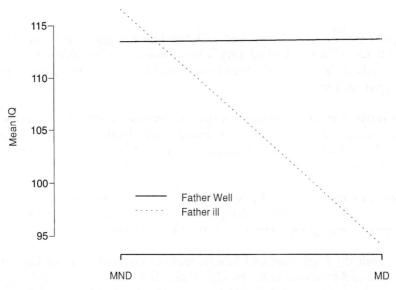

Fig. 4.5 Interaction plot of IQ for the post-natal depression data: MND, mother no depression; MD, mother depression.

4. Unbalanced factorial designs need care in their analyses. It is important to be aware of what procedure for calculating sums of squares is being employed by whatever statistical software is to be used.

Table 4.15 Multivariate analysis of variance of perceptual, verbal and quantitative variables in post-natal depression data

Criterion	Value	F	DF1	DF2	P
Test for mother's depression					
Wilk	0.929	2.18	3	86	0.0962
Pillai	0.071	2.18	3	86	0.0962
Hotelling	0.076	2.18	3	86	0.0962
Test for father's illness					
Wilk	0.926	2.29	3	86	0.0843
Pillai	0.075	2.29	3	86	0.0843
Hotelling	0.080	2.29	3	86	0.0843
Test for interaction					
Wilk	0.938	1.88	3	86	0.1390
Pillai	0.062	1.88	3	86	0.1390
Hotelling	0.065	1.88	3	86	0.1390

Exercises

4.1 Survival times are generally not normally distributed. Suggest a transformation of the survival times in Table 4.1 which may help to overcome this problem. Carry out a two-way analysis of variance on the transformed observations and compare the results with those given in Table 4.5.

4.2 In the survival time data assume that both the levels of treatment and the levels of poison form an ordered scale with equally spaced points. Find the analysis of variance table in which the sums of squares represent the appropriate orthogonal polynomial contrasts.

4.3 Using the slimming data in Table 4.7 construct the appropriate 95% confidence interval for the difference in weight change between novice and experienced slimmers when members of both groups have access to a slimming manual.

4.4 Apply both the Bonferroni and Scheffé multiple comparison procedures to the levels of poison and treatment in the survival times data.

4.5 In the survival times example, assume that the first treatment level is a control and carry out an appropriate series of planned comparisons to test each of the other treatments against it.

Table 4.16 Blood pressure, family history and smoker status

Family history	Blood pressure		
	Non-smoker	Ex-smoker	Current smoker
Present	125	114	135
	156	107	120
	103	134	123
	129	140	113
	110	120	165
	128	115	145
	135		120
Absent	114	110	140
	110	128	125
	91	105	123
	136	90	108
	105		113
	125		160
	103		
	110		

From Boniface (1995).

4.6 In the drug, biofeed and diet example, carry out separate two-way analyses of variance of the data corresponding to each drug. What conclusions do you reach from your analysis?

4.7 In the post-natal depression data, analyse separately each of the three variables used in the multivariate analysis of variance in Section 4.8. Comment on the results.

4.8 The data in Table 4.16 (Boniface 1995) were collected during a survey of systolic blood pressure of individuals classified according to smoking status and family history of circulation and heart problems. Carry out an analysis of variance of the data and state your conclusions.

4.9 In the model for a balanced two-way fixed effects design (see Display 4.1), suggest sensible estimators for the main effect and interaction parameters. Use your suggested estimators to determine the parameter estimates for the survival time data in Table 4.1.

4.10 The observations in Table 4.17 are part of the data collected in a clinical trial of the use of oestrogen patches in the treatment of postnatal depression. (The full data set

Table 4.17 Data from a trial of oestrogen patches in the treatment of post-natal depression

Treatment	Baseline 1	Baseline 2	Depression score
Placebo	18	18	15
	25	27	10
	24	17	12
	19	15	5
	22	20	5
	27	28	9
	21	16	11
	26	26	13
	20	19	6
	24	20	18
	24	22	10
Active	27	27	7
	19	15	8
	25	28	2
	19	18	6
	21	20	11
	21	21	5
	25	24	11
	25	25	6
	15	22	6
	27	26	10

will be considered in more detail in the next chapter.) Carry out an analysis of variance of the post-treatment measure of depression using both pre-treatment values as covariates.

Further reading

Jackson, S. and Brashers, D.E. (1994). *Random factors in ANOVA*. Sage, Beverly Hills, California.

Keren, G. (1993). A balanced approach to unbalanced designs. In *A handbook for data analysis in the behavioural sciences: statistical issues* (ed. G. Keren and C. Lewis). Lawrence Erlbaum, Hilllsdale, NJ.

Searle, S.R. (1987). *Linear models for unbalanced data*. Wiley, New York.

5

Analysis of variance: repeated measures designs

5.1 Introduction

Many studies undertaken in the behavioural sciences and related disciplines involve observing a response variable for each subject on more than one occasion. In some cases, particularly in clinical trials or learning experiments, the different occasions simply relate to the passing of time; however, in others they also involve changes in some condition manipulated by the experimenter. Both types of study are said to lead to **repeated measurements** and therefore both are labelled **repeated measures designs**, although perhaps the former should be more properly termed **longitudinal designs**. Some examples will help to illustrate the distinction more clearly:

1. **Visual acuity and lens strength:** Seven subjects had their response times measured when a light was flashed into each eye through lenses of powers 6/6, 6/18, 6/36 and 6/60 (a lens of power a/b means that the eye will perceive as being at a feet an object actually positioned at b feet). Measurements were made in milliseconds, and the question of interest was whether response time varied with lens strength. The data from this experiment are shown in Table 5.1.
2. **Field independence and a reverse Stroop task:** Subjects selected randomly from a large group of subjects identified as having field-independent or field-dependent cognitive style were required to read two types of words (colour and form names) under three cue conditions, i.e. normal, congruent and incongruent. The dependent measure was the time (milliseconds) taken to read the stimulus words. The data are shown in Table 5.2.

Table 5.1 Visual acuity and lens strength. (Taken with permission from Crowder and Hand, 1990.)

Subject	Left eye				Right eye			
	6/6	6/18	6/36	6/60	6/6	6/18	6/36	6/60
1	116	119	116	124	120	117	114	122
2	110	110	114	115	106	112	110	110
3	117	118	120	120	120	120	120	124
4	112	116	115	113	115	116	116	119
5	113	114	114	118	114	117	116	112
6	114	115	94	116	100	99	94	97
7	110	110	105	118	105	105	115	115

Table 5.2 Observations (times in msec) from a $2 \times 2 \times 3$ factorial design with repeated measures on the last two factors

Subject	b_1 form			b_2 colour		
	c_1 (N)	c_2 (C)	c_3 (I)	c_1 (N)	c_2 (C)	c_3 (I)
a_1 (Field-independent)						
1	191	206	219	176	182	196
2	175	183	186	148	156	161
3	166	165	161	138	146	150
4	206	190	212	174	178	184
5	179	187	171	182	185	210
6	183	175	171	182	185	210
7	174	168	187	167	160	178
8	185	186	185	153	159	169
9	182	189	201	173	177	183
10	191	192	208	168	169	187
11	162	163	168	135	141	145
12	162	162	170	142	147	151
a_2 (Field-dependent)						
13	277	267	322	205	231	255
14	235	216	271	161	183	187
15	150	150	165	140	140	156
16	400	404	379	214	223	216
17	183	165	187	140	146	163
18	162	215	184	144	156	165
19	163	179	172	170	189	192
20	163	159	159	143	150	148
21	237	233	238	207	225	228
22	205	177	217	205	208	230
23	178	190	211	144	155	177
24	164	186	187	139	151	163

N, normal; C, congruent; I, incongruent.

3. **Alcohol dependence and salsolinol excretion:** Two groups of subjects, one with severe and one with moderate dependence on alcohol, had their salsolinol excretion levels (in mmol) recorded on four consecutive days (for those readers without the necessary expertise in chemistry, salsolinol is an alkaloid with a structure similar to that of heroin). Primary interest centres on whether the groups behaved differently over time. The data are shown in Table 5.3.

4. **Trial of oestrogen patches in the treatment of post-natal depression:** Women who had suffered an episode of post-natal depression were randomly allocated to two groups; the members of one group received an oestrogen patch, and the members of the other group received a 'dummy' patch—the placebo. The dependent variable was a composite measure of depression, which was recorded on two occasions prior

Table 5.3 Salsolinol excretion rates (mmol) for moderately and severely dependent alcoholic patients. (Taken with permission from Crowder and Hand, 1990.)

Subject	Day			
	1	2	3	4
Group 1 (moderate dependence)				
1	0.33	0.70	2.33	3.20
2	5.30	0.90	1.80	0.70
3	2.50	2.10	1.12	1.01
4	0.98	0.32	3.91	0.66
5	0.39	0.69	0.73	2.45
6	0.31	6.34	0.63	3.86
Group 2 (severe dependence)				
7	0.64	0.70	1.00	1.40
8	0.73	1.85	3.60	2.60
9	0.70	4.20	7.30	5.40
10	0.40	1.60	1.40	7.10
11	2.50	1.30	0.70	0.70
12	7.80	1.20	2.60	1.80
13	1.90	1.30	4.40	2.80
14	0.50	0.40	1.10	8.10

to randomization and six occasions after treatment commenced. The data are shown in Table 5.4. Note that a number of the women in each group do not have observations on all eight possible occasions.

Superficially, these examples look quite different. However, what they do have in common is that the subjects or patients involved have the response variable of interest recorded more than once. In some cases the repeated measurements on each subject correspond simply to a time sequence of observations (as in the last two examples above); in other cases the investigator varies systematically the conditions under which the measurements are made (as in the first two examples above). These conditions are known as the **within-subject** factors in the experiment. In addition, there may be **between-subject** factors corresponding to different groups of subjects; for example different treatments, gender, diagnostic group etc.

In a longitudinal design (such as the third and fourth examples above) the repeated measures on the same subject are a necessary part of the design. In the other examples, however, it would be quite possible to use different groups of subjects for each condition combination, giving rise to a factorial design as discussed in the previous chapter. The primary purpose of using a repeated measures design in such cases is the control that this approach provides over individual differences between subjects. In the area of behavioural sciences, such differences are often quite large relative to differences produced by manipulation of the experimental conditions or treatments which the investigator is trying to evaluate.

Table 5.4 Data from a trial of oestrogen patches in the treatment of post-natal depression

Group	Baseline		Visit					
	BL1	BL2	V1	V2	V3	V4	V5	V6
0	18.00	18.00	17.00	18.00	15.00	17.00	14.00	15.00
0	25.11	27.00	26.00	23.00	18.00	17.00	12.00	10.00
0	19.00	16.00	17.00	14.00	−9.00	−9.00	−9.00	−9.00
0	24.00	17.00	14.00	23.00	17.00	13.00	12.00	12.00
0	19.08	15.00	12.00	10.00	8.00	4.00	5.00	5.00
0	22.00	20.00	19.00	11.54	9.00	8.00	6.82	5.05
0	28.00	16.00	13.00	13.00	9.00	7.00	8.00	7.00
0	24.00	28.00	26.00	27.00	−9.00	−9.00	−9.00	−9.00
0	27.00	28.00	26.00	24.00	19.00	13.94	11.00	9.00
0	18.00	25.00	9.00	12.00	15.00	12.00	13.00	20.00
0	23.00	24.00	14.00	−9.00	−9.00	−9.00	−9.00	−9.00
0	21.00	16.00	19.00	13.00	14.00	23.00	15.00	11.00
0	23.00	26.00	13.00	22.00	−9.00	−9.00	−9.00	−9.00
0	21.00	21.00	7.00	13.00	−9.00	−9.00	−9.00	−9.00
0	22.00	21.00	18.00	−9.00	−9.00	−9.00	−9.00	−9.00
0	23.00	22.00	18.00	−9.00	−9.00	−9.00	−9.00	−9.00
0	26.00	26.00	19.00	13.00	22.00	12.00	18.00	13.00
0	20.00	19.00	19.00	7.00	8.00	2.00	5.00	6.00
0	20.00	22.00	20.00	15.00	20.00	17.00	15.00	13.73
0	15.00	16.00	7.00	8.00	12.00	10.00	10.00	12.00
0	22.00	21.00	19.00	18.00	16.00	13.00	16.00	15.00
0	24.00	20.00	16.00	21.00	17.00	21.00	16.00	18.00
0	−9.00	17.00	15.00	−9.00	−9.00	−9.00	−9.00	−9.00
0	24.00	22.00	20.00	21.00	17.00	14.00	14.00	10.00
0	24.00	19.00	16.00	19.00	−9.00	−9.00	−9.00	−9.00
0	22.00	21.00	7.00	4.00	4.19	4.73	3.03	3.45
0	16.00	18.00	19.00	−9.00	−9.00	−9.00	−9.00	−9.00
1	21.00	21.00	13.00	12.00	9.00	9.00	13.00	6.00
1	27.00	27.00	8.00	17.00	15.00	7.00	5.00	7.00
1	24.00	15.00	8.00	12.27	10.00	10.00	6.00	5.96
1	28.00	24.00	14.00	14.00	13.00	12.00	18.00	15.00
1	19.00	15.00	15.00	16.00	11.00	14.00	12.00	8.00
1	17.00	17.00	9.00	5.00	3.00	6.00	0.00	2.00
1	21.00	20.00	7.00	7.00	7.00	12.00	9.00	6.00
1	18.00	18.00	8.00	1.00	1.00	2.00	0.00	1.00
1	24.00	28.00	11.00	7.00	3.00	2.00	2.00	2.00
1	21.00	21.00	7.00	8.00	6.00	6.50	4.64	4.97
1	19.00	18.00	8.00	6.00	4.00	11.00	7.00	6.00
1	28.00	27.46	22.00	27.00	24.00	22.00	24.00	23.00
1	23.00	19.00	14.00	12.00	15.00	12.00	9.00	6.00
1	21.00	20.00	13.00	10.00	7.00	9.00	11.00	11.00
1	18.00	16.00	17.00	26.00	−9.00	−9.00	−9.00	−9.00
1	22.61	21.00	19.00	9.00	9.00	12.00	5.00	7.00

Table 5.4 Data from a trial of oestrogen patches in the treatment of post-natal depression – *cont'd*

Group	Baseline		Visit					
	BL1	BL2	V1	V2	V3	V4	V5	V6
1	24.24	23.00	11.00	7.00	5.00	8.00	2.00	3.00
1	23.00	23.00	16.00	13.00	−9.00	−9.00	−9.00	−9.00
1	24.84	24.00	16.00	15.00	11.00	11.00	11.00	11.00
1	25.00	25.00	20.00	18.00	16.00	9.00	10.00	6.00
1	−9.00	28.00	−9.00	−9.00	−9.00	−9.00	−9.00	−9.00
1	15.00	22.00	15.00	17.57	12.00	9.00	8.00	6.50
1	26.00	20.00	7.00	2.00	1.00	0.00	0.00	2.00
1	22.00	20.00	12.13	8.00	6.00	3.00	2.00	3.00
1	24.00	25.00	15.00	24.00	18.00	15.19	13.00	12.32
1	22.00	18.00	17.00	6.00	2.00	2.00	0.00	1.00
1	27.00	26.00	1.00	18.00	10.00	13.00	12.00	10.00
1	22.00	20.00	27.00	13.00	9.00	8.00	4.00	5.00
1	24.00	21.00	−9.00	−9.00	−9.00	−9.00	−9.00	−9.00
1	20.00	17.00	20.00	10.00	8.89	8.49	7.02	6.79
1	22.00	22.00	12.00	−9.00	−9.00	−9.00	−9.00	−9.00
1	20.00	22.00	15.38	2.00	4.00	6.00	3.00	3.00
1	21.00	23.00	11.00	9.00	10.00	8.00	7.00	4.00
1	17.00	17.00	15.00	−9.00	−9.00	−9.00	−9.00	−9.00
1	18.00	22.00	7.00	12.00	15.00	−9.00	−9.00	−9.00
1	23.00	26.00	24.00	−9.00	−9.00	−9.00	−9.00	−9.00

0 = Placebo, 1 = active; −9.00 indicates a missing value.

Another advantage often claimed for repeated measure designs is that of economy of subjects. In many respects, this is a somewhat dubious advantage since using different subjects under each of the treatment combinations is very likely to be the best way of increasing the precision of the results. By having each subject serve as his or her own control, the experimenter attempts to work with a smaller sample size, but this increases the problems of analysis because the observations are no longer necessarily independent; the repeated measures, which involve the same subjects on different occasions, are very likely to be correlated.

There are variety of ways in which repeated measures data can be analysed. In fact, recent years have seen a considerable increase in the number of suitable methods, particularly for data from studies such as the trial of oestrogen patches where there are a considerable number of missing values; such observations (or perhaps non-observations is more appropriate) can arise for a number of reasons which will be discussed later (see Section 5.6). The pattern of correlations between the repeated measurements is of considerable importance in determining which methods of analysis are appropriate, as will be seen in Section 5.5. First, however, a number of relatively simple but informative methods of plotting repeated measures data will be considered.

5.2   Plotting repeated measures data

A useful initial step in the analysis of certain types of repeated measures is to plot the data in some way. This applies particularly to studies in which the repeated measurements arise from simply recording the values of a dependent variable on a number of occasions over time (longitudinal studies). Graphical methods may be less helpful in experimental studies in which the repeated measures arise from the crossing of within-subject factors, as in the first two examples considered in Section 5.1.

A graphical procedure commonly employed, particularly in the medical literature, is to plot means of the response variable, by group if applicable, for every time point at which a recording is made. Such plots for the salsolinol and oestrogen patch data are shown in Figs 5.1 and 5.2. (Since the salsolinol data are clearly very skewed, Fig. 5.1 uses the logarithmically transformed observations.) Figure 5.1 suggests that the salsolinol excretion level of the severely alcohol-dependent group is consistently larger than in the moderately dependent group over all four days, with the difference apparently increasing with time. Figure 5.2 shows that the average depression score in both the placebo and the active groups decreases over time, but the decrease in the active group is considerably greater between the start of treatment and the first visit. From the first visit onwards, the difference between the average depression scores of the two groups remains relatively constant. (Standard error 'bars' are frequently added to such plots (e.g. Fig. 5.3), although the resulting diagrams can often become quite cluttered.)

To supplement plots involving means, it is usually quite helpful to produce separate graphs of the dependent variable against time for each subject, differentiat-

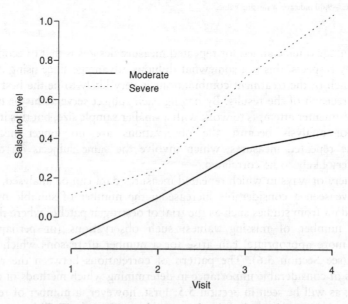

Fig. 5.1 Means by group for the salsolinol example.

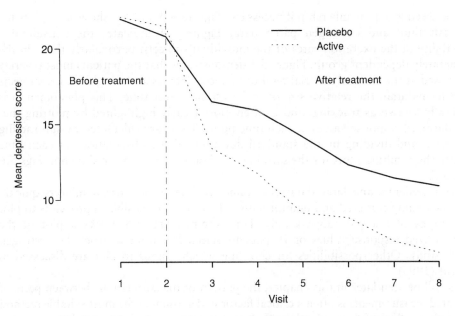

Fig. 5.2 Means by treatment group for the oestrogen patch example.

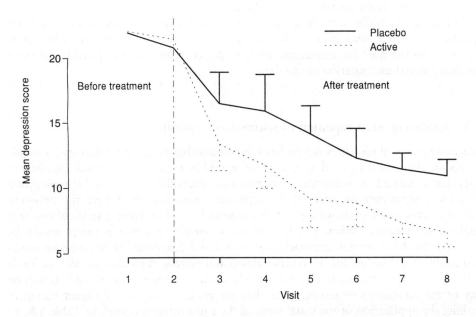

Fig. 5.3 Means by treatment group for oestrogen patch data with standard error 'bars'.

ing between group membership if necessary. Figures 5.4 and 5.5 show such plots for the salsolinol and oestrogen patch data. Figure 5.4 indicates the considerable variability in the excretion rates of the individual subjects, particularly those in the moderately dependent group. Figure 5.5 demonstrates that the patients most severely depressed at the start of the trial tend to be most depressed throughout, i.e. subjects tend to maintain the relative size of their response over time. This phenomenon is generally known as **tracking**, and is often more clearly highlighted by plotting the **standardized** response values at each time point. These are calculated by subtracting the mean and dividing by the standard deviation of the observations at each time point. The resulting plots for the salsolinol and oestrogen data are shown in Figs 5.6 and 5.7.

With moderate and large data sets, connected line graphs for all subjects quickly become unduly cluttered and uninformative. Thus a more sensible approach is to plot the graphs of selected subjects only. For example, Fig. 5.8 shows a plot of the standardized response values of 10 patients selected at random from the oestrogen patch study. Other possibilities for choosing which graphs to plot are discussed in Everitt (1995).

As will be seen later in this chapter, the pattern of the correlations between pairs of repeated measurements is often a critical factor in determining the most suitable method of analysis. A useful graphical procedure for examining these correlations is the draughtsman's plot introduced in Chapter 2. Figure 5.9 shows such a diagram for the oestrogen patch data. The pattern that emerges from this plot is that of decreasing correlations between the depression scores with an increasing amount of time between the visits on which the measures were taken.

(In practice, in addition to the graphical displays described in this section which are specific to repeated measures data, it will also be wise to consider the use of box plots etc. to assess the need for transformations, to detect outliers and to provide the usual necessary initial examination of the data.)

5.3 Analysing each repeated measurement separately

When the repeated measures design has a between-subjects factor (or factors), a simple procedure that could be used in its analysis would be to perform separate significance tests (or construct a sequence of confidence intervals) to assess between-group differences separately on each of the repeated measurements. Where the between-subjects factor has g levels with $g > 2$ this approach would involve a series of one-way analyses of variance. When $g = 2$, a series of simple two-sample t-tests would be required. To illustrate this approach, Tables 5.5 and 5.6 show the appropriate t-tests and confidence intervals for the reverse stroop and oestrogen patch examples. In Table 5.5, none of the tests are significant at the 5% level, suggesting no group differences on any of the conditions of testing (note that the groups have very different variances making the application of the usual form of the t-test rather suspect). In Table 5.6, all the separate confidence intervals suggest that there is a difference between the active and placebo groups. (Note that in the results given in Table 5.6, missing values have simply been excluded.)

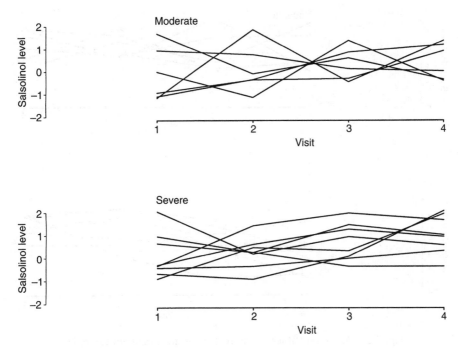

Fig. 5.4 Individual response profiles for subjects in the salsolinol example.

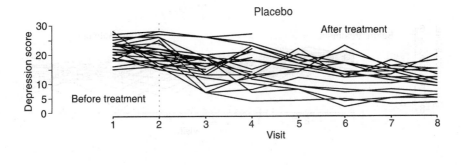

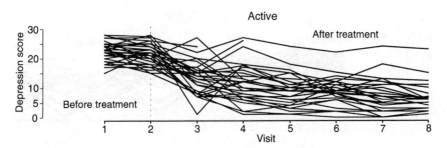

Fig. 5.5 Individual profiles for subjects in the oestrogen patch trial.

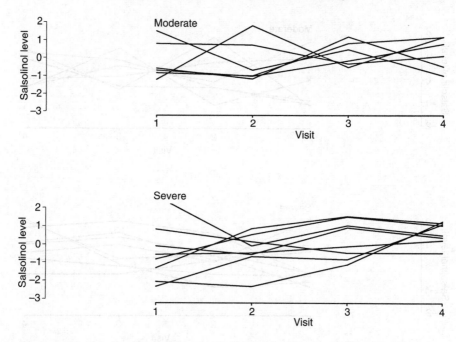

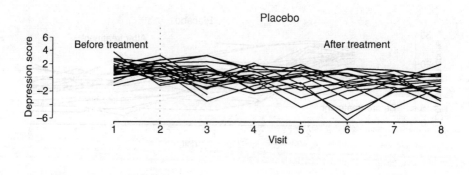

Fig. 5.6 Deviation values for individuals in the salsolinol example.

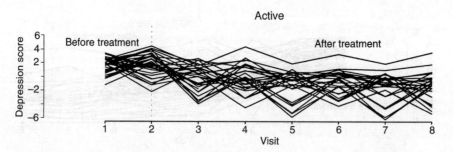

Fig. 5.7 Deviation values for subjects in oestrogen patch trial example.

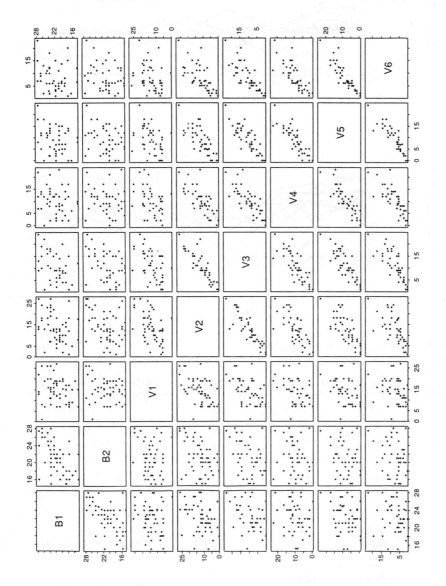

Fig. 5.9 Draughtsman's plot of repeated measures from the oestrogen patch trial data.

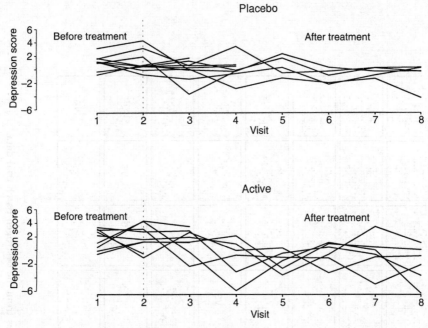

Fig. 5.8 Deviation values for a random sample of 10 subjects in the oestrogen patch trial example.

Table 5.5 *t*-tests for the data in Table 5.2

	Group 1	Group 2	*t*-value	95% CI	P
b_1c_1					
Mean	179.7	209.7			
SD	13.0	71.4	−1.43	(−73.45, 13.45)	0.16
b_1c_2					
Mean	180.5	211.2			
SD	13.8	69.4	−1.50	(−73.06, 11.66)	0.15
b_1c_3					
Mean	188.7	224.3			
SD	18.9	68.1	−1.74	(−77.91, 6.71)	0.09
b_2c_1					
Mean	159.5	167.7			
SD	16.1	31.3	−0.81	(−29.27, 12.87)	0.42
b_2c_2					
Mean	163.2	179.7			
SD	14.8	34.4	−1.52	(−38.92, 5.92)	0.14
b_2c_3					
Mean	173.5	190.0			
SD	19.8	34.5	−1.43	(−40.31, 7.31)	0.17

Table 5.6   *t*-tests for the data in Table 5.4

	Placebo	Active	*t*-value	95% CI	P
Visit 1					
Mean	16.48	13.37			
SD	5.28	5.56			
n	27	34	2.22	(0.31, 5.91)	0.030
Visit 2					
Mean	15.89	11.74			
SD	6.12	6.57			
n	22	31	2.33	(0.59, 7.71)	0.024
Visit 3					
Mean	14.13	9.13			
SD	4.97	5.47			
n	17	29	3.09	(1.77, 8.23)	0.003
Visit 4					
Mean	12.27	8.83			
SD	5.85	4.67			
n	17	28	2.18	(0.28, 6.60)	0.035
Visit 5					
Mean	11.40	7.31			
SD	4.44	5.74			
n	17	28	2.51	(0.83, 7.34)	0.016
Visit 6					
Mean	10.89	6.59			
SD	4.68	4.73			
n	17	28	2.97	(1.40, 7.20)	0.005

Since the analysis described above is so straightforward, readers might ask: 'Why not use it in every case?' The answer is that the method has a number of flaws and weaknesses. The first is that the series of tests performed are not independent of one another, making interpretation difficult. For example, a succession of marginally significant group mean differences might be collectively compelling if the repeated measurements are only weakly correlated, but much less so if there are strong correlations between successive observations on subjects. It is also assumed that each repeated measurement is of separate interest in its own right. This is unlikely in general, since the real concern is likely to involve something more global. For example, in Table 5.5 the separate *t*-tests fail to give any answer to the obvious questions about differences between the levels of the type factor or the cue condition; in particular the tests in Table 5.5 give no clue to the importance or otherwise of the interaction between the two within-subject factors. In Table 5.6, the series of tests shown provide very little information about the longitudinal development of the mean response profiles. In addition, the separate significance tests do not give an overall answer to whether or not there is a group difference and, of particular importance, do not provide a useful estimate of the overall treatment effect.

5.4   Response feature analysis: the use of summary measures

A relatively straightforward but often extremely informative approach to the analysis of repeated measures data (particularly when 'time' is the only within-subject factor) is that which makes use of **summary measures**. This procedure is often known as **response feature analysis**. Here the repeated measurements for each subject are combined in some way to produce a single value (or in some cases two or three such values) summarizing some *relevant* aspect of the subject's response profile. Having identified a suitable summary measure (see later), the analysis of group differences will now involve only simple analysis of variance or, when only two groups are involved, the application of a two-sample *t*-test (or, in some cases, its non-parametric equivalent; see Chapter 9). Alternatively (and preferably), the corresponding confidence interval for the chosen summary measure can be constructed.

Which summary measure is most relevant will largely depend on the particular questions of interest. A list of potentially useful measures taken from Matthews *et al.* (1990) is shown in Table 5.7.

The summary measure approach to repeated measures data will first be illustrated on the salsolinol excretion data. The first question to consider is: 'What is a suitable summary measure for these data?' Since the difference in average excretion level is likely to be one of the questions of interest here, the most obvious summary measure to use is simply the average response of each subject over the four measurement occasions (after the responses have been logarithmically transformed for the reasons given earlier). Display 5.1 gives this measure for each subject in the study together with the results of constructing a 95% confidence interval for the difference between the two alcohol-dependent groups. The confidence interval contains the value zero and so, strictly, no

Table 5.7   Possible summary measures

Type of data	Question of interest	Summary measure
Peaked	Is overall value of outcome variable the same in different groups?	Overall mean (equal time intervals); or area under curve (unequal time intervals)
Peaked	Is maximum (minimum) response different between groups?	Maximum (minimum) value
Peaked	Is time to maximum (minimum) response different between groups?	Time to maximum (minimum) response
Growth	Is rate of change of outcome variable different between groups?	Regression coefficient
Growth	Is eventual value of outcome variable the same between groups?	Final value of outcome measure, or difference between last and first values, or percentage change between first and last values
Growth	Is response in one group delayed relative to the other?	Time to reach a particular value (e.g. a fixed percentage of baseline)

From Matthews *et al.* (1990).

Display 5.1 Application of summary measure approach to data in Table 5.3 case: average response over 4 days (averages of log transformed values)

- Average response is as follows:

Group	Subject	Average response
Group 1 (moderate)	1	0.06
	2	0.19
	3	0.19
	4	−0.02
	5	−0.08
	6	0.17
Group 2 (severe)	1	−0.05
	2	0.28
	3	0.52
	4	0.20
	5	0.05
	6	0.41
	7	0.37
	8	0.06

- Means and standard deviations are as follows:

Group	Mean	SD	n
Moderate	0.0858	0.1186	6
Severe	0.2301	0.1980	8

- The 95% confidence interval for the difference between the two groups is

$$(0.2301 - 0.0858) \pm 2.18 \times s \times (1/6 + 1/8)^{1/2}$$

where s^2 is the estimate of the assumed common variance in the two groups and is given by

$$s^2 = \frac{5 \times 0.1186^2 + 7 \times 0.1980^2}{8 + 6 - 2}.$$

- These calculations lead to the interval

$$(-0.0552, 0.3438).$$

claim can be made that the data give any evidence of a difference between the average excretion levels of those people who are moderately dependent and those who are severely dependent on alcohol. However, taking a more pragmatic view, it does appear that subjects who are severely dependent on alcohol tend to have a somewhat higher salsolinol excretion level.

A further summary measure that might be relevant for these data is the maximum salsolinol level amongst the four observations for each subject (again after a logarithmic transformation of the raw data). These values and a confidence interval for the difference in the two groups are shown in Display 5.2. Here there really does appear to be very little evidence of a difference.

Display 5.2 Summary measures approach to data in Table 5.3: maximum response over 4 days (after logarithmic transformation of raw data)

- The maximum response over 4 days is as follows:

Group	Subject	Maximum response
Group 1 (moderate)	1	0.51
	2	0.72
	3	0.40
	4	0.59
	5	0.39
	6	0.80
Group 2 (severe)	7	0.15
	8	0.56
	9	0.86
	10	0.85
	11	0.41
	12	0.89
	13	0.64
	14	0.91

- Means and standard deviations are as follows:

Group	Mean	SD	n
Moderate	0.5685	0.1701	6
Severe	0.6595	0.2748	8

- The 95% confidence interval for the difference between groups is
$$(-0.37, 0.19).$$

The response feature procedure can also be applied to the oestrogen patch data, but here there is a complication caused by the absence of values for some patients. How should the missing observations be dealt with? The simplest answer to this question is to remove patients with such values from the analysis and use only those for whom all six post-treatment measures are present. This may be simple but it is not good! Using only subjects with a complete set of measurements has obvious and less obvious weaknesses. The obvious part is that such an approach reduces the number of subjects in the analysis. When only one or two subjects have missing values this may not be too devastating; however, if it results in a 20% reduction in the sample size (a not uncommon event), it is clearly very damaging. The less obvious weakness of the 'complete cases' approach is that the results from this subset of subjects might give a distorted picture of what happens to subjects in general.

An alternative to simply removing offending subjects when using the summary measure procedure for repeated measures data containing missing values is to calculate the chosen summary measure from the available measurements on a subject. In this way subjects with different numbers of repeated measurements can all contribute to the analysis. These mean values for each subject in the oestrogen patch trial are shown in Table 5.8. (Also shown in this table are the means of the available pre-treatment values for each subject which will be used later in this chapter.) The 95% confidence interval of (−6.79, −1.61) for the difference between the active and placebo groups shows clearly that there is a difference in average depression in the two groups, with the active group being considerably lower.

(It should be noted here that if the configuration of repeated measures for each subject varies, the summary measures calculated are likely to have differing precisions. Analysis of the summary measures should ideally take this into account by some form of **weighting**. This was not attempted in the analysis reported above since it involves techniques outside the scope of this text. For those readers courageous enough to tackle a little mathematics, a description of a technically more satisfactory procedure is given by Gorbein *et al.*, 1992.)

Longitudinal studies often involve one or more measurements of the dependent variable taken before any treatment commences. The oestrogen patch study provides an example. These pretreatment values can be used in association with the response feature procedure in a number of ways. For example, if the average response to treatment over time is the chosen summary, there are three possible methods of analysis (Frison and Pocock, 1992).

1. Post-treatment means (POST): a simple analysis ignoring completely the measures taken prior to the formation of the treatment groups.
2. Mean changes (CHANGE): again, a relatively simple analysis using the difference between the post-treatment and pre-treatment means for each subject (the latter often consists of the 'mean' of a single pre-treatment value).
3. Analysis of covariance (ANCOVA): a more complicated approach in which the mean of the pre-treatment values is used as a covariate in the analysis of the post-treatment values.

Frison and Pocock (1992) compared these three methods for the analysis of repeated measures data when pre-treatment values are available, and with a single pre-treatment

Table 5.8 Means of usable post-treatment and pre-treatment values for oestrogen patch trial data

Group	Mean pre-treatment	Mean post-treatment
Placebo	18.00	16.00
	26.06	17.67
	17.50	15.50
	25.00	15.17
	17.04	7.33
	21.00	9.90
	22.00	9.50
	26.00	26.50
	27.50	17.16
	21.50	13.50
	23.50	14.00
	18.50	15.83
	24.50	17.50
	21.00	1.00
	21.50	18.00
	22.50	18.00
	26.00	16.17
	19.50	7.83
	21.00	16.79
	15.50	9.83
	21.50	16.17
	22.00	18.17
	17.00	15.00
	23.00	16.00
	21.50	17.50
	21.50	4.40
	17.00	19.00
Active	21.00	10.33
	27.00	9.83
	19.50	8.70
	26.00	14.33
	17.00	12.67
	17.00	4.17
	20.50	8.00
	18.00	2.17
	26.00	4.50
	21.00	6.18
	18.50	7.00
	27.73	23.67
	21.00	11.33
	20.50	10.17
	17.00	21.50
	21.81	10.17

Table 5.8 Means of usable post-treatment and pre-treatment values for oestrogen patch trial data – *cont'd*

Group	Mean pre-treatment	Mean post-treatment
Active	23.62	6.00
	23.00	14.50
	24.42	12.50
	25.00	13.17
	18.50	11.35
	23.00	2.00
	21.00	5.69
	24.50	16.25
	20.00	4.67
	26.50	10.67
	21.00	11.00
	18.50	10.20
	22.00	12.00
	21.00	5.56
	22.00	8.17
	17.00	15.00
	20.00	11.33
	24.50	24.00

measure found that the analysis of covariance is more powerful than either the analysis of change scores or the analysis of post-treatment means, except when the correlations between the repeated measurements are small. If there is substantial correlation between the repeated measures, using the mean of several pre-treatment recordings of the response variable as covariate makes the analysis of covariance even more efficient. (Everitt, 1995, gives a comparison of the three approaches in terms of their power for various values of the correlations between the repeated measurements.)

The results of applying each of POST, CHANGE and ANCOVA to the oestrogen patch data, using the pre-treatment and post-treatment means of the available values of each subject (see Table 5.8) are shown in Tables 5.9 and 5.10. Here, all three analyses clearly demonstrate a difference between the levels of depression in the active and placebo groups.

The response feature method, although not suitable for all types of repeated measures data, has a number of advantages. Three given by Matthews (1993) are as follows:

1. Appropriate choice of summary measure ensures that the analysis is focused on relevant and interpretable aspects of the data.
2. The method is statistically respectable (!).
3. To some extent, missing and irregularly spaced observations can be accommodated.

5.5 Analysis of variance for repeated measures data

All the examples presented in Section 5.1 are, superficially at least, similar in form to the type of factorial design data met in the previous chapter. For example, in the salsolinol

Table 5.9　POST and CHANGE analyses for oestrogen patch data

	Placebo	Active	*t*	DF	*P*
POST					
Mean	14.76	10.55			
SD	4.56	5.36			
n	27	34	3.25	59	0.0019
CHANGE					
Mean	−6.51	−11.07			
SD	4.38	5.49			
n	27	34	3.51	59	0.0009

Table 5.10　ANCOVA analysis for oestrogen patch data

Source	SS	DF	MS	*F*	*P*
Group	287.76	1	287.76	12.36	0.0009
Baseline	138.02	1	138.02	5.93	0.018
Error	1350.65	58	23.29		

data time could be regarded as a factor with four levels, and type of dependency could be regarded as a second factor with two levels. Consequently, why not simply apply the analysis of variance procedures described in Chapter 4 to the repeated measures data? Of course, the answer is that the data sets described in the introduction to this chapter only appear to be similar to factorial design data. In fact, there is, one very important difference. The observations in a factorial design involve different subjects in each cell; the observations in Tables 5.1–5.4 involve the same subjects observed under a number of different conditions. Consequently, the observations are likely to be dependent rather than independent, as assumed for the observations in the designs discussed in Chapters 3 and 4.

However, it is possible to use relatively straightforward analysis of variance procedures for repeated measures data, *if* three particular assumptions about the observations are valid. The first two of these have been met in previous chapters and will not be discussed any further here (of course, this does not mean that they can be disregarded in a repeated measures analysis). They are as follows:

1. Normality: the data arise from populations with normal distributions.
2. Homogeneity of variance: the variances of the normal populations are assumed to be the same.

The third and most critical assumption about the observations concerns the form of the relationship between the repeated measures; it is known as **sphericity** and requires that the variances of the differences between all pairs of repeated measurements are

Table 5.11 Analysis of variance for the 45 complete observations in the oestrogen patch trial data

Source	SS	DF	MS	F	P
Treatment groups	1054.39	1	1054.39	8.81	0.0049
Error	5147.56	43	119.71		
Time	1108.94	5	221.79	20.12	< 0.0001
Groups × time	21.35	5	4.27	0.39	0.8571
Error	2369.91	215	11.02		

equal. This condition implies that the correlations between pairs of repeated measurements are also equal, the so-called **compound symmetry** pattern of correlations (see Appendix A). In addition, sphericity must hold in all levels of the between-subjects part of the design.

The sphericity condition has not been met before and is particularly critical in the analysis of variance of repeated measures data, as will be seen in the discussion later in this section. However, for the moment let us assume that this is that 'best of all possible worlds' where data are always normal, variances are always equal and repeated measures always satisfy sphericity.

To begin, a suitable model for longitudinal data with a number of treatment groups will be considered (such a study is often referred to as involving a two-factor design with repeated measures on one of the factors) and then applied to the *complete* observations in the data from the oestrogen patch trial. The model and the associated analysis of variance table are outlined in Display 5.3. The model allows for correlations between the repeated measurements, but only of the compound symmetry pattern (the effect of departures from this pattern is discussed later). The variation in the observations is simply divided into a part arising from variation *between subjects* and a part due to variation *within subjects*. The former corresponds essentially to differences between different subjects, and the latter to differences between the observations made on the same subject. The between-subjects variation can be further divided into a part representing differences between group means and an 'error' variance which simply measures variation between subjects within groups. The within-subjects term can be further partitioned into components due to differences between the time points, a groups × time interaction and 'error' (which actually corresponds to the subjects within the groups × time interaction). The analysis of variance table resulting from applying this model to the oestrogen patch trial data is shown in Table 5.11. Both the time effect and the treatment group effect are highly significant, but the group × time interaction is non-significant. These effects indicate that both groups of patients change similarly over time, with a relatively constant difference maintained between them. The relevant graphs shown in Section 5.2 (see Figs 5.2 and 5.3) show that the depression score of the active group remains well below that of the group given the placebo patch throughout the course of the trial.

Display 5.3   Repeated measures analysis of variance model for two-factor design (A and B) with repeated measures on one factor (B)

- In general terms the model is

  observation = mean + factor A effect + factor B effect + AB interaction effect
  + constant associated with a particular subject + error.

- In algebraic terms, let y_{ijk} represent the observation on the ith person for factor A level j and factor B level k. The model for the observations is

$$y_{ijk} = \mu + \alpha_j + \beta_k + \gamma_{jk} + \tau_i + \epsilon_{ijk}$$

  where α_j represents the effect for the jth level of factor A (with a levels), β_k is the effect for the kth level of factor B (with b levels) and γ_{jk} the interaction effect of the two factors. The term τ_i is a constant associated with subject i and there are assumed to be n_j subjects in level j of factor A. Finally, ϵ_{ijk} is the random error term.

- The factor A and factor B terms are assumed to be fixed effects, but the subject terms and error terms are assumed to be random effects that are normally distributed with mean zero and particular variances. (For complete details, see Maxwell and Delaney, 1990.)

- This is an example of a **mixed model**. This model allows correlations between the repeated measures (these arise from the presence of the term τ_i, which is common to all the observations on the same subject), but only of the compound symmetry pattern, i.e. the correlations between each pair of repeated measures take a common value.

- The analysis of variance table is as follows:

Source	SS	DF	MS	MSR(F)
Between subjects		$N-1$		
A	ASS	$a-1$	ASS/$(a-1)$	AMS/EMS1
Subjects within A (Error1)	ESS1	$N-a$	ESS1/$(N-a)$	
Within subjects	WSSS	$N(b-1)$		
B	BSS	$b-1$	ASS/$(b-1)$	BMS/EMS2
AB	ABSS	$(a-1)(b-1)$	ABSS/$(a-1)(b-1)$	ABMS/EMS2
B × Subjects within A (Error2)	ESS2	$(N-a)(b-1)$	ESS2/$(N-a)(b-1)$	

- N is the total number of subjects, i.e. $N = n_1 + n_2 + \ldots . n_a$.

Table 5.12   Analysis of variance of visual acuity data

Source	SS	DF	MS	F	P
Between subjects	1379.43	6	229.90		
Eyes	46.45	1	46.45	0.78	0.41
Error	357.43	6	59.57		
Lenses	140.77	3	46.92	2.25	0.12
Error	375.86	18	20.88		
Eyes × lenses	40.62	3	13.54	1.06	0.39
Error	231.00	18	12.83		

Table 5.13   Analysis of variance table for reverse Stroop experiment

Source	SS	DF	MS	F	P
Groups (G)	18 906.25	1	18 906.25	2.56	0.12
Error	162 420.08	22	7382.73		
Type (T)	25 760.25	1	25 760.25	12.99	0.0016
G × T	3061.78	1	3061.78	1.54	0.23
Error	43 622.30	22	19 82.83		
Cue (C)	5697.04	2	2848.52	22.60	< 0.0001
G × C	292.62	2	146.31	1.16	0.32
Error	5545.00	44	126.02		
T × C	345.37	2	172.69	2.66	0.08
G × T × C	90.51	2	45.26	0.70	0.50
Error	2860.78	44	65.02		

Similar, but rather more complicated, models can be formulated for the first two examples in Section 5.1, the first of which involves a two-factor design with repeated measurements on both factors, with the second being a three-factor design with repeated measurements on two of the factors. Details of the appropriate models are given by Winer (1971) and by Maxwell and Delaney (1990). Only the corresponding analysis of variance tables for the two examples will be considered here; these appear in Tables 5.12 (visual acuity) and 5.13 (reverse Stroop). Detailed examination and interpretation of the results in these two displays are left as exercises for the reader.

It now becomes necessary to return to considering the sphericity assumption on which the within-subject F-tests in the analysis of variance of repeated measures are based (the between-subjects F-tests are not affected by departures from sphericity). Box (1954) showed that if the sphericity assumption is not met, the F-tests are positively biased so that the result of a departure from the assumption will be an increase in the probability of rejecting the null hypothesis when it is true, i.e. an increase in the type I error. This will lead to an investigator claiming a greater number of 'significant' results than is actually justified by the data. (No doubt, some readers will see this as a distinct advantage in their search for statistical significance.) It is possible to perform a formal test of the sphericity assumption (Crowder and Hand, 1990), but this is of limited practical value for a variety of reasons, not least of which is that the assumption is very unlikely to be valid in the majority of situations. The reasoning behind this apparently dogmatic statement is that, intuitively, variances of the differences between those measurements taken close together in time are likely to be *less* than the corresponding variance of measurements taken a considerable time apart; measurements on the same subject will have a kind of 'inertia' which is likely to lessen as time passes. For example, in the oestrogen patch data the variance of the difference between the measurements taken at visits 1 and 2 in the placebo group is 27, whereas for the measurements taken at visits 1 and 6 it is 55.

Since it appears, without recourse to formal testing, that sphericity is very rarely likely to hold, the F-tests in the analysis of repeated measures designs will not be valid. So what can be done? Two possibilities are as follows:

(1) the use of **correction factors**;
(2) the use of multivariate analysis of variance.

5.5.1 *Correction factors in the analysis of variance of repeated measures designs*

The extent to which a set of repeated measures data deviates from the sphericity assumption can be summarized in terms of a parameter ϵ which is used to decrease the degrees of freedom of the within-subjects F-tests, with the consequence that larger values will be needed to claim statistical significance than in the uncorrected version. In this way the increased risk of falsely rejecting the null hypothesis is removed. When sphericity holds, ϵ takes its maximum value of unity and the number of degrees of freedom is unchanged. The minimum value of ϵ is $1/(p-1)$ where p is the number of repeated measurements. Some authors, for example Greenhouse and Geisser (1959), have suggested using this lower bound in all cases so as to avoid the need to estimate ϵ from the data (see below). However, such an approach is very conservative, i.e. it will too often fail to reject the null hypothesis when it is false. The procedure is not recommended.

For those readers who enjoy wallowing in gory mathematical details, the formula for ϵ is given in Display 5.4. Two suggestions for estimating ϵ from sample data have been made:

1. Greenhouse and Geisser (1959): simply substitute corresponding sample values in the formula given in Display 5.4.

2. Huynh and Feldt (1976): take $\min(1, a/b)$ where $a = n(p-1)\hat{\epsilon} - 2$ and $b = (p-1)[(n-1) - (p-1)\hat{\epsilon}]$, with n being the number of subjects and $\hat{\epsilon}$ being the Greenhouse and Geisser estimate.

Display 5.4   Greenhouse and Geisser correction factor

$$\epsilon = \frac{p^2(\bar{\sigma}_{tt} - \bar{\sigma}^2)}{(p-1)\left[\sum \sum \sigma_{ts}^2 - 2p \sum \bar{\sigma}_t^2 + p^2\bar{\sigma}^2\right]}$$

where p is the number of repeated measures on each subject, $(\sigma_{ts}, t = 1, \ldots, p, s = 1, \ldots, p)$ represent the elements of the population covariance matrix of the repeated measures and the remaining terms are as follows: $\bar{\sigma}$ is the mean of all elements of the covariance matrix, $\bar{\sigma}_{tt}$ is the mean of the elements on the main diagonal, and $\bar{\sigma}_t$ is the mean of the elements in row t. (Covariance matrices are defined in Chapter 10.)

To illustrate the application of the correction factor approach to the analysis of variance of repeated measures, the data from the oestrogen patch trial will again be used. The results are shown in Table 5.14. Here the adjusted tests lead to the same conclusions as those of the unadjusted tests given earlier.

5.5.2 *Multivariate analysis of variance for repeated measures designs*

An alternative approach to the use of correction factors in the analysis of repeated measures data, when the sphericity assumption is judged to be inappropriate, is to use multivariate analysis of variance (MANOVA). This technique has already been considered briefly in Chapters 3 and 4, in the analysis of studies in which a series of different response variables are observed on each subject. However, this method can also be applied in the repeated measures situation, where a single response variable is observed under a number of different conditions and/or at a number of different times. The main advantage of using MANOVA for the analysis of repeated measures designs is that no assumptions now need to be made about the pattern of correlations between

Table 5.14   Correction factors applied to the analysis of variance of oestrogen patch trial data

	Greenhouse and Geisser	Huynh and Feldt
Estimated correction term $\hat{\epsilon}$	0.5532	0.6088
Adjusted degrees of freedom for time and groups × time	2.766, 118.938	3.044, 130.892

Here the application of the correction factor does not alter the conclusions drawn from the 'uncorrected' analysis of variance.

the repeated measures. In particular, these correlations need not satisfy the compound symmetry condition. A disadvantage of using MANOVA for repeated measures is often stated to be the technique's relatively low power when the assumption of compound symmetry is actually valid. However, Davidson (1972) compares the power of the univariate and multivariate analysis of variance approaches when compound symmetry holds and concludes that the latter is nearly as powerful as the former when the number of observations exceeds the number of repeated measures by more than 20.

As a simple illustration of the application of the MANOVA approach to the analysis of repeated measures data, the salsolinol data given in Table 5.3 will be used (again the logarithmically transformed values will be analysed).

For the moment forget the division of the data into the two groups, severe and moderately dependent, and assume that the null hypothesis of interest is whether the means of the salsolinol levels are the same on all four days of the study. The multivariate approach to testing this hypothesis (using a version of Hotelling's T^2-statistic) is described in Display 5.5. The test gives no evidence of a difference between the mean salsolinol levels on the four days of testing.

Display 5.5 Multivariate test of equality of day means for the salsolinol example (after logarithmic transformation)

- The null hypothesis of interest is that the means of the four days are the same, i.e.

$$H_0 : \mu_1 = \mu_2 = \mu_3 = \mu_4$$

where $\mu_1, \mu_2, \mu_3,$ and μ_4 are the population day means.
- This is equivalent to

$$H_0 : \mu_1 - \mu_2 = 0; \mu_2 - \mu_3 = 0; \mu_3 - \mu_4 = 0$$

(see Exercise 5.6).
- To assess whether these three differences are *simultaneously* equal to zero gives the multivariate test of whether the day means are the same.
- The appropriate test statistic is Hotelling's T^2 applied to the sample means of the following differences:

$$d_1 = \text{day1 level} - \text{day2 level}$$
$$d_2 = \text{day2 level} - \text{day3 level}$$
$$d_3 = \text{day3 level} - \text{day4 level}.$$

- The test statistic in general is

$$F = \frac{n - p + 1}{(n - 1)(p - 1)} T^2$$

with $p - 1$ and $n - p - 1$ degrees of freedom.
- The T^2 term is given by

$$T^2 = n\bar{d}' S_d^{-1} \bar{d}.$$

- In these formulae, n is the sample size, p is the number of repeated measures, $\bar{d}$ is the vector of sample mean differences and S_d is the covariance matrix of these differences.
- For the salsolinol data

$$\bar{d}' = [-0.16, -0.38, -0.22]$$

$$S_d = \begin{pmatrix} 1.86 & & \\ -0.85 & 1.25 & \\ 0.88 & -0.71 & 1.20 \end{pmatrix}.$$

- For the salsolinol data, $T^2 = 0.39257$ and the corresponding F-value is 1.5502 with 3 and 10 degrees of freedom; the associated P-value is 0.2568.

Now what about the multivariate equivalent of the group $\times$ day interaction test? Again, this involves Hotelling's T^2-test, the same version as introduced in Chapter 3. Details are given in Display 5.6. The conclusion from the test is that there is no group $\times$ day interaction.

Display 5.6   Multivariate test for groups $\times$ day interaction for salsolinol example

- Here the null hypothesis can be expressed as follows:

$$H_0 : \mu_1^{(1)} - \mu_2^{(1)} = \mu_1^{(2)} - \mu_2^{(2)}$$
$$\mu_2^{(1)} - \mu_3^{(1)} = \mu_2^{(2)} - \mu_3^{(2)}$$
$$\mu_3^{(1)} - \mu_4^{(1)} = \mu_3^{(2)} - \mu_4^{(2)}$$

where the superscripts refer to groups 1 and 2.

- Testing these equalities **simultaneously** gives the multivariate test for the group $\times$ day interaction.
- The relevant test is Hotelling's T^2 of the same form as that described in Display 3.8, with the $\bar{x}_1$ and $\bar{x}_2$ terms being replaced by the group mean vectors of the difference variables defined in Display 5.5.
- For the salsolinol data the relevant group mean vectors and covariance matrices are as follows:

(a) Moderate dependence

$$\bar{d}' = [-0.21, -0.25, -0.09]$$

$$S_d = \begin{pmatrix} 2.83 & & \\ -2.05 & 2.71 & \\ 1.99 & -1.78 & -1.78 \end{pmatrix}$$

(b) Severe dependence

$$\bar{d}' = [-0.13, -0.48, -0.31]$$

$$S_d = \begin{pmatrix} 1.44 & & \\ -0.11 & 0.36 & \\ 0.22 & -0.07 & 0.93 \end{pmatrix}.$$

- The resulting F-value is 0.1967 with an associated P-value of 0.8963.

Keselman, Keselman and Lix (1995) give some detailed comparisons of univariate and multivariate approaches to the analysis of repeated measure designs, and, for balanced designs, recommend the degrees of freedom adjusted univariate F-test, since the multivariate is more affected by non-normality.

5.6   Other approaches to the analysis of repeated measures designs

The analysis of repeated measures data when all subjects have the same number of observations measured at equivalent time intervals is relatively straightforward. The summary measure procedure and univariate (or multivariate) analysis of variance procedures will usually be adequate. However, in many cases the number of repeated measures on each subject may not be the same, or they may not be taken at the same time interval. Additionally, gaps in the data may occur because some subjects cease to comply with their assigned treatment and drop out of the study, or they simply fail to show up for some appointed visit. (Such problems may be more likely to occur with the longitudinal data arising from a clinical trial than with the data from experimental situations in psychology. Nevertheless, irregular repeated measures can still arise in the latter.)

   A possible approach to such repeated measures data is to 'fill in' or **impute** the missing values using any one of a variety of methods that have been suggested. For example, appropriate mean values obtained from the non-missing observations might be inserted, or the last recorded value of a subject might be carried forward to produce a 'complete' set of repeated measures. Such methods are not to be recommended. Imputation invents data, and analysing filled-in data as if they were complete leads to overstatement of precision, i.e. standard errors are underestimated, stated P-values are too small and confidence levels do not cover the true parameter at the stated rate.

   The preferred approach to incomplete repeated measures data is to apply recently developed regression type models which allow for the missing values and for various patterns of correlations between the observations. Details of these methods are outside the scope of this text, but readers should be aware that such methods exist and that software is available for applying them.

5.7   Summary

1. Repeated measures data arise frequently in many areas of psychological research and require special care in their analysis.

2. As always, the first stage in the examination of repeated measures data should involve some graphical displays.
3. The summary measure approach is simple to perform and simple to understand (not insubstantial advantages). *Relevant* summary measures need to be chosen.
4. Univariate analysis of variance of repeated measures designs depends on the assumption of sphericity. This assumption is unlikely to be valid in most situations.
5. When sphericity does not hold, either a correction factor approach or a MANOVA approach can be used (other possibilities are described by Goldstein, 1995).
6. The analysis of variance approach to the analysis of repeated measures data where the repeated measurements occur for only a single factor, usually time (for example the salsolinol and oestrogen data sets) is often referred to as a **profile analysis**.
7. Specialized methods are available when the repeated measures contain missing values (Diggle *et al.*, 1994).
8. An excellent account of the analysis of repeated measures is given by Hand and Taylor (1987).
9. Recently developed methods for the analysis of repeated measure designs having a non-normal response variable are described in Davis (1991).

Exercises

5.1 Reanalyse the oestrogen patch data using orthogonal polynomial contrasts to represent the change of the response variable over time. What are your conclusions?

Table 5.15 Skin resistance and electrode type

Subject	Electrode type				
	1	2	3	4	5
1	500	400	98	200	250
3	660	600	600	75	310
4	250	370	220	250	220
5	135	300	450	430	70
6	27	84	135	190	180
7	100	50	82	73	78
8	105	180	32	58	32
9	90	180	220	34	64
10	200	290	320	280	135
11	15	45	75	88	80
12	160	200	300	300	220
13	250	400	50	50	92
14	170	310	230	20	150
15	66	1000	1050	280	220
16	107	48	26	45	51

5.2 Reanalyse the reverse Stroop data using a multivariate analysis of variance approach and compare your results with those given in Tables 5.9 and 5.10. By plotting suitable measures of the cue × type interaction for each subject investigate the difference between the univariate and multivariate results.

5.3 Carry out an analysis of covariance of the oestrogen patch data using each pretreatment measure of depression as a separate covariate.

5.4 Analyse the oestrogen patch trial data by the response feature approach using the following summary statistics: (1) mean; (2) measure of linear trend; (3) last value recorded. What are your conclusions?

5.5 Apply the correction factor approach to the analysis of the visual acuity and reverse Stroop examples shown in Tables 5.1 and 5.2. Do the conclusions differ from the results given by the analyses of variance shown in Tables 5.12 and 5.13? What happens if you use the conservative procedure advocated by Greenhouse and Geisser?

5.6 Show the equivalence of the two forms of the null hypothesis given in Display 5.5.

5.7 Five different types of electrodes were applied to the arms of 16 subjects and the resistance measured in kilohms. The data are given in Table 5.15. The experiment was designed to see whether all electrode types performed similarly. Carry out any analysis you think appropriate, paying careful attention to the possibility of extreme observations. Give a possible explanation of any outliers detected.

Further reading

Eskstrom, D., Quade, D. and Golden, R.N. (1990). Statistical analysis of repeated measures in psychiatric research. *Archives of General Psychiatry*, **47**, 770–2.

Jennings, J.R., Cohen, M.J., Ruchkin, D.S. and Fridlund, A.J. (1989). Editorial policy on analysis of variance with repeated measures. *Psychophysiology*, **24**, 474–8.

Lewis, C. (1993). Analysing means from repeated measures data. In *A handbook for data analysis in the behavioural sciences: statistical issues*, (ed. G. Keren and C. Lewis). Lawrence Erlbaum, Hillsdale, NJ.

6

Simple linear regression and multiple regression analysis

6.1 Introduction

In Chapter 2 a small set of data giving the average vocabulary size of children at various ages appeared in Table 2.4. Is it possible (or indeed sensible) to try to use these data to construct a procedure for *predicting* the vocabulary size of children older than six, and what would be the appropriate method to use? Such questions serve to introduce one of the most widely used of statistical techniques, i.e. **regression analysis**. (It has to be admitted that the method is often also widely misused.) In very general terms regression analysis involves the development and use of statistical techniques designed to reflect the way in which variation in an observed random variable changes with changing circumstances. More specifically, the aim of a regression analysis is to derive an equation relating a dependent and an explanatory variable (or, more commonly, several explanatory variables). The derived equation may sometimes be used for prediction purposes, but more often its primary use is as a way of establishing the relative importance of the explanatory variables in determining the response variable.

No doubt most readers will have covered simple **linear regression**, involving a response variable and a single explanatory variable, in their introductory statistics course. Nevertheless, at the risk of a little boredom it is worth covering the topic relatively briefly as an initial step in dealing with the more complex model needed when several explanatory variables are of interest.

6.2 Simple linear regression

The essential components of the simple linear regression model involving a single explanatory variable are shown in Display 6.1. (Those readers who require a more detailed account of the model should consult Daly *et al.*, 1995.) Fitting the model to the vocabulary size data gives the results shown in Table 6.1. A plot of the fitted equation and the original data are shown in Fig. 6.1. The confidence interval calculated for the slope parameter (**regression coefficient**) from the results given in Table 6.1, (513.35, 610.51) indicates that there is a very strong relationship between vocabulary size and age. Since the estimated regression coefficient is positive, the relationship is such that as age increases so does vocabulary size; of course, this is all rather obvious from a simple plot of the data. The estimated regression coefficient is interpreted as the estimated increase in average vocabulary size corresponding to an increase in age of 1 year.

Table 6.1 Results of fitting simple linear regression model to vocabulary data

Parameter estimates

Coefficient	Estimate	SE
Intercept	−763.86	88.25
Slope	561.93	24.29

Analysis of variance table

Source	SS	DF	MS	F
Regression	7 294 087.0	1	7 294 087.0	539.19
Residual	109 032.2	8	1369.0	

Display 6.1 The simple linear regression model

- The basic idea of simple linear regression is that the means of a response variable y lie on a straight line when plotted against values of an explanatory variable x.
- The variance of y at a given x is assumed to be the same for all values of x.
- More specifically, the model can be written as;

$$y_i = \alpha + \beta x_i + \epsilon_i$$

where $y_1, y_2, \ldots, y_n$ are the n observed values of the response variable, and $x_1, x_2, \ldots, x_n$ are the corresponding values of the explanatory variable. The ϵ_i are residual or error terms measuring how much an observed value, y_i, differs from the value predicted by the model, namely $\alpha + \beta x_i$.

- The two parameters of the model, α and β, are the **intercept** and **slope** of the line. Estimators of the parameters are found by minimizing the sum of squared vertical deviations from each point in the sample to the point on the line corresponding to the x value. The procedure is known as **least squares**, and the resulting estimators are the following functions of the observed x and y values:

$$\hat{\alpha} = \bar{y} - \hat{\beta}\bar{x}$$

$$\hat{\beta} = \frac{\sum_{i=1}^{n}(x_i - \bar{x})(y_i - \bar{y})}{\sum_{i=1}^{n}(x_i - \bar{x})^2}$$

where the circumflex accent means 'estimator of'.

- The residual terms ϵ_i, are assumed to have a normal distribution with mean zero and variance σ^2.

- An estimator of σ^2 is s^2 given by

$$s^2 = \frac{\sum_{i=1}^n (y_i - \hat{y}_i)^2}{n - 2}$$

where $\hat{y}_i = \hat{\alpha} + \hat{\beta} x_i$ is known as the **fitted value** of y_i.
- Estimators of the standard errors of the estimated slope and estimated intercept are given by

$$s_{\hat{\alpha}} = \left(\frac{s^2}{n} + \frac{\bar{x}^2 s^2}{\sum_{i=1}^n (x_i - \bar{x})^2} \right)^{1/2}$$

$$s_{\hat{\beta}} = \frac{s}{\left(\sum_{i=1}^n (x_i - \bar{x})^2 \right)^{1/2}} \ .$$

- Confidence intervals for, and tests of hypotheses about, the slope and intercept parameters can be constructed in the usual way from the standard errors given above.
- The variance in the response variable can be partioned into a part due to regression on the explanatory variable and a residual. The terms can be arranged in an analysis of variance table as shown below:

Source	SS	DF	MS	F
Regression	RGSS	1	RGSS/1	MSRG/MSR
Residual	RSS	$n-2$	RSS/$(n-2)$	

- The F-statistic from the analysis of variance table provides a test of the hypothesis that the slope parameter β is zero.
- The residual mean square gives the estimate of σ^2.

It is possible to use the derived equation relating average vocabulary size to age to predict vocabulary size for different ages. For example, for age 5.5 the prediction would be

average vocabulary size $= -763.86 + 561.93 \times 5.5 = 2326.7$.

As always, an estimate of this kind is of little use without some measure of its variance which will enable a confidence interval to be constructed. Some relevant formulae are given in Display 6.2, together with a number of predicted values and their confidence intervals for various ages. Note that the confidence intervals become wider as the age at which a prediction is made departs further from the mean of the observed ages.

Therefore the derived regression equation does allow predictions to be made, but it is of great importance to consider whether such predictions are sensible. A little thought shows that, in this particular example at least, this is most unlikely. Using the fitted relationship to predict future vocabulary sizes is based on the assumption that the

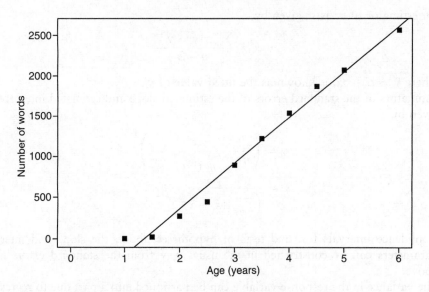

Fig. 6.1 Vocabulary size data and fitted regression of vocabulary size on age.

observed upward trend in the data will continue into future ages at the same rate as observed between ages 1 and 6, namely between 513 and 610 words per year. This assumption is clearly false, since the rate of vocabulary acquisition will gradually decrease. Extrapolation outside the range of the observed values of the explanatory variable is known, in general, to be a risky procedure and this particular example is no exception.

Display 6.2 Using the simple linear regression model for prediction

- The predicted response value corresponding to a value of the explanatory variable of, say, x_0 is

$$y_{\text{predicted}} = \hat{\alpha} + \hat{\beta} x_0.$$

- An estimator of the variance of a predicted value is provided by

$$s^2_{\text{predicted}} = s^2 \left[\frac{(x_0 - \bar{x})^2}{\sum_{i=1}^{n} (x_i - \bar{x})^2} + \frac{1}{n} + 1 \right].$$

- A confidence interval for a prediction can be constructed from the above variance as follows:

$$y_{\text{predicted}} \pm s_{\text{predicted}}\, t$$

where t is the appropriate Student's t-value for the chosen interval size with $n - 2$ degrees of freedom.

- Some predictions and their confidence intervals for the vocabulary size data are given below.

Age	Predicted vocabulary size	SE of prediction	95% CI
5.5	2326.7	133.59	(2018, 2635)
7.0	3169.6	151.88	(2819, 3520)
10.0	4855.4	203.66	(4385, 5326)
20.0	1 0474.7	423.72	(9496, 11 453)

Now you might remember that in Chapter 1 it was remarked that if you do not believe in a model you should not perform operations and analyses which assume that it is true. Bearing this in mind, is the simple linear regression model fitted to the vocabulary data really believable? A little thought shows that of course it is not. The estimated vocabulary size at age zero, i.e. the estimated intercept on the y axis is −763.86, with an approximate confidence interval of (−940.34, −587.38). This is clearly a silly estimate for a value which is known a priori to be zero. It reflects the inappropriate nature of the simple linear regression model for these data. An apparently more suitable model would be one in which the intercept was constrained to be zero. Estimation for such a model in general, and for the vocabulary, data in particular is described in Display 6.3. The zero intercept line is plotted together with the original data in Fig. 6.2. It is apparent from this plot that our supposedly more appropriate

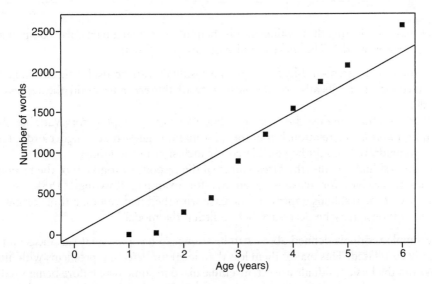

Fig. 6.2 Vocabulary size data and fitted zero intercept regression of vocabulary size on age.

model does not fit the data as well as the one rejected as being unsuitable on logical grounds. So what has gone wrong? The answer is that the relationship between age and vocabulary size is more complex than is allowed by either of the two models considered. One way of investigating the failings of a model is to examine what are known as **residuals**, which in their basic form are simply defined as

$$\text{residual} = \text{observed response value} - \text{fitted   response   value}. \qquad (6.1)$$

Display 6.3   The simple linear regression model with zero intercept

- The model is now

$$y_i = \beta x_i + \epsilon_i.$$

- Application of least squares gives the following estimator of the single parameter β:

$$\hat{\beta} = \frac{\sum_{i=1}^{n} x_i y_i}{\sum_{i=1}^{n} x_i^2}.$$

- An estimate of the variance of $\hat{\beta}$ is given by

$$s_{\hat{\beta}}^2 = \frac{s^2}{\sum_{i=1}^{n} x_i^2}$$

where s^2 is the residual mean square from the analysis of variance table.
- The estimated value of β for the vocabulary size data is 370.96 with an estimated standard error of 30.84.

Various ways of plotting these values can be helpful in assessing particular components of the regression model. The most useful plots are as follows:

1. A histogram or stem-and-leaf plot of the residuals can be useful in checking for symmetry and specifically for the normality of the error terms in the regression model.
2. Plot the residuals against the corresponding value of the explanatory variable. Any sign of a *non-linear* relationship in this plot might suggest that a higher-order term (e.g. a quadratic) should be considered for inclusion in the model.
3. Plot the residuals against the *fitted* values of the response variable (not the response values themselves for reasons given by, for example, Rawlings, 1988). If the variance of the residuals appears to increase with the fitted values, a transformation of the response may be necessary before fitting the model.

(The simple residuals defined above can be shown to have unequal variances and to be slightly correlated. This makes them less than ideal for detecting problems with fitted models, and the basic residuals are often **standardized** in some way before being used in a graphical examination of the regression model. The details of this procedure are

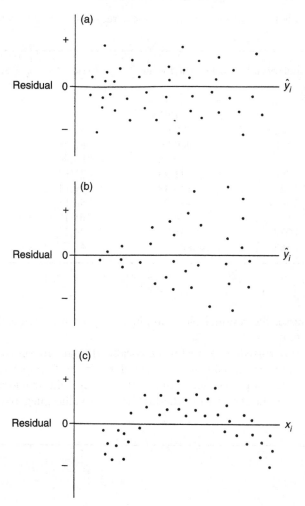

Fig. 6.3 Idealized residual plots.

outside the scope of this text, but are given by Rawlings, 1988, and Everitt and Dunn, 1991). Most regression software automatically produces standardized residuals, and these are preferable to the unstandardized values in most situations. Ideally, standardized residuals should fall roughly in the interval $(-2, 2)$.)

Figure 6.3 shows some idealised residual plots that indicate particular points about models.

1. Figure 6.3(a) is what might be expected with an adequate fitted model.
2. Figure 6.3(b) suggests that the assumption of constant variance is not justifed so that transforming the response variable before fitting the model may be justifiable.
3. Figure 6.3(c) implies that the model needs an additional quadratic term in the explanatory variable.

Table 6.2 Residuals from fitting the simple linear regression model to the vocabulary data

Age	Vocabulary size	Predicted value	Residual	Standardized residual
1.0	3	–201.93	204.93	2.14
1.5	22	79.03	–57.03	–0.56
2.0	272	360.00	–87.99	–0.83
2.5	446	640.96	–194.96	–1.79
3.0	896	921.93	–25.92	–0.23
3.5	1222	120.89	19.11	0.17
4.0	1540	1483.86	56.15	0.51
4.5	1870	1764.82	105.19	0.98
5.0	2072	2045.79	26.22	0.25
6.0	2562	2607.72	–45.70	–0.51

(In practice, of course, the residual plots obtained may be more difficult to interpret than those in Fig. 6.3.)

The basic and standardized residuals for the vocabulary data are shown in Table 6.2. Plots of the latter against the fitted value of vocabulary size and against age are given in Fig. 6.4. Both plots show a pattern indicating that the simple linear regression model is not suitable for these data. Apart from the first and last values, negative residuals are

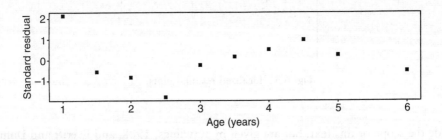

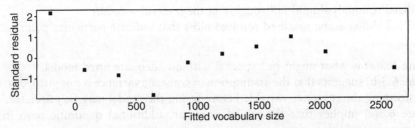

Fig. 6.4 Standardized residual plots for vocabulary size data.

found for the young ages and positive residuals for the older ages. The standardized residual for the observation at age 1 is greater than 2. Determining a more suitable model for these data is the subject of Exercise 6.1.

6.3   Multiple regression

The multiple regression model involves a single response variable and several explanatory variables. (Although the data used in multiple regression consist of more than a single variable value for each subject, they are not usually referred to as multivariate in the sense that the term was defined in Chapter 2, since only the response variable is considered to be random.) Details of the model, including the estimation of parameters and their standard errors, are given in Display 6.4. (Readers to whom a matrix is still a mystery should avoid this table at all costs.) The regression coefficients in the multiple regression model give the change in the response variable associated with a unit change in the corresponding explanatory variable, *conditional* on the other explanatory variables in the model remaining unchanged; this is often referred to as 'partialling out' or 'controlling' for the other variables, although such terms are best avoided. As in the simple linear regression model described in the previous section, the variation in the response variable can be partitioned into a part due to regression on the explanatory variables and a residual. The resulting *F*-test can be used to test the hypothesis that *all* the regression coefficients are zero.

Display 6.4   The multiple regression model

- The multiple regression model for a response variable y with observed values $y_1, y_2, \ldots, y_n$ and p explanatory variables, $x_1, x_2, \ldots, x_p$, with observed values $x_{i1}, x_{i2}, \ldots, x_{ip}$ for $i = 1, 2, \ldots, n$, is

$$y_i = \beta_0 + \beta_1 x_{i1} + \beta_2 x_{i2} + \cdots + \beta_p x_{ip} + \epsilon_i.$$

- The regression coefficients $\beta_1, \beta_2, \cdots, \beta_p$ give the amount of change in the response variable associated with a unit change in the corresponding explanatory variable, *conditional* on the other explanatory variables in the model remaining unchanged.
- The explanatory variables are strictly assumed to be fixed, i.e. are not random variables. In practice, where this is rarely the case, the results from a multiple regression analysis are interpreted as being *conditional* on the observed values of the explanatory variables.
- The residual terms in the model are assumed to have a normal distribution with mean zero and variance σ^2. This implies that, for given values of the explanatory variables, the response variable is normally distributed with a mean that is a linear function of the explanatory variables and a variance that is not dependent on these variables.
- The aim of multiple regression is to arrive at a set of values for the regression coefficients which make the values of the response variable predicted from the model as close as possible to the observed response values.

- As in the simple linear regression model, the least-squares estimation procedure is used.
- By introducing a vector $y' = [y_1, y_2, \ldots, y_n]$ and an $n \times (p+1)$ matrix $\mathbf{X}$ given by

$$\mathbf{X} = \begin{pmatrix} 1 & x_{11} & x_{12} & \cdots & x_{1p} \\ 1 & x_{21} & x_{22} & \cdots & x_{2p} \\ \vdots & \vdots & \vdots & \vdots & \vdots \\ 1 & x_{n1} & x_{n2} & \cdots & x_{np} \end{pmatrix}$$

the multiple regression model for the n observations can be written concisely as

$$y = \mathbf{X}\boldsymbol{\beta} + \boldsymbol{\epsilon}$$

where $\boldsymbol{\epsilon}' = [\epsilon_1, \epsilon_2, \ldots, \epsilon_n]$ and $\boldsymbol{\beta}' = [\beta_0, \beta_1, \ldots, \beta_p]$.

- The least-squares estimators of the parameters in the multiple regression are given by the set of equations

$$\hat{\boldsymbol{\beta}} = (\mathbf{X}'\mathbf{X})^{-1}\mathbf{X}'y.$$

(More details of the model in matrix form and the least-squares estimation of the parameters are given by Rawlings, 1988.)

- The variation in the response variable can be partitioned into a part due to regression on the explanatory variables and a residual. These can be arranged in an analysis of variance table as follows:

Source	DF	SS	MS	F
Regression	p	RGSS	RGSS/p	RGMS/RSMS
Residual	$n - p - 1$	RSS	RSS/$(n - p - 1)$	

- The residual mean square s^2 is an estimator of σ^2.
- The covariance matrix of the parameter estimates in the multiple regression model is estimated as

$$S_{\hat{\boldsymbol{\beta}}} = s^2(\mathbf{X}'\mathbf{X})^{-1}.$$

The diagonal elements give the variances of the estimated regression coefficients and the off-diagonal elements give their covariances.

6.3.1 *A simple example of multiple regression*

As a gentle introduction, the multiple regression model will be applied to the data shown in Table 6.3. Here the response variable is the consumption of ice cream measured over 30 4-week periods. The explanatory variables believed to influence consumption of ice cream include price and mean temperature. (I am sure that most

Table 6.3 Ice cream consumption

Observation	Consumption	Price	Mean temperature (°F)
1	0.386	0.270	41
2	0.374	0.282	56
3	0.393	0.277	63
4	0.425	0.280	68
5	0.406	0.272	69
6	0.344	0.262	65
7	0.327	0.275	61
8	0.288	0.267	47
9	0.269	0.265	32
10	0.256	0.277	24
11	0.286	0.282	28
12	0.298	0.270	26
13	0.329	0.272	32
14	0.318	0.287	40
15	0.381	0.277	55
16	0.381	0.287	63
17	0.470	0.280	72
18	0.443	0.277	72
19	0.386	0.277	67
20	0.342	0.277	60
21	0.319	0.292	44
22	0.307	0.287	40
23	0.284	0.277	32
24	0.326	0.285	27
25	0.309	0.282	28
26	0.359	0.265	33
27	0.376	0.265	41
28	0.416	0.265	52
29	0.437	0.268	64
30	0.548	0.260	71

readers will recognize the subtle psychological points that analysis of these data is aiming to illustrate.)

A draughtsman's plot of the three variables in Table 6.3 (Fig. 6.5) suggests that temperature is of most importance in determining consumption. The results of applying multiple regression analysis to the data are shown in Display 6.5. The F-value of 23.27 with 2 and 27 degrees of freedom has an associated P-value which is very small. Clearly, the hypothesis that both regression coefficients are zero is not tenable.

An index of the fit of the model is provided by the proportion of the variance in the response variable accounted for by the explanatory variables. This is given by

$$I = (\text{TSS} - \text{RSS})/\text{TSS} = 1 - \text{RSS}/\text{TSS}. \qquad (6.2)$$

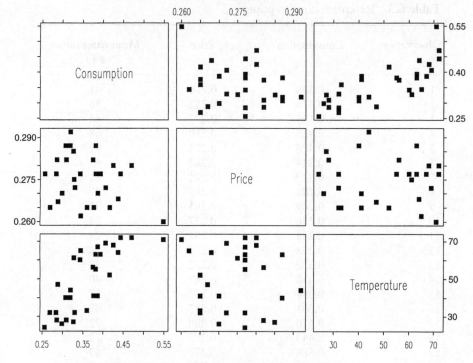

Fig. 6.5 Draughtsman's plot of the ice cream data.

Models with high values of I indicate that the explanatory variables 'explain' much of the variation in the response variable.

A further important quantity in multiple regression is the **multiple correlation coefficient, R,** which is simply the Pearson correlation coefficient between the observed values of the response variable and its values as predicted by the fitted model. The coefficients I and R are related, with $I = R^2$. For the ice cream data, $R = 0.7955$ and $I = 0.6328$. The two explanatory variables, price and temperature, together account for approximately 63% of the variance in consumption. The negative regression coefficient for price indicates that, for a given mean temperature, consumption decreases with price. The positive coefficient for temperature implies that, for a given price, consumption increases with temperature. The sizes of the regression coefficients might appear to imply that price was of most importance in determining consumption; this is an illusion since the raw regression coefficients given in Display 6.5 cannot be used to judge the relative importance of the explanatory variables. A rough guide to the latter can, however, be obtained from the **standardized regression coefficients** which are the regression coefficients obtained from analysing the standardized response variable and standardized explanatory variables; that is, the original variables divided by their respective standard deviations. Now each regression coefficient represents the change in the standardized response variable produced by a change of one standard deviation unit in the corresponding explanatory variable. The standardized regression coefficients can, in fact, be found by multiplying the raw regression coefficient by the standard deviation of the response variable and dividing by the standard deviation of the response variable. In the ice cream example the relevant standard deviations are consumption (0.06579), price (0.00834) and temperature (16.422). The standardized regression coefficients are therefore:

1. Standardized regression coefficient for price $= \dfrac{-1.4018 \times 0.00834}{0.06579} = -0.1777.$

2. Standardized regression coefficient for temperature $= \dfrac{0.00303 \times 16.422}{0.06579} = 0.7563.$

Display 6.5 Multiple regression model for ice cream consumption data

- The model for the data is

$$\text{consumption} = \beta_0 + \beta_1 \times \text{price} + \beta_2 \times \text{temperature}.$$

- The least-squares estimates of the regression coefficients in the model are as follows:

Parameter	Estimates	SE
β_1	−1.4018	0.9251
β_2	0.00303	0.00047

- The analysis of variance table is as follows:

Source	SS	DF	MS	F
Regression	0.07943	2	0.03972	23.27
Residual	0.04609	27	0.001707	

Comparing the sizes of the standardized coefficients indicates that the mean temperature is more important than price in determining consumption.

One further point about the multiple regression model which can usefully be illustrated on this simple example, is the effect of entering the explanatory variables into the model in *different* orders. This will become of more relevance in discussing selection procedures in Section 6.3.4, but simply examining the numerical results from the ice cream data is helpful for now; these results are given in Display 6.6. The change produced in a previously estimated regression coefficient when an additional variable is included in the model results from the correlation between the explanatory variables. If these variable were independent (sometimes the term **orthogonal** is used), their regression coefficients would remain unchanged as other variables were added. (Some examples illustrating this point are given in Chapter 8.)

Display 6.6   Multiple regression for ice cream data: the effect of order

- *Entering price followed by temperature*
  (a) The first model fitted is

$$\text{consumption} = \beta_0 + \beta_1 \times \text{price}.$$

The parameter estimates in this model are $\hat{\beta}_0 = 0.9230$, $\hat{\beta}_1 = -2.0472$. The multiple correlation coefficient, $R = 0.2596$. The analysis of variance table for the model is as follows:

Source	SS	DF	MS	F
Regression	0.00846	1	0.00846	2.02
Residual	0.1171	28	0.00418	

  (b) Temperature is now added to the model, i.e. the following new model is fitted:

$$\text{consumption} = \beta_0 + \beta_1 \times \text{price} + \beta_2 \times \text{temperature}.$$

The parameter estimates and analysis of variance table are now as in Display 6.5. Note that the estimated regression coefficient for price is now different from its value in (a).

- *Entering temperature followed by price*
  (a) The first model fitted is now

$$\text{consumption} = \beta_0 + \beta_1 \times \text{temperature}.$$

The parameter estimates are $\hat{\beta}_0 = 0.2069$, $\hat{\beta}_1 = 0.00311$. The multiple correlation coefficient $R = 0.7756$. The analysis of variance table is as follows:

Source	SS	DF	MS	F
Regression	0.07551	1	0.07551	42.28
Residual	0.05001	28	0.001786	

  (b) Adding price to the model gives the results in Display 6.5.

Table 6.4 Human age and fatness

Age	Percentage fat	Sex*
23	9.5	0
23	27.9	1
27	7.8	0
27	17.8	0
39	31.4	1
41	25.9	1
45	27.4	0
49	25.2	1
50	31.1	1
53	34.7	1
53	42.0	1
54	20.0	0
54	29.1	1
56	32.5	1
57	30.3	1
57	21.0	0
58	33.0	1
58	33.8	1
60	41.1	1
61	34.5	1

*0 = female; 1 = male.

6.3.2 An example of multiple regression in which one of the explanatory variables is categorical

The data shown in Table 6.4 were taken from a study investigating a new method of measuring body composition, and give the body fat percentage, age and sex for 20 normal adults aged between 23 and 61 years. The question of interest is: 'How are percentage fat, age and sex related?'

The data in Table 6.4 include the **binary variable** sex. Should such a explanatory variable be included in a multiple regression model and, if so, how? In fact it is quite appropriate to include a categorical variable such as sex in a multiple regression model. The distributional assumptions in the model (see Display 6.4) apply only to the response variable. Indeed the explanatory variables are strictly not considered random variables at all. Consequently they can, in theory at least, be *any* type of variable. However, care is often needed in deciding how particular types of categorical or ordinal variable should be included in the model (as will be seen in the next section). But for a two-category variable such as sex there are no real problems, and details of suitable multiple regression models for the human fat data are given in Display 6.7.

Display 6.7   Possible multiple regression models for the human fat data in Table 6.4

- The first model that might be considered is the simple linear regression model relating percentage fat to age:

$$\% \text{ fat} = \beta_0 + \beta_1 \times \text{age}.$$

- After such a model has been fitted, a further question of interest might be: 'Allowing for the effect of age does a person's sex have any bearing on their percentage fatness?'. The appropriate model would be

$$\% \text{ fat} = \beta_0 + \beta_1 \times \text{age} + \beta_2 \times \text{sex}$$

where sex is a **dummy variable** that takes values of zero for men and unity for women; it is merely a way of distinguishing between males and females. The model now describes the situation shown in the diagram below, namely two parallel lines with a vertical separation of β_2. Since in this case the effect of age on fatness is the same for both sexes, or, equivalently, the effect of a person's sex is the same for all ages, the model assumes that there is no *interaction* between age and sex.

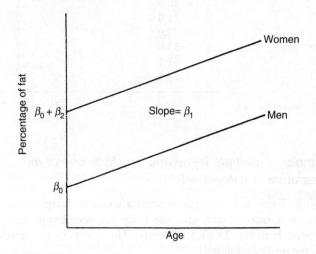

- Suppose now that a model is required which *does* allow for the possibility of an age × sex interaction effect on percentage fatness. Such a model needs to include a new variable, defined as the product of the variables age and sex. Therefore the new model is

$$\% \text{ fat} = \beta_0 + \beta_1 \times \text{age} + \beta_2 \times \text{sex} + \beta_3 \times \text{age} \times \text{sex}.$$

- To understand this equation, first consider the percentage fatness of men; here the values of both sex and sex × age are zero and the model reduces to

$$\% \text{ fat} = \beta_0 + \beta_1 \times \text{age}.$$

However, for women, sex = 1 and so sex × age = age and the model becomes

$$\% \text{ fat} = (\beta_0 + \beta_2) + (\beta_1 + \beta_3) \times \text{age}.$$

Thus the new model allows the lines for males and females to be other than parallel (see diagram below). The parameter β_3 is a measure of the difference between the slopes of the two lines.

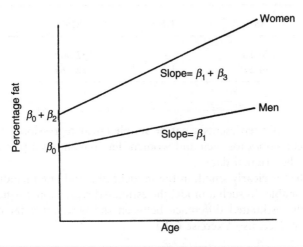

The results of fitting a multiple regression model to the human fat data, with age, sex and the interaction of age and sex as explanatory variables, are shown in Display 6.8. The fitted model can be interpreted as follows:

1. For men, where sex = 0 and sex × age = 0, the fitted model is

$$\% \text{ fat} = 3.470 + 0.3547 \times \text{age}. \tag{6.3}$$

2. For women, where sex = 1 and so sex × age = age, the fitted model is

$$\% \text{ fat} = 3.470 + 0.3547 \times \text{age} + 16.6376 - 0.1147 \times \text{age}. \tag{6.4}$$

Thus

$$\% \text{ fat} = 20.108 + 0.240 \times \text{age}. \tag{6.5}$$

Display 6.8 Multiple regression model for percentage fatness data

- The model fitted is

$$\% \text{ fat} = \beta_0 + \beta_1 \times \text{age} + \beta_1 \times \text{sex} + \beta_3 \times \text{age} \times \text{sex}.$$

- The least-squares estimates of the regression coefficients in the model are as follows:

Parameter	Estimate	SE
β_1	0.3547	0.1420
β_2	16.6376	8.8436
β_3	-0.1147	0.1912

- The value of the multiple correlation coefficient is 0.8738.
- The analysis of variance table is as follows:

Source	SS	DF	MS	F
Regression	1176.181	3	392.060	17.22
Residual	364.279	16	22.767	

The fitted model actually represents separate simple linear regressions with different intercepts and different slopes for men and women. Fig. 6.6 shows a plot of the fitted model together with the original data.

The interaction effect is clearly small, in the model fitted and one including only sex and age is more reasonable. In such a model the estimated regression coefficient for sex (11.567) is simply the estimated difference between the percentage fat of men and women of a given age. (See also Exercise 6.4.)

6.3.3 *A more complex example of a multiple regression model*

The data shown in Table 6.5 were obtained in a learning experiment on eye-blink conditioning. The aim of the experiment was to condition the subjects to react to an audio tone by blinking; this was achieved by presenting the audio tone together with an electric shock. The extent of learning was assessed by the number of conditioned

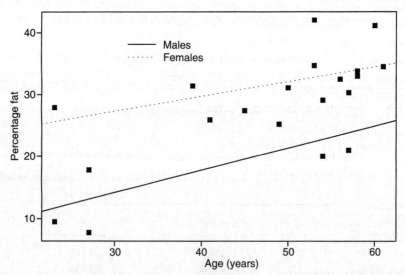

Fig. 6.6 Human fat data and a fitted regression model which allows different slopes and different intercepts for males and females.

Table 6.5　Eye-blink conditioning data

totcr	apr	psy	extr	canr	thre	Q20
0	31	6	16	9	2	1
0	36	3	16	9	2	1
0	38	1	16	7	1	2
0	41	2	19	14	1	2
0	24	1	21	−16	1	1
0	32	0	15	14	1	1
0	31	7	14	4	2	2
1	30	8	15	14	1	1
1	35	5	4	14	2	1
1	37	8	17	9	1	1
1	31	8	7	9	2	1
1	42	5	19	14	1	1
1	23	1	19	14	2	1
1	41	5	8	−2	2	3
1	33	2	19	11	2	1
1	47	3	9	9	2	2
2	32	4	18	−18	2	3
2	35	1	11	−1	1	1
2	41	5	19	−13	1	3
2	49	4	6	−18	2	1
2	31	5	5	9	1	1
3	43	9	17	9	2	3
3	21	1	16	−2	2	1
3	37	4	2	14	2	3
3	33	2	14	14	2	1
4	49	8	20	14	1	1
4	35	9	14	−19	1	1
5	23	6	16	−11	2	1
5	45	4	15	−1	1	1
5	37	1	11	9	2	4
5	41	2	7	14	2	4
6	49	4	15	14	1	3
6	43	6	18	14	2	3
6	39	8	12	9	2	3
7	30	7	19	−19	1	2
8	26	1	16	4	1	3
9	27	3	16	−1	2	1
9	32	3	11	9	2	3
9	32	9	13	14	2	1
9	30	2	15	14	2	1
9	33	3	10	14	1	1
9	30	2	3	9	1	1
9	33	6	18	9	1	3
10	34	4	12	4	1	4

Table 6.5   Eye-blink conditioning data – *cont'd*

totcr	apr	psy	extr	canr	thre	Q20
11	40	10	7	–18	2	1
11	34	6	16	9	1	4
11	56	5	5	9	2	4
12	25	4	14	14	1	2
12	36	1	19	–24	1	2

totcr, total number of conditioned responses given in 50 acquisition trials; apr, score for anxiety; psy, score for psychoticism; extr, score for extraversion; cawr, contingency awareness assessment; thre, binary variable indicating whether the subject's threshold for a blink reflex is over a given shock level; Q20, ordinal scale indicating frequency with which the subject blinked purposely to avoid the shock.

responses (eye blinks) given in 500 acquisition trials. Six variables that might influence the extent of conditioning were also recorded for each subject. One of these (thre) is a binary variable indicating whether the subject's threshold for a blink reflex is over a given shock level, and another (Q20) is categorical with the four levels corresponding to the increasing frequency with which a subject blinked purposely to avoid the shock.

Before applying a multiple regression model to these data, it is necessary to consider how to deal with the ordinal variable Q20. If included as given in Table 6.5, i.e. as the values 1 to 4, it implies that equal changes in any part of the scale have equal effects on the response variable. In other words a change in Q20 from 1 to 2, for example, is considered equivalent to a change from 3 to 4 in its effect on the total number of conditioned responses. This may be reasonable, but it is quite a strong assumption, and so an alternative way of using Q20 might be worth considering. In general, categorical explanatory variables with more than two categories are best recoded into a series of what are usually known as **dummy variables**. These are simply binary variables indicating which category of the original variable an observation is in. A categorical variable with k categories can be recoded into $k - 1$ dummy variables. Therefore the three required dummy variables d_1, d_2 and d_3 for Q20 in the eye-blink example can be defined as follows:

	Value of Q20			
	1	2	3	4
d_1	1	0	0	0
d_2	0	1	0	0
d_3	0	0	1	0

The estimated regression coefficients corresponding to d_1, d_2 and d_3 will represent a comparison of the mean of the response variable in category 1, 2 or 3 of Q20 with the mean in category 4, conditional on the other variables in the model being fixed. (See the explanation of the regression coefficient for sex in the model for human fat discussed in the previous section.)

Table 6.6 Results of fitting a multiple regression model to the eye-blink conditioning data in Table 6.5

Parameter estimates and standard errors

Variable	Coefficient	SE
apr	−0.14	0.14
psy	−0.68	0.36
extr	−0.26	0.22
cawr	−0.14	0.09
thre	−6.35	2.16
d_1	−9.89	2.59
d_2	−12.78	3.77
d_3	−5.59	3.08

• *Analysis of variance table*

Source	SS	DF	MS	F
Regression	2977.34	8	372.17	4.42
Residual	6315.61	75	84.21	

The results of fitting a multiple regression model to the eye-blink data with Q20 recoded in terms of three dummy variables are given in Table 6.6. The global test that all the regression coefficients are zero has an associated P-value less than 0.05, and so the hypothesis can be rejected. The multiple correlation coefficient is 0.57, so that the explanatory variables together explain 32% of the variance in the number of conditioned responses. This example will be discussed further in the next section.

6.3.4 *Selecting subsets of explanatory variables*

The overall test that all regression coefficients in a multiple regression model are zero is seldom of great interest. In most applications it will be rejected, since it is unlikely that *all* the explanatory variables selected by an investigator to study will be unrelated to the response variable. The investigator is more likely to be concerned with assessing whether some *subset* of the explanatory variables might be as successful as the full set in explaining the variation in the response variable. If a small number of explanatory variables produces a model that fits the data only marginally worse than a larger set, then a more parsimonious description of the data is the result, which is the aim of most scientific investigations (see Chapter 1). How can the most important explanatory variables be identified? Readers might look again at the results in Table 6.6 and imagine that the answer to this question is relatively straightforward; namely, select those variables for which the corresponding *t*-value is significant and drop the remainder. Unfortunately, such a procedure is of only limited use, since the regression coefficients and their associated standard errors are estimated *conditional* on the other variables in the model. If a variable is removed from a model, the regression coefficients of the remaining variables (and their standard errors) need to be re-estimated from a further analysis. (Of course, if the explanatory variables happened to be orthogonal, there would be no problem; the *t*-statistics in Table 6.6 could then be used to select the most important explanatory variables. However, this is of little consequence in most practical applications of multiple regression.)

The procedures generally used for identifying important subsets of explanatory variables are the **selection** methods, namely **forward selection, backward selection** and a combination of these known as **stepwise regression**. In forward selection, variables are considered for adding to an existing model, beginning with a model containing none of the explanatory variables. In backward selection, variables are considered for removal from an existing model, beginning with the model in which all the explanatory variables under investigation are included. The criterion used for assessing whether a variable should be added to an existing model in forward selection, or removed in backward selection, is based on the change in the residual sum of squares produced by the inclusion or exclusion of a variable. Details of the criterion, and of how forward and backward selection are applied in practice, are given in Display 6.9.

Display 6.9   Forward and backward selection

- The criterion used for assessing whether a variable should be added to an existing model in forward selection or removed from an existing model in backward selection is as follows:

$$F = \frac{(SS_{\text{residual},k} - SS_{\text{residual},k+1})}{SS_{\text{residual},k+1}/(n - k - 2)}$$

where $SS_{\text{residual}, k} - SS_{\text{residual}, k+1}$ is the decrease in the residual sum of squares when a variable is added to an existing k-variable model (forward selection), or the increase in the residual sum of squares when a variable is removed from an existing $(k + 1)$-variable model (backward selection), and $SS_{\text{residual},k+1}$ is the residual sum of squares for the model including $k + 1$ explanatory variables.

- The calculated F-value is then compared with a preset term known as the F-to-enter (forward selection) or the F-to-remove (backward selection). In the former, calculated F-values greater than the F-to-enter lead to the addition of the candidate variable to the existing model. In the latter a calculated F-value less than the F-to-remove leads to discarding the candidate variable currently in the model.

In the stepwise selection procedure, variables are entered into an existing model according to the rules for forward selection, but after the addition of each new variable variables currently in the model are considered for removal using the backward selection process. In this way it is possible that variables included in the model at some early stage may be removed at some later stage, because the presence of new variables has made their contribution to the model no longer significant.

Table 6.7   Forward selection applied to the eye-blink conditioning data (F-to-enter set at 4.00)

Variables in equation			Variables not in equation	
Variable	Coefficient		Variable	F
Step 0				
(Constant)	11.81		apr	0.02
			psy	3.93
			extr	0.03
			cawr	2.62
			thre	8.52
			d_1	4.23
			d_2	1.92
			d_3	0.01
Step 1				
(Constant)	21.35		apr	0.10
thre	−6.46		psy	2.29
			extr	0.98
			cawr	1.52
			d_1	4.36
			d_2	3.09
			d_3	0.07
Step 2				
(Constant)	23.32		apr	0.43
thre	−6.37		psy	2.80
d_1	−4.54		extr	1.48
			cawr	1.47
			d_2	7.17
			d_3	0.64
Step 3				
(Constant)	26.04		apr	0.68
thre	−6.92		psy	3.80
d_1	−6.45		extr	0.90
d_2	−9.60		cawr	2.17
			d_3	4.24
Step 4				
(Constant)	28.86		apr	0.56
thre	−6.76		psy	3.59
d_1	−9.50		extr	0.66
d_2	−12.62		cawr	2.01
d_3	−6.46			

No further variables are entered since their calculated F-values are less than the chosen F-to-enter value of 4.00.

In the best of all possible worlds, the final model selected by applying each of the three procedures outlined above would be the same. Often this does occur, but it is in no way guaranteed. Certainly none of the automatic procedures for selecting subsets of variables are foolproof. They must be used with care! (See McKay and Campbell, 1982*a,b*, for some more thoughts on automatic selection procedures in regression.)

To illustrate the use of variable selection methods in regression, the results of applying forward selection to the eye-blink example are given in Table 6.7. The method selects the explanatory variable thre and the three dummy variables representing Q20 as contributing significantly to the regression model for the total number of conditioned responses. The negative coefficient for thre indicates that the number of conditioned responses is less for those subjects whose threshold is over a given shock level, conditional on the category of Q20 to which they belong. The negative coefficients of the dummy variables d_1, d_2 and d_3 indicate that categories 1, 2 and 3 of Q20 give rise to fewer conditioned responses than category 4, conditional on the value of thre.

6.3.5 *Assessing the multiple regression model: residuals and other diagnostics*

The use of residuals in the case of simple linear regression was discussed in Section 6.2. Residual analysis is equally, if not more, important in assessing the appropriateness of a multiple regression model. However, in addition to simple or standardized residuals, the researcher making a detailed investigation of a multiple regression model can now turn to a host of other 'diagnostics' developed during the last decade. Particularly important are those quantities which aim to quantify the influence of each observation on the estimates of the regression coefficients and consequently on the regression analysis itself. A number of measures of influence are mentioned briefly in Display 6.10. A detailed account of regression diagnostics is given by Lovie (1991).

Display 6.10　Measures of influence in multiple regression

- The general procedure for assessing the influence of an observation in regression analysis is to determine the changes that occur in some statistic of interest (for example, the multiple correlation coefficient or a particular regression coefficient estimate) when the observation is omitted from the sample.
- Several measures of influence have been developed using this approach. They differ in the particular regression result on which the effect of the deletion of an observation is measured and the standardization used to make them comparable over observations.
- The four most commonly used influence measures are as follows:
  - (a) Cook's distance which measures the effect of the deletion of an observation on the estimated regression coefficients—values of Cook's distance greater than unity give most cause for concern;
  - (b) DFFIT which measures the effect of deletion on the fitted values of the response;
  - (c) DFBETA which measures the effect of deletion on a particular regression coefficient;

(d) COVRATIO which measures the effect of deletion on the covariance matrix of the parameter estimates.

- In general, the value of a chosen diagnostic is calculated for each sample observation and the values plotted in some appropriate way; for example, as an index plot as described in the text.
- These measures are defined explicitly by Rawlings (1988).

Returning to the ice cream data analysed in Section 6.3.1, Table 6.8 gives the observed values of ice cream consumption, the predicted values from a regression model

Table 6.8 Residuals and Cook's distances from multiple regression model fitted to the ice cream data

Consumption	Predicted	Residual	Standardized residual	Cook's distance
0.385	0.3423	0.0437	1.0895	0.0367
0.374	0.3710	0.0030	0.0763	0.0002
0.393	0.3992	−0.0062	−0.1542	0.0008
0.425	0.4101	0.0149	0.3787	0.0008
0.406	0.4244	−0.0184	−0.4650	0.0102
0.344	0.4263	−0.0823	−2.1507	0.3861
0.327	0.3959	−0.0689	−1.7127	0.0796
0.288	0.3647	−0.0767	−1.9245	0.1381
0.269	0.3221	−0.0531	−1.3799	0.1474
0.256	0.2810	−0.0250	−0.6426	0.0265
0.286	0.2861	−0.0001	−0.0026	0.0000
0.298	0.2969	0.0011	0.0294	0.0001
0.329	0.3122	0.0168	0.4228	0.0077
0.318	0.3155	0.0025	0.0651	0.0002
0.381	0.3749	0.0061	0.1500	0.0005
0.381	0.3852	−0.0042	−0.1082	0.0009
0.470	0.4222	0.0478	1.2310	0.1015
0.443	0.4264	0.0166	0.4235	0.0105
0.386	0.4113	−0.0253	−0.6375	0.0172
0.340	0.3901	−0.0481	−1.1947	0.0385
0.319	0.3206	−0.0016	−0.0417	0.0018
0.307	0.3155	−0.0085	−0.2166	0.0028
0.284	0.3052	−0.0212	−0.5332	0.0109
0.326	0.2789	0.0471	1.2244	0.1139
0.309	0.2861	0.0229	0.5860	0.0203
0.359	0.3251	0.0339	0.8797	0.0574
0.376	0.3493	0.0267	0.6804	0.0256
0.416	0.3827	0.333	0.8441	0.0335
0.437	0.4148	0.0222	0.5606	0.0142
0.548	0.4472	0.1108	2.7168	0.8898

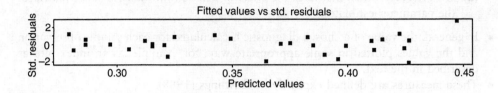

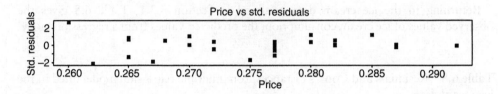

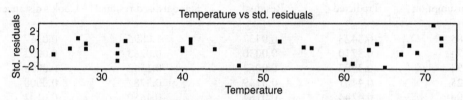

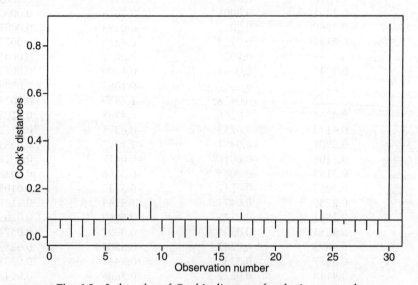

Fig. 6.7 Standardized residuals for the ice cream data.

Fig. 6.8 Index plot of Cook's distances for the ice cream data.

including explanatory variables, price and mean temperature, the values of both raw and standardized residuals and the values of Cook's distance. Plots of the standardized residuals against the fitted consumption values and against the values of the two explanatory variables are shown in Fig. 6.7. The three plots give little cause for concern; there is no discernible pattern in the residuals and most fall between the required limits of (–2, 2).

A useful method of producing a graphical display of Cook's distances is the **index plot**, which is simply distance measure plotted against observation number. It is also useful to include a horizontal line on the plot at the average distance value and to draw vertical lines joining each observed distance to the average. The plot for the ice cream data is shown in Fig. 6.8; observations 6 and 30, particularly the latter, have relatively large values of Cook's distance. Observation 30 has an observed consumption which is far higher than that predicted by the fitted regression model. (See also Exercise 6.5.)

6.4 Multicollinearity

One of the problems that often occurs when using multiple regression in practice is **multicollinearity**. The term is used to describe situations in which there are moderate to high intercorrelations amongst the explanatory variables. Multicollinearity gives rise to a number of difficulties when applying multiple regression:

1. It severely limits the size of the multiple correlation coefficient R because the explanatory variables are largely attempting to explain much of the same variance in the response variable (see Dizney and Gromen, 1967, for an example).
2. It makes determining the importance of a given explanatory variable difficult because the effects of the explanatory variables are confounded due to their inter-correlations.
3. It increases the variances of the regression coefficients, making use of the fitted model for prediction less stable.

Spotting multicollinearity amongst a set of explanatory variables may not be easy. The obvious course of action is to examine the correlations between these variables, but whilst this is often helpful, it is by no means foolproof—more subtle forms of multicollinearity may be missed. An alternative and generally far more useful approach is to examine what are known as the **variance inflation factors** of the explanatory variables. The variance inflation factor VIF_j for the jth variable is given by

$$\text{VIF}_j = \frac{1}{1 - R_j^2} \tag{6.6}$$

where R_j^2 is the square of the multiple correlation from the regression of the jth explanatory variable on the remaining explanatory variables. The variance inflation factor of an explanatory variable indicates the strength of the linear relationship between the variable and the remaining explanatory variables. A rough rule of thumb is that variance inflation factors greater than 10 give some cause for concern.

How can multicollinearity be combated? One way is to combine explanatory variables that are highly correlated, for example by taking their sum. An alternative is simply to select one of the set of correlated variables for use in the regression analysis. Two more complex procedures are **regression on principal components** and **ridge regression**, both of which are described by Chatterjee and Price (1991).

6.5   Summary

1. Multiple regression is used to assess the relationship between a set of explanatory variables and a response variable.
2. The response variable is assumed to be normally distributed with a mean that is a linear function of the explanatory variables and a variance that is independent of the explanatory variables.
3. The explanatory variables are strictly assumed to be fixed variables. In practice, where the explanatory variables are rarely fixed, the results of the multiple regression are conditional on the observed values of these variables.
4. Automatic selection procedures can be used to identify important subsets of explanatory variables, although they need to be used with care if results are to be replicable.
5. An extremely important part of any regression analysis involves the graphical examination of residuals and other diagnostics in a bid to identify possible departures from an assumed model, to indicate outliers etc.

Exercises

6.1   Explore the vocabulary size data further using models which allow a quadratic effect of age and a cubic effect of age, i.e.

$$\text{vocabulary size} = \beta_0 + \beta_1 \times \text{age} + \beta_2 \times \text{age}^2$$
$$\text{vocabulary size} = \beta_0 + \beta_1 \times \text{age} + \beta_2 \times \text{age}^2 + \beta_3 \times \text{age}^3.$$

Examine the residuals from such models to determine which is the most reasonable.

6.2   Examine the four data sets shown in Table 6.9 and show that the estimates of the slope and intercept parameters in a simple linear regression are the same for each. Find the value of the multiple correlation coefficient in each case. (This example illustrates the dangers of blindly fitting a regression model without the use of additional graphical material.)

6.3   Reanalyse the eye-blink data using a square-root transformation on the response variable.

6.4   Reanalyse the human fat data using sex as the single explanatory variable. What does the estimated regression coefficient now represent?

6.5   Reanalyse the ice cream data leaving out observation number 30. How do the results compare with those obtained in Section 6.3.1?

Table 6.9 Four hypothetical data sets each comparing 11 observations for two variables

Data set	1–3	1	2	3	4	4
Variable	x	y	y	y	x	y
Observation						
1	10.0	8.04	9.14	7.46	8.0	6.58
2	8.0	6.95	8.14	6.77	8.0	5.76
3	13.0	7.58	8.74	12.74	8.0	7.71
4	9.0	8.81	8.77	7.11	8.0	8.84
5	11.0	8.33	9.26	7.81	8.0	8.47
6	14.0	9.96	8.10	8.84	8.0	7.04
7	6.0	7.24	6.13	6.08	8.0	5.25
8	4.0	4.26	3.10	5.39	19.0	12.50
9	12.0	10.84	9.13	8.15	8.0	5.56
10	7.0	4.82	7.26	6.42	8.0	7.91
11	5.0	5.68	4.74	5.73	8.0	6.89

6.6 The data in Table 6.10 are for 47 states in the USA. Apply multiple regression to investigate how the crime rate depends on the other variables. Pay particular attention to checking the assumptions of the model.

6.7 The data shown in Table 6.11 were collected from a sample of 24 primary school children in Sydney, Australia. Each child had completed the Embedded Figures Test (EFT) which measures 'field dependence', i.e. the extent to which a person can abstract the logical structure of a problem from its context. Then the children were allocated to two experimental groups. They were timed as they constructed a 3×3 pattern for nine coloured blocks, taken from the Wechsler Intelligence Scale for Children (WISC). The two groups received different instructions for the task: the 'row group' were told to start with a row of three blocks, and the 'corner group' were told to start with a corner of three blocks. The experimenter was interested in whether the different instructions produced any change in the average time to complete the pattern and in whether this time was affected by field dependence. Use a suitable multiple regression model in an attempt to answer these questions.

6.8 The data shown in Table 6.12 give the average percentage memory retention p measured against passing time t (minutes). The measurements were taken five times during the first hour after subjects memorized a list of disconnected items, and then at various times up to a week later. Plot the data (after a suitable transformation if necessary) and investigate the relationship between retention and time using a suitable regression model.

Table 6.10   Crime in the USA, 1960

R	Age	S	Ed	Ex0	Ex1	LF	M	N	NW	U_1	U_2	W	X
79.1	151	1	91	58	56	510	950	33	301	108	41	394	261
163.5	143	0	113	103	95	583	1012	13	102	96	36	557	194
57.8	142	1	89	45	44	533	969	18	219	94	33	318	250
196.9	136	0	121	149	141	577	994	157	80	102	39	673	167
123.4	141	0	121	109	101	591	985	18	30	91	20	578	174
68.2	121	0	110	118	115	547	964	25	44	84	29	689	126
96.3	127	1	111	82	79	519	982	4	139	97	38	620	168
155.5	131	1	109	115	109	542	969	50	179	79	35	472	206
85.6	157	1	90	65	62	553	955	39	286	81	28	421	239
70.5	140	0	118	71	68	632	1029	7	15	100	24	526	174
167.4	124	0	105	121	116	580	966	101	106	77	35	657	170
84.9	134	0	108	75	71	595	972	47	59	83	31	580	172
51.1	128	0	113	67	60	624	972	28	10	77	25	507	206
66.4	135	0	117	62	61	595	986	22	46	77	27	529	190
79.8	152	1	87	57	53	530	986	30	72	92	43	405	264
94.6	142	1	88	81	77	497	956	33	321	116	47	427	247
53.9	143	0	110	66	63	537	977	10	6	114	35	487	166
92.9	135	1	104	123	115	537	978	31	170	89	34	631	165
75.0	130	0	116	128	128	536	934	51	24	78	34	627	135
122.5	125	0	108	113	105	567	985	78	94	130	58	626	166
74.2	126	0	108	74	67	602	984	34	12	102	33	557	195
43.9	157	1	89	47	44	512	962	22	423	97	34	288	276
121.6	132	0	96	87	83	564	953	43	92	83	32	513	227
96.8	131	0	116	78	73	574	1038	7	36	142	42	540	176
52.3	130	0	116	63	57	641	984	14	26	70	21	486	196
199.3	131	0	121	160	143	631	1071	3	77	102	41	674	152
34.2	135	0	109	69	71	540	965	6	4	80	22	564	139
121.6	152	0	112	82	76	571	1018	10	79	103	28	537	215
104.3	119	0	107	166	157	521	938	168	89	92	36	637	154
69.6	166	1	89	58	54	521	973	46	254	72	26	396	237
37.3	140	0	93	55	54	535	1045	6	20	135	40	453	200
75.4	125	0	109	90	81	586	964	97	82	105	43	617	163
107.2	147	1	104	63	64	560	972	23	95	76	24	462	233
92.3	126	0	118	97	97	542	990	18	21	102	35	589	166
65.3	123	0	102	97	87	526	948	113	76	124	50	572	158
127.2	150	0	100	109	98	531	964	9	24	87	38	559	153
83.1	177	1	87	58	56	638	974	24	349	76	28	382	254
56.6	133	0	104	51	47	599	1024	7	40	99	27	425	225
82.6	149	1	88	61	54	515	953	36	165	86	35	395	251
115.1	145	1	104	82	74	560	981	96	126	88	31	488	228
88.0	148	0	122	72	66	601	998	9	19	84	20	590	144
54.2	141	0	109	56	54	523	968	4	2	107	37	489	170
82.3	162	1	99	75	70	522	996	40	208	73	27	496	224
103.0	136	0	121	95	96	574	1012	29	36	111	37	622	162
45.5	139	1	88	46	41	480	968	19	49	135	53	457	249

Table 6.10 Crime in the USA, 1960 – *cont'd*

R	Age	S	Ed	Ex0	Ex1	LF	M	N	NW	U_1	U_2	W	X
50.8	126	0	104	106	97	599	989	40	24	78	25	593	171
84.9	130	0	121	90	91	623	1049	3	22	113	40	588	160

R, crime rate (number of offences known to police per 1 000 000 population); Age, age distribution (the number of males aged 14–24 per 1000 of total state population); S, binary variable distinguishing southern states (S = 1) from the rest; Ed, educational level (mean number of years of schooling × 10 of the population aged 25 years and above); Ex0, police expenditure (per capita expenditure on police protection by state and local government in 1960); Ex1, police expenditure (as Ex0, but for 1959); LF, labour force participation rate per 1000 civilian urban males in the age group 14–24; M, number of males per 1000 females; N, state population in hundred thousands; NW, number of non-whites per 1000; U_1, unemployment rate of urban males per 1000 in the age group 14–24; U_2, unemployment rate of urban males per 1000 in the age group 35–39; W, wealth as measured by the median value of transferable goods and assets or family income (in units $10); X, income inequality (number of families per 1000 earning less than half the median income).

Table 6.11 WISC blocks

Row Group											
Time	317	464	525	298	491	196	268	372	370	739	430	410
EFT	59	33	49	69	65	26	29	62	31	139	74	31

Corner Group											
Time	342	222	219	513	295	285	408	543	298	494	317	407
EFT	48	23	9	128	44	49	87	43	55	58	113	7

Table 6.12 Memory retention

t	p
1	0.84
5	0.71
15	0.61
30	0.56
60	0.54
120	0.47
240	0.45
480	0.38
720	0.36
1440	0.26
2880	0.20
5760	0.16
10 080	0.08

Further reading

Atkinson, A.C. (1985). *Plots, transformations and regression*. Oxford University Press.

Cook, R.D. (1977). Detection of influential observations in linear regression. *Journal of the American Statistical Association*, **74**, 169–74.

Cook, R.D. and Weisberg, S. (1994). *An introduction to regression graphics*. Wiley, New York.

Hocking, R.R. and Pendleton, O.J. (1983). The regression dilemma. *Communications in Statistics*, **A12**, 497–527.

Lewis-Beck, M.S. (ed.) (1993). *Regression analysis*. Sage, Beverly Hills, California.

7

The analysis of categorical data: log–linear models and logistic regression

7.1 Introduction

Categorical data occur frequently in the social and behavioural sciences, where information is often collected on variables such as marital status, sex, occupation, ethnicity etc. In many cases the researcher collecting such data is most interested in looking at how such variables are related, in particular whether they are independent of one another. Cross-classification of pairs of categorical variables, i.e. **two-dimensional contingency tables**, are commonly the starting point for assessing independence and no doubt will be familiar to most readers. Examples of such tables appear in Tables 7.1 and 7.2.

However, cross-classifications of more than two categorical variables will not usually have been encountered in an introductory statistics course, and it is such tables (usually known as **multidimensional contingency tables** or **multiway frequency tables**) that are the main concern in this chapter. An example of such a table involving four categorical variables is shown in Table 7.3. A variety of hypotheses can be formulated about the

Table 7.1 Classification of psychiatric patients by sex and diagnosis

Diagnosis	Male	Female
Schizophrenia	43	32
Other	15	52

Table 7.2 Snoring and heart disease

Heart disease	Snoring behaviour				Total
	Non-snorer	Occasional snores	Nearly every night	Every night	
Yes	24	35	21	30	110
No	1355	603	192	224	2374
Total	1379	538	213	254	2484

Table 7.3   Degree of depression in adolescents: a four-way contingency table

Age group	Type	Sex	Depression	
			Low	High
1 (12–14)	LD	Male	90	36
		Female	40	33
	SED	Male	18	8
		Female	10	12
2 (15–16)	LD	Male	70	30
		Female	33	28
	SED	Male	39	15
		Female	25	14
3 (17–18)	LD	Male	41	35
		Female	21	21
	SED	Male	40	12
		Female	18	9

SED, seriously emotionally disturbed; LD, learning disabled.

variables that give rise to such tables, and for this reason the analysis of multiway tables is often considerably more complex than that involved in dealing with two-dimensional tables. Consequently, it may be helpful to begin with a brief review of the (hopefully) familiar chi-squared test of the independence of the two variables forming a two-dimensional table; this will act as a gentle introduction to the more difficult material to come.

7.2.   The two-dimensional contingency table

The simplest form of two-dimensional contingency table is obtained when a sample of observations is cross-classified according to the values taken by two dichotomous variables, i.e. categorical variables with only two categories. The general form of such a 2×2 contingency table is shown in Display 7.1, which also includes the hypothesis of most interest about such tables and the details of the chi-squared test of this hypothesis. The application of the chi-squared test to the schizophrenia data in Table 7.1 is shown in Display 7.2. The results given there indicate clearly that sex and psychiatric diagnosis are associated in the sense that a higher proportion of men than women are diagnosed as schizophrenic.

For larger contingency tables where the number r of rows and/or the number c of columns are greater than 2, the chi-squared test of the independence of the two variables forming the table is best developed in terms of the concept of **estimated expected values**, more often simply referred to as **expected values**, although the former name is preferable and will generally be used in this chapter. The calculation of such

Display 7.1 The 2 × 2 contingency table

- The general form of a 2 × 2 contingency table (observed frequencies in a sample of size N) is as follows:

Variable 2	Variable 1		
	Category 1	Category 2	Total
Category 1	a	b	$a + b$
Category 2	c	d	$c + d$
Total	$a + c$	$b + d$	$a + b + c + d = N$

- The null hypothesis in such a table is that there is no association between the two dichotomous variables. More specifically, the hypothesis is that the conditional probability of being in category 1 of variable 2 is the same for both categories of variable 1.
- The test statistic for assessing the hypothesis is

$$X^2 = \frac{N(ad - bc)^2}{(a + b)(c + d)(a + c)(b + d)}.$$

- If the null hypothesis is true, then X^2 has a chi-squared distribution with a single degree of freedom.

Display 7.2 Analysis of cross-classification of sex and diagnosis

- The hypothesis is that the probability p_1 of a man being diagnosed as schizophrenic is the same as the probability p_2 of a woman being diagnosed as schizophrenic.
- The relevant chi-squared statistic is calculated as

$$X^2 = \frac{142 \times (43 \times 52 - 32 \times 15)^2}{58 \times 84 \times 75 \times 67} = 17.88.$$

- The associated P-value is very small, and a strong association between sex and a diagnosis of schizophrenia is clearly indicated. This implies that the proportion of men who are diagnosed as schizophrenic is different from the corresponding proportion of women. In fact, the estimates of these two proportions obtained from the data in Table 7.1, namely

$$\hat{p}_1 = \frac{43}{58} = 0.74$$

$$\hat{p}_2 = \frac{32}{84} = 0.38,$$

indicate that men are diagnosed as schizophrenic considerably more frequently than women.

- An estimate of the standard error of the difference $\hat{p}_1 - \hat{p}_2$ is given by

$$s = \left(\frac{\hat{p}_1(1 - \hat{p}_1)}{n_1} + \frac{\hat{p}_2(1 - \hat{p}_2)}{n_2} \right)^{1/2}$$

  where n_1 and n_2 are the sample sizes from which the estimated proportions are calculated.

- An approximate 95% confidence interval for the difference $p_1 - p_2$ between the two population probabilities, can be calculated as follows:

$$(\hat{p}_1 - \hat{p}_2) \pm 2s.$$

- The resulting interval for the schizophrenia data is (0.204, 0.516).

values and the associated chi-squared statistic are outlined in Display 7.3. Details of applying these calculations to the snoring and heart disease data (Table 7.2) are shown in Display 7.4. It appears that the more prolific snorers are considerably over-represented in the heart disease category and that the two variables are not independent. Of course, these data do not tell us whether snoring increases the chance of suffering from heart disease or whether people liable to heart disease snore more.

Display 7.3   The $r \times c$ contingency table

- The general form of a two-dimensional contingency table is as follows:

Variable 1	Variable 2				Total
	1	2	$\cdots$	c	
1	n_{11}	n_{12}	$\cdots$	n_{1c}	$n_{1.}$
2	n_{21}	n_{22}	$\cdots$	n_{2c}	$n_{2.}$
$\vdots$	$\vdots$	$\vdots$		$\vdots$	$\vdots$
r	n_{r1}	n_{r2}	$\cdots$	$n_{r}c$	$n_{r.}$
Total	$n_{.1}$	$n_{.2}$	$\cdots$	$n.c$	N

- Here n_{ij} represents the observed frequency in the ijth cell of the table. Subscript points are used to indicate summation over a subscript; for example, $n_{1.} = n_{11} + n_{12} + \ldots + n_{1c}$, is the sum of the frequencies in the first row of the table. The row and column totals are usually known as **marginal totals**.
- The hypothesis that the two variables forming the table are independent can be formulated as follows:

$$H_0 : p_{ij} = p_{i.}p_{.j}$$

where p_{ij} is the probability of an observation falling in the ijth cell of the table, $p_{i.}$ is the probability of being in the ith category of variable 1 and $p_{.j}$ is the probability of being in the jth category of variable 2. (Note that, as usual, the null hypothesis is specified in terms of population values, i.e. the various probabilities of interest.)

- Under H_0 the number of observations that would be expected to fall into the ijth cell when a sample of N observations is cross-classified

$$F_{ij} = N p_{i.} p_{.j}$$

(note that F_{ij} is also a population value).
- The 'intuitively' sensible estimators of $p_{i.}$ and $p_{.j}$ are given by

$$\hat{p}_{i.} = \frac{n_{i.}}{N}; \qquad \hat{p}_{.j} = \frac{n_{.j}}{N}.$$

(Intuition here also matches the mathematics; these are also the **maximum likelihood estimators**; see Everitt, 1992).
- The estimated expected values are

$$\hat{F}_{ij} = E_{ij} = N \frac{n_{i.}}{N} \frac{n_{.j}}{N} = \frac{n_{i.} n_{.j}}{N},$$

i.e. $\dfrac{\text{row total} \times \text{column total}}{\text{sample size}}.$

- The test statistic for assessing H_0 is calculated as

$$X^2 = \sum_{i=1}^{r} \sum_{j=1}^{c} \frac{(n_{ij} - E_{ij})^2}{E_{ij}}.$$

- Under H_0, X^2 has a chi-squared distribution with $(r-1)(c-1)$ degrees of freedom.
- Note that the marginal totals of the estimated expected values under the hypothesis of independence will be equal to the corresponding marginal totals of the observed values.

Display 7.4 The chi-squared test of independence for the snoring and heart disease data

- The estimated expected values under independence are given below

Heart disease	Snoring behaviour				Total
	Non-snorer	Occasional snores	Nearly every night	Every night	
Yes	61.1	28.3	9.4	11.2	110.0
No	1317.9	609.7	203.6	242.8	2374.0
Total	1379	638	213	254	2484

- The chi-squared statistic takes the value 72.78 with three degrees of freedom. The associated P-value is very small, and it would appear that the amount of snoring and the occurrence of heart disease are related.

Defining the independence of the two variables forming a contingency table is relatively straightforward, but measuring the degree of dependence is not so clear cut, and many measures have been proposed (Everitt 1992). In a 2×2 table one possible measure might be thought to be the difference between the estimates of the two probabilities of interest, as illustrated in Display 7.2. An alternative, and in many respects a more acceptable, measure is the **odds ratio** which is explained in Display 7.5 and illustrated for the schizophrenia data in Display 7.6. This statistic is of considerable practical importance in the application of both **log–linear models** (see Section 7.4) and **logistic regression** (see Section 7.5); further examples of its use and interpretation will be given later.

Display 7.5   The odds ratio

- The general 2 × 2 contingency table can be summarized in terms of the population probabilities of an observation being in each of the following four cells:

Variable 1	Variable 2	
	Category 1	Category 2
Category 1	p_{11}	p_{12}
Category 2	p_{21}	p_{22}

- The ratios p_{11}/p_{12} and p_{21}/p_{22} are known as **odds**. The first is the odds of being in category 1 of variable 1 for the two categories of variable 2. The second is the corresponding odds for category 2 of variable 1. (Odds will be familiar to those readers who are regular visitors to their local betting shop.)
- A possible measure of the degree of dependence between the two variables forming a 2 × 2 contingency table is the so-called **odds ratio** given by

$$\alpha = \frac{p_{11}}{p_{12}} \bigg/ \frac{p_{21}}{p_{22}} = \frac{p_{11}p_{22}}{p_{21}p_{12}}.$$

- Note that α may have any value between zero and ∞, with a value of 1 corresponding to independence (why?).
- The odds ratio α has a number of desirable properties for representing dependence amongst categorical variables that other competing measures do not have. These properties include the following:

  (a) α remains unchanged if the rows and columns are interchanged;
  (b) if the levels of a variable are changed (e.g. listing category 2 before category 1), α becomes $1/\alpha$;
  (c) multiplying either row by a constant or either column by a constant leaves α unchanged.

- The odds ratio is estimated from the four frequencies in an observed table (see Display 7.1) as

$$\hat{\alpha} = \frac{ad}{bc}.$$

- Confidence intervals for α can be determined relatively simply by using the following estimator of the variance of $\ln \hat{\alpha}$:

$$\text{vâr}(\ln \hat{\alpha}) = \frac{1}{a} + \frac{1}{b} + \frac{1}{c} + \frac{1}{d}.$$

- An approximate 95% confidence interval for $\ln \alpha$ is given by

$$\ln \hat{\alpha} \pm 2.0 \times [\text{vâr}(\ln \hat{\alpha})]^{1/2}.$$

- The required confidence interval for α can now be found by exponentiating the limits found for $\ln \alpha$.

Display 7.6 Estimating the odds ratio for the psychiatric diagnosis by sex data in Table 7.1

- The estimate of the odds ratio is

$$\hat{\alpha} = \frac{43 \times 52}{32 \times 15} = 4.66.$$

- The odds in favour of being diagnosed schizophrenic amongst males is nearly five times the corresponding odds for females.
- The estimated variance of the logarithm of the estimated odds ratio is

$$\frac{1}{4} + \frac{1}{52} + \frac{1}{15} + \frac{1}{32} = 0.1404.$$

- An approximate confidence interval for $\ln \alpha$ is

$$\ln(4.66) \pm 2.0\sqrt{0.1404} = (0.8045, 2.2884).$$

- Consequently, the limits for α are

$$(\exp(0.8045), \exp(2.2884)) = (2.235, 9.859).$$

A comprehensive account of the analysis of two-dimensional contingency tables is given by Everitt (1992).

7.3 Three-dimensional contingency tables

The analysis of three-dimensional contingency tables poses entirely new conceptual problems compared with the analysis of two-dimensional tables. However, the extension from tables of three dimensions to those of four or more, whilst often increasing the complexity of both analysis and interpretation, presents no further new problems. Consequently, this section is concerned only with three-dimensional tables and will form the necessary basis for the discussion of **models** for multiway tables to be undertaken in the next section.

The first question that might be asked about a three-dimensional contingency table is: 'Why not simply attempt its analysis by examining the two-dimensional tables resulting from summing the observed counts over one of the variables?' The example shown in Display 7.7 illustrates why such a procedure is not to be recommended: it can often lead to erroneous conclusions being drawn about the data. For example, analysing the data collapsed over clinics gives a chi-squared statistic of 5.26 with a single degree of freedom; the associated P-value is less than 0.05, and the apparent conclusion to be drawn is that infant survival and the amount of prenatal care received are related. However, the separate analyses of the data from Clinic A only and from Clinic B only lead to chi-squared values of approximately zero in each case and the conclusion that, within each clinic, survival and amount of prenatal care are independent. The reason for these different conclusions will become clear later. However, this example should make it clear why consideration of two-dimensional tables resulting from collapsing a three-dimensional table is not a sufficient procedure for analysing the latter.

Display 7.7   Survival of infants and amount of prenatal care

- Data collected in two clinics are given below:

Place where care received	Infants' survival			
	Died		Survived	
	Less prenatal care	More prenatal care	Less prenatal care	More prenatal care
Clinic A	3	4	176	293
Clinic B	17	2	197	23

- Collapsing over clinics gives the following two-dimensional table:

Amount of prenatal care	Infants' survival		Total
	Died	Survived	
Less	20	373	393
More	6	316	322
Total	26	689	715

Only a single hypothesis, namely that of the independence of the two variables involved, is of interest in a two-dimensional table. However, the situation is more complex for a three-dimensional table, and several hypotheses about the three variables may need to be assessed. For example, an investigator may wish to test that some variables are independent of some others, or that a particular variable is independent of the remainder. More specifically, the following hypotheses may be of interest in a three-dimensional table;

(1) **mutual independence** of the three variables, i.e. none of the variables are related;
(2) **partial independence**, i.e. an association exists between two of the variables, both of which are independent of the third;
(3) **conditional independence**, i.e. two of the variables are independent in each level of the third, but each may be associated with the third variable (this is the situation that holds in the case of the clinic data discussed above).

In addition, the variables in a three-way contingency table may display a more complex form of association, namely what is known as a **second-order relationship**; this occurs when the degree and/or direction of the dependence of each pair of variables is different in some or all levels of the remaining variable.

As will be demonstrated later, each hypothesis is tested in a fashion exactly analogous to that used when testing for independence in a two-dimensional table, namely by comparing the estimated expected frequencies corresponding to the particular hypothesis with the observed frequencies via the usual chi-squared statistic, or an alternative known as the **likelihood ratio statistic** given by

$$X_L^2 = 2 \sum \text{observed} \times \ln(\text{observed}/\text{expected}) \qquad (7.1)$$

where 'observed' refers to the observed frequencies in the table and 'expected' refers to the estimated expected values corresponding to a particular hypothesis (see later). In many cases X^2 and X_L^2 will have similar values, but there are a number of advantages to the latter (Williams 1976) which make it particularly suitable in the analysis of more complex contingency tables, as will be illustrated later.

Under the hypothesis of independence, the estimated expected frequencies in a two-dimensional table are found from simple calculations involving the marginal totals of the observed frequencies (see Display 7.3). In some cases the required expected frequencies corresponding to a particular hypothesis about the variables in a three-dimensional table can also be found from straightforward calculations on certain marginal totals (this will be illustrated in Displays 7.8 and 7.9). Unfortunately, estimated expected values in multiway tables cannot always be found so simply. For example, in a three-dimensional table estimated expected values for the hypothesis of no second-order relationship amongst the three variables have to be obtained from a relatively complex **iterative procedure**. The details are outside the scope of this text, but can be found in Everitt (1992). In general, of course, investigators analysing multiway contingency tables will obtain the required expected values and associated test statistics from a suitable piece of statistical software, and so will not need to be too concerned with the details of the arithmetic.

The data on suicide behaviour, cross-tabulated against age and sex, shown in Table 7.4 will be used to illustrate the analysis of a three-dimensional contingency table. The first hypothesis that will be considered is that the three variables are **mutually independent**. The calculation of estimated expected values, the chi-squared statistic and

Table 7.4 Cross-classification of method of suicide by age and sex

Age (Years)	Sex	Method					
		1	2	3	4	5	6
10–40	Male	398	121	455	155	55	124
41–70	Male	399	82	797	168	51	82
> 70	Male	93	6	316	33	26	14
10–40	Female	259	15	95	14	40	38
41–70	Female	450	13	450	26	71	60
> 70	Female	154	5	185	7	38	10

1, Solid or liquid matter; 2, gas; 3, hanging, suffocating or drowning; 4, guns, knives or explosives; 5, jumping; 6, other.

the likelihood ratio statistic are detailed in Display 7.8. The number of degrees of freedom corresponding to each test statistic is 27 (see Everitt, 1992, for an explanation of how to determine the number of the degrees of freedom corresponding to a particular hypothesis). Clearly, the three variables used to form Table 7.4 are not mutually independent.

Display 7.8 Testing the mutual independence hypothesis for the suicide data in Table 7.4

- Using an obvious extension of the nomenclature introduced in Display 7.3 for the general two-dimensional contingency table, we can formulate the hypothesis of mutual independence as

$$H_0 : p_{ijk} = p_{i..}p_{.j.}p_{..k}$$

where p_{ijk} represents the probability of an observation being in the ijkth cell of the table and $p_{i..}, p_{.j.}$ and $p_{..k}$ are the marginal probabilities for the three variables.
- The estimated expected values under this hypothesis in a sample of N observations are given by

$$E_{ijk} = N\hat{p}_{i..}\hat{p}_{.j.}\hat{p}_{..k}$$

where $\hat{p}_{i..}, \hat{p}_{.j.}$ and $\hat{p}_{..k}$ are estimates of the corresponding probabilities.
- The intuitive (and fortunately also the maximum likelihood) estimators of the marginal probabilities are

$$\hat{p}_{i..} = \frac{n_{i..}}{N}, \hat{p}_{.j.} = \frac{n_{.j.}}{N}, \hat{p}_{..k} = \frac{n_{..k}}{N}$$

where the $n_{i..}, n_{.j.}$ and $n_{..k}$ are single variable marginal totals for each variable obtained by summing the observed frequencies over the other two variables.

- For the suicide data, for example, the estimated expected value E_{111} is obtained as

$$E_{111} = 5305 \times \frac{3375}{5305} \times \frac{1769}{5305} \times \frac{1753}{5305} = 371.89.$$

- The full set of expected values for the suicide data under the mutual independence hypothesis is as follows:

Age (Years)	Sex	Method					
		1	2	3	4	5	6
10–40	Male	371.9	51.3	487.5	85.5	59.6	69.6
41–70	Male	556.9	76.9	730.0	128.0	89.3	104.2
> 70	Male	186.5	25.7	244.4	42.9	29.9	34.9
10–40	Female	212.7	29.4	278.8	48.9	34.1	39.8
41–70	Female	318.5	44.0	417.5	73.2	51.0	59.6
> 70	Female	106.6	14.7	139.8	24.5	17.1	20.0

- The values of the two test statistics are

$$X^2 = 747.37, \qquad X_L^2 = 790.30.$$

- The independence hypothesis has 27 degrees of freedom.
- Note that the single-variable marginal totals of the estimated expected values under the hypothesis of mutual independence are equal to the corresponding marginal totals of the observed values, for example

$$n_{1..} = 398 + 399 + 93 + 259 + 450 + 154 = 1753$$
$$E_{1..} = 371.9 + 556.9 + 186.5 + 212.7 + 318.5 + 106.6 = 1753.$$

Now consider a more complex **partial independence hypothesis** about the three variables, namely that sex is independent of method of suicide and age is independent of sex, but sex is associated with method. Display 7.9 gives details of the calculation of the estimated expected values under this hypothesis and the values of both the familiar chi-squared statistic and the likelihood ratio statistic. Clearly, even this more complicated hypothesis is not adequate for these data. Comparison of the observed values with the estimates of the values to be expected under this partial independence hypothesis shows that women in all age groups are under-represented in the use of guns, knives or explosives (explosives!) to perform the tragic task. (A more detailed account of how best to compare observed and expected values is given later.)

Display 7.9 Testing a hypothesis of partial independence on the suicide data

- The hypothesis is that method of suicide is independent of sex, and that age and sex are also unrelated. However, an association between age and method is allowed.

Using the nomenclature adopted in previous tables, we can write this hypothesis in two equivalent forms:

$$H_0 : p_{ijk} = p_{..k}.p_{ij.}$$

or

$$H_0 : p_{i.k} = p_{i..}.p_{..k} \quad \text{and} \quad p_{.jk} = p_{.j.}.p_{..k}$$

where $p_{..1}$ is the probability of being male, $p_{12.}$ is the probability of being in the method 1 – age group 2 cell of the table etc.

- The estimators of the probabilities involved are

$$\hat{p}_{..k} = \frac{n_{..k}}{N}, \qquad \hat{p}_{ij.} = \frac{n_{ij.}}{N}$$

where the $n_{ij.}$ are the **two variable marginal totals** obtained by summing the observed frequencies over the third variable (sex in the case of the suicide data).

- Using these probability estimates leads to the following estimated expected values:

$$E_{ijk} = \frac{n_{..k}n_{ij.}}{N}.$$

For example,

$$E_{111} = \frac{3375 \times 657}{5305} = 417.98.$$

- The full set of estimated expected values under the hypothesis is as follows:

Age (years)	Sex	Method					
		1	2	3	4	5	6
10–40	Male	417.98	86.52	349.91	107.52	60.44	103.06
41–70	Male	540.13	60.44	793.33	123.42	77.61	90.34
> 70	Male	157.14	6.99	318.73	25.45	40.72	15.27
10–40	Female	239.02	49.48	200.09	61.48	34.56	58.94
41–70	Female	308.87	34.56	453.67	70.58	44.38	51.66
> 70	Female	89.86	4.00	182.25	14.55	23.28	8.73

- Note that in this case the marginal totals $n_{ij.}$ and $E_{ij.}$ are equal; for example, $n_{11.} = 398 + 259 = 657$ and $E_{11.} = 417.98 + 239.02 = 657$.
- The values of the two test statistics are

$$X^2 = 485.33, \qquad X_L^2 = 520.41.$$

- The statistics have 17 degrees of freedom.

Finally, consider the hypothesis of no second-order relationship between the variables in the suicide data. This allows each pair of variables to be associated, but constrains the degree and direction of the association to be the same in each level of the third variable. Details of testing the hypothesis are given in Display 7.10. Note that in this case estimated expected values cannot be found directly from any set of marginal totals. They are found from the iterative procedure referred to earlier. (The technical reason for requiring an iterative process is that, in this case, the maximum likelihood equations from which estimates arise have no explicit solution. The equations have to be solved iteratively.) Both test statistics are non-significant, demonstrating that this particular hypothesis is acceptable for the suicide data. Further comments on this result will be given in the next section.

Display 7.10 Testing the hypothesis of no second-order relationship between the variables in the suicide data

- The hypothesis to be tested is that the association between any two of the variables does not differ in degree or direction in each level of the remaining variable. More specifically this means that the odds ratios corresponding to the 2×2 tables that can be derived from the cross-classification of two of the variables are the same in all levels of the remaining variable. (Details are given in Everitt, 1992.)
- Estimates of expected values under this hypothesis cannot be found from simple calculations on marginal totals of observed frequencies as in Displays 7.8 and 7.9. Instead the estimates have to be obtained iteratively using a procedure described in Everitt (1992).
- The estimated expected values derived from the iterative procedure are as follows:

Age (years)	Sex	Method					
		1	2	3	4	5	6
10–40	Male	410.9	122.7	439.2	156.4	56.8	122.0
41–70	Male	379.4	77.6	819.9	166.3	51.1	84.7
> 70	Male	99.7	8.7	308.9	33.4	24.1	13.3
10–40	Female	246.1	13.3	110.8	12.6	38.2	40.0
41–70	Female	496.6	17.4	427.1	27.7	70.9	57.3
> 70	Female	1473	2.3	192.1	6.6	39.9	10.7

- The two test statistics take the values
$$X^2 = 15.40, \qquad X_L^2 = 14.90.$$
- The statistics have 10 degrees of freedom.

7.4 Models for contingency tables

Statisticians are very fond of models! In previous chapters the majority of analyses have been based on the assumption of a suitable model for the data of interest. The analysis of categorical data arranged in the form of a multiway frequency table may also be based on a particular type of model, not dissimilar to those used in the analysis of variance. As will be seen, each particular model corresponds to a specific hypothesis about the variables forming the table, but the advantages to be gained from a model-fitting procedure are that it provides a systematic approach to the analysis of complex multidimensional tables and, in addition, gives estimates of the magnitude of effects of interest. The models used for contingency tables can be introduced most simply (if a little clumsily) in terms of a two-dimensional table; details are given in Display 7.11. The model introduced in the latter is analogous to the model used in a two-way analysis of variance (see Chapter 4), but differs in a number of respects:

1. The data now consist of counts, rather than a score for each subject on some dependent variable.
2. The model does not distinguish between independent and dependent variables. All variables are treated alike as 'response' variables whose mutual associations are to be explored.

Display 7.11   Log–linear model for a two-dimensional contingency table with r rows and c columns

- Again, the general model considered in previous chapters, i.e.

$$\text{observed response} = \text{expected response} + \text{error}$$

  is the starting point.
- Here the observed response is the observed count n_{ij} in a cell of the table, and the expected response is the frequency F_{ij} expected under a particular hypothesis. Hence

$$n_{ij} = F_{ij} + \text{error}.$$

- Unlike the corresponding terms in previous chapters, the error terms here will not be normally distributed. Appropriate distributions are discussed by Everitt and Dunn (1991) and briefly in Chapter 8 of this text.
- Under the independence hypothesis the population frequencies F_{ij} are given by

$$F_{ij} = N p_{i.} p_{.j}$$

  which can be rewritten, using an obvious dot notation, as

$$F_{ij} = N \times \frac{F_{i.}}{N} \times \frac{F_{.j}}{N} = \frac{F_{i.} F_{.j}}{N}.$$

- By taking logarithms, the following linear model for the expected frequencies is derived:

$$\ln F_{ij} = \ln F_{i.} + \ln F_{.j} - \ln N.$$

- By some simple algebra (it is simple, but see Everitt, 1992, for details), the model can be written in the form

$$\ln F_{ij} = u + u_{1(i)} + u_{2(j)}$$

where

$$u = \frac{\sum_{i=1}^{r} \sum_{j=1}^{c} \ln F_{ij}}{rc}$$

$$u_{1(i)} = \frac{\sum_{j=1}^{c} \ln F_{ij}}{c} - u$$

$$u_{2(j)} = \frac{\sum_{i=1}^{r} \ln F_{ij}}{r} - u.$$

- This model is very similar to those used in the analysis of variance. Consequently, analysis of variance terms are used for the parameters, and u is said to represent an 'overall mean effect', $u_{1(i)}$ is the 'main effect' of category i of the row variable and $u_{2(j)}$ is the 'main effect' of the jth category of the column variable.
- The main effect parameters are measured as deviations of row or column means of log frequencies from the overall mean. Therefore, using an obvious dot notation,

$$u_{1(.)} = 0, \qquad u_{2(.)} = 0.$$

- The values taken by the main effects parameters in this model simply reflect differences between the row or the column marginal totals and so are of little concern in the context of the analysis of contingency tables. They could be estimated by replacing the F_{ij} in the formulae above with the estimated expected values E_{ij}.
- The log–linear model can be fitted by estimating the parameters, and hence the expected frequencies, and comparing these with the observed values using either the usual chi-squared statistic or the likelihood ratio statistic. This would be exactly equivalent to the usual procedure for testing independence in a two-dimensional table as described in Section 7.2.
- If the independence model fails to give a satisfactory fit to a two-dimensional table, extra terms need to be added to the model to represent the association between the variables. This leads to consideration of the model

$$\ln F_{ij} = u + u_{1(i)} + u_{2(j)} + u_{12(ij)}.$$

where the parameter $u_{12(ij)}$ represents the association between category i of variable 1 and category j of variable 2.

- This is known as the *saturated model* for a two-dimensional table since the number of parameters in the model is equal to the number of independent cells in the table (see Everitt, 1992, for details). Estimated expected values under this model would simply be the observed frequencies, and the model provides a perfect fit to the observed data. The interaction parameters are related to odds ratios (see Exercise 7.5).

3. Whereas a linear combination of parameters is used in the analysis of variance and regression models of previous chapters, in multiway tables the natural model is **multiplicative** and hence logarithms are used to obtain a model in which parameters are combined additively.
4. In previous chapters the underlying distribution assumed for the data was the normal; with frequency data the appropriate distribution is **binomial** or **multinomial** (see Appendix A and Everitt and Dunn, 1991).

Now consider how the log linear model in Display 7.11 needs to be extended to be suitable for a three-way table. The saturated model will now need to contain main effect parameters for each variable, parameters to represent the possible associations between each pair of variables and finally parameters to represent the possible second-order relationship between the three variables. The model is

$$\ln F_{ijk} = u + u_{1(i)} + u_{2(j)} + u_{3(k)} + u_{12(ij)} + u_{13(ik)} + u_{23(jk)} + u_{123(ijk)}. \qquad (7.2)$$

The parameters in this model are as follows:

(1) u is the overall 'mean' effect;
(2) $u_{1(i)}$ is the 'main effect' of variable 1;
(3) $u_{2(j)}$ is the 'main effect' of variable 2;
(4) $u_{3(k)}$ is the 'main effect' of variable 3;
(5) $u_{12(ij)}$ is the interaction between variables 1 and 2;
(6) $u_{13(ik)}$ is the interaction between variables 1 and 3;
(7) $u_{23(jk)}$ is the interaction between variables 2 and 3;
(8) $u_{123(ijk)}$ is the second-order relationship between the three variables.

The purpose of modelling a three-way table would be to find the **unsaturated** model with fewest parameters that adequately predicts the observed frequencies. To assess whether some simpler model would fit a given table, particular parameters in the saturated model are set to zero and the reduced model is assessed for fit. However, it is important to note that, in general, attention must be restricted to what are known as **hierarchical models**. These are such that whenever a higher-order effect is included in a model, the lower-order effects composed from variables in the higher effect are also included. For example, if terms u_{123} are included, so also must terms $u_{12}, u_{13}, u_{23}, u_1, u_2$ and u_3. Therefore, models such as

$$\ln F_{ijk} = u + u_{2(j)} + u_{3(k)} + u_{123(ijk)} \qquad (7.3)$$

are not permissible. (This restriction to hierarchical models arises from the constraints imposed by the maximum likelihood estimation procedures used in fitting log–linear models, details of which are too technical to be included in this text. In practice, the restriction is of little consequence since most tables can be described by a series of hierarchical models.)

Each model that can be derived from the saturated model for a three-dimensional table is equivalent to a particular hypothesis about the variables forming the table; the equivalence is illustrated in Display 7.12. Particular points to note about the material in this display are as follows:

1. The first three models are of no consequence in the analysis of a three-dimensional table. Model 4 is known as the **minimal** model for such a table.
2. The **fitted marginals** or 'bracket' notation is frequently employed to specify the series of models fitted when examining a multidimensional contingency table. The notation reflects the fact noted earlier that, when testing particular hypotheses about a multiway table (or fitting particular models), certain marginal totals of the estimated expected values are constrained to be equal to the corresponding marginals of the observed values. (This arises because of the form of the maximum likelihood equations.) The terms used to specify the model with the bracket notation are the marginals fixed by the model.

Display 7.12   Hierarchical models for a general three-dimensional contingency table

- A series of log–linear models for a three-way table is shown below:

Log–linear model	Bracket notation
1. $\ln F_{ijk} = u$	
2. $\ln F_{ijk} = u + u_{1(i)}$	[1]
3. $\ln F_{ijk} = u + u_{1(i)} + u_{2(j)}$	[1], [2]
4. $\ln F_{ijk} = u + u_{1(i)} + u_{2(j)} + u_{3(k)}$	[1], [2], [3],
5. $\ln F_{ijk} = u + u_{1(i)} + u_{2(j)} + u_{3(k)} + u_{12(ij)}$	[12], [3]
6. $\ln F_{ijk} = u + u_{1(i)} + u_{2(j)} + u_{3(k)} + u_{12(ij)} + u_{13(ik)}$	[12], [13]
7. $\ln F_{ijk} = u + u_{1(i)} + u_{2(j)} + u_{3(k)} + u_{12(ij)} + u_{13(ik)} + u_{23(jk)}$	[12], [13], [23]
8. $\ln Fijk = u + u_{1(i)} + u_{2(j)} + u_{3(k)} + u_{12(ij)} + u_{13(ik)} + u_{23(jk)} + u_{123(ijk)}$	[123]

- The hypotheses corresponding to each model are as follows:
  1. All frequencies are the same.
  2. Marginal totals for variable 2 and for variable 3 are equal.
  3. Marginal totals for variable 3 are equal. (Since the above three models do not allow the observed frequencies to reflect observed differences in the marginal totals of each variable, they are of no interest in the analysis of three-dimensional tables.)
  4. The variables are mutually independent.
  5. Variables 1 and 2 are associated and both are independent of variable 3.
  6. Variables 2 and 3 are conditionally independent given variable 1.
  7. There is no second-order relationship between the three variables.
- Model 8 of the saturated model for a three-dimensional table.

   To illustrate the use of log-linear models in practice a series of such models will be fitted to the suicide data given in Table 7.4. Details are given in Display 7.13. The aim of the procedure is to arrive at a model which gives an adequate fit to the observed data and, as shown in Display 7.13, differences in the likelihood ratio statistic for different models are used to assess whether models of increasing complexity (larger number of parameters) are needed.

Display 7.13 Log–linear models for suicide data

- The goodness-of-fit of a series of log–linear models is given below (variable 1 = method, variable 2 = age and variable 3 = sex):

Model	DF	LR Statistic	P
[1] [2] [3]	27	790.30	< 0.001
[12] [3]	17	520.41	< 0.001
[13] [2]	22	424.59	< 0.001
[23] [1]	25	658.88	< 0.001
[12] [13]	12	154.70	< 0.001
[12] [23]	15	389.00	< 0.001
[12] [13] [23]	10	14.90	0.14

- The difference in the likelihood ratio statistics can be used to compare models. For example, the mutual independence model

$$\ln F_{ijk} = u + u_{1(i)} + u_{2(j)} + u_{3(k)}$$

and the model which allows for an association between variables 1 and 2

$$\ln F_{ijk} = u + u_{1(i)} + u_{2(j)} + u_{3(k)} + u_{12(ij)}$$

have $X_L^2 = 790.30$ with 27 degrees of freedom, and $X_L^2 = 520.41$ with 17 degrees of freedom respectively. The hypothesis that the extra parameters in the more complex model are all zero, i.e. $H_0 : u_{12(ij)} = 0$ for all i and j ($H_0 : u_{12} = 0$ for short), is tested by the difference in the two likelihood ratio statistics, with degrees of freedom equal to the difference in the degrees of freedom of each model. Here this gives the value $X_L^2 = 790.30 - 520.41 = 269.89$ with $27 - 17 = 10$ degrees of freedom. The result is highly significant and the second model provides a significantly improved fit compared with that provided by the first.
- A useful way of judging a series of log–linear models is via an analogue of the square of the multiple correlation coefficient as used in multiple regression (see Chapter 6). The measure L is defined as

$$L = \frac{X_L^2 \text{ baseline model} - X_L^2 \text{ model of interest}}{X_L^2 \text{ baseline model}}.$$

- L lies in the range $(0, 1)$ and indicates the percentage improvement in goodness-of-fit of the model being tested over the base model.
- The choice of baseline model is not fixed. It will often be the mutual independence model, but it could be the simpler of two models to be compared.

- For comparing the mutual independence and no second-order relationship models on the suicide data, L is

$$L = \frac{790.30 - 14.90}{790.30} = 98.1\%.$$

The results given in Display 7.13 demonstrate that only model 7 provides an adequate fit for the suicide data. This model states that the association between age and method of suicide is the same for males and females, and that the association between sex and method is the same for all age groups. The parameter estimates (and the ratio of the estimates to their standard errors) for the fitted model are given in Display 7.14. The estimated 'main effects' parameters are not of great interest; their values simply reflect differences between the marginal totals of the categories of each variable. For example, the largest effect for method ($\hat{u}_{1(3)} = 1.55$) arises only because more people use hanging, suffocating or drowning as a method of suicide than the other five possibilities. The estimated interaction parameters are of more interest, particularly those for age and method and for sex and method. For example, the latter reflect that males use 'solid' and 'jump' less and women use them more than if sex was independent of method. The reverse is true for 'gas' and 'gun'.

Display 7.14 Parameter estimates in the final model selected for suicide data

- The final model derived for the suicide data is that of no second-order relationship among the three variables, i.e.

$$\ln F_{ijk} = u + u_{1(i)} + u_{2(j)} + u_{3(k)} + u_{12(ij)} + u_{13(ik)} + u_{23(jk)}.$$

- The estimated main effect parameters are as follows:

Variable	Parameter	Category	Estimate	Ratio of estimate to its SE
Method	$u_{1(1)}$	Solid	1.33	34.45
	$u_{1(2)}$	Gas	−1.27	−11.75
	$u_{1(3)}$	Hang	1.55	41.90
	$u_{1(4)}$	Gun	−0.64	−8.28
	$u_{1(5)}$	Jump	−0.42	−7.00
	$u_{1(6)}$	Other	−0.55	−7.64
Age	$u_{2(1)}$	10–40	0.25	7.23
	$u_{2(2)}$	41–70	0.56	16.77
	$u_{2(3)}$	> 70	−0.81	−16.23
Sex	$u_{3(1)}$	male	0.41	15.33
	$u_{3(2)}$	female	−0.41	−15.33

(Note that the parameter estimates for each variable sum to zero.)

- The estimated interaction parameters for method and age are as follows:

Age (years)	Method					
	Solid	Gas	Hanging	Gun	Jump	Other
10–40	−0.02	0.52	−0.61	−0.03	−0.20	0.34
41–70	−0.05	0.11	0.07	0.09	−0.25	0.03
> 70	0.07	−0.63	0.54	−0.06	0.45	−0.37

- The ratios of the estimated values to their standard errors are as follows:

Age (years)	Method					
	Solid	Gas	Hanging	Gun	Jump	Other
10–40	−0.48	4.93	−14.18	−0.35	−2.52	4.18
41–70	−1.09	1.04	1.69	1.27	−3.38	0.36
> 70	1.10	−3.57	9.57	−0.62	4.84	−2.95

- The estimated interaction parameters for method and sex are as follows:

Sex	Method					
	Solid	Gas	Hanging	Gun	Jump	Other
Male	−0.42	0.43	0.01	0.58	−0.48	−0.12
Female	0.42	−0.43	−0.01	−0.58	0.48	0.12

- The ratios of the estimated values to their standard errors are as follows:

Sex	Method					
	Solid	Gas	Hanging	Gun	Jump	Other
Male	−13.07	5.32	0.32	8.44	−8.58	−2.19
Female	13.07	−5.32	−0.32	−8.44	8.58	2.19

- The estimated interaction parameters for age and sex are as follows:

Sex	Age		
	10–40	41–70	> 70
Male	0.27	−0.09	−0.18
Female	−0.27	0.09	0.18

- The ratios of the estimated values to their standard errors are as follows:

Sex	Age		
	10–40	41–70	> 70
Male	11.48	–4.51	–6.83
Female	–11.48	4.51	6.83

As always when fitting models to observed data, it is essential to examine the fit in more detail than is provided by a single goodness-of-fit statistic such as the likelihood ratio criterion. With log–linear models, differences between the observed and estimated expected frequencies form the basis for this more detailed examination as described in Display 7.15. The residuals for the final model selected for the suicide data are also given in Display 7.15. All of them are small, suggesting that the chosen model does give an adequate representation of the observed frequencies.

Display 7.15 Residuals in the analysis of multidimensional contingency tables

- Differences between the observed (O) and estimated expected values under an assumed model (E) can be used as an aid in judging a model's fit.
- Generally, the following standardized residual is used:

$$\frac{O - E}{\sqrt{E}}.$$

- For the final model chosen for the suicide data, these are given by the following:

Age (years)	Sex	Method					
		1	2	3	4	5	6
10–40	Male	–0.6	–0.2	0.8	–0.1	–0.2	0.2
41–70	Male	1.0	0.5	–0.8	0.1	–0.0	–0.3
> 70	Male	–0.7	–0.9	0.4	–0.1	0.4	0.2
10–40	Female	0.8	0.5	–1.5	0.4	0.3	–0.3
41–70	Female	–0.9	–1.1	1.1	-0.3	0.0	0.4
> 70	Female	0.6	1.8	-0.5	0.1	–0.3	–0.2

7.5 Logistic regression

In many multidimensional contingency tables (I am tempted to say in almost all), there is one variable of particular interest–and it is the effects of the remaining variables on this variable that need to be assessed. Situations in which the variable of primary interest is dichotomous are most common, and an example is provided by the data on depression in adolescents given in Table 7.3. Here the dependent variable is whether or not an individual suffers from high depression, and interest centres on assessing the effect of age, type and sex on this variable. The situation is analogous to that encountered in Chapter 6, where the effects of explanatory variables on a dependent variable were modelled by multiple regression. But here the dependent variable is *binary* rather than continuous, and the question arises: 'What is a suitable model now?' One possibility that springs to mind would be to consider modelling the probability p that a person has a high level of depression. In terms of the general model encountered in earlier chapters and in Display 7.11, i.e.

$$\text{observed response} = \text{expected response} + \text{error},$$

this probability would be the expected response, and the corresponding observed response would be the proportion of individuals in the sample with a high degree of depression. Therefore a possible model is

$$p = \beta_0 + \beta_1 \text{age} + \beta_2 \text{sex} + \beta_3 \text{type}$$

and

$$\text{observed response} = p + \text{error}.$$

Such a model could be fitted as described in Chapter 6, but there are a number of problems which make it essentially unsuitable for data such as those given in Table 7.3. These are as follows:

1. In multiple regression models the random disturbance terms are assumed to have a normal distribution. Such an assumption is clearly not realistic for dichotomous dependent variables.
2. It would be quite possible to arrive at estimates of the parameters in the model which led to fitted probabilities *outside* the range $(0,1)$.

It is clearly not very sensible to contemplate using a model which is known a priori to have serious disadvantages, and so an alternative approach must be employed. That most frequently adopted is the **linear logistic model**, or **logistic model** for short, in which the **logistic transformation** of p is modelled rather than modelling p directly. Details of this model are given in Display 7.16.

The logistic regression model will now be applied to the data in Table 7.3, beginning with a model with a single explanatory variable, namely sex. Details of fitting the model and its interpretation are given in Display 7.17. Note that the estimated regression parameter for sex is simply the odds ratio calculated from the 2×2 cross-classification of sex and depression.

Display 7.16 The logistic regression model

- The **logistic transformation** of a probability p is defined as follows:

$$\lambda = \ln \frac{p}{1-p}.$$

In other words, λ is the logarithm of an odds ratio.
- As p varies from 0 to 1, λ varies between $-\infty$ and ∞.
- The logistic regression model is a linear model for λ, i.e.

$$\lambda = \ln \frac{p}{1-p} = \beta_0 + \beta_1 x_1 + \beta_2 x_2 + \ldots + \beta_q x_q$$

where $x_1, x_2, \ldots, x_q$ are explanatory variables.
- Modelling the logistic transformation rather than the probability itself avoids problems with fitted values outside their permitted range.
- The parameters in the model are estimated by maximum likelihood (see Collett, 1991, for details).
- The parameters in the model give the change in the ln (odds) produced by a change of one unit in the corresponding explanatory variable, conditional on the remaining variables remaining constant.
- The model can be written directly in terms of the probability p in the following non-linear form:

$$p = \frac{\exp(\beta_0 + \beta_1 x_1 + \ldots + \beta_q x_q)}{1 + \exp(\beta_0 + \beta_1 x_1 + \ldots + \beta_q x_q)}.$$

Display 7.17 Fitting a logistic model to the adolescent depression data using sex as the only explanatory variable

- The model to be fitted is

$$\ln \left(\frac{p}{1-p} \right) = \beta_0 + \beta_1 \text{sex}$$

where p is the probability that an individual has a high degree of depression and sex is coded 1 for men and 2 for women.
- The parameter estimates obtained are

$$\hat{\beta}_0 = -0.784$$
$$\hat{\beta}_1 = 0.556.$$

- The fitted model can be written in the following form:

  (1) males : ln(estimated odds) $= -0.784 + 0.556 \times 1$

  (2) females : ln(estimated odds) $= -0.784 + 0.556 \times 2$.

- On subtraction this leads to:

$$\text{ln(estimated odds ratio)} = 0.556$$

  leading to an estimate of the odds ratio itself of $e^{0.556}$, i.e. 1.74.

- The standard error of $\hat{\beta}_1$ is 0.161, and so an approximate 95% confidence interval of the ln(odds ratio) is $0.556 \pm 2 \times 0.161$. Exponentiating these limits leads to the corresponding confidence interval for the odds ratio itself, namely (1.27, 2.39).

- The odds of an adolescent girl having a high degree of depression are between 1.27 and 2.39 times the equivalent odds for a teenage boy.

- In this simple case with a single explanatory variable, the odds ratio estimate derived from the logistic regression analysis is the same as would be obtained using the formulae in Display 7.6 applied to the 2×2 table obtained from the data in Table 7.3 by summing over age and type, i.e. the following table:

	Depression	
	Low	High
Male	298	136
Female	147	117

As with the multiple regression model considered in Chapter 6, when applying the logistic model interest often centres on identifying those variables most important in determining or explaining the response variable. Techniques similar to those described in Chapter 6, namely forward, backward and stepwise selection, are used, but the criterion for assessing whether or not a variable should be included in a model is now essentially the likelihood ratio statistic described in the previous section. The details of applying forward selection to the adolescent depression data are shown in Display 7.18. The results indicate that it is the sex of the adolescent that is most strongly related to suffering a high degree of depression, although type may have some small additional effect.

Display 7.18 Fitting a logistic regression model to the adolescent depression data using a stepwise procedure to select variables

- The stepwise procedure operates in an exactly analogous way to that described in Chapter 6 for multiple regression.

- The criterion used for entering and excluding variables is essentially the change in the likelihood ratio statistic as discussed in Display 7.13 in connection with log–linear models.

- Applying the procedure to the adolescent depression data results in the following steps:
    1. Sex is entered; the improvement in the likelihood ratio statistic is 11.875 which with a single degree of freedom has an associated P-value of 0.001. The likelihood ratio statistic for judging the fit of the model is 13.83 which with 10 degrees of freedom has an associated P-value of 0.181.
    2. Type is entered; the improvement in the likelihood ratio statistic is 3.174 with an associated P-value of 0.075. The likelihood ratio statistic for judging the fit of the model is 10.660 with nine degrees of freedom and a P-value of 0.30.

- It appears that sex has the greatest effect in predicting the degree of depression that an adolescent will suffer, although type may also have some small additional effect.
- Values of 1, 2 and 3 were used in the logistic regression for the three age groups (see Exercise 7.7 for an alternative approach).

7.6 Summary

1. The analysis of cross-classifications of three or more categorical variables can now be undertaken routinely using log–linear models.
2. The log–linear models fitted to multidimensional tables correspond to particular hypotheses about the variables forming the tables.
3. Expected values and parameters in log–linear models are estimated by maximum likelihood methods. In some cases the former consist of simple functions of particular marginal totals of observed frequencies. However, in many examples, the estimated frequencies have to be obtained by an iterative process.
4. The fit of a log–linear model is assessed by comparing the observed and estimated expected values under the model via the chi-squared statistic or, more commonly, the likelihood ratio statistic.
5. In a data set in which one of the categorical variables can be considered to be the response variable, logistic regression can be applied to investigate the effects of explanatory variables. The regression parameters in such models can be interpreted in terms of odds ratios.
6. Two useful references for detailed discussions of log–linear models and logistic regression are Everitt (1992) and Collett (1991).

Exercises

7.1 The data in Table 7.5 were obtained from a study of the relationship between car size and car accident injuries. Accidents were classified according to their type, severity and whether or not the driver was ejected. Using 'severity' as the response variable, derive and interpret a suitable logistic model for these counts.

Table 7.5 The effect of car weight, accident type and ejection of driver on the severity of accidents

Car weight	Driver ejected	Accident type	Number hurt severely	Number hurt not severely
Small	No	Collision	150	350
Small	No	Roll-over	112	60
Small	Yes	Collision	23	26
Small	Yes	Roll-over	80	19
Standard	No	Collision	1022	1878
Standard	No	Roll-over	404	148
Standard	Yes	Collision	161	111
Standard	Yes	Roll-over	265	22

7.2   The data below show the incidence of 'suicidal feelings' in samples of psychotic and neurotic patients. Calculate a confidence interval for the odds ratio. Does the incidence of suicidal feelings differ in the two diagnostic groups?

	Psychotics	Neurotics	Total
Suicidal feelings	2	6	8
No suicidal feelings	18	14	32

7.3   The data shown in Table 7.6 arise from a study in which a sample of 1008 people were asked to compare two detergents, brand M and brand X. In addition to stating their preference, the sample members provided information on previous use of brand M, the degree of softness of the water that they used and the temperature of the water. Use log–linear models to explore the associations between the four variables.

7.4   Examine the effects of previous use, degree of softness and temperature on brand preference for the data in Table 7.6 using logistic regression.

7.5   Show that the interaction parameter in the saturated log–linear model for a 2×2 table is related to the odds ratio of the table.

7.6   Explore further the adolescent depression data (Table 7.3) using logistic models which allow for possible interaction effects between the explanatory variables.

7.7   Fit a further logistic regression model to the adolescent depression data, recoding age group in terms of two dummy variables.

7.8   Show that the marginal totals of estimated expected values $E_{ij.}$, $E_{i.k}$ and $E_{.jk}$, corresponding to the no second-order relationship hypothesis for the suicide data, are equal to the corresponding marginal totals of the observed values.

Table 7.6 Cross-classification of a sample of 1008 consumers according to water softness, previous use of detergent brand M, water temperature and preference for brand M

Water softness	Brand preferred	Previous user of M		Not previous user	
		High temperature	Low temperature	High temperature	Low temperature
Soft	X	19	57	29	63
	M	29	49	27	53
Medium	X	23	47	33	66
	M	47	55	23	50
Hard	X	24	37	42	68
	M	43	52	30	42

Further reading

Bishop, Y.M.M., Fienberg, S.E. and Holland, P.W. (1975). *Discrete multivariate analysis.* MIT Press, Cambridge, MA.

Fienberg, S.E. (1980). *The analysis of cross-classified data* (2nd edn). MIT Press, Cambridge, MA.

Freeman, D.H. (1987). *Applied categorical data analysis.* Dekker, New York.

8

An introduction to the generalized linear model

8.1 Introduction

That (hopefully) ubiquitous creature 'the more observant reader' will have noticed that the models described in Displays 6.1 and 6.4 look similar in many respects to the models used in the analysis of variance (e.g. Displays 3.2 and 4.1). In fact it can now be revealed that the analysis of variance models used in Chapters 3 and 4 are *exactly* equivalent to the multiple regression model discussed in Chapter 6. More surprisingly perhaps, the log–linear and logistic regression models covered in the previous chapter can also be included in the same class of models that describe both analysis of variance and multiple regression. All these models, and many others not dealt with in this text, are special cases of what is known as the **generalized linear model** (GLM). During the last two decades GLMs have become of central importance in statistics since, as well as unifying a number of areas, they have provided a rich source of alternative models for analysing data. Psychologists should be familiar with at least the basic ideas behind such models and imparting such familiarity will be the main aim of this chapter. However, it is first necessary to clarify the distinction between **linear** and **non-linear** models.

8.2 Linear and non-linear models

Display 8.1 shows a number of models specifying the relationship between the expected value of a response variable and a number of explanatory variables. (The corresponding models for an observed response will include some random disturbance term.) The first three models in Display 8.1 are all **linear models**. This may appear odd to some readers, since two of the three models contain non-linear functions of the explanatory variables. The explanation is that the 'linear' in linear models refers to the parameters in the model, and not to the explanatory variables. **Non-linear models** proper (which are far more difficult to deal with than linear models) contain non-linear functions of the parameters. Models 4 and 5 in Display 8.1 are of this type. However, a distinction can be made between these two models since the first is an example of what can be termed **intrinsically non-linear models,** meaning that there is no transformation available that will convert them into linear form. However, model 5 in Display 8.1 can be converted into linear form simply by taking logarithms throughout

8.3 Analysis of variance and multiple regression models

In Chapter 3 the following model was introduced for a one-way design (see Table 3.3):

Display 8.1   Linear and non-linear models

- Linear models:

    (1) expected response $= \beta_0 + \beta_1 x_1 + \beta_2 x_2$

    (2) expected response $= \beta_0 + \beta_1 x + \beta_2 x^2$

    (3) expected response $= \beta_0 + \beta_1 x_1 + \beta_2 x_2 + \beta_3 x_1^2 + \beta_4 x_1 x_2$.

- Non-linear models:

    (4) expected response $= \beta_0 + \beta_1 e^{\beta_2 x_1} + \beta_3 e^{\beta_4 x_2}$

    (5) expected response $= \beta_0 x_1^{\beta_1} x_2^{\beta_2}$.

$$y_{ij} = \mu + \alpha_i + \epsilon_{ij}. \tag{8.1}$$

Without some constraints on the parameters, the model is overparameterized (see Chapter 3). The constraint adopted in Chapter 3 to overcome the problem was to require that

$$\sum_{i=1}^{k} \alpha_i = 0. \tag{8.2}$$

Consequently

$$\alpha_k = -\alpha_1 - \alpha_2 - \cdots - \alpha_{k-1}. \tag{8.3}$$

(Other constraints could be used to deal with the overparameterization problem; see Exercise 8.2.)

How can this model be put into an equivalent form to the multiple regression model given in Display 6.4? The answer is provided in Display 8.2, using an example where there are $k = 5$ groups. Display 8.3 uses the teaching styles data (see Table 3.1) to show how the multiple regression model in Display 8.2 can be used to find the relevant sums of squares in a one-way analysis of variance of the data. Note that the parameter estimates given in Display 8.3 are those to be expected when the model is as specified in eqns (8.1) and (8.2), with $\hat{\mu}$ being the overall mean of the arithmetic test scores, and the estimates of the α_i being simply the deviations of the corresponding group mean from the overall mean.

Moving on now to the two-way analysis of variance, the simplest way of illustrating the equivalence of the model given in Display 4.1 to the multiple regression model is to use an example in which each of the two factors has only two levels. Display 8.4 gives the details, and Display 8.5 gives a numerical example of performing a two-way analysis of variance for a balanced design using multiple regression. Notice that in this case the estimates of the parameters in the multiple regression model do not change when other 'explanatory' variables are added to the model. The explanatory variables for a balanced two-way design are orthogonal (uncorrelated). But now consider what

Display 8.2 The multiple regression model for a one-way design with five groups

- Introduce four variables, x_1, x_2, x_3 and x_4, defined below, to label the group to which an observation belongs.

	Group				
	1	2	3	4	5
x_1	1	0	0	0	−1
x_2	0	1	0	0	−1
x_3	0	0	1	0	−1
x_4	0	0	0	1	−1

- The usual one-way analysis of variance model for this situation is

$$y_{ij} = \mu + \alpha_i + \epsilon_{ij}$$

which, allowing for the constraint $\sum_{i=1}^{5} \alpha_i = 0$, can now be written as

$$y_{ij} = \mu + \alpha_1 x_1 + \alpha_2 x_2 + \alpha_3 x_3 + \alpha_4 x_4 + \epsilon_{ij}.$$

This is exactly the form of the multiple regression model given in Display 6.4.

Display 8.3 One-way analysis of variance of teaching styles data using a multiple regression approach

- Define four new variables as specified in Display 8.2.
- Regress the arithmetic score on x_1, x_2, x_3 and x_4.
- The analysis of variance table from the regression is as follows:

Source	SS	DF	MS	F
Regression	722.67	4	180.67	15.27
Residual	473.33	40	11.83	

- This is exactly the same as the one-way analysis of variance table given in Table 3.3.
- The estimates of the regression coefficients from the analysis are

$$\hat{\mu} = 21.00$$
$$\hat{\alpha}_1 = -1.33$$
$$\hat{\alpha}_2 = -2.67$$
$$\hat{\alpha}_3 = 6.44$$
$$\hat{\alpha}_4 = 2.44.$$

- The estimates of the α_i are simply the differences between each group mean and the grand mean.

happens when the multiple regression approach is used to carry out an analysis of variance of an unbalanced two-factor design, as shown in Display 8.6. In this case the order in which the explanatory variables enter the multiple regression model is of importance; both the sums of squares corresponding to each variable and the parameter estimates depend on what variables have already been included in the model. This highlights the point made previously in Chapter 4 that the analysis of unbalanced designs is not straightforward.

Display 8.4   Multiple regression model for a 2×2 factorial design (factor A at levels A1 and A2, factor B at levels B1 and B2)

- The usual model for a 2×2 design is

$$y_{ijk} = \mu + \alpha_i + \beta_j + \gamma_{ij} + \epsilon_{ijk}$$

(see Chapter 4).

- The usual constraints on the parameters introduced to deal with the over-parametrized model above are as follows:

$$\sum_{i=1}^{2} \alpha_i = 0$$

$$\sum_{j=1}^{2} \beta_j = 0$$

$$\sum_{i=1}^{2} \gamma_{ij} = 0$$

$$\sum_{j=1}^{2} \gamma_{ij} = 0.$$

- The constraints imply that the parameters in the model satisfy the following equations:

$$\alpha_1 = -\alpha_2$$
$$\beta_1 = -\beta_2$$
$$\gamma_{1j} = -\gamma_{2j}$$
$$\gamma_{i1} = -\gamma_{i2}.$$

- The last two equations imply the following:

$$\gamma_{12} = -\gamma_{11}$$
$$\gamma_{21} = -\gamma_{11}$$
$$\gamma_{22} = \gamma_{11}.$$

- In other words there is only one interaction parameter for this design.
- The model for the observations in each of the four cells of the design can now be written explicitly as follows:

	A1	A2
B1	$\mu + \alpha_1 + \beta_1 + \gamma_{11}$	$\mu - \alpha_1 + \beta_1 - \gamma_{11}$
B2	$\mu + \alpha_1 - \beta_1 - \gamma_{11}$	$\mu - \alpha_1 - \beta_1 + \gamma_{11}$

- Now define two variables x_1 and x_2 as follows:

  $x_1 = 1$ if first level of A, $x_1 = -1$ if second level of A;
  $x_2 = 1$ if first level of B, $x_2 = -1$ if second level of B.

- The model can now be written in multiple regression form as

$$y_{ijk} = \mu + \alpha_1 x_1 + \beta_1 x_2 + \gamma_{11} x_3 + \epsilon_{ijk}$$

where $x_3 = x_1 x_2$.

Display 8.5 The analysis of a balanced two-way design using multiple regression

- Consider the following data which have four observations in each cell:

	A1	A2
B1	23	22
	25	23
	27	21
	29	21
B2	26	37
	32	38
	30	40
	31	35

- Introduce the three variables x_1, x_2 and x_3 as defined in Display 8.4 and perform a multiple regression, firstly entering the observations in the order x_1, followed by x_2 followed by x_3. This gives the following series of results.

  Step 1: x_1 entered. The analysis of variance is as follows:

Source	SS	DF	MS
Regression	12.25	1	12.25
Residual	580.75	14	41.48

The regression sum of squares gives the between levels of A sum of squares that would be obtained in a two-way analysis of variance of these data. The estimates of the regression coefficients at this stage are

$$\hat{\mu} = 28.75$$
$$\hat{\alpha}_1 = -0.875.$$

Step 2: x_1 and x_1 entered. The analysis of variance is as follows.

Source	SS	DF	MS
Regression	392.50	2	196.25
Residual	200.50	13	15.42

The difference in the regression sum of squares between steps 1 and 2, i.e. 380.25, gives the sum of squares corresponding to the factor B that would be obtained in a conventional two-way analysis of variance of these data. The estimates of the regression coefficients this stage are

$$\hat{\mu} = 28.75$$
$$\hat{\alpha}_1 = -0.875$$
$$\hat{\beta}_1 = -4.875.$$

Step 3: x_1 and x_2 and x_3 entered. The analysis of variance is as follows:

Source	SS	DF	MS
Regression	536.50	3	178.83
Residual	56.50	12	4.71

The difference in the regression sum of squares between steps 2 and 3, i.e. 144.00, gives the sum of squares corresponding to the A × B interaction in a conventional analysis of variance of these data. The residual sum of squares in this final table corresponds to the error sum of squares in the usual analysis of variance table. The estimates of the regression coefficients at this final stage are

$$\hat{\mu} = 28.75$$
$$\hat{\alpha}_1 = -0.875$$
$$\hat{\beta}_1 = -4.875$$
$$\hat{\gamma}_{11} = 3.000.$$

- Note that the estimates of the regression coefficients do not change as extra variables are included in the model.

Display 8.6 The analysis of an unbalanced two-way design using multiple regression

- In this case consider the following data:

	A1	A2
B1	23	22
	25	23
	27	21
	29	21
	30	19
	27	23
	23	17
	25	
B2	26	37
	32	38
	30	40
	31	35
		39
		35
		38
		41
		32
		36
		40
		41
		38

- Three new variables x_1, x_2 and x_3 are defined as specified in Display 8.4 and used in a multiple regression of the data, firstly in the order x_1, followed by x_2 followed by x_3. This leads to the following series of results.

  Step 1: x_1 entered. The analysis of variance is as follows:

Source	SS	DF	MS
Regression	149.63	1	149.63
Residual	1505.87	30	50.19

The regression sum of squares gives the A sum of squares for an unbalanced design (see Chapter 4). The estimates of the regression coefficients at this stage are

$$\hat{\mu} = 29.567$$
$$\hat{\alpha}_1 = -2.233.$$

Step 2: x_1 and x_2 entered. The analysis of variance is as follows.

Source	SS	DF	MS
Regression	1180.86	2	590.42
Residual	476.65	29	16.37

The increase in the regression sum of squares, i.e. 1031.23, is the sum of squares due to B, conditional on A, i.e. B|A as encountered in Chapter 4. The estimates of the regression coefficients at this stage are

$$\hat{\mu} = 29.667$$
$$\hat{\alpha}_1 = -0.341$$
$$\hat{\beta}_1 = -5.977.$$

Step 3: x_1 and x_2 and x_3 entered. The analysis of variance is as follows:

Source	SS	DF	MS
Regression	1474.25	3	491.42
Residual	181.25	28	6.47

The increase in the regression sum of squares, i.e. 293.39, is the sum of squares due to the interaction of A and B, conditional on A and B, i.e. AB|A,B. The estimates of the regression coefficients at this stage are

$$\hat{\mu} = 28.606$$
$$\hat{\alpha}_1 = -0.667$$
$$\hat{\beta}_1 = -5.115$$
$$\hat{\gamma}_{11} = 3.302.$$

- Now enter the variables in the order x_2 followed by x_1 (adding x_3 after x_1 and x_2 will give the same results as step 3 above):

Step 1: x_2 entered. The analysis of variance is as follows:

Source	SS	DF	MS
Regression	1177.70	1	1177.70
Residual	477.80	30	15.93

The regression sum of squares gives the B sum of squares for an unbalanced design. The estimates of the regression coefficients at this stage are

$$\hat{\mu} = 29.745$$
$$\hat{\beta}_1 = -6.078.$$

Step 2: x_2 and x_1 entered. The analysis of variance is as follows.

Source	SS	DF	MS
Regression	1180.85	2	590.42
Residual	474.65	29	16.37

The increase in the regression sum of squares, i.e. 3.15, gives the sum of squares of A conditional on B, i.e. A|B. The estimates of the regression coefficients are

$$\hat{\mu} = 29.667$$
$$\hat{\alpha}_1 = -0.341$$
$$\hat{\beta}_1 = -5.977.$$

8.4   Link functions and the generalized linear model

The models used in analysis of variance and multiple regression are equivalent versions of a linear model in which an observed response is expressed as a linear function of explanatory variables plus some random disturbance term, often referred to as the 'error' even though in many cases it may not have anything to do with measurement error. Therefore the general form of such models, as outlined in several previous chapters, is

$$\text{observed response} = \text{expected response} + \text{error} \qquad (8.4)$$
$$\text{expected response} = \text{linear function of explanatory variables.} \qquad (8.5)$$

Specification of the model is completed by assuming some specific distribution for the error terms. In the case of analysis of variance and multiple regression models, for example, the assumed distribution is the normal with mean zero and a constant variance σ^2.

Now consider the log–linear model and the logistic regression model introduced in the previous chapter. How can those models be put into a similar form to the models used in the analysis of variance and multiple regression? The answer is, by a relatively simple adjustment of the equation given above that allows some **transformation** of the expected response to be modelled as a linear function of explanatory variables, i.e. by introducing a model of the form

$$\text{observed response} = \text{expected response} + \text{error} \qquad (8.6)$$
$$f(\text{expected response}) = \text{linear function of explanatory variables} \qquad (8.7)$$

where f represents some suitable transformation. In the context of the generalized linear model, f is known as a **link function**. By also allowing the error terms to have distributions other than the normal, both log–linear models and logistic regression can be included in the same framework as analysis of variance and multiple regression models. Details are given in Display 8.7.

Display 8.7   Link functions

- The generalized linear model can be formulated in very general terms as

    observed response = expected response + error

    f(expected response) = linear function of explanatory variables.

- A particular model is selected by specifying the link function f and the appropriate distribution of the error terms.
- In the analysis of variance and multiple regression, the appropriate link function f is simply an identity function, i.e. no transformation of the expected response is made, and the error distribution is assumed to be normal with mean zero and variance σ^2.
- In the analysis of multiway tables by log–linear models, the expected response is a frequency, the link function f is logarithmic and the error distribution may be **Poisson** or **multinomial** (see Appendix A).
- In the analysis of a dichotomous response variable using logistic regression, the expected response is a probability, the link function f is logistic and the error distribution is **binomial** (see Appendix A).
- Many other models can be included in the general framework (McCullagh and Nelder 1989).

The generalized linear model allowing a variety of link functions and corresponding error distributions was first suggested by Nelder and Wedderburn (1972). Such a model is fitted to data using a general maximum likelihood approach, details of which are outside the scope of this text (but can be found in, for example, McCullagh and Nelder, 1989,). Apart from the unifying perspective of the generalized linear model, its main advantage is that it provides opportunities to carry out analyses that make more realistic assumptions about particular data sets than the normality assumption made explicitly or implicitly in the past.

8.5 Summary

1. The generalized linear model unifies many seemingly different models, including those used in analysis of variance, multiple regression and the analysis of multidimensional contingency tables.
2. Software based upon the generalized linear model has been developed that enables a far more flexible approach to be adopted to the modelling of data. An example is the GLIM package (see Further reading below).

Exercises

8.1 Using a multiple regression approach on the survival time data given in Table 4.1, reproduce the analysis of variance table shown in Table 4.5.

8.2 As mentioned in Chapter 3, analysis of variance models are usually presented in overparametrized form. For example, in a one-way analysis of variance, the constraint $\sum_{i=1}^{k} \alpha_i = 0$ is often introduced to overcome the problem. However, the over-parametrization in the one-way analysis of variance model can also be dealt with by setting one of the α_i equal to zero. Carry out a multiple regression analysis of the teaching styles data in Table 3.1 which is equivalent to applying the analysis of variance model with $\alpha_5 = 0$. In terms of group means, what are the parameter estimates in this case?

Further reading

Aitkin, M., Anderson, D., Francis, B. and Hinde, J. (1989). *Statistical modelling in GLIM.* Oxford University Press.

Thompson, R. and Baker, R.J. (1981). Composite link functions in generalized linear models. *Applied Statistics*, 30, 125–31.

9
Distribution-free, computer-intensive methods

9.1 Introduction

The statistical methods discussed in the previous chapters make inferences about a population based on the assumption that the error terms in an assumed model for the data are random variables with a particular type of distribution, in many cases a normal distribution. The inferences made by such an approach are generally about parameters characterizing the assumed distributional types; they are **parametric inferences**. Analysis of variance methods, for example, lead to inferences about the means of assumed normal distributions.

Of course, an assumption that samples come from a specific distribution type may be wrong, and although inferences based on, say, an assumed normal distribution are often **robust** even if the assumption is incorrect, this is not always so. Consequently a large number of techniques have been developed that can be applied to data arising from populations having any of a wide class of distributions which need only be specified in broad terms, for example as being continuous, symmetrical etc. Such techniques are usually labelled as either **non-parametric** or **distribution-free**; the latter term will be used in this chapter.

Distribution-free methods are most useful in the following particular circumstances:

(1) when the sample size is small and therefore evidence for any distributional assumption is not available empirically;
(2) when the observations simply specify order, ranks or categories;
(3) when there is considerable doubt about the appropriateness of the distributional assumptions of a parametric test.

Distribution-free tests are usually introduced in introductory statistics courses as alternatives to well-known parametric methods, such as the *t*-test, for use when data are non-normal. Accounts of the many distribution-free tests available are given by, for example, Meddis (1984) and Sprent (1993). The purpose of this chapter is not to duplicate this material and give a lengthy list of the tests available for many different situations. Instead, the aim is to illustrate a more general distribution-free approach, namely that involving **computationally intensive techniques**. Nevertheless, one well-known distribution-free method, the **Wilcoxon–Mann–Whitney test**, is a useful starting point for the general discussion that will come later.

9.2   The Wilcoxon–Mann–Whitney test

Firstly the question of 'what's in a name' should be dealt with. The literature refers to equivalent tests formulated in different ways as the **Wilcoxon rank sum test** and the **Mann–Whitney test**. The two names arise because the formulations were developed independently by Wilcoxon (1945) and by Mann and Whitney (1947). Both were intended as distribution-free alternatives to the independent samples t-test. The main points to remember about the Wilcoxon–Mann–Whitney test are the following:

1. The null hypothesis to be tested is that the two populations being compared have identical distributions.
2. The alternative hypothesis is that the population distributions differ in location (i.e. mean or median).
3. Samples of observations are available from each of the two populations to be compared.
4. The test is based on a joint ranking of observations from the two samples.
5. The test statistic is the sum of the ranks associated with one sample (the lower of the two sums is generally used).

If both samples come from the same population (which may be of any continuous form and need not be symmetric), a mixture of low, medium and high ranks is to be expected in each. However, if the alternative hypothesis is true, one of the samples would be expected to have lower ranks than the other. P-values are available from tables for small samples. Alternatively, the large-sample approximation described later (Display 9.3) can be used. (The distribution of the test statistic under the null hypothesis can be found using a **permutational** approach; this will be discussed further in the next section.)

The two data sets given in Display 9.1 will be used to illustrate the application of the Wilcoxon–Mann–Whitney test, in particular the two methods of deriving P-values mentioned above. The first of these is taken from a study of organization in the memory of mildly retarded children attending a special school. A bidirectional subjective organization measure (SO2) was used to assess the amount of intertrial consistency in a memory task given to children from two groups, one of which had received a considerable amount of training in sorting tasks. The question of interest here is whether there is evidence of an increase in the organization in the group which had received training. (More details of the study are given by Robertson, 1991.) The details of the application of the Wilcoxon–Mann–Whitney test to these data are given in Display 9.2. The conclusion reached from the data is that the two groups do differ with respect to their SO2 scores.

The second data set in Display 9.1 consists of the times in seconds taken by the children in two experimenal groups to construct a pattern from nine coloured blocks taken from the Wechsler Intelligence Scale for Children (WISC). The two groups were given different instructions for the task. The 'row group' were told to start with a row of three blocks, and the 'corner group' were told to start with a corner of three blocks. Box plots of the observations for each group are shown in Fig. 9.1. There is some evidence of an outlier in the row group and of considerable skewness in the corner group. A t-test applied to the data gives a P-value of 0.03; however, since the box plots indicate that the assumptions of a *t*-test are not valid here, it is of interest to compare this result with that obtained from the application of the Wilcoxon–Mann–Whitney test. Details of the results from the latter, using a large-sample approximation to derive the *P*-value, are given in Display 9.3. The calculated *z*-value is significant beyond the 5% level, implying that the times taken in the two groups differ.

Display 9.1 Two data sets

- Data from a study of organization in the memory of mildly retarded children (SO2 scores)

  Training group: 0.35, 0.40, 0.41, 0.46, 0.49
  No training group: 0.33, 0.34, 0.35, 0.37, 0.39

- WISC blocks data (times to completion (seconds))

  Row group: 675, 510, 490, 850, 317, 464, 525, 298, 491, 196, 268, 372, 370, 739, 430, 410
  Corner group: 342, 222, 219, 513, 295, 285, 408, 543, 298, 494, 317, 407, 290, 301, 325, 360

Display 9.2 Application of the Wilcoxon–Mann–Whitney test to the SO2 scores of two groups of children

- The observations are first jointly ranked and the smaller of the sum of the ranks in the two samples is used as the test statistic.
- The ranked observations, with those in the training group labelled T, are as follows:

Observation	Rank
0.33	1
0.34	2
0.35 (T)	3
0.35	4
0.37	5
0.39	6
0.40 (T)	7
0.41 (T)	8
0.45 (T)	9
0.49 (T)	10

- The sum of the ranks associated with the training group observations is 37, and that associated with the no training group is 18.
- The significance of the results is judged using appropriate tables (e.g. Table VI of Sprent, 1993). Here *S* is significant beyond the 5% value and a difference between the two groups can be claimed.

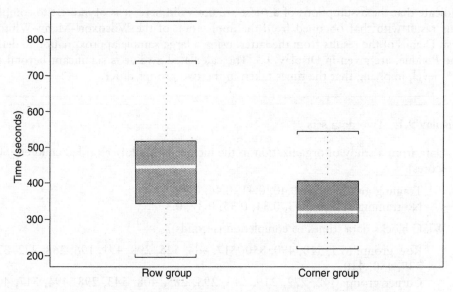

Fig. 9.1 Boxplots of WISC data.

Display 9.3 Large-sample procedure for the Wilcoxon–Mann–Whitney test

- When the two sample sizes (n_1, n_2) exceed 15, a normal approximation can be used.
- Under the null hypothesis, if S is the smaller of S_1 and S_2, where S_1 is the sum of the ranks in the first group and S_2 the corresponding sum in the second group, then

$$Z = \frac{S + 0.5 - 0.5 n_1 n_2}{(n_1 n_2 (n_1 + n_2 + 1)/12)^{1/2}}$$

has approximately a standard normal distribution.

- The ordered WISC data are as follows:

Rank	Observation	Group
1	196	1
2	219	2
4	222	2
5	268	1
6	285	2
7	295	2
8.5	298	1
8.5	298	2
10	301	2
11.5	317	1
11.5	317	2

13	325	2
14	342	2
15	360	2
16	370	1
17	372	1
18	407	2
19	408	2
20	410	1
21	430	1
22	464	1
23	490	2
24	491	1
25	494	2
26	510	2
27	513	2
28	525	1
29	543	2
30	675	2
31	739	1
32	850	2

- 'Tied' observations are given the average of the ranks that they would have occupied.
- For the WISC data $S = 184$, and z is calculated as

$$z = \frac{184 + 0.5 - 0.5 \times 16 \times 16}{[16 \times 16(16 + 16 + 1)/12]^{1/2}} = 2.12.$$

Before the advent of high-speed personal computers, significance levels for the Mann–Whitney test for relatively small sample sizes were always obtained from specialized tables (e.g. Tables V and VI in Sprent (1993)). The approximation illustrated in Display 9.3 could be used for larger sample sizes. Both methods have now largely been superseded by the development of appropriate software that implements the approach described in the next section.

The *efficiency* of the Wilcoxon–Mann–Whitney test is 95.5% relative to an independent samples t-test when the populations have normal distributions. In other words, under ideal conditions for the t-test, the Wilcoxon test will require about 5% more observations than the t-test to achieve the same power.

9.3 Permutation tests

The Wilcoxon–Mann–Whitney test described in the previous section is a simple example of a general class of tests known as either **permutation** or **randomization** tests. Such procedures were first introduced in the 1930s by Fisher and Pitman, but initially they were largely of theoretical rather than practical interest because of the lack of the computer technology needed to undertake the extensive computation often needed in their application. However, with each increase in computer speed and power, the permutation approach is being applied to a wider and wider variety of problems, and with today's more powerful generation of personal computers, it is often faster to calculate a *P*-value for an exact permutation test than to look up an asymptotic approximation in a book of tables. Additionally, the statistician (or the psychologist!) is not limited by the availability of tables, but is free to choose a test statistic exactly matched to testing a particular null hypothesis against a particular alternative. Significance levels are then, so to speak, 'computed on the fly' (Good 1994). The stages in a general permutation test are as follows:

1. Choose a test statistic *S*.
2. Compute *S* for the original set of observations.
3. Obtain the **permutation distribution** of *S* by repeatedly rearranging the observations. When two or more samples are involved (for example when assessing the difference between groups), all the observations are combined into a single large sample before they are rearranged.
4. For a chosen significance level α obtain the upper α-percentage point of the permutational distribution and accept or reject the null hypothesis according to whether the value of *S* calculated for the orginal observations is smaller or larger than this value. The resultant *P*-value is often referred to as **exact**.

To illustrate the application of a permutation test, consider a situation involving two treatments in which three observations of some dependent variable of interest are made under each treatment. Suppose that the observed values are as follows:

Treatment 1: 121, 118, 110
Treatment 2: 34, 22, 12.

The null hypothesis is that there is no difference between the treatments in their effect on the dependent variable. The alternative is that the first treatment results in higher values of the dependent variable. (The author is aware that the result in this case is pretty clear without any test!)

The first step in a permutation test is to choose a test statistic that discriminates between the hypothesis and the alternative. An obvious candidate is the sum of the observations for the first treatment group. If the alternative hypothesis is true, this sum ought to be larger than the sum of the observations in the second treatment group. If the null hypothesis is true, then the sum of the observations in each group should be approximately the same. One sum might be smaller or larger than the other by chance, but the two should not be very different.

The value of the chosen test statistic for the observed values is $121 + 118 + 110 = 349$. To generate the necessary permutation distribution, remember that under the null hypothesis the labels 'treatment 1' and 'treatment 2' provide no information about the test statistic, as the observations are expected to have almost the same values in each of the two treatment groups. Consequently, to permute the observations, simply reassign the six labels, three ' treatment 1 ' and three 'treatment 2', to the six observations; for example, treatment 1, 121, 118, 34, treatment 2, 110, 12, 22 and so on. Repeat the process until all the possible 20 distinct arrangements have been tabulated as shown in Table 9.1.

Table 9.1 Permutation distribution of example with three observations in each group

	First group			Second group			Sum
1.	121	118	110	34	22	12	349
2.	121	118	34	110	22	12	273
3.	121	110	34	118	22	12	265
4.	118	110	34	121	22	12	262
5.	121	118	22	110	34	12	261
6.	121	110	22	118	34	12	253
7.	121	118	12	110	34	22	251
8.	118	110	22	121	34	12	250
9.	121	110	12	118	34	22	243
10.	118	110	12	121	34	22	240
11.	121	34	22	118	110	12	177
12.	118	34	22	121	110	12	174
13.	121	34	12	118	110	22	167
14.	110	34	22	121	118	12	166
15.	118	34	12	121	110	22	164
16.	110	34	12	121	118	22	156
17.	121	22	12	118	110	34	155
18.	118	22	12	121	110	34	152
19.	110	22	12	121	118	34	144
20.	34	22	12	121	118	110	68

From the results given in Table 9.1 it is seen that the sum of the observations in the original treatment 1 group, i.e. 349, is equalled only once and never exceeded in the distinct random relabellings. If chance alone is operating, then such an extreme value has a 1 in 20 chance of occurring, i.e. 5%. Therefore at the conventional 0.05 significance level, the test leads to the rejection of the null hypothesis in favour of the alternative.

The Wilcoxon–Mann–Whitney test described in the previous section is also an example of a permutation test, but one applied to the ranks of the observations rather than their actual values. Originally the advantage of this procedure was that, since ranks always take the same values (1, 2 and so forth), previously tabulated distributions could be used to derive P-values, at least for small samples. Consequently lengthy computations were avoided. However, it is now relatively simple to calculate the required permutation distribution directly as shown in Display 9.4. As can be seen, this leads to an exact P-value for the test of a group difference on the SO2 scores of 0.028.

An advantage of the use of ranks is that it diminishes the effects of outliers. However, there is a disadvantage, and that is a loss of power, i.e. a diminished probability of detecting a real difference between the populations under investigation. In general, however, this loss of power is not great; for example, it is about 5% for the Wilcoxon–Mann–Whitney test.

Tests which lead to exact P-values have had great success in the analysis of categorical data, in particular in the analysis of contingency tables in which many of the

Display 9.4   Permutational distribution for the Wilcoxon–Mann–Whitney test statistic applied to SO2 scores

- There are a total of 252 possible permutations of pupils to groups (i.e. $\binom{10}{5}$).
- The distribution of the sum S of the ranks in the training group for all possible 252 permutations is as follows:

S	15	16	17	18	19	20	21	22	23	24	25	26	27
f	1	1	2	3	5	7	9	11	14	16	18	19	20

S	28	29	30	31	32	33	34	35	36	37	38	39	40
f	20	19	18	16	14	11	9	7	5	3	2	1	1

- Thus, for example, there is one arrangement where the ranks sum to 15, one where they sum to 16, two where they sum to 17 etc.
- From this distribution we can determine the probability of finding a value of the sum of ranks equal to or greater than the observed value of 37, if the null hypothesis is true:

$$P(S \geq 37) = \frac{3 + 2 + 1 + 1}{252} = 0.028.$$

frequencies are rather small. Such values cause problems for the usual chi-squared test (see Chapter 7) because the chi-squared distribution with $(r-1)(c-1)$ degrees of freedom is only an approximation to the distribution of the test statistic under the null hypothesis of independence, and this approximation is notoriously inexact for small and unevenly distribution samples. (This is the reason for the widely quoted and often used, but essentially arbitrary, 'rule' that estimated expected values must all be greater than 5 for the chi-squared test to be valid.)

An obvious answer to the problem would be the development of an appropriate permutation test, but until recently the computational effort required has prevented any real progress. However, in the last 5 years algorithms have been constructed and software developed which allow the routine calculation of exact P-values for sparse contingency tables. Details of the algorithm are well outside the level of this text, but are available for the keen and mathematically well-equipped reader in Mehta and Patel (1983). However, it is of some interest to compare the application of exact procedures with the usual chi-squared test applied to a contingency table. Consider, for example, the following 3×9 contingency table:

Row category	Column category								
	1	2	3	4	5	6	7	8	9
1	0	7	0	0	0	0	0	1	1
2	1	1	1	1	1	1	1	0	0
3	0	8	0	0	0	0	0	0	0

The chi-squared test statistic for this table takes a value of 22.9 with 16 degrees of freedom. The associated *P*-value is 0.1342. However, the exact *P*-value, obtained by a permutational approach, is 0.0013. The exact analysis suggests strongly that the row and column classification are not independent. The asymptotic analysis fails to show this relationship.

Perhaps a more interesting example is provided by the table below, presented in the case of *US versus Lansdowne Swim Club*, as an example of racial discrimination at the club. Analysed in the usual way by the Pearson chi-squared statistic, the results are statistically significant. The goverment, however, lost the case, because of applying the statistic when the expected count in two cells was less than five—the defendant argued that the software used to analyse the date printed out a warning that the chi-squared test might not be valid. An exact test would have settled the question—the associated *P*-value is less than 0.000001.

Racial discrimination at the Lansdowne Swimming Club?

	Black applicants	White applicants
Accepted for membership	1	379
Rejected for membership	5	0
Total applicants	6	379

9.4 The bootstrap

The **bootstrap** is a data-based method for statistical inference. Its introduction into statistics is relatively recent since the method is computationally intensive. According to Efron and Tibshirani (1993), the term 'bootstrap' derives from the phrase 'to pull oneself up by one's bootstraps', widely considered to be based on the eighteenth century adventures of Baron Munchausen by Rudolph Erich Raspe. (The relevant adventure is one where the Baron had fallen into the bottom of a deep lake. Just when it looked as if all was lost, he thought he could pick himself up by his own bootstraps.)

The bootstrap looks like the permutational approach in many respects, requires a minimal number of assumptions for its applications and derives critical values for testing and constructing confidence intervals from the data at hand. The stages in the bootstrap approach are as follows:

1. Choose a test statistic *S*.
2. Calculate *S* for the original set of observations.
3. Obtain the **bootstrap distribution** of *S* by repeatedly resampling from the observations. In the multigroup situation samples are not combined, but are resampled separately. Sampling is *with* replacement.
4. Obtain the upper α-percentage point of the bootstrap distribution and accept or reject the null hypothesis according to whether *S* for the original observations is smaller or larger than this value.
5. Alternatively, construct a confidence interval for the test statistic using the bootstrap distribution (see the example given later).

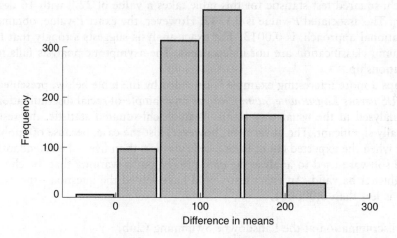

Fig. 9.2 Histogram of mean differences for 1000 bootstrap samples.

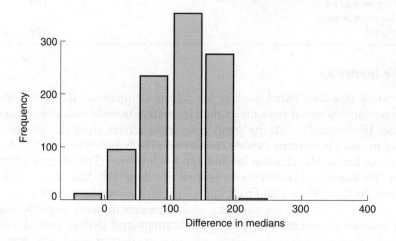

Fig. 9.3 Histogram of median differences for 1000 bootstrap samples.

Unlike a permutation test, the bootstrap does not provide exact *P*-values. In addition, it is generally less powerful than a permutation test. However, it may be possible to use a bootstrap procedure when no other statistical method is applicable. Full details of the bootstrap, including many fascinating examples of its application, are given by Efron and Tibshirani (1993). Here, we merely illustrate its use in the construction of confidence intervals for the difference in means and in medians of the groups involved in the WISC data in Display 9.1. The results are summarized in Display 9.5. The confidence interval for the mean difference obtained using the bootstrap is seen to be narrower than the corresponding interval obtained conventionally with the t statistic. Histograms of the mean and median differences obtained from the bootstrap samples are shown in Figs 9.2 and 9.3.

Display 9.5 Construction of confidence intervals for the WISC data in Display 9.1 using the bootstrap

- The procedure is based on drawing random samples of 16 observations with replacement from each of the row and corner groups.
- The random samples are found by labelling the observations in each group with the integers 1, 2, ..., 16 and selecting random samples of these integers (with replacement) using an appropriate computer algorithm (these are generally available in most statistical software packages).
- The mean difference or median difference is calculated for each bootstrap sample.
- In this study, 1000 bootstrap samples were taken from each group, resulting in 1000 differences in means and 1000 differences in medians.
- The first five bootstrap samples in terms of the integers 1, 2, ..., 16, were as follows:

$$1, 2, 2, 6, 7, 7, 8, 9, 11, 11, 13, 13, 14, 15, 16, 16$$
$$1, 2, 3, 3, 5, 6, 7, 10, 11, 11, 12, 13, 14, 15, 16$$
$$1, 1, 3, 3, 3, 4, 5, 6, 8, 8, 9, 14, 14, 15, 16, 16$$
$$1, 2, 4, 4, 4, 5, 5, 5, 6, 10, 11, 11, 12, 12, 12, 14$$
$$1, 2, 3, 3, 5, 5, 6, 6, 9, 9, 12, 13, 14, 15, 15, 16.$$

- A rough 95% confidence interval can be derived by taking the 25th and 975th largest of the 1000 replicates. This leads to the following confidence intervals:

  mean   (16.06, 207.81)
  median (7.5, 193.0).

- The confidence interval for the mean difference derived in the usual way, assuming normality of the population distributions and homogeneity of variance, is (11.65, 211.59).

9.5 Summary

1. Permutation tests and the bootstrap offer alternative approaches to making distribution-free inferences. Both methods are computationally intensive.
2. This chapter has given only a brief account of this increasingly important area of modern applied statistics. Comprehensive accounts are given by Good (1994) and Efron and Tibshirani (1993).

Exercises

9.1 Reanalyse the SO2 scores using a permutational approach, taking as the test statistic the sum of the scores in the group that had received training.

9.2 Investigate how the bootstrap confidence intervals for both the mean and median differences in the WISC data change with the size of the bootstrap sample.

9.3 Use the bootstrap approach to produce an approximate 95% confidence interval for the ratio of the two population variances of the WISC data given in Display 9.1. Investigate how the confidence interval changes with the number of bootstrap samples used.

Further reading

Edgington, E.S. (1987). *Randomization tests* (2nd edn). Dekker, New York.

Efron, B. and Gong, G. (1983). A leisurely look at the bootstrap, the jackknife and cross-validation. *American Statistician*, 37, 36–48.

Norren, E.W. (1989). *Computer intensive methods for testing hypotheses: an introduction*. Wiley, New York.

10

Multivariate analysis I: the analysis of covariances and correlations (principal components and exploratory factor analysis)

10.1 Introduction

In Chapter 1 attention was drawn to the existence of two relatively separate disciplines of scientific psychology: in one the psychologist tests general principles about human and animal behaviour by performing experiments, and in the other the investigator's interest lies in describing and interpreting individual differences using data collected in questionnaire surveys or interview studies, for example. The statistical techniques described in earlier chapters are largely the armoury of the experimental psychologist. In this chapter and in Chapters 11 and 12, methods of most use to what can loosely be called the observational psychologist will be described. The latter invariably collects data that are multivariate, with the variables not generally divided into dependent and independent as in previous chapters (with the exception of Chapter 7), instead all variables are considered on the same footing.

The discussion of multivariate data in this chapter centres around methods which aim to simplify the data in particular ways in an attempt to learn more about their structure and to uncover any interesting 'patterns' present. Of central importance to the methods to be described are the **covariances** and **correlations** between the observed variables. These quantities should be familiar to most readers, but the next section will help to refresh those whose memories of the terms have perhaps faded a little.

10.2 Covariances and correlations

The concept of expressing the relationship between two variables in terms of a correlation coefficient was introduced by Galton in the nineteenth century, and such coefficients (and corresponding measures of covariance) continue to be of fundamental importance in the analysis of multivariate data. Both correlations and covariances are described in detail in Display 10.1.

Unless the correlations between all pairs of variables in a set of multivariate data are zero (in which case the correlation matrix would be an **identity matrix**), there are dependencies in the data which may allow them to be described and summarized more simply in terms of a smaller number of **composite** or **derived** variables. This can often be a great aid in achieving an understanding of the data, which is the main objective in many investigations where multivariate data have been collected. The two approaches of primary importance here are **principal components analysis** and **factor analysis**. In general terms, techniques of both types seek to reduce the number of variables needed for the adequate description of a set of multivariate data, so that, any structure becomes more apparent. Many descriptions of this area do not differentiate principal components from factor analysis, with the latter term often being used as a label for all methods of this type. However, there are several good reasons why they are best discussed separately, and this is the policy adopted here.

Display 10.1   Covariances and correlations

- A set of multivariate data is generally represented by a matrix $\mathbf{X}$ where

$$\mathbf{X} = \begin{pmatrix} x_{11} & x_{12} & \cdots & x_{1p} \\ x_{21} & x_{22} & \cdots & x_{2p} \\ \vdots & \vdots & \vdots & \vdots \\ x_{n1} & x_{n2} & \cdots & x_{np} \end{pmatrix}$$

where n is the number of observations in the data, p is the number of variables and x_{ij} represents the value of variable j for observation i.

- The sample covariance s_{ij} of variables i and j is given by

$$s_{ij} = \frac{1}{n-1} \sum_{k=1}^{n} (x_{ki} - \bar{x}_i)(x_{kj} - \bar{x}_j)$$

where $\bar{x}_i$ and $\bar{x}_j$ are the sample means of the two variables.

- A covariance can take any value from $-\infty$ to ∞. A value of zero indicates that there is no association (strictly, no *linear* association) between the variables. A positive value occurs when as one of the variables increases in value then, on average, so does the other. A negative covariance indicates that as one variable increases, the other decreases, and vice versa.

- The sample **covariance matrix** is a matrix with the variances of each variable on the main diagonal and the covariances of each pair of variables as off-diagonal elements.

- The sample **correlation** r_{ij} between variables i and j is given by

$$r_{ij} = \frac{s_{ij}}{(s_{ii}s_{jj})^{\frac{1}{2}}}$$

where s_{ii} and s_{jj} are used to denote the variances of the two variables.

- A correlation takes values between -1 and 1, with the two extremes indicating that the two variables are perfectly linearly related.

- The sample **correlation matrix** is

$$\mathbf{R} = \begin{pmatrix} 1 & r_{12} & \cdots & r_{1p} \\ r_{21} & 1 & \cdots & r_{2p} \\ \vdots & \vdots & \vdots & \vdots \\ r_{p1} & r_{p2} & \cdots & 1 \end{pmatrix}.$$

10.3 Principal components analysis

Principal components analysis is a multivariate technique in which a number of related (correlated) variables are transformed into a smaller set of unrelated (uncorrelated) variables. The rationale behind the method is that the number of variables in a set of multivariate data is often large and the sheer volume of the raw data can be daunting. In such circumstances the researcher would welcome a reduction in the complexity of the data by reducing the number of variables in some way. Of course, one approach would be simply to choose a subset of the original variables by, for example, dropping variables highly correlated with several others. However, principal components analysis constructs a number of new variables which are composites of those originally available, and uses a small number of these derived variables to describe and summarize the data. To many readers this may not appear as immediately convincing as simply using a subset of the original variables; however, the method does have considerable advantages as will be seen later.

The new variables derived by a principal components analysis are **linear combinations** of the original variables. The coefficients defining each such new variable are chosen so that the derived variables (the principal components) account for maximal amounts of the variation in the original data and are themselves uncorrelated. A summary of principal components analysis is given in Display 10.2. A more detailed account of the model is given by Everitt and Dunn (1991), but the essence of the method can also be gleaned from the examples that follow.

Display 10.2   Principal components analysis

- Principal components analysis is essentially a method of **data reduction** which aims to produce a small number of derived variables that can be used in place of the larger number of original variables to simplify subsequent analysis of the data.
- The principal component variables $y_1, y_2, \ldots, y_p$ are defined to be linear combinations of the original variables $x_1, x_2, \ldots, x_p$ that are uncorrelated and account for maximal proportions of the variation in the original data, i.e. y_1 accounts for the maximum amount of the variance amongst all possible linear combinations of $x_1, \ldots, x_p$, y_2 accounts for maximum variance subject to being uncorrelated with y_1 and so on.
- Explicitly, the principal component variables are obtained from $x_1, \ldots, x_p$ as follows:

$$y_1 = a_{11}x_1 + a_{12}x_2 + \ldots + a_{1p}x_p$$
$$y_2 = a_{21}x_1 + a_{22}x_2 + \ldots + a_{2p}x_p$$
$$\vdots$$
$$y_p = a_{p1}x_1 + a_{p2}x_2 + \ldots + a_{pp}x_p$$

where the coefficients $a_{ij}(i = 1, \ldots, p, j = 1, \ldots, p)$ are chosen such that the required maximal variance and uncorrelated conditions hold.
- The coefficients defining the principal components are given by what are known as

the **latent vectors** or **eigenvectors** of either the sample covariance or the correlation matrix (for which of these matrices should be used in general, see below).

- The variances of the components are given by the **latent roots** or **eigenvalues** of the covariance or correlation matrix. (For more details about eigenvectors and eigenvalues see, for example, Everitt and Dunn, 1991.)
- The sum of the variances of the principal components equals the sum of the diagonal elements of the matrix from which they are extracted. Therefore in the case of the analysis of a correlation matrix, for example, the sum equals p, the number of variables (think about it!).
- The coefficients defining the components are usually derived initially in a form where their sums of squares equal unity, i.e.

$$\sum_{j=1}^{p} a_{ij}^2 = 1 \quad \text{for all } i.$$

- It is often useful to rescale the coefficients so that they represent correlations between observed variables and components (for details, see Everitt and Dunn, 1991). For coefficients derived from a correlation matrix this involves nothing more than multiplying the original coefficients defining a component by the square root of the component's variance (examples are given later). Such a rescaling often aids in the interpretation of the components. Most statistical software packages present the results of a principal components analysis in this way.
- Components extracted from the sample covariance matrix may differ considerably from those derived from the corresponding correlation matrix, and there is not necessarily any simple relationship between them. In most practical applications of principal components, the analysis is based on the correlation matrix, i.e. on the standardized variables, simply because the observed variables will generally be on very different scales so that linear combinations of the unstandardized variables will make little sense.
- The number of principal components needed to adequately represent a set of multivariate data is generally selected according to one of the following relatively arbitrary procedures:

  (a) The proportion of variance accounted for; in most practical applications, values over 60% usually correspond to a reasonable solution.
  (b) A **scree plot** of the variances of the components, i.e. a plot of variance against component number. An 'elbow' in the plot is often indicative of the appropriate number of components.
  (c) If the components are derived from the correlation matrix, choose those with variances greater than unity, i.e. greater than the 'average' variance in this case.

- Scores for each of the individuals on each of the selected principal components are found by simply applying a component's defining coefficients to the individuals' observed variable values (after standardization when the components are extracted from the correlation matrix).

10.3.1 *A simple example of principal components analysis*

Many points about principal components analysis can be illustrated using a simple example with only two variables. Therefore consider the data plotted in Fig. 10.1, which consist of the heights (inches) and weights (pounds) of 100 men aged 20–30 years. In this example it should be clear that deriving new variables which are linear combinations of the raw height and weight values would not be very sensible; linear

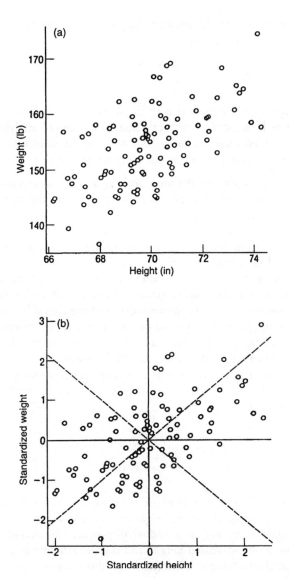

Fig. 10.1 (a) Heights and weights for 100 young men and (b) standardized data showing principal components.

combinations of the *standardized* heights and weights are required, and so the analysis should involve the correlation between the two variables rather than their covariance. For two variables with correlation, $r > 0$, it can be shown that the principal component variables y_1 and y_2 are given by

$$y_1 = \frac{1}{\sqrt{2}} x_1 + \frac{1}{\sqrt{2}} x_2 \qquad (10.1)$$

$$y_2 = \frac{1}{\sqrt{2}} x_1 - \frac{1}{\sqrt{2}} x_2 \qquad (10.2)$$

where x_1 and x_2 represent the standardized height and weight variables. It can also be shown that the variances of y_1 and y_2 are

$$\text{var}(y_1) = 1 + r \qquad (10.3)$$

$$\text{var}(y_2) = 1 - r. \qquad (10.4)$$

The principal components are plotted with the standardized height and weight data in Fig. 10.1. This plot demonstrates that principal components analysis is essentially a simple rotation of the axes used to describe a multivariate data set.

The following points about the principal component variables should be noted:

1. The squares of the coefficients defining both y_1 and y_2 sum to unity.
2. The sum of the variances of each component is 2, i.e. the sum of the diagonal elements of the correlation matrix.
3. The first component y_1 accounts for a proportion $(1 + r)/2$ of the variance of x_1 and x_2. Clearly, the greater the value of r, the greater is this proportion. When $r = 1$, y_1 accounts for all the variation in the original two variables, i.e. the observations lie on a straight line. When $r = 0$, y_1 accounts for 50% of the total variation. Clearly there is little point in a principal components analysis in such a situation.
4. The principal component scores for an individual are found by simply substituting his standardized height and weight values in the equations defining y_1 and y_2.
5. Interpretation of the components can often be made simpler if the defining coefficients are rescaled so that they are the correlations between variables and components. Such rescaling is achieved by multiplying a component's coefficients by the square root of the component's variance. In this example this leads to the following components:

$$y_1 = \frac{\sqrt{1 + r}}{\sqrt{2}} (x_1 + x_2) \qquad (10.5)$$

$$y_2 = \frac{\sqrt{1 - r}}{\sqrt{2}} (x_1 - x_2). \qquad (10.6)$$

How should the two derived variables be interpreted? The first component, y_1, is essentially the sum of the standardized height and weight values; it is a measure of the 'size' of an individual, separating large and small people. The second component, y_2, is the difference between standardized height and standardized weight; essentially, it is a measure of an individual's 'shape', distinguishing 'short heavy' people from those who are tall and light. If r is reasonably large, the variance due to size is predominant and y_1

could be used in place of height and weight in subsequent analyses of the data, thus reducing the number of variables by 50%.

10.3.2 Principal components of occupations data

The values of four variables for each of 36 occupations in the United States were given in Chapter 2 (Table 2.6). The variables are on very different scales, and again it appears sensible to apply principal components analysis to their correlation matrix rather than to the matrix of covariances. The results of the analysis are shown in Display 10.3. The first two components both have variances greater than unity and together account for

Display 10.3 Results from a principal components analysis of the occupations data in Table 2.6

- The correlation matrix of the four observed variables is as follows:

$$
\mathbf{R} = \begin{array}{c} 1 \\ 2 \\ 3 \\ 4 \end{array}
\begin{array}{cccc}
1 & 2 & 3 & 4 \\
\left(\begin{array}{cccc}
1.00 & & & \\
0.11 & 1.00 & & \\
0.78 & 0.26 & 1.00 & \\
0.86 & -0.15 & 0.65 & 1.00
\end{array} \right)
\end{array}.
$$

- The principal components solution is as follows:

Variable	PC1	PC2	PC3	PC4
Prestige	0.60	0.03	−0.26	0.75
Suicide	0.08	−0.93	−0.33	−0.14
Income	0.56	−0.20	0.78	−0.17
Education	0.56	0.31	−0.45	−0.61
Variance	2.55	1.10	0.25	0.10

- Note that the sum of squares of the coefficients defining each component is unity.
- The scree plot of the results (see below) perhaps indicates that the two-component solution as the one to choose.

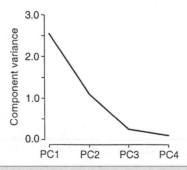

91% of the variation of the original four variables. Clearly, these two components will give a very adequate representation of the data. The first component is essentially a weighted average of the standardized prestige, income and education scores. The second component is primarily the standardized suicide score.

The first two principal component scores of each occupation can now be used both to summarize the data concisely and in subsequent analysis of the data. For example, the scores can be used to produce a graphical display of the data by simply plotting them to form a scattergram as shown in Fig. 10.2. Two features of this plot are particularly striking.

1. Occupation 13 (self-employed manufacturing workers) appears as an outlier, primarily because of its very high suicide rate.
2. The occupations are divided into two (or perhaps three) groups. The two-group division largely corresponds to 'professions' and 'non-professions'. (The classification aspect of these data is taken up again in Chapter 12.)

10.3.3 A principal components analysis of drug usage among American students

The majority of adult and adolescent Americans use psychoactive substances during an increasing proportion of their lifetime. Various forms of licit and illicit psychoactive substance use are prevalent, suggesting that patterns of psychoactive substance taking are major components of the individual's behavioural repertoire and have pervasive implications for the performance of other behaviours. In an investigation of these

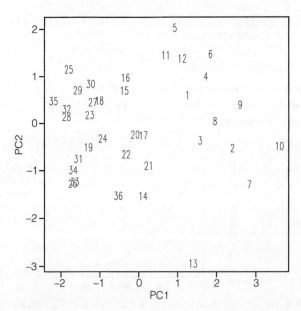

Fig. 10.2 Plot of the first two principal components scores for occupations data.

phenomena, Huba *et al.* (1981) collected data on drug usage rates for 1634 students in the seventh to ninth grades in 11 schools in the greater metropolitan area of Los Angeles. Each participant completed a questionnaire about the number of times that he or she had ever used a particular substance. The substances for which data were collected were as follows:

(1) cigarettes;
(2) beer;
(3) wine;
(4) spirits;
(5) cocaine;
(6) tranquillizers;
(7) drug-store medications used to get high;
(8) heroin and other opiates;
(9) marijuana;
(10) hashish;
(11) inhalants (glue, petrol etc.);
(12) hallucinogenics (LSD, mescalin etc.);
(13) amphetamine stimulants.

Responses were recorded on a five-point scale which ranged from 'never tried' to 'used regularly'. The correlations between the usage rates of the 13 substances are shown in Table 10.1. The results of applying principal components analysis to these correlations are shown in Table 10.2. Note that, in this example, the coefficients defining each component are scaled so that they represent correlations between the

Table 10.1 correlations between usage rates for 13 substances

						Substance							
	1	2	3	4	5	6	7	8	9	10	11	12	13
1	1.000												
2	0.447	1.000											
3	0.422	0.619											
4	0.436	0.604	0.583	1.000									
5	0.114	0.068	0.583	0.115	1.000								
6	0.203	0.146	0.139	0.258	0.349	1.000							
7	0.091	0.103	0.110	0.122	0.209	0.221	1.000						
8	0.082	0.063	0.066	0.097	0.321	0.355	0.201	1.000					
9	0.513	0.445	0.365	0.482	0.186	0.316	0.150	0.154	1.000				
10	0.304	0.318	0.240	0.368	0.303	0.377	0.163	0.219	0.53	1.000			
11	0.245	0.203	0.183	0.255	0.272	0.323	0.310	0.288	0.301	0.302	1.000		
12	0.101	0.088	0.074	0.139	0.279	0.367	0.232	0.320	0.204	0.368	0.340	1.000	
13	0.245	0.199	−0.184	0.293	0.278	0.545	0.232	0.314	0.394	0.467	0.392	0.511	1.000

For key to substances see text.

Table 10.2   Results from a principal components analysis of drug usage data

Substance	PC1	PC2	PC2	PC4	PC5	PC6	PC7	PC8	PC9	PC10	PC11	PC12	PC13
1	0.58	0.40	−0.06	0.01	0.27	0.38	0.10	−0.02	0.45	−0.08	−0.09	−0.13	−0.12
2	0.60	0.57	0.13	0.09	−0.15	−0.12	−0.09	−0.04	−0.04	−0.06	−0.05	0.38	−0.30
3	0.55	0.56	0.21	0.13	−0.27	−0.13	−0.05	−0.06	0.07	−0.28	−0.17	0.09	−0.34
4	0.66	0.46	0.05	0.06	−0.15	−0.13	0.00	−0.09	−0.15	0.40	−0.07	−0.30	−0.08
5	0.44	−0.41	0.05	0.53	0.38	−0.29	−0.24	−0.18	0.13	0.05	0.10	0.02	−0.00
6	0.61	−0.37	−0.17	0.08	−0.11	−0.04	−0.44	−0.38	−0.06	−0.06	0.28	0.11	−0.08
7	0.37	−0.27	−0.71	0.30	0.22	0.22	0.27	0.16	0.05	−0.00	−0.00	−0.02	−0.02
8	0.42	−0.45	−0.14	0.48	0.28	−0.32	0.13	0.39	−0.08	−0.01	0.03	−0.04	−0.003
9	0.71	0.23	−0.23	−0.10	0.31	0.12	−0.12	0.20	−0.10	0.23	0.13	0.24	0.28
10	0.69	−0.07	−0.35	−0.11	0.22	−0.20	0.01	0.29	−0.26	−0.27	−0.16	−0.18	−0.07
11	0.58	−0.24	0.31	−0.18	0.07	0.42	−0.38	−0.28	−0.28	−0.05	0.04	0.01	0.02
12	0.52	−0.47	−0.11	−0.26	−0.31	−012	−0.32	015	0.36	0.13	−0.17	0.07	0.10
13	0.69	−0.33	−0.23	−0.24	−018	−0.02	0.11	−0.14	0.04	−0.05	0.45	−0.06	−0.18
Variance	4.38	2.04	0.95	0.82	0.76	0.69	0.64	0.61	0.56	0.40	0.40	0.39	0.37

Note that the coefficients are scaled so that their sums of squares equal the corresponding variance. Consequently, these coefficients represent correlations between observed variables and components. The scree plot of variances is shown below.

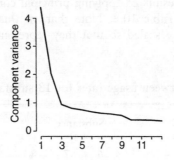

observed variables and the derived components; consequently, the sum of squares of each set of coefficients equals the variance of the corresponding component. (When scaled in this way the coefficients are usually referred to as **loadings** since they are analogous to the factor loadings of the factor analysis model to be described in the next section.) The results given in Table 10.2 show that only the first two components have variances greater than unity; these two components together account for nearly 50% of the variation in the original 13 usage rates. The scree plot shown in Table 10.2, however, indicates that a three-component solution might be more appropriate. But the moment we shall look in more detail at only the first two components.

How should the first two components be interpreted? The first, which has relatively high positive loadings on all 13 substances, clearly measures overall drug usage. Such a size component always arises when the elements of a correlation matrix are all positive. The second component largely contrasts usage of 'legal' and 'illegal' substances (although marijuana appears to have slipped into the former category—no doubt good news for many readers). Alternatively this component might be seen as contrasting usages rates of so-called 'soft' and 'hard' drugs. Therefore, once overall usage has been accounted for, the main source of variation in these data arises from the individuals consuming substances of two largely different classes.

Most users of principal components analysis search for an interpretation of the components in this fashion, but this is not without its difficulties and critics, and the following quotation from Marriot (1974) serves to act as a salutory warning against the dangers of overinterpretation.

> It must be emphasised that no mathematical method is, or could be, designed to give physical meaningful results. If a mathematical expression of this sort has an obvious physical meaning, it must be attributed to a lucky chance, or to the fact that the data have a strongly marked structure that shows up in analysis. Even in the latter case, quite small sampling fluctuations can upset the interpretation; for example, the first two principal components may appear in reverse order, or may become confused altogether. Reification, then, requires considerable skill and experience if it is to give a true picture of the physical meaning of the data.

10.4 Exploratory factor analysis

Factor analysis is rather like religion—different things to different people. (In fact, factor analysis is not a single technique, but a collection of methods; however, it will be referred to here in the singular.) In one sense the method is similar in character to principal components analysis in that it seeks to simplify multivariate data by reducing the number of variables needed for their description. However, factor analysis is more ambitious than principal components analysis since it postulates a particular model to explain the correlations between the observed variables (also often known as the **manifest variables** in this context). The proposed model involves a (hopefully) small number of more fundamental underlying variables that cannot be measured directly.

A point that needs to be made at the outset is that factor analysis is used in two distinct modes. In the first, the method is used as an 'exploratory' technique for examining the possible structure or pattern in a set of observed correlations. However, factor analysis can also be used as a 'confirmatory' technique, seeking to establish whether or not a specific model is compatible with the observed correlations. In this chapter it will be exploratory factor analysis that is of concern. Confirmatory factor analysis and associated techniques will be dealt with in Chapter 11.

So what is the factor analysis model? Essentially, it is a model that postulates that the covariances or correlations between the observed variables are generated by their relationships with a small number of underlying variables or concepts, not directly measurable, known either as **common factors** or, more generally, as **latent variables**. The model implies that, given the latent variables, the **partial correlations** (see Appendix A) between the manifest variables are all zero.

Some of the mathematical details behind factor analysis are given in Display 10.4, but once again for those readers whose matrix algebra is a little shaky, much can still be learnt from examining some examples.

Display 10.4 The factor analysis model

- In general terms factor analysis is concerned with whether the covariances or correlations between a set of observed variables $x_1, x_2, \ldots, x_p$ can be 'explained' in terms of a smaller number of unobservable latent variables or common factors $f_1, f_2, \ldots, f_k$, where $k < p$ (hopefully k, the number of common factors, will be much less than the number of original variables).

- In mathematical terms the factor analysis model is

$$x_1 = \lambda_{11}f_1 + \lambda_{12}f_2 + \ldots + \lambda_{ik}f_k + u_1$$
$$x_2 = \lambda_{21}f_1 + \lambda_{22}f_2 + \ldots + \lambda_{2k}f_k + u_2$$
$$\vdots$$
$$x_p = \lambda_{p1}f_1 + \lambda_{p2}f_2 + \ldots + \lambda_{pk}f_k + u_p.$$

Essentially, this is a multiple regression type model for each observed variable with, in each case, the 'explanatory' variables being the common factors. In the context of factor analysis, the random disturbance terms of regression (the $u_1, u_2, \ldots, u_p$ in the equations above) are known as **specific variates**. They represent that part of an observed variable *not* accounted for by the common factors.

- We make the following assumptions:

  (a) The common factors are in standardized form, i.e. have variances of unity.
  (b) The common factors are uncorrelated.
  (c) The specific variates are uncorrelated.
  (d) The common factors are uncorrelated with the specific variates.

- Then the factor analysis model implies that the population variances σ_i^2 and covariances σ_{ij} of the observed variables can be written as follows:

$$\sigma_i^2 = \sum_{j=1}^{k} \lambda_{ij}^2 + \psi_i$$

$$\sigma_{ij} = \sum_{l=1}^{k} \lambda_{il}\lambda_{jl}$$

where ψ_i is the variance of specific variate u_i, i.e. the **specific variance** of variable x_i (for full details, see Everitt and Dunn, 1991).

- The model implies that the variance σ_i^2 of an observed variable can be split into two parts, $\sum_{j=1}^{k} \lambda_{ij}^2$ and ψ_i. The first of these is known as the **communality** of variable i; it is the variance in the variable shared with the other observed variables via their relationships with the common factors.

- Note that the covariances of the observed variables are generated solely from their relationship with the common factors. The specific variates play no part in determining the covariances of the observed variables; they contribute only to the variances of these variables.

- If the common factors are assumed to be uncorrelated (often the term **orthogonal** is used), then the coefficients $\lambda_{ij}(i = 1, \ldots, p, j = 1, \ldots, k)$ are the correlations between the common factors and the observed variables. The coefficients are generally termed **factor loadings**.
- The factor analysis model can be written more concisely as

$$x = \Lambda f + u$$

where

$$\Lambda = \begin{pmatrix} \lambda_{11} & \lambda_{12} & \cdots & \lambda_{1k} \\ \vdots & \vdots & \vdots & \vdots \\ \lambda_{p1} & \lambda_{p2} & \cdots & \lambda_{pk} \end{pmatrix}$$

and $f' = [f_1, f_2, \ldots, f_k]$ and $u' = [u_1, u_2, \ldots, u_p]$.

- Given the assumptions listed earlier, the model implies that the covariance matrix Σ of the observed variables can be written in the form

$$\Sigma = \Lambda\Lambda' + \Psi$$

where the matrix Ψ is diagonal and contains the specific variances on its main diagonal.

- If the assumption that the factors are uncorrelated is dropped (see the discussion of oblique rotation in Section 10.5), then the factor analysis model implies that the covariance matrix of the observed variables is

$$\Sigma = \Lambda\Phi\Lambda' + \Psi$$

where Φ is the correlation matrix of the common factors.

- The factor analysis model is fitted to an observed covariance or correlation matrix by estimating the loadings matrix Λ and the specific variances, so that the covariances or correlations predicted by the model are as 'close' as possible in some sense to the corresponding observed values.
- The two main estimation methods used are **principal factor analysis** and **maximum likelihood factor analysis**.

  (a) Principal factor analysis is essentially equivalent to a principal components analysis performed on what is known as the **reduced covariance matrix** S^*, which is obtained by replacing the observed diagonal elements of the sample covariance matrix S with estimated communalities for each variable. Possible estimators for these communalities are the square of the multiple correlation coefficient of a variable with all other variables, and the largest of the absolute values of the correlation coefficients between a variable and one of the other variables. Each of these will give a higher communality estimate when a variable is highly correlated with the other variables, which is what is required.

  (b) In maximum likelihood factor analysis it is assumed that the data have a **multivariate normal distribution** (see Appendix A) and estimates of loadings and variances of specific variates to maximize what is known as the **likelihood function** are determined.

- Details of both principal factor analysis and maximum likelihood factor analysis are given by Everitt and Dunn (1991).

10.4.1 A simple example of factor analysis

As a first illustration of the application of the factor analysis model, a simple example originally discussed by Spearman (1904) will be used. The example involves children's examination scores in three subjects; the details and the relevant correlation matrix are given in Display 10.5. Spearman's interest was in a one-factor model, with the single factor presumably being labelled 'intelligence'. In Display 10.5 it is demonstrated that, in this simple example, such a model will fit the observed correlations exactly. Here the model contains the same number of parameters as there are observed variances and covariances. In general, of course, factor analysis models with fewer parameters than the number of variances and correlations will be sought, since these represent a genuine simplification of the data.

Display 10.5   A simple factor analysis example taken from Spearman (1904)

- The data consisted of children's examination scores in three subjects: Classics (x_1), French (x_2) and English (x_3).
- The observed correlation matrix is

$$\mathbf{R} = \begin{array}{c} \\ x_1 \\ x_2 \\ x_3 \end{array} \begin{array}{c} x_1 \quad\; x_2 \quad\; x_3 \\ \left(\begin{array}{ccc} 1.00 & & \\ 0.83 & 1.00 & \\ 0.78 & 0.67 & 1.00 \end{array} \right) \end{array}.$$

- If a single underlying factor f is assumed, the factor model to be fitted to the observed correlations is

$$x_1 = \lambda_1 f + u_1$$
$$x_2 = \lambda_2 f + u_2$$
$$x_3 = \lambda_3 f + u_3.$$

- In this example, estimates of the parameters in the model can be found by simply equating the observed correlation matrix $\mathbf{R}$ to the matrix predicted by the model, i.e. $\hat{\mathbf{R}}$ which, assuming that f is uncorrelated with u and that f has variance unity, is given by

$$\hat{\mathbf{R}} = \begin{array}{c} \\ x_1 \\ x_2 \\ x_3 \end{array} \begin{array}{c} x_1 \qquad\qquad x_2 \qquad\qquad x_3 \\ \left(\begin{array}{ccc} \hat{\lambda}_1^2 + \hat{\psi}_1 & & \\ \hat{\lambda}_1 \hat{\lambda}_2 & \hat{\lambda}_2^2 + \hat{\psi}_2 & \\ \hat{\lambda}_1 \hat{\lambda}_3 & \hat{\lambda}_2 \hat{\lambda}_3 & \hat{\lambda}_3^2 + \hat{\psi}_3 \end{array} \right) \end{array}.$$

- Therefore the model implies the following relationships:

$$\hat{\lambda}_1 \hat{\lambda}_2 = 0.83$$
$$\hat{\lambda}_1 \hat{\lambda}_3 = 0.78$$
$$\hat{\lambda}_1 \hat{\lambda}_3 = 0.67$$
$$\hat{\lambda}_1^2 + \hat{\psi}_1 = 1.00$$
$$\hat{\lambda}_2^2 + \hat{\psi}_2 = 1.00$$
$$\hat{\lambda}_3^2 + \hat{\psi}_3 = 1.00.$$

- Solving these equations leads to the following solution for the parameters of the one-factor model:

$$\hat{\lambda}_1 = 0.99$$
$$\hat{\lambda}_2 = 0.84$$
$$\hat{\lambda}_3 = 0.79$$
$$\hat{\psi}_1 = 0.02$$
$$\hat{\psi}_2 = 0.30$$
$$\hat{\psi}_3 = 0.38.$$

- Here the predicted correlation matrix from the one-factor model and the observed correlation matrix are identical, since the model has six parameters $(\lambda_1, \lambda_2, \lambda_3, \psi_1, \psi_2, \psi_3)$ and is used to represent a total of six correlations and variances.

10.4.2 *Maximum likelihood factor analysis for the drug usage correlations given in Table 10.1*

The results of fitting a two-factor model to the drug usage correlations are shown in Display 10.6. Here the parameters of the model were estimated by maximum likelihood (maximum likelihood factor analysis is available in most statistical software packages). The estimated factor loadings given in Display 10.6 are seen to be very similar to the principal component solution for those data (see Table 10.2). (A more general comparison of principal components analysis and factor analysis is given in Section 10.6.) The specific variances of, for example, heroin and drug-store medication, indicate that a large proportion of the variance of these variables is not shared with the other variables via the common factors.

Display 10.6   Maximum likelihood factor analysis: two-factor solution for drug usage data

- Factor loadings, communalities and specific variances are as follows:

Substance	Factor 1	Factor 2	Communality	Specific variance
1. Cigarettes	0.57	−0.20	0.36	0.64
2. Beer	0.67	−0.43	0.63	0.37
3. Wine	0.61	−0.42	0.55	0.45
4. Spirits	0.71	−0.31	0.60	0.40
5. Cocaine	0.32	0.35	0.22	0.78
6. Tranquillizers	0.51	0.43	0.45	0.55
7. Drug-store medication	0.28	0.22	0.13	0.87
8. Heroin	0.31	0.37	0.23	0.77
9. Marijuana	0.68	−0.03	0.46	0.54
10. Hashish	0.62	0.21	0.43	0.57
11. Inhalants	0.47	0.27	0.29	0.71
12. Hallucinogenics	0.41	0.48	0.40	0.60
13. Amphetamines	0.60	0.45	0.56	0.44
Variance	3.78	1.54		

- Note that the variances are less than for the first two principal components of these data; factor analysis attempts to explain the covariances between the observed variables and only the variance shared with other variables through the common factors. In contrast, principal components analysis attempts to account for the total variation of the observed variables.

The drug usage data can also be used to illustrate the test for the number of common factors available in association with the maximum likelihood method of fitting the factor analysis model. Details are given in Display 10.7. The test remains significant for the drug usage data even when the number of common factors is increased to five. For this example, where the sample size is large, the test appears to lead to a model which includes a number of relatively unimportant factors. Perhaps 'formal' tests for number of factors are out of place in an exploratory factor analysis.

Display 10.7   Maximum likelihood factor analysis; test for number of common factors

- The test statistic is based on what is known as the **likelihood function,** which is essentially a measure of how well the estimated factor model fits the observed correlations (see Everitt and Dunn, 1991, for a specific definition).

- A sequential procedure is used to determine the number k of common factors. Starting with some small value for k (usually 1), the parameters in the factor analysis model are estimated using the maximum likelihood method. If the test statistic is not significant, the current model is accepted; otherwise k is increased by 1 and the process is repeated until an acceptable solution is reached.
- This procedure gives the following series of results for the drug usage data.

Model	Test statistic	DF
One-factor	2287.26	65
Two-factor	477.57	53
Three-factor	230.21	42
Four-factor	115.87	32

- According to this formal test, all four solutions are unacceptable for these data. It seems likely that the large sample size makes even small discrepancies between observed and predicted correlations significant.

In addition to using the test described in Display 10.7, the goodness of fit of a factor analysis model can (and should) be examined by comparing the observed correlation matrix with that predicted by the model, i.e. the **reproduced correlation matrix** or **predicted correlation matrix** (Display 10.8). For the drug usage data, for example, the fitted two-factor model shown in Display 10.6 leads to the reproduced correlation matrix shown in Display 10.8. Also shown in Display 10.8 is the **residual correlation matrix**, the entries of which are simply the differences between the observed and reproduced correlations. If the factor analysis model fits well the elements of the residual correlation matrix will all be small. Here, the values of the elements in the residual correlation matrix are probably sufficiently small to claim that, despite the evidence from the test described in Display 10.7, the two-factor model gives an adequate description of the data. Note that the elements on the main diagonal of the reproduced correlation matrix are the communalities of each variable and those on the diagonal of the residual correlation matrix are 1-communality, i.e. the specific variances.

(A similar reproduced correlation matrix can also be obtained from the results of a principal components analysis as described in Display 10.9. This display also contains both the reproduced and the residual correlations matrices resulting from the first two principal components of the drug usage data—see Table 10.1. Note that the residual correlations although relatively small, are generally larger than the corresponding terms from the two-factor model given in Display 10.8. This will also be the case generally because the factor analysis model essentially seeks to explain the correlations between the observed variables, whilst principal components analysis aims to explain the variation in these variables.)

10.5 Factor rotation

In the mathematical description of factor analysis given in Display 10.6 one important point was conveniently ignored, namely that, as described, the loadings in the factor

Display 10.8 Reproduced correlation matrix and residual correlation matrix for two-factor model estimated by maximum likelihood

- *Reproduced correlation matrix*
  The correlation matrix reproduced from the estimated loadings of a fitted factor analysis model, $\hat{\mathbf{R}}$, is given by:

$$\hat{\mathbf{R}} = \hat{\mathbf{\Lambda}}\hat{\mathbf{\Lambda}}'$$

  where $\hat{\mathbf{\Lambda}}$ is the estimated loadings matrix.

- For the two-factor solution on the drug usage data this leads to the matrix:

	1	2	3	4	5	6	7	8	9	10	11	12	13
1	0.36												
2	0.47	0.63											
3	0.43	0.59	0.55										
4	0.47	0.60	0.56	0.59									
5	0.11	0.06	0.05	0.12	0.23								
6	0.21	0.16	0.13	0.23	0.32	0.45							
7	0.11	0.09	0.08	0.13	0.16	0.23	0.12						
8	0.10	0.04	0.03	0.19	0.23	0.32	0.17	0.24					
9	0.39	0.47	0.43	0.49	0.20	0.33	0.18	0.20	0.46				
10	0.31	0.32	0.29	0.37	0.27	0.40	0.21	0.27	0.41	0.42			
11	0.27	0.20	0.18	0.25	0.24	0.36	0.19	0.25	0.31	0.35	0.29		
12	0.14	0.07	0.05	0.15	0.30	0.41	0.22	0.31	0.26	0.35	0.32	0.40	
13	0.25	0.20	0.18	0.29	0.35	0.50	0.27	0.36	0.39	0.47	0.41	0.46	0.57

- *Residual correlation matrix*
  The residual correlation matrix is simply, $\mathbf{R} - \hat{\mathbf{R}}$; for this example it is given by

	1	2	3	4	5	6	7	8	9	10	11	12	13
1	0.64												
2	-0.02	0.37											
3	-0.01	0.03	0.45										
4	-0.03	0.00	0.02	0.40									
5	0.00	0.01	0.01	-0.01	0.77								
6	0.00	-0.01	0.01	0.02	0.03	0.55							
7	-0.02	0.01	0.03	-0.01	0.04	0.01	0.88						
8	-0.02	0.02	0.03	-0.01	0.09	0.03	0.03	0.76					
9	0.12	-0.02	-0.06	-0.01	-0.02	-0.02	-0.03	-0.04	0.54				
10	-0.01	0.00	-0.05	-0.01	0.03	-0.03	-0.05	-0.05	0.12	0.58			
11	0.03	0.00	0.01	0.00	0.03	-0.03	0.12	0.04	-0.01	-0.05	0.70		
12	-0.04	0.02	0.02	-0.01	-0.02	-0.05	0.02	0.01	-0.06	0.02	0.02	0.60	
13	-0.01	-0.01	0.01	0.00	-0.07	0.04	-0.03	-0.04	0.00	0.00	-0.01	0.05	0.43

Display 10.9 Reproduced correlation matrix and residual correlation matrix for two-component solution for drug usage data

- Reproduced correlation matrix: if the components are scaled so that their coefficients represent correlations between observed variables and components, then

$$\hat{R} = AA'$$

where A is the matrix containing the rescaled coefficients as its columns. The number of columns of A is the number of components selected by one or other of the criteria described in Display 10.2.

- For example, matrix A for the two-component solution for the drug usage data is given by

$$A = \begin{pmatrix} 0.58 & 0.40 \\ 0.60 & 0.57 \\ 0.55 & 0.56 \\ 0.66 & 0.46 \\ 0.44 & -0.41 \\ 0.61 & -0.37 \\ 0.37 & -0.27 \\ 0.42 & -0.45 \\ 0.71 & 0.23 \\ 0.69 & -0.07 \\ 0.58 & -0.24 \\ 0.52 & -0.47 \\ 0.69 & -0.33 \end{pmatrix}.$$

- This leads to the following predicted correlation matrix:

	1	2	3	4	5	6	7	8	9	10	11	12	13
1	0.50												
2	0.58	0.68											
3	0.55	0.65	0.62										
4	0.57	0.66	0.63	0.66									
5	0.09	0.03	0.01	0.10	0.36								
6	0.21	0.16	0.13	0.23	0.42	0.51							
7	0.10	0.07	0.05	0.12	0.27	0.33	0.21						
8	0.06	0.00	-0.02	0.07	0.37	0.42	0.28	0.38					
9	0.51	0.56	0.53	0.58	0.21	0.35	0.20	0.19	0.56				
10	0.37	0.37	0.34	0.42	0.33	0.45	0.27	0.32	0.47	0.48			
11	0.24	0.21	0.18	0.27	0.35	0.44	0.28	0.35	0.35	0.41	0.39		
12	0.11	0.04	0.02	0.13	0.42	0.49	0.32	0.43	0.26	0.39	0.41	0.49	
13	0.27	0.22	0.20	0.30	0.44	0.54	0.34	0.44	0.41	0.50	0.48	0.51	0.58

- The residual correlation matrix is as follows:

	1	2	3	4	5	6	7	8	9	10	11	12	13
1	0.50												
2	0.13	0.32											
3	−0.13	−0.03	0.38										
4	−0.14	−0.06	−0.05	0.34									
5	0.02	0.04	0.04	0.02	0.64								
6	−0.01	−0.01	0.01	0.02	−0.07	0.49							
7	−0.02	0.04	0.06	0.00	−0.06	−0.10	0.79						
8	0.02	0.07	0.08	0.03	−0.05	−0.07	−0.08	0.62					
9	0.01	−0.11	−0.16	−0.10	−0.03	−0.03	−0.05	−0.04	0.44				
10	−0.07	−0.05	−0.10	0.06	0.03	−0.07	−0.11	−0.10	0.06	0.52			
11	0.01	−0.01	0.00	−0.02	−0.08	−0.12	0.03	−0.06	−0.05	−0.11	0.61		
12	−0.01	0.04	0.05	0.01	−0.14	−0.13	−0.09	−0.11	−0.06	−0.02	−0.07	0.51	
13	−0.02	−0.02	−0.01	−0.01	−0.16	0.00	−0.11	−0.13	−0.02	−0.03	−0.09	0.00	0.42

analysis model are not uniquely defined. An **orthogonal matrix** (see Appendix A) which alters the factor loadings, but leaves the ability of the model to account for the correlations between the observed variables unchanged, can be introduced into the model. The mathematical details are given in Display 10.10. The process of transforming the factor loadings by multiplying them by an orthogonal matrix is usually known as **factor rotation**.

Display 10.10 The non-uniqueness of the factor analysis model

- The basic k-common-factor analysis model implies that the population covariance matrix of the observed variables is

$$\Sigma = \Lambda\Lambda' + \Psi.$$

- Let $\mathbf{M}$ be any orthogonal matrix of order $k \times k$; since $\mathbf{MM'} = \mathbf{I}$, the factor analysis model can be rewritten as

$$\mathbf{x} = \Lambda\mathbf{MM'f} + \mathbf{u}.$$

- This satisfies all the requirements of a k-factor model with new factors $\mathbf{f}^* = \mathbf{M'f}$ and new factor loadings $\Lambda\mathbf{M}$. This 'new' model implies the following for the covariance matrix Σ of the observed variable:

$$\Sigma = (\Lambda\mathbf{M})\Lambda\mathbf{M}' + \Psi.$$

- Since $\mathbf{MM'} = \mathbf{I}$ this reduces to the value given previously. The implication is that factors $\mathbf{f}$ with loadings Λ and factors $\mathbf{f}^*$ with loadings $\Lambda\mathbf{M}$ provide identical explanations for the covariance matrix of the observed variables.

The lack of uniqueness of the factor loadings once caused many statisticians to view factor analysis with grave suspicion, since apparently it allows investigators licence to consider a large number of solutions (each corresponding to a different rotation of the factors) and to select the one closest to their a priori expectations (or prejudices) about the factor structure of the data. However, in general, such suspicion is misplaced, and factor rotation can be a useful procedure for simplifying an exploratory factor analysis solution. Factor rotation merely allows the fitted factor analysis model to be described as simply as possible. Rotation does not alter the overall structure of a solution, but only how the solution is described; rotation of factors is a process by which a solution is made more interpretable without changing its underlying mathematical properties.

The rotation methods usually employed are designed to lead to a solution with the properties that Thurstone (1947) labelled as **simple structure**. In very general terms such a structure is achieved when the common factors involve subsets of the original variables with as little overlap as possible, i.e. variables have high loadings on a particular factor and negligible loadings on the others. In this way the original variables are divided into groups relatively independent of each other. Rotation is particularly valuable in such fields as psychology and educational measurement, where the original variables represent a battery of tests and simple structure attempts to reduce this battery to groups of tests with the most in common.

In fact, there are two general classes of rotation, **orthogonal** and **oblique**. The first produces factors which are uncorrelated and are interpreted via their loadings as was done for the drug usage example in Display 10.6. However, oblique rotation procedures produce correlated factors, and an interpretation of the solution needs to consider both the factor correlation matrix and the loadings matrix. An added complication is that the latter now splits into two matrices—a **structure** matrix of correlations between factors and variables and a **pattern** matrix of unique relationships (i.e. uncontaminated by overlap among factors) between each factor and each observed variable. The consequence of allowing correlations between factors is that the sum of squares of a factor's loadings can no longer be used to determine the amount of variance attributable to the factor. Additionally, the sums of squares of factor loadings for each variable no longer give the communality of a variable. With an oblique solution, more complex calculations are required to arrive at communalities and factor variances as will be demonstrated in Display 10.11.

Methods of rotation operate by seeking a solution that essentially tries to make large loadings larger and small loadings smaller. This rather vague aim is translated into more specific mathematical terms by selecting a rotated solution in which the loadings optimize some suitable numerical criterion. For example, a well-known method of orthogonal rotation, **varimax**, attempts to maximize the within-factor variance of the squared loadings. An oblique method, **direct quartimin**, uses a similar approach. Details of both methods are given in Jackson (1991).

The drug usage example will be used once again to illustrate the use of factor rotation. The results of applying both varimax and direct quartimin to the two-factor solution are shown in Display 10.11. For both solutions the first factor might be labelled as 'serious drugs' and the second as 'recreational drugs'. (The proper place for marijuana and hashish is, as in real life, ambiguous in such an interpretation.)

When an oblique solution is derived, it is important to give both the structure and pattern matrices. Substantial correlations between the factors make the interpretation of an oblique solution more difficult than a corresponding orthogonal solution. The oblique solution would only usually be preferred if it led to a far clearer divison of the variables into non-overlapping groups.

A useful rotated solution for a two-factor solution can often be found by simply examining a scatter plot of the factor loadings. Such a plot for the two-factor solution of the drug usage data is shown in Fig. 10.3. The relatively distinct 'grouping' of the variables can be seen clearly, and can be described in simpler terms by rotating the axis to the position shown in Fig. 10.4. Since the new axes are not at right angles, this corresponds to an oblique rotation. The relationship between the original loadings and the values after oblique rotation can be obtained with the aid of some relatively simple geometry; details are given in Display 10.12. The interpretation in terms of 'hard' and 'soft' drugs remains largely unchanged.

Display 10.11   Orthogonal and oblique rotation of the maximum likelihood two-factor solution for the drug usage data

- The orthogonal rotation is as follows:

Substance	F1	F2
1. Cigarettes	0.18	0.58
2. Beer	0.05	0.79
3. Wine	0.03	0.74
4. Spirits	0.18	0.75
5. Cocaine	0.47	0.05
6. Tranquillizers	0.65	0.15
7. Drug-store medication	0.34	0.09
8. Heroin	0.49	0.02
9. Marijuana	0.38	0.56
10. Hashish	0.53	0.37
11. Inhalants	0.50	0.22
12. Hallucinogenics	0.63	0.04
13. Amphetamines	0.72	0.21
Variance	2.66	2.65

- The communalities of each variable in this rotated solution will be the same as those for the unrotated solution given in Display 10.6 (apart from possible rounding errors). The total variance accounted for by the two solutions is also the same; in the rotated solution the variance has been redistributed more equally between the two factors.

- The oblique rotation is as follows. First, the loading matrix (pattern) is given by the following:

Substance	F1	F2
1. Cigarettes	0.09	0.57
2. Beer	−0.09	0.82
3. Wine	−0.11	0.77
4. Spirits	0.05	0.75
5. Cocaine	0.49	−0.05
6. Tranquillizers	0.66	0.02
7. Drug-store medication	0.34	0.02
8. Heroin	0.51	−0.08
9. Marijuana	0.30	0.51
10. Hashish	0.50	0.27
11. Inhalants	0.48	0.13
12. Hallucinogenics	0.66	−0.09
13. Amphetamines	0.73	0.07

Second, the factor structure (correlations) is given by the following:

Substance	F1	F2
1. Cigarettes	0.29	0.60
2. Beer	0.21	0.79
3. Wine	0.17	0.74
4. Spirits	0.32	0.77
5. Cocaine	0.47	0.13
6. Tranquillizers	0.67	0.26
7. Drug	0.35	0.15
8. Heroin	0.48	0.11
9. Marijuana	0.48	0.62
10. Hashish	0.60	0.46
11. Inhalants	0.53	0.30
12. Hallucinogenics	0.62	0.15
13. Amphetamines	0.75	0.33

- The estimated correlation between the two factors is 0.36.
- The communality of a variable now involves a part attributable to the joint influence of the two factors. For example, the communality of cigarettes is now calculated as

$$(0.09)^2 + (0.57)^2 + 2 \times 0.36 \times 0.09 \times 0.57 = 0.37.$$

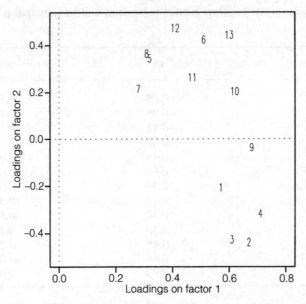

Fig. 10.3   Plot of factor loadings for the two-factor model fitted to drug usage data.

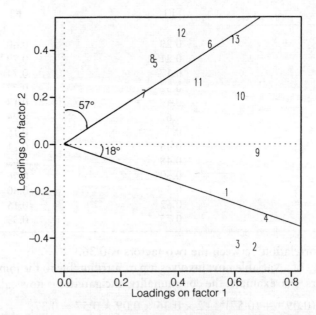

Fig. 10.4   Plot of factor loadings for the two-factor model fitted to drug usage data, showing the proposed oblique rotation of axes.

A final point to note about rotation is that the process is often applied to principal component solutions. Now, although this may be acceptable in many situations, it does have a number of disadvantages which are detailed by Jolliffe (1989). One in particular that should be mentioned here is that, when rotated, one of the defining properties of principal components, namely that of accounting for maximal proportions of the variation in the observed variables, is lost. This point is illustrated in Display 10.13, which shows the varimax rotated two-component solution for the drug usage data. Note that the variance attributable to the two components has been redistributed between them in the rotated solution. The first component is no longer the linear combination of the original variables that accounts for the maximum amount of the variance of the observed variables.

10.6 Comparison of exploratory factor analysis and principal components

Exploratory factor analysis, like principal components analysis, attempts to explain the correlations between a set of variables in a smaller number of dimensions than in the

---

Display 10.12   Rotation of factors for a two-factor solution

- In an oblique rotation suppose that one factor is rotated by an angle of θ and the other factor by an angle α.
- If the original loadings of a variable on the two factors are λ_1 and λ_2, then the rotated loadings λ'_1 and λ'_2 are given by

$$\lambda'_1 = \lambda_1 \cos \theta + \lambda_2 \sin \theta$$
$$\lambda'_2 = \lambda_2 \cos \alpha - \lambda_1 \sin \alpha.$$

- For the example in Fig. 10.4, the angles θ and α are 57° and 18°.
- Consequently the rotated loadings are as follows:

Substance	F1	F2
1	0.14	−0.37
2	0.00	−0.62
3	−0.02	−0.59
4	0.13	−0.51
5	0.47	0.23
6	0.64	0.25
7	0.34	0.12
8	0.48	0.26
9	0.35	−0.24
10	0.51	0.01
11	0.48	0.11
12	0.63	0.33
13	0.70	0.24

Display 10.13 Varimax rotated principal components

• The rotated loadings are as follows:

Substance	PC1	PC2
1	0.13	0.69
2	0.02	0.82
3	0.00	0.79
4	0.14	0.80
5	0.60	0.01
6	0.70	0.17
7	0.45	0.07
8	0.62	−0.02
9	0.34	0.67
10	0.54	0.43
11	0.58	0.24
12	0.70	0.03
13	0.72	0.25
Variance	3.22	3.21

• Note that in the unrotated principal components solution the first component had variance 4.38 and the second 2.04. The total variance of the two components in the rotated and unrotated solutions is the same, but the rotated components no longer account for maximal proportions of the total variance.

original data. However, the approaches used to achieve this goal are quite different. Factor analysis, unlike principal components analysis, begins with a model or hypothesis about the data, namely that a small set of latent variables is sufficient to account for the interrelationships of the manifest variables but not for their full variances. In contrast, principal components analysis is merely a transformation of the data; in particular, the method has no part corresponding to the specific variates in factor analysis. Consequently, if the factor model holds but the variances of the specific variates are small, both forms of analysis might be expected to give similar results. However, if the specific variances are large, they will be absorbed into all the principal components, both those retained and those rejected. In such circumstances, since factor analysis makes special provision for such variance, its solutions are likely to be easier to interpret.

It should be remembered that principal components analysis and factor analysis are exactly equivalent in at least one respect, namely that both are pointless if the observed variables are uncorrelated; factor analysis because it has nothing to explain and principal components because it would lead to a simple rearrangement of the original variables in terms of the sizes of their variances.

10.7   Summary

1. Principal components analysis and factor analysis both attempt to simplify multivariate data by reducing their dimensionality.
2. Principal components analysis involves a straightforward mathematical transformation of the observed variables.
3. Factor analysis proposes a model for the correlations or covariances of the observed variables, which seeks to 'explain' them in terms of the relationship of the observed variables to a small number of underlying latent variables.
4. Exploratory factor solutions can be subjected to the process of rotation in order to make the solution more interpretable. Rotated solutions aim to achieve simple structure and such solutions may be either orthogonal or oblique.

Exercises

10.1   Rescale the principal components solution given in Display 10.3 so that the coefficients represent correlations between components and variables.

10.2   The matrix given in Display 10.14 shows the correlations between ratings on nine statements about pain made by 123 people suffering from extreme pain.

(a) Perform a principal components analyses on these data and use a scree test plot to decide on the appropriate number of components.
(b) Apply maximum likelihood factor analysis, using the test described in the chapter to select the number of common factors.
(c) Rotate the chosen factor solution using both an orthogonal and oblique procedure and interpret the results.

Display 10.14   Correlations between nine statements about pain

- Each statement was scored on a scale of 1 to 6 ranging from agreement to disagreement.
- The nine statements were as follows:

  (a) Whether or not I am in pain in the future depends on the skills of the doctors.
  (b) Whenever I am in pain, it is usually because of something I have done or not done.
  (c) Whether or not I am in pain depends on what doctors do for me.
  (d) I cannot get any help for my pain unless I go to seek medical advice.
  (e) When I am in pain I know that it is because I have not been taking proper exercise or eating the right food.
  (f) People's pain results from their own carelessness.
  (g) I am directly responsible for my pain.
  (h) Relief from pain is chiefly controlled by the doctors.
  (i) People who are never in pain are just plain lucky.

- The observed correlation matrix obtained from ratings made by 123 people is as follows:

$$R = \begin{pmatrix}
1.0000 & & & & & & & & \\
-0.0385 & 1.0000 & & & & & & & \\
0.6066 & -0.0693 & 1.0000 & & & & & & \\
0.4507 & -0.1167 & 0.5916 & 1.0000 & & & & & \\
0.0320 & 0.4881 & 0.0317 & -0.0802 & 1.0000 & & & & \\
-0.2877 & 0.4271 & -0.1336 & -0.2073 & 0.4731 & 1.0000 & & & \\
-0.2974 & 0.3045 & -0.2404 & -0.1850 & 0.4138 & 0.6346 & 1.0000 & & \\
0.4526 & -0.3090 & 0.5886 & 0.6286 & -0.1397 & -0.1329 & -0.2599 & 1.0000 & \\
0.2952 & -0.1704 & 0.3165 & 0.3680 & -0.2367 & -0.1541 & -0.2893 & 0.4047 & 1.0000
\end{pmatrix}$$

10.3 Find the reproduced and residual correlation matrices for both the chosen principal components solution and the factor analysis solution in the previous question. Which solution appears to give the best fit?

10.4 In the example due to Spearman discussed in Section 10.4.1, suppose that the correlation matrix of the three observed variables had been as follows:

$$\begin{array}{ccc}
 & x_1 & x_2 & x_3 \\
\end{array}$$
$$R = \begin{array}{c} x_1 \\ x_2 \\ x_3 \end{array} \begin{pmatrix}
1.00 & & \\
0.84 & 1.00 & \\
0.60 & 0.35 & 1.00
\end{pmatrix}$$

Find the parameter estimates for a one-factor model using the procedure described in Display 10.5. Are there any problems with the solution?

10.5 Find the correlation corresponding to the rotated factors for the drug usage data derived using the simple graphical procedure shown in Fig. 10.4.

Further reading

Gorsuch, R.L. (1983). *Factor analysis*. Lawrence Erlbaum, Hillsdale, NJ.
Hair, J.F, Anderson, R.E., Tatham, R.L. and Black, W.C. (1992). *Multivariate data analysis with readings*. Macmillan, New York.
Stewart, D.W. (1981). The application and misapplication of factor analysis in marketing research. *Journal of Marketing Research*, **18**, 51–62.

11

Multivariate analysis II: confirmatory factor analysis and covariance structure models

11.1 Introduction

According to Cliff (1983), the last 20 years have seen 'the most important and influential statistical revolution to have occurred in the social sciences'. The revolution referred to in this quotation is the ability to fit, almost routinely, models which can include both dependent and explanatory **latent** variables linked by a series of linear equations. Such models are known as either **structural equation models** or **covariance structure models**, and represent the convergence of relatively independent research traditions in psychometrics, econometrics and biometrics. Specifically, covariance structure models involve a combination of the following topics:

(1) the concept of latent variables and the factor analysis model from psychometrics;
(2) the concept of simultaneous directional influences of some variables on others modelled by a series of multiple regressions which has been used extensively by economists for several decades, but only for **manifest** variables;
(3) a graphical tool known as **path analysis** introduced by Wright (1934) in a biometrics context for indicating the postulated relationships between both latent and manifest variables.

Much like the exploratory factor analysis model described in the previous chapter, covariance structure models attempt to 'explain' the covariances or correlations of the observed variables by the relationships of these variables to the postulated latent variables and by the assumed relationships between the latter. Much of the mathematical detail behind the models is outside the scope of this text; consequently, in this chapter we give a relatively non-mathematical account of the models, concentrating once again on the interpretation of examples of their practical application. However, such an approach means that a number of problems associated with using the models will be conveniently ignored; therefore readers contemplating applying the models to their own data are advised to read this chapter in association with one of the more specialized texts in the area such as Everitt (1984) or Dunn *et al.* (1993).

11.2 Path diagrams

When planning to fit a covariance structure model in practice, it is often of considerable help to formulate the proposed model initially in terms of what is known as a **path diagram**. This gives a graphical illustration of the model which is useful for communicating its essential points in a direct and appealing fashion. Additionally, the path diagram provides a useful guide to setting up the mathematical equations that will explicitly define a model. The fundamental concepts of path diagrams are illustrated in Fig. 11.1. The following conventions are generally adopted:

1. A one-way arrow between two variables indicates a postulated direct influence of one variable on another. A two-way arrow indicates that the variables may be correlated.
2. All direct influences of one variable on another must be included in the path diagram. Therefore the non-existence of an arrow between two variables means that it is assumed in the model that these two variables are not directly related.

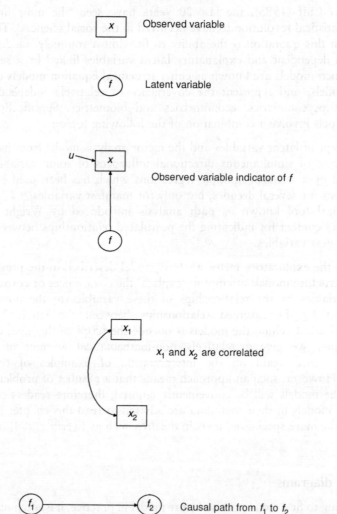

Fig. 11.1 Basic features of path diagrams.

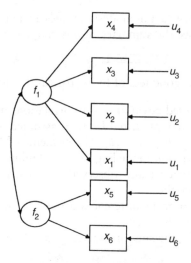

Fig. 11.2 Example of a path diagram for a confirmatory factor analysis model.

3. Manifest variables are enclosed in a square box, and latent variables are enclosed within a circle. 'Error' terms in the model are not enclosed in this way.

A simple example of a path diagram which illustrates what is known as a **confirmatory correlated two-factor model** (see Section 11.3) is given in Fig. 11.2. Detailed explanation of the diagram will be left until an appropriate example is discussed in the next section.

11.3 Confirmatory factor analysis models

Perhaps the simplest examples of covariance structure models are what are generally known as **confirmatory factor analysis models**. Such models arise in investigations involving the correlational structure of a set of multivariate data in which, perhaps on the basis of previous work, the researcher wishes to postulate a specific factor analysis model to explain the relationships between the observed variables. For example, such a model would specify that some of the observed variables had fixed zero loadings on some of the common factors, whilst on the other factors their loadings are free parameters to be estimated in some way. Additionally, the model might fix some correlations between the common factors to be zero, with the remaining correlations again allowed to be free parameters that have to be estimated. Note that this approach is very different from the exploratory use of factor analysis as described in the previous chapter, where all variables were considered to load on all factors, and where all pairs of factors were assumed to be either uncorrelated (an orthogonal solution) or correlated (an oblique solution).

A confirmatory factor analysis model is fitted to a set of data by estimating its free parameters so that the predicted variances and covariances of the observed variables are as 'close' as possible, in some sense, to the corresponding observed values. Some details of the estimation process are given in Display 11.1. Specialized software is generally needed for fitting confirmatory factor analysis models in particular, and covariance structure models in general (see the summary of this chapter, Section 11.6).

Display 11.1 Estimation and goodness of fit in structural equation models

- Suppose that S is the observed covariance (or correlation) matrix with elements s_{ij} and $\hat{\Sigma}$ is the covariance matrix predicted from an assumed model which has t free-parameter values, denoted as $\theta_1, \theta_2, \cdots, \theta_t$. The elements of $\hat{\Sigma}$ are $\hat{\sigma}_{ij}$.
- Estimation in structural equation modelling involves finding parameter estimates so that the corresponding predicted and observed covariances and variances are as 'close' as possible to one another.
- More specifically, a function of the differences between s_{ij} and σ_{ij} is minimized with respect to the parameters $\theta_1, \theta_2, \cdots, \theta_t$.
- One such function would be the sum of squares of the differences; this corresponds to **least-squares** estimation.
- Other estimation criteria are discussed in Everitt (1984).
- Having decided on a measure of 'closeness', some type of mathematical optimization algorithm is applied to find the values of the parameters that minimize the measure.
- The fitting procedure leads not only to parameter estimates but also to the standard errors of these estimates.
- A chi-squared statistic measuring the discrepancies between the observed variances and covariances and those predicted by the model is one of the methods that can be used to assess the fit of the model. The degrees of freedom are

$$\nu = p(p+1)/2 - t$$

where p is the number of observed variables and t the number of free parameters in the model.

- Fit can (and should) also be assessed by examining the differences between the corresponding elements of the observed and predicted covariance or correlation matrix.

As ever, much can be learnt about even an advanced topic such as confirmatory factor analysis by examining a number of examples; these should also help readers to appreciate the differences between fitting a confirmatory factor analysis model and the exploratory use of factor analysis as described in Chapter 10.

11.3.1 *Ability and aspiration*

Caslyn and Kenny (1977) observed the values of the following six variables for 556 white eighth-grade students:

self-concept of ability (x_1);
perceived parental evaluation (x_2);
perceived teacher evaluation (x_3);
perceived friends' evaluation (x_4);

educational aspiration (x_5);
college plans (x_6).

The model postulated to explain the correlations between the six variables involves two latent variables, **ability** and **aspiration**. The first four observed variables are assumed to be 'indicators' of ability, and the last two observed variables are assumed to be indicators of aspiration. The two latent variables are assumed to be correlated. The path diagram for this **correlated two-factor model** is given in Fig. 11.2. The mathematical equations corresponding to this path diagram appear in Display 11.2. Note that, unlike the exploratory factor analysis model, certain loadings here are fixed a priori to be zero. The results of fitting the model to the correlation matrix of the observed variables (Table 11.1) are shown in Table 11.2. (The EQS package was used to estimate the parameters of the model.)

Display 11.2 Equations specifying proposed model for ability and aspiration

- The two common factors or latent variables are ability (f_1) and aspiration (f_2). Both are assumed to have variances of unity.
- The proposed model postulates that the relationships between the observed variables and the latent variables are as follows:

$$x_1 = \lambda_1 f_1 + 0\, f_2 + u_1$$
$$x_2 = \lambda_2 f_1 + 0\, f_2 + u_2$$
$$x_3 = \lambda_3 f_1 + 0\, f_2 + u_3$$
$$x_4 = \lambda_4 f_1 + 0\, f_2 + u_4$$
$$x_5 = 0\, f_1 + \lambda_5 f_2 + u_5$$
$$x_6 = 0\, f_1 + \lambda_6 f_2 + u_6$$

which can be rewritten as

$$x_1 = \lambda_1 f_1 + u_1$$
$$x_2 = \lambda_2 f_1 + u_2$$
$$x_3 = \lambda_3 f_1 + u_3$$
$$x_4 = \lambda_4 f_1 + u_4$$
$$x_5 = \lambda_5 f_2 + u_5$$
$$x_6 = \lambda_6 f_2 + u_6.$$

- Note that, unlike an exploratory factor analysis, a number of loadings are fixed a priori at zero, i.e. they play no part in the estimation process.
- The model also allows for f_1 and f_2 to be correlated.
- The model has a total of 13 free parameters (six loadings, six error variances and one correlation). The observed correlation matrix has six variances and 15 correlations, a total of 21 terms. Consequently, the postulated model has $21 - 13 = 8$ degrees of freedom.

Of particular note among the results given in Table 11.2 is the estimate of the correlation between the two postulated latent variables, ability and aspiration. This estimate (0.666 with a standard error of 0.03) is the **disattenuated correlation**, which represents the correlation between 'true' ability and 'true' aspiration uncontaminated by measurement error in the observed indicators of these concepts. Note that the value of the disattenuated correlation is considerably higher than the correlations between the observed variables, which range from 0.37 to 0.61. An approximate 95% confidence interval for the disattenuated correlation is (0.60, 0.72).

The estimated factor loadings shown in Table 11.2 show that the self-concept of ability is the strongest indicator of ability and college plans is the strongest indicator of aspiration. Comparing each estimated loading with its estimated standard error shows that all are significantly different from zero. In this context, the square of the loading is known as the **reliability** of the corresponding variable, a point which is taken up in more detail in Chapter 13.

Table 11.1 Observed correlations for the ability and aspiration example

	x_1	x_2	x_3	x_4	x_5	x_6
x_1	1.00					
x_2	0.73	1.00				
x_3	0.70	0.68	1.00			
x_4	0.58	0.61	0.57	1.00		
x_5	0.46	0.43	0.40	0.37	1.00	
x_6	0.56	0.52	0.48	0.41	0.72	1.00

Table 11.2 Results from fitting the correlated two-factor model to the correlations in Table 11.1

Parameter	Estimate	SE	Estimate/SE
λ_1	0.863	0.035	24.558
λ_2	0.849	0.035	23.961
λ_3	0.805	0.035	22.115
λ_4	0.695	0.039	18.000
λ_5	0.775	0.040	19.206
λ_6	0.929	0.039	23.569
var(u_1)	0.255	0.023	19.911
var(u_2)	0.279	0.024	11.546
var(u_3)	0.352	0.027	13.070
var(u_4)	0.516	0.035	14.876
var(u_5)	0.399	0.038	10.450
var(u_6)	0.137	0.044	3.152
corr(f_1, f_2)	0.667	0.031	21.521

The fit of the correlated two-factor model can be partially judged by the chi-squared statistic mentioned in Display 11.1; here the statistic takes a value of 9.26 with eight degrees of freedom. The associated P-value is 0.32, suggesting that the model provides a good fit for the observed correlations. As always, however, it is essential not to rely on a single goodness-of-fit index for assessing the fit of a model. A single statistic can rarely 'tap' all aspects of the fit of model. Here, for example, the overall chi-squared statistic might be supplemented by examining the residual correlations, i.e. the differences between the observed values and those predicted by the model; these residuals are shown in Table 11.3, and since they are all very small, the adequacy of the fitted model is confirmed. It appears that the correlated two-factor model with 13 parameters explains the 21 elements of the correlation matrix of the observed variables reasonably well.

Table 11.3 Residual correlations from fitting the correlated two-factor model to the correlations in Table 11.1

	x_1	x_2	x_3	x_4	x_5	x_6
x_1	0.000					
x_2	−0.003	0.000				
x_3	0.005	−0.004	0.000			
x_4	−0.020	0.019	0.100	0.000		
x_5	0.014	−0.009	−0.016	0.011	0.000	
x_6	0.026	−0.006	−0.018	−0.020	0.000	0.000

11.3.2 *A confirmatory factor analysis model for drug usage data*

In the previous chapter a number of exploratory factor analysis models were considered for the correlations between drug usage rates given in Table 10.1. However, in the original investigation of these data reported by Huba *et al.* (1981), a confirmatory factor analysis model was of most interest. The model proposed arose from considering previously reported research in the area, and postulated the following three latent variables.

1. **Alcohol use** (f_1) with non-zero loadings on beer, wine, spirits and cigarettes.
2. **Cannabis use** (f_2) with non-zero loadings on marijuana, hashish, cigarettes and wine. The cigarette variable is assumed to load on both the first and second latent variables because it sometimes occurs with both alcohol and marijuana use and at other times does not. The non-zero loading on wine was allowed because of reports that wine is frequently used with marijuana and that consequently some of the use of wine may be an indicator of tendencies towards cannabis.
3. **Hard drug use** (f_3) with non-zero loadings on amphetamines, tranquillizers, hallucinogenics, hashish, cocaine, heroin, drug-store medication, inhalants and spirits. The use of each of these substances was considered to suggest a strong commitment to the notion of psychoactive drug use.

The path diagram of the proposed model is given in Fig. 11.3, and the corresponding equations defining the model are shown in Display 11.3. Note that, in this example, each pair of the postulated latent variables is allowed to be correlated.

Display 11.3   Structure of the correlated three-factor model for the drug usage data

- Three latent variables, alcohol use (f_1), cannabis use (f_2) and hard drug use (f_3), are proposed. All are assumed to have a variance of unity.
- The proposed model postulates the following relationships between the observed and latent variables:

$$\text{cigarettes} = \lambda_1 f_1 + \lambda_2 f_2 + u_1$$
$$\text{beer} = \lambda_3 f_1 + u_2$$
$$\text{wine} = \lambda_4 f_1 + \lambda_5 f_2 + u_3$$
$$\text{spirits} = \lambda_6 f_1 + \lambda_7 f_3 + u_4$$
$$\text{cocaine} = \lambda_8 f_3 + u_5$$
$$\text{tranquillizers} = \lambda_9 f_3 + u_6$$
$$\text{drug-store medication} = \lambda_{10} f_3 + u_7$$
$$\text{heroin} = \lambda_{11} f_4 + u_8$$
$$\text{marijuana} = \lambda_{12} f_2 + u_9$$
$$\text{hashish} = \lambda_{13} f_2 + \lambda_{14} f_3 + u_{10}$$
$$\text{inhalants} = \lambda_{15} f_3 + u_{11}$$
$$\text{hallucinogenics} = \lambda_{16} f_3 + u_{12}$$
$$\text{amphetamines} = \lambda_{17} f_3 + u_{13}.$$

- The proposed model also allows for non-zero correlations between each pair of latent variables.
- The proposed model has a total of 33 parameters to estimate (17 loadings, 13 error variances and three between-factor correlations). Consequently, the model has $91 - 33 = 58$ degrees of freedom.

The results of fitting the proposed model (again using the EQS software) are shown in Table 11.4. The chi-squared goodness-of-fit statistic takes a value of 323.96 with 58 degrees of freedom and has a very small associated P-value. It appears that the proposed model does not provide an adequate fit for the correlations between the recorded usage rates of the 13 substances. However, before jumping to such a conclusion it will be helpful to cast an eye over the residual correlations given in Table 11.5. The majority of the residuals are small, with the most notable exception being that corresponding to the correlation of inhalants and drug-store medication. The model predicts a correlation between these two substances which is substantially lower than the observed value of 0.310. However, on the whole, the size of the residuals appears to indicate that the proposed model accounts for the observed correlations reasonably

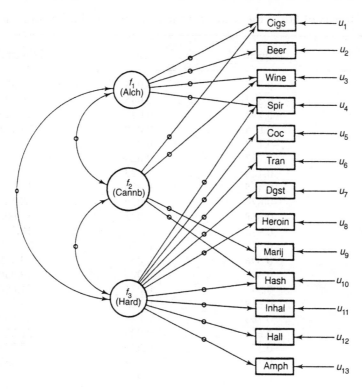

Fig. 11.3 Path diagram for the correlated three-factor model for drug usage data.

well. Perhaps the chi-squared statistic is significant here because, with the large sample size involved ($n = 1634$), even relatively trivial discrepancies between observed and predicted correlations are judged to be significant.

11.4 An example of a structural equation model for longitudinal data: the stability of alienation

The characteristic feature of a longitudinal research design is that measurements on a set of variables are obtained from the same people on two or more occasions. One particular aspect of the analysis of such designs was discussed in Chapter 5. Here the use of structural equation modelling will be illustrated using data from a longitudinal study reported by Wheaton *et al.* (1977) which was concerned with the stability over time of attitudes such as alienation and their relationship to background variables such as education and occupation. In the investigation, data on attitude scales were collected from 932 people in two rural regions in Illinois at three points in time (1966, 1967 and 1971). Only that part of the data collected in 1967 and 1971 is of concern here, and Table 11.6 shows the covariances between six observed variables. The anomia and powerlessness subscales are taken to be indicators of a latent variable, **alienation**,

Table 11.4 Results of fitting the correlated three-factor model to the drug usage data

Parameter	Estimate	SE	Estimate/SE
λ_1	0.358	0.035	10.371
λ_2	0.332	0.035	9.401
λ_3	0.792	0.023	35.021
λ_4	0.875	0.038	23.285
λ_5	−0.152	0.037	−4.158
λ_6	0.722	0.024	30.673
λ_7	0.123	0.023	5.439
λ_8	0.465	0.026	18.079
λ_9	0.676	0.024	28.182
λ_{10}	0.359	0.025	13.602
λ_{11}	0.476	0.026	18.571
λ_{12}	0.912	0.030	29.958
λ_{13}	0.396	0.030	13.379
λ_{14}	0.381	0.029	13.050
λ_{15}	0.543	0.025	21.602
λ_{16}	0.618	0.025	25.233
λ_{17}	0.763	0.023	32.980
$\mathrm{var}(u_1)$	0.611	0.024	25.823
$\mathrm{var}(u_2)$	0.374	0.020	18.743
$\mathrm{var}(u_3)$	0.379	0.024	16.052
$\mathrm{var}(u_4)$	0.408	0.019	21.337
$\mathrm{var}(u_5)$	0.784	0.029	26.845
$\mathrm{var}(u_6)$	0.544	0.023	23.222
$\mathrm{var}(u_7)$	0.871	0.032	27.653
$\mathrm{var}(u_8)$	0.773	0.029	26.735
$\mathrm{var}(u_9)$	0.169	0.044	3.846
$\mathrm{var}(u_{10})$	0.547	0.022	24.593
$\mathrm{var}(u_{11})$	0.705	0.027	25.941
$\mathrm{var}(u_{12})$	0.618	0.025	24.655
$\mathrm{var}(u_{13})$	0.418	0.021	19.713
$\mathrm{corr}(f_1, f_2)$	0.634	0.027	23.369
$\mathrm{corr}(f_1, f_3)$	0.313	0.029	10.674
$\mathrm{corr}(f_2, f_3)$	0.499	0.027	18.412

and the two background variables education (years of schooling completed) and Duncan's socio-economic index (SEI) which are assumed to indicate a respondent's **socio-economic status**. The path diagram for the model proposed to explain the covariances between the observed variables is shown in Fig. 11.4. Here the model involves a combination of a confirmatory factor analysis model with a regression model for the latent variables. One of the important questions here involves the size of the regression coefficient of alienation in 1971 on alienation in 1967, since this reflects the stability of the attitude over time. (Note that the error terms of anomia and

Table 11.5 Residual correlations from fitting the correlated three-factor model to the drug usage data

	1	2	3	4	5	6	7	8	9	10	11	12	13
1	0.000												
2	-0.003	0.000											
3	0.009	0.002	0.000										
4	-0.008	0.002	-0.004	0.000									
5	-0.015	-0.047	-0.039	-0.047	0.000								
6	0.015	-0.021	0.005	0.022	0.035	0.000							
7	-0.009	0.014	0.039	-0.003	0.042	-0.021	0.000						
8	-0.050	-0.055	-0.028	-0.069	0.099	0.033	0.030	0.000					
9	0.004	-0.012	-0.002	0.009	-0.026	0.008	-0.013	-0.063	0.000				
10	-0.023	0.025	0.005	0.029	0.034	-0.014	-0.045	-0.057	-0.001	0.000			
11	0.094	0.068	0.075	0.065	0.019	-0.044	0.115	0.029	0.054	-0.013	0.00		
12	-0.071	-0.065	-0.049	-0.077	-0.009	-0.051	0.010	0.025	-0.077	0.010	0.004	0.000	
13	0.033	0.010	0.033	0.026	-0.077	0.030	-0.042	-0.049	0.047	0.025	-0.022	0.039	0.000

Table 11.6 Covariances of manifest variables in the stability of alienation example

	x_1	x_2	x_3	x_4	x_5	x_6
x_1	11.834					
x_2	6.947	9.364				
x_3	6.819	5.09	12.532			
x_4	4.783	5.028	7.495	9.986		
x_5	-3.839	-3.841	-3.625	9.610	3.552	
x_6	-2.190	-1.883	-2.175	-1.878		4.503

x_1, anomia in 1967; x_2, powerlessness in 1967; x_3, anomia in 1971; x_4, powerlessness in 1971; x_5, years of education; x_6, Duncan's socio-economic index.

powerlessness are allowed to be correlated over time to account for possible memory or other retest effects.) Some of the results of fitting the proposed model are shown in Display 11.4.

The chi-squared goodness-of-fit statistic takes a value of 4.73 with four degrees of freedom and suggests that the proposed model fits the observed covariances extremely well. The regression coefficient of alienation on socio-economic status in both 1967 and 1971 is negative, as might be expected since higher socio-economic status is likely to result in lower alienation and vice versa. The regression coefficient for alienation in 1971 on alienation in 1967 is positive and highly significant. Clearly, the attitude remains relatively stable over the time period. The error covariance for anomia in 1967 and 1971 is significantly different from zero; that for powerlessness in the two years is not significant.

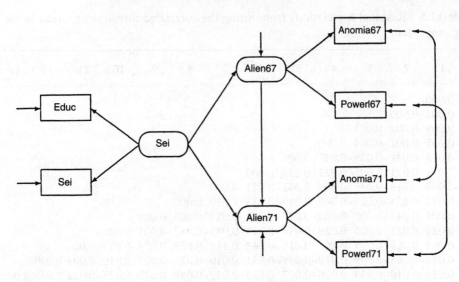

Fig. 11.4 Path diagram for the stability of alienation example.

Display 11.4   Results of fitting the model specified by the path diagram in Fig. 11.4 to the covariances in Table 11.6.

- The most interesting part of the model specified in Fig. 11.4 is that involving the regression equations relating the latent variables:

    alienation $67 = \beta_1 \times$ socio-economic status

    alienation $71 = \beta_2 \times$ alienation $67 + \beta_3 \times$ socio-economic status.

- The estimated regression coefficients and their standard errors are

$$\hat{\beta}_1 = -1.500, \quad SE = 0.124$$
$$\hat{\beta}_2 = 0.607, \quad\ \ SE = 0.051$$
$$\hat{\beta}_3 = -0.592, \quad SE = 0.131.$$

11.5   Latent variables and structural equation models—some caveats

Like many earlier methodological advances, the fusion of factor analysis, multiple regression and path analysis achieved by the creators of covariance structure models in the 1970s has not been without its difficulties. Many social and behavioural scientists appear to have received the advance with an enthusiasm which has, on occasions, overcome their usual critical faculties. In disciplines such as psychology and sociology, still essentially seeking the first steps along the road to some type of unifying theory, models which suggest that 'causal' mechanisms might be demonstrable from correlational data have often proved difficult to resist. That old, but still apposite, aphorism 'correlation does not imply causation' appears to have been conveniently shelved among the mass of path diagrams, parameter estimates and models for everything from intelligence to sexual behaviour that have appeared in the literature. Latent variables are given names and tested as if they had an independent existence and might even be experimentally manipulated if necessary. In many cases little attention is paid to the purpose that the model finally accepted is intended to serve.

Of course, all of this is an extremely unsatisfactory state of affairs, and readers with an interest in using covariance structure models in practice should make themselves familiar with the criticisms of the approach voiced by, among others, Cliff (1983), Lenk (1986) and Fergusson and Horwood (1986). However, despite such critics the covariance structure approach provides, potentially at least, a rich source of models for many areas of psychology and related disciplines.

11.6 Summary

1. Structural equation models represent a fusion of factor analysis, multiple regression and path analysis.
2. Complex models can now be fitted routinely (although not always appropriately!) using one of the specialized software packages available. The two main packages are EQS and LISREL. Detailed descriptions of how to use these are given by Dunn *et al.* (1993) and Jöreskog and Sörborm (1993) respectively.
3. A problem with covariance structure models that has been conveniently ignored throughout this chapter is that not all such models can be tested. Models can only be tested if the parameters of the model can be uniquely specified or **identified**. The question of identification of a model is important and is well described by Bentler (1980) and Dunn *et al.* (1993).

Exercises

11.1 Find the predicted covariance matrix corresponding to a confirmatory factor analysis model with the following structure.

Pattern of free and fixed loadings

f_1	f_2	f_3
X	0	0
X	0	0
0	X	0
0	X	0
0	X	0
0	X	0
0	X	X
0	0	X

X represents a free parameter. The factors are all assumed to have variance unity, and only f_2 and f_3 can have a non-zero correlation.

11.2   Huba *et al.* (1981), in their analysis of the drug usage data, extend the correlated three-factor model considered in Section 11.3 to allow for correlation of the error terms of particular variables. The new model allows for correlations between the error terms corresponding to the following substances, for the reasons given:

1. Amphetamines and cocaine: these share a subjective 'rush' effect so that the respective error terms can be correlated.
2. Tranquillizers and heroin: these both show a sedative effect, so that again a correlation between the appropriate error terms should be allowed.
3. Tranquillizers and amphetamines: these are both used in pill form by young adolescents, and a preference might be expressed for pills regardless of their psychoactive effect. Therefore a correlation between the error terms of these variables might be appropriate.

Construct a path diagram for the new model and, if possible, fit the model and compare its fit with the model described in Section 11.3.

11.3   In the ability and aspiration example discussed in Section 11.3.1, use the results given to show that a one-dimensional model for the observed correlations (i.e. a model with a single common factor) would not be adequate.

Further reading

Cudeck, R. (1989). Analysis of correlation matrices using covariance structure models. *Psychological Bulletin*, 105, 317–27.
Lochlin, J.C. (1987). *Latent variable models: an introduction to factor, path and structural analysis*. Lawrence Erlbaum, Hillsdale, NJ.

12

Multivariate analysis III: cluster analysis, discriminant analysis and multidimensional scaling

12.1 Introduction

Some further multivariate analysis techniques useful in particular types of psychological research are described in this chapter. The first two, **cluster analysis** and **discriminant analysis**, deal with various aspects of the **classification** of the phenomena under investigation in a research study. Such classification is an important component of virtually all scientific research. In the behavioural sciences, for example, the phenomena of concern are often individuals, but may in other cases be societies, or even patterns of behaviour, for which the investigator is interested in developing a classification in which the items of interest are sorted into a small number of relatively homogeneous groups or **clusters**. At the very least, such a classification should provide a convenient summary of the multivariate data from which it arises, but often it will yield much more than this; for example, it may aid in the understanding of the data and in communication between different groups of research workers. In some cases the classification will have important theoretical and/or practical implications. In psychiatry, for example, a suitable classification of mental disturbances could help in the search for both causes and appropriate treatments.

Statistical techniques concerned with classification are essentially of two types. The first are those that attempt to produce a sensible and informative classification from an initially unclassified set of multivariate data using the variable values observed on the phenomenon being studied. For example, Paykel and Rassaby (1978) studied 236 individuals who had attempted suicide. Each suicide attempter was described by 14 variables including age, number of previous suicide attempts, severity of depression etc. A number of clustering methods were applied to the data, and a final classification which divided the individuals into three groups appeared potentially valuable as a basis for future studies into the causes and possible treatment of attempted suicide.

The second type of classification problem is that dealt with by the so-called **discriminant analysis** or **assignment** methods. Here the classification scheme is known a priori, and the main questions of interest become the development of a rule for assigning as yet unclassified individuals to one or other of the known classes and the identification of subsets of variables that are the most useful for discrimination. The classic example of where such an approach is needed occurs in medicine when there is a disease of interest which can only be accurately diagnosed via a post-mortem examination. It is clearly highly desirable to have a procedure for allocating patients to either the disease or no-disease class which minimizes the chance of misclassification and allows appropriate therapeutic action to be taken whilst the patient is still alive. In such a case, a classification rule could be derived from observations taken prior to death on patients now dead, and thus diagnosed without error; the group of patients from which the rule is derived is usually known as the **training set**.

The third topic that will be briefly discussed in this chapter is **multidimensional scaling**. Techniques of this type are particularly useful in the analysis of data from experiments where subjects are asked to assess the similarity or dissimilarity of pairs of objects, people, stimuli etc. An example of such data, arising from an experiment in which subjects were asked to judge pairs of Morse code signals for the integers from 0 to 9, is shown in Table 12.1. The entries in the table give the percentage of times that pairs of signals were declared to be the same by 598 subjects. The primary aim of a multidimensional scaling of such judgements is to display them graphically so that any structure or pattern becomes apparent.

Table 12.1 Percentage of times that pairs of Morse code signals for two numbers were declared to be the same by 598 subjects

Signal	1	2	3	4	5	6	7	8	9	0
(· − − − −) 1	84									
(· · − − −) 2	62	89								
(· · · − −) 3	16	59	86							
(· · · · −) 4	6	23	38	89						
(· · · · ·) 5	12	8	27	56	90					
(− · · · ·) 6	12	14	33	34	30	86				
(− − · · ·) 7	20	25	17	24	18	65	85			
(− − − · ·) 8	37	25	16	13	10	22	65	88		
(− − − − ·) 9	57	28	9	7	5	8	31	58	91	
(− − − − −) 0	52	18	9	7	5	18	15	39	79	94

Data taken from Rothkopf (1957).

12.2 Cluster analysis

Consider the data listed in Table 12.2 giving the age and body fat percentage of 18 normal adults. A scatter plot of the data is shown in Fig. 12.1. It is clear, without applying any complex statistical techniques, that the observations fall into two groups. In fact the two groups correspond to males and females, as shown in Fig. 12.2.

In this very simple example, the groups or clusters of observations present in the data can be discovered very easily by merely plotting the data (and the two derived clusters even validated by reference to an external criterion!). For multivariate data sets involving only two or three variables, examination of such scatter plots often provides a very effective method of cluster analysis since the human eye–brain system is an excellent pattern recognition device. Identifying groups from such plots involves an assessment of the relative distances between the points in the diagram. In practice, however, most data sets to be analysed will contain many more than two variables, and

Table 12.2 Age and body fat

Age	Percentage fat	Age	Percentage fat
39	31.4	52	14.0
40	12.3	53	34.7
41	11.8	53	42.0
42	14.5	53	14.6
41	25.9	54	29.1
45	27.4	56	32.5
45	13.9	56	13.1
45	12.4	57	30.3
46	14.3	58	33.0
49	25.2	58	33.8
50	31.1	60	41.1
51	10.8	61	34.5

establishing whether the data contain relatively distinct groups of observations will not be so straightforward. Consequently, more complex methods of cluster analysis are likely to be needed. Many methods have been suggested, and a comprehensive review is given by Everitt (1993). Here, attention will be concentrated on one particular class of methods, which are generally known as **agglomerative hierarchical clustering techniques**. However, before describing a number of these methods, it is necessary to spend a little time discussing the measurement of distance in a set of multivariate data since such measurement is fundamental in the operation of the clustering procedures.

12.2.1 *Distance measures*

A set of multivariate data consists of a sample of, say, n individuals each having measurements on p variables. Of primary interest in the clustering situation is how to measure the distance between each pair of individuals using their observed variable values. To begin, suppose that each individual had only two recorded variable values so that the data for a pair of individuals i and j can be plotted as shown in Fig. 12.3. Also shown in this figure is the **Euclidean distance** between the two individuals; such a distance should be familiar to most readers since, locally at least, they live in an Euclidean universe! The Euclidean distance between the two individuals i and j can be calculated from their coordinate values as follows:

$$d_{ij} = [(0.5 - 1.5)^2 + (2.5 - 1.5)^2]^{1/2} = 1.41. \tag{12.1}$$

When there are p variable values for individual i, i.e. $x_{i1}, x_{i2}, \ldots, x_{ip}$, and similarly for individual j, $x_{j1}, x_{j2}, \ldots, x_{jp}$, the Euclidean distance between them is defined as follows:

$$d_{ij} = [(x_{i1} - x_{j1})^2 + (x_{i2} - x_{j2})^2 + \ldots + (x_{ip} - x_{jp})^2]^{1/2}, \tag{12.2}$$

i.e.

$$d_{ij} = [\sum_{k=1}^{p} (x_{ik} - x_{jk})^2]^{1/2}. \tag{12.3}$$

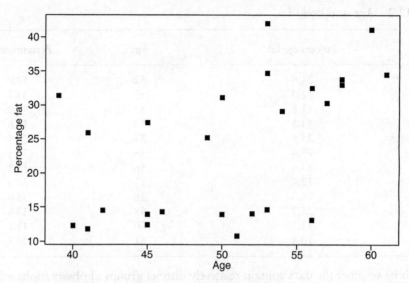

Fig. 12.1 Scatter plot of percentage body fat against age.

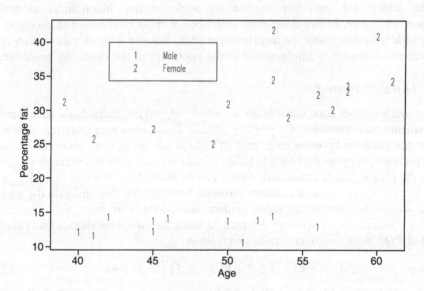

Fig. 12.2 Scatter plot of percentage body fat against age, with sex of individual indicated.

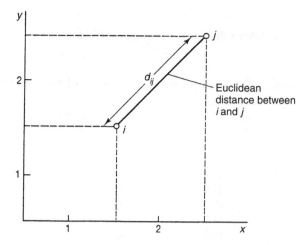

Fig. 12.3 Euclidean distance in two dimensions.

The Euclidean distances between each pair of individuals in a set of multivariate data can be arranged in a matrix **D**, which is symmetric since $d_{ij} = d_{ji}$ and has zeros on the main diagonal. Such a matrix is the starting point of many clustering procedures, although the calculation of Euclidean distances from the raw data may not be sensible when the variables are on very different scales. In such cases a more acceptable, but still not completely satisfactory, approach is to standardize each variable to have the same variance (usually unity) before calculating the required distances. (The difficult problem of the most appropriate standardization of variables prior to a cluster analysis is discussed in more detail by Everitt, 1993.)

Display 12.1 illustrates the calculation of an Euclidean distance matrix for a small set of data both before and after standardization of the variables to variance unity. Notice that the ordering of the distances has changed, a point that has fairly obvious implications in a clustering context.

When the distance between two locations A and B is referred to in everyday conversation, it is generally Euclidean distance that is implied, and certainly this is the distance measure most often used in clustering applications. But what about city dwellers in general, and New Yorkers in particular? Here a much more relevant measure of the distance between two points is the so-called city block or Manhattan distance; this measure is described in Display 12.2 and is occasionally used in the clustering of multivariate data for reasons described by Everitt (1993), who also discusses other possible distance measures.

12.2.2 Agglomerative hierarchical clustering methods

The techniques known as agglomerative hierarchical clustering are among the most commonly applied methods of cluster analysis. All such methods proceed by a series of steps in which progressively larger groups are formed by joining together groups

Display 12.1 Euclidean distances for a set of multivariate data before and after standardization

- The data consist of four variable values for each of six individuals as follows:

Individual	Variable			
	1	2	3	4
1	39.8	38.0	22.2	23.2
2	53.7	37.2	18.7	18.5
3	47.3	39.8	23.3	22.1
4	41.7	37.6	22.8	22.3
5	44.7	38.5	24.8	24.4
6	47.9	39.8	22.0	23.3

- The matrix $\mathbf{D}$ of Euclidean distances for the raw data, is given by

$$
\mathbf{D} = \begin{array}{c}
\begin{array}{ccccccc} \quad & 1 & 2 & 3 & 4 & 5 & 6 \end{array} \\
\begin{array}{c} 1 \\ 2 \\ 3 \\ 4 \\ 5 \\ 6 \end{array}
\left(\begin{array}{cccccc}
0.00 & & & & & \\
15.01 & 0.00 & & & & \\
7.86 & 9.05 & 0.00 & & & \\
2.22 & 13.24 & 6.04 & 0.00 & & \\
5.70 & 12.44 & 4.00 & 4.27 & 0.00 & \\
8.30 & 8.62 & 1.87 & 6.70 & 4.58 & 0.00
\end{array}\right)
\end{array}
$$

- The matrix $\mathbf{D_s}$ of Euclidean distances for the data after standardizing each variable to have variance unity is given by

$$
\mathbf{D_s} = \begin{array}{c}
\begin{array}{ccccccc} \quad & 1 & 2 & 3 & 4 & 5 & 6 \end{array} \\
\begin{array}{c} 1 \\ 2 \\ 3 \\ 4 \\ 5 \\ 6 \end{array}
\left(\begin{array}{cccccc}
0.00 & & & & & \\
4.08 & 0.00 & & & & \\
2.35 & 3.93 & 0.00 & & & \\
0.75 & 3.68 & 2.30 & 0.00 & & \\
1.78 & 4.70 & 1.86 & 1.75 & 0.00 & \\
2.31 & 3.88 & 0.88 & 2.43 & 2.00 & 0.00
\end{array}\right)
\end{array}
$$

- Note that the ordering of distances in $\mathbf{D}$ and $\mathbf{D_s}$ is not the same. For example, in $\mathbf{D}$ the distance between individuals 4 and 2 is more than that between individuals 5 and 2; in $\mathbf{D_s}$ the reverse is the case.

Display 12.2   City block distance

- Mathematically, the distance measure is defined as

$$d_{ij} = \sum_{k=1}^{p} |x_{ik} - x_{jk}|.$$

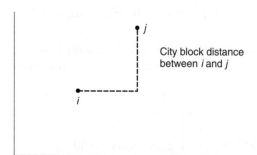

City block distance
between i and j

formed earlier in the process. The initial step involves combining the two individuals who are closest (according to whatever distance measure is being used) into a 'group' with two members, and the final stage occurs when all the individuals are contained within a single 'cluster'. The progression from single individuals to a single cluster is made by joining together, at each stage, the two individuals or the two groups of individuals that are closest at that stage. It is the different possibilities for defining distance between individuals and multimember groups, and between groups, that gives rise to the variety of agglomerative hierarchical techniques available. Two methods which are widely used, **complete linkage clustering** and **average linkage clustering**, are described in detail in Displays 12.3 and 12.4.

Display 12.3   Complete linkage cluster analysis

- In complete linkage cluster analysis, the distance between groups is defined as the distance between the two individuals, one in one group and one in the other, that are farthest apart.
- To illustrate the application of the complete linkage clustering method it will be applied to the matrix $\mathbf{D}_s$ of Euclidean distances, given in Display 12.1.
- The first stage is the merger of individuals 1 and 4 into a group with two members, since d_{14} is the smallest entry in $\mathbf{D}_s$. At this stage the groups are

$$\{1,4\}, \{2\}, \{3\}, \{5\}, \{6\}.$$

- The distances between the group formed by individuals 1 and 4 and the remaining individuals are calculated as follows:

$$d_{(14)2} = \max[d_{12}, d_{24}] = d_{12} = 4.08$$
$$d_{(14)3} = \max[d_{13}, d_{34}] = d_{13} = 2.35$$
$$d_{(14)5} = \max[d_{15}, d_{45}] = d_{15} = 1.78$$
$$d_{(14)6} = \max[d_{16}, d_{46}] = d_{46} = 2.43.$$

- A new distance matrix $\mathbf{D}_s^{(1)}$, which includes the distances between individuals 2, 3, 5, and 6, and the two-member group $\{1, 4\}$, is now constructed:

$$\mathbf{D}_s^{(1)} = \begin{array}{c} \\ (14) \\ 2 \\ 3 \\ 5 \\ 6 \end{array} \begin{array}{c} (14) \quad 2 \quad\quad 3 \quad\quad 5 \quad\quad 6 \\ \left(\begin{array}{ccccc} 0.00 & & & & \\ 4.08 & 0.00 & & & \\ 2.35 & 4.04 & 0.00 & & \\ 1.78 & 4.65 & 1.78 & 0.00 & \\ 2.43 & 3.78 & 1.05 & 1.97 & 0.00 \end{array} \right) \end{array}$$

- The smallest entry in $\mathbf{D}_s^{(1)}$ is that between individuals 3 and 6, and these are merged to give a second two-member group. Thus the groups at this stage are

$$\{14\}, \{2\}, \{3, 6\}, \{5\}.$$

- The distance between the two two-membered groups is given by

$$d_{(14)(36)} = \max[d_{13}, d_{16}, d_{34}, d_{46}] = d_{46} = 2.43.$$

- The relevant distance matrix $\mathbf{D}_s^{(2)}$ at this stage is

$$\mathbf{D}_s^{(2)} = \begin{array}{c} \\ (14) \\ 2 \\ (36) \\ 5 \end{array} \begin{array}{c} (14) \quad\; 2 \quad\; (36) \quad\; 5 \\ \left(\begin{array}{cccc} 0.00 & & & \\ 4.08 & 0.00 & & \\ 2.43 & 3.78 & 0.00 & \\ 1.78 & 4.65 & 1.78 & 0.00 \end{array} \right) \end{array}$$

- The smallest entry in $\mathbf{D}_s^{(2)}$ is between individual 5 and the group containing individuals 1 and 4. Consequently at this stage the groups become:

$$\{1, 4, 5\}, \{2\}, \{3, 6\}.$$

- The procedure continues in this way until all individuals are joined in a single group.
- The series of steps can be conveniently summarized in a diagram known as a **dendrogram**. The complete linkage dendogram corresponding to the example here is shown below:

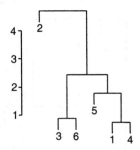

Display 12.4   Average linkage cluster analysis

- With average linkage clustering the distance between two groups is defined as the average of the interindividual distances of pairs of individuals made up of members of the different groups. The distance measure is illustrated in the diagram below:

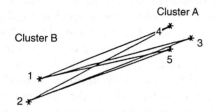

$$d_{AB} = \frac{1}{6}(d_{13} + d_{14} + d_{15} + d_{23} + d_{24} + d_{25}).$$

- In the application of average linkage to the standardized distance matrix in Display 12.1, the first stage is again to form a group with individuals 1 and 4. The distances between this group and the remaining individuals are given by

$$d_{(14)2} = (d_{12} + d_{24})/2 = 3.86$$
$$d_{(14)3} = (d_{13} + d_{34})/2 = 2.37$$
$$d_{(14)5} = (d_{15} + d_{45})/2 = 1.74$$
$$d_{(14)6} = (d_{16} + d_{46})/2 = 2.36.$$

- As with complete linkage, individuals 3 and 6 are joined at the next stage. The distance between the two two-membered groups is calculated as

$$d_{(14)(36)} = (d_{13} + d_{16} + d_{34} + d_{46})/4 = 2.37.$$

- In this case the average linkage dendrogram is as follows.

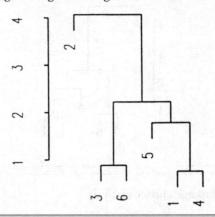

After studying Displays 12.3 and 12.4, it will be apparent to readers that each of the agglomerative hierarchical techniques described (and the same applies to other methods of the class) give a series of what might be called **clustering solutions** containing n clusters (n is the number of individuals) all the way down to one cluster, whereas in practice most investigators are looking for a specific number of clusters that best describes the structure of their data. Choosing a single 'best' solution from the series given by an agglomerative hierarchical clustering method is not a simple task. In fact, it is largely an unresolved problem and is discussed in detail by Everitt (1979, 1993) and by Milligan and Cooper (1985). One very informal method for assessing the most appropriate number of groups is to examine the dendrogram corresponding to the series of solutions and identify a 'large' change in level. Such a change may be indicative of the number of clusters to select.

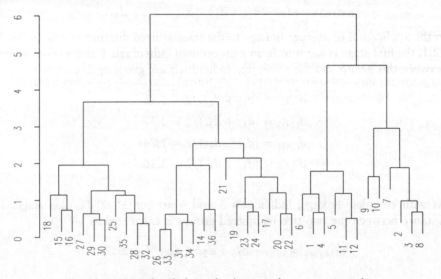

Fig. 12.4 Complete linkage dendrogram for occupations data.

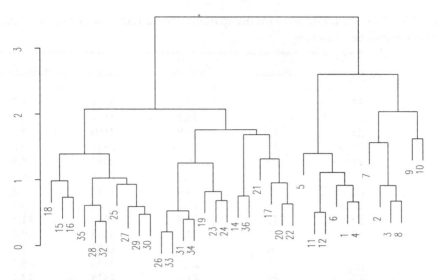

Fig. 12.5 Average linkage dendrogram for occupations data.

To illustrate the application of cluster analysis in practice, both complete linkage and average linkage will be applied to the occupations data introduced in Chapter 2 (see Table 2.6) after removal of occupation 13, since this occupation was identified as a possible outlier in Chapter 10 and such points often cause problems for clustering techniques. Since the four variables describing each occupation are on very different scales, they were each standardized to have a variance of unity before using them to calculate the Euclidean distances between each pair of occupations. The dendrograms resulting from applying complete linkage and average linkage clustering to the Euclidean distances are shown in Figs 12.4 and 12.5. Both dendrograms suggest that the two-group solution might be most appropriate for these data. Details of this solution (which is the same for both methods) are given in Table 12.3. The two groups correspond essentially to 'professional' occupations and others. A simple graphical display of the derived clusters can be produced by plotting cluster labels on the scattergram of the first two principal component scores of each observation (see Chapter 10). Such a diagram is shown in Fig. 12.6.

Cluster analysis techniques are potentially very valuable aids in attempts both to describe and ultimately to explain complex multivariate data; however, they require considerable care in their application if misleading artifactual solutions are to be avoided. Many of the problems are discussed by Everitt (1993), but the following two quotations should help readers to adopt a sensible attitude with respect to the clustering of multivariate data:

> Cluster analysis is a tool for exploring data and should be supplemented by techniques for visualizing data. (Jain and Dubes, 1988)

> What purpose do clusters serve? Presumably purposes of description, where they may help with either graphical or verbal description, and, to a degree, purposes of

Table 12.3 Two-cluster solution for occupations data resulting from complete linkage and average linkage clustering

Cluster	Occupation	Prestige	Suicide	Income	Education
1	33	16	42.2	2249	8.7
	34	11	38.2	2551	8.5
	29	13	17.9	2590	9.6
	30	24	15.7	2915	9.6
	31	20	36.0	2357	8.8
	28	10	24.9	2213	8.9
	32	7	24.4	1942	9.8
	27	19	19.2	3424	9.2
	20	53	30.8	3447	11.1
	22	57	34.5	3303	9.6
	23	26	24.4	2693	9.4
	24	29	29.4	3353	9.3
	15	39	21.9	2828	12.7
	16	34	16.5	3480	12.2
	26	15	41.7	2410	8.2
	35	8	20.3	1866	8.2
	19	33	32.7	2450	8.7
	18	16	24.1	2543	12.1
	25	10	14.4	1898	10.3
	17	41	32.4	3771	12.7
	36	41	47.6	2866	10.6
	14	45	47.3	3806	11.6
	21	67	34.2	4648	8.8
2	11	59	16.0	3176	15.8
	12	73	16.8	3456	16.0
	4	90	20.7	4091	16.0
	6	93	14.2	4366	16.0
	3	76	37.0	4303	15.6
	8	88	31.9	4590	16.0
	1	82	23.8	3977	14.4
	2	90	37.5	5509	16.0
	5	87	10.6	2410	16.0
	7	90	45.6	6448	16.0
	9	89	24.3	6284	16.0
	10	97	31.9	8302	16.0

prediction or prognosis—as where we try to separate persons with an upper respiratory infection (cold) from those who do not, even though there is a continuous graduation, in some patients, from one state to the other. If we can avoid asking too much of clustering techniques, they can serve us better. (Hansen and Tukey, 1992)

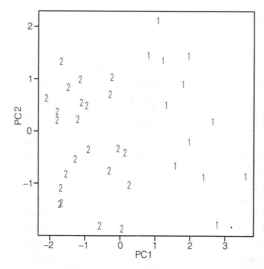

Fig. 12.6 Plot of occupations data in the space of the first two principal components with the two-cluster solution from complete linkage and average linkage indicated.

12.3 Discriminant function techniques

Discriminant function techniques are concerned with deriving rules for classifying an object or individual into one of a number of predefined groups, using the information provided by a number of variable values recorded on the object or individual. Some possible applications are as follows:

1. Determining what category of credit risk (e.g. low risk or high risk) an individual falls into.
2. Predicting the success or failure of a new product.
3. Classifying mentally ill patients into one of a number of diagnostic categories.

The most commonly occurring situation is that involving just two groups, and the most widely applied method of discrimination is known as **Fisher's linear discriminant function**, the details of which are described in Display 12.5. The data shown in Table 12.4 are used to illustrate the use of Fisher's linear discriminant function. These data were collected by Spicer *et al.* (1987) in an investigation of the tragic occurrence of sudden infant death syndrome (SIDS). The two groups here consist of 16 SIDS victims and 49 controls. The **factor 68** variable arises from a particular aspect of 24-hour recordings of electrocardiograms and respiratory movements made for each child (see the original paper for more details). The SIDS victims and controls were matched for the age at which these recordings were made, and all the infants had a gestational age of 37 or more weeks and were regarded as full term. Here the primary purpose of using discriminant analysis is to derive a rule which may be able to identify children at risk of SIDS.

Table 12.4   SIDS data

Group	1	2	3	4
1	115.5	3060	0.291	39
1	108.2	3570	0.277	40
1	114.2	3950	0.390	41
1	118.8	3480	0.339	40
1	76.9	3370	0.248	39
1	132.6	3260	0.342	40
1	107.7	4420	0.310	42
1	118.2	3560	0.220	40
1	126.6	3290	0.233	38
1	138.0	3010	0.309	40
1	127.0	3180	0.355	40
1	127.7	3950	0.309	40
1	106.8	3400	0.250	40
1	142.1	2410	0.368	38
1	91.5	2890	0.223	42
1	151.1	4030	0.364	40
1	127.1	3770	0.335	42
1	134.3	2680	0.356	40
1	114.9	3370	0.374	41
1	118.1	3370	0.152	40
1	122.0	3270	0.356	40
1	167.0	3520	0.394	41
1	107.9	3340	0.250	41
1	134.6	3940	0.422	41
1	137.7	3350	0.409	40
1	112.8	3350	0.241	39
1	131.3	3000	0.312	40
1	132.7	3960	0.196	40
1	148.1	3490	0.266	40
1	118.9	2640	0.310	39
1	133.7	3630	0.351	40
1	141.0	2680	0.420	38
1	134.1	3580	0.366	40
1	135.5	3800	0.503	39
1	148.6	3350	0.272	40
1	147.9	3030	0.291	40
1	162.0	3940	0.308	42
1	146.8	4080	0.235	40
1	131.7	3520	0.287	40
1	149.0	3630	0.456	40
1	114.1	3290	0.284	40
1	129.2	3180	0.239	40
1	144.2	3580	0.191	40
1	148.1	3060	0.334	40
1	108.2	3000	0.321	37
1	131.1	4310	0.450	40

Table 12.4 SIDS data – *cont'd*

Group	1	2	3	4
1	129.7	3975	0.244	40
1	142.0	3000	0.173	40
1	145.5	3940	0.304	41
2	139.7	3740	0.409	40
2	121.3	3005	0.626	38
2	131.4	4790	0.383	40
2	152.8	1890	0.432	38
2	125.6	2929	0.347	40
2	139.5	2810	0.493	39
2	117.2	3490	0.521	38
2	131.5	3030	0.343	37
2	137.3	2000	0.359	41
2	140.9	3770	0.349	40
2	139.5	2350	0.279	40
2	128.4	2780	0.409	39
2	154.2	2980	0.309	40
2	140.7	2120	0.372	38
2	105.5	2700	0.314	39
2	121.7	3060	0.405	41

Group 1, controls; group 2, cases.
Variables: 1, heart rate (beats/minute); 2, birth weight (g); 3, factor 68; 4, gestational age (weeks).

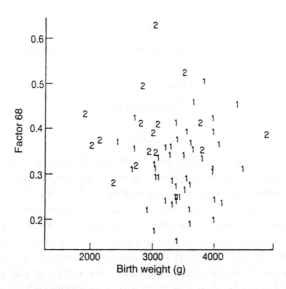

Fig. 12.7 Scatter plot of birth weight and factor 68 from SIDS data with controls (1) and cases (2) identified.

Display 12.5   Fisher's linear discriminant function

- The linear discriminant function was originally derived by Fisher (1936) as a technique for classifying an individual into one of two groups on the basis of a set of measurements $x_1, x_2, \ldots, x_p$.
- Fisher's suggestion was to seek a linear transformation of the variables

$$z = a_1 x_1 + a_2 x_2 + \ldots + a_p x_p$$

such that the separation between the group means on the transformed scale, $\bar{z}_1$ and $\bar{z}_2$, would be maximized relative to the within-group variation on the z scale.

- Fisher showed the coefficients that give such a transformation to be

$$a = S^{-1}(\bar{x}_1 - \bar{x}_2)$$

where $a' = [a_1, a_2, \cdots, a_p]$, $\bar{x}_1$ and $\bar{x}_2$ are the vectors of sample means in the two groups and S is the **pooled within-groups covariance matrix**, calculated from the separate within-group covariance matrices S_1 and S_2 as

$$S = \frac{1}{n_1 + n_2 - 2}[(n_1 - 1)S_1 + (n_2 - 1)S_2].$$

n_1 and n_2 are the sample sizes of each group.

- If an individual has a discriminant score closer to $\bar{z}_1$ than to $\bar{z}_2$, assignment is to group 1; otherwise it is to group 2.
- The classification rule can be formalized by defining a cut-off value z_c given by

$$z_c = \frac{\bar{z}_1 + \bar{z}_2}{2}.$$

- Now, assuming that $\bar{z}_1$ is the larger of the two means, the classification rule for an individual with discriminant score z_i is

  assign individual to group 1 if $z_i - z_c > 0$

  assign individual to group 2 if $z_i - z_c \leq 0$.

To begin only the factor 68 variable and birth weight will be used. Display 12.6 shows the means of each of these variables for the cases and controls, and what is known as the **pooled within-group covariance matrix** of the data. A scatter plot of the two variables in which cases and controls are identified is shown in Fig. 12.7. The details of Fisher's linear discriminant function for the data are shown in Display 12.7.

A deficiency of the allocation rule derived in Display 12.7 is that it takes no account of the **prior probability** of class membership in the population under study. Therefore, if it is used in this simple form as a screening device for babies at risk of SIDS, many more infants would be considered at risk than is genuinely merited since, fortunately, SIDS is known to be a relatively rare condition. To accommodate prior probabilities

Display 12.6 Means and pooled covariance matrix for SIDS data variables factor 68 and birth weight only

• The mean vectors of the two groups on the two variables are as follows:

Variable	Controls	Cases
Birth weight	3437.86	2964.69
Factor 68	0.31	0.40

• The pooled within-group covariance matrix **S** is

$$S = \begin{array}{c} \text{birth weight} \\ \text{factor 68} \end{array} \begin{array}{cc} \text{birth weight} & \text{factor 68} \\ \left(\begin{array}{cc} 278612.28 & \\ 4.32 & 0.0062 \end{array} \right) \end{array}$$

into Fisher's linear discriminant function, the derived allocation rule must be amended to the following:

$$\text{assign subject to group 1 if } z_i - z_c > \ln Q$$
$$\text{assign subject to group 2 if } z_i - z_c \leq \ln Q$$

where

$$Q = \frac{\text{prior probability of group 1}}{\text{prior probability of group 2}}.$$

Prior probabilities are often ignored in published accounts of the application of discriminant function analysis; thus it is implicitly assumed that that $P(\text{group 1}) = P(\text{group 2}) = 0.5$.

A question of some importance about a discriminant function allocation rule is: 'How well does it perform?' An obvious method of evaluating performance is to apply the derived rule to the original data to see how many individuals are misclassified. The table below shows the results of applying this procedure to the classification rule derived for the SIDS data using only the factor 68 and birth weight variables.

Actual group	Percentage correct	Allocation rule group	
		Controls	Cases
Controls	83.7	41	8
Cases	81.3	3	13
Total	83.1	44	21

Display 12.7   Fisher's linear discriminant function for birth weight and factor 68 from the SIDS data

- The discriminant function coefficients derived from the information in Display 12.6 are birth weight (0.001948) and factor 68 (-16.0846), giving the discriminant function

$$z = 0.001948 \times \text{birth weight} - 16.0846 \times \text{factor 68}.$$

- Means on the transformed variable are needed to derive the classification rule. These are obtained by simply applying the derived discriminant function coefficients to the group mean vectors, i.e.

$$\bar{z}_1 = 0.001948 \times 3437.857 - 16.0846 \times 0.31082 = 1.696$$
$$\bar{z}_2 = 0.001948 \times 2964.688 - 16.0846 \times 0.40181 = -0.6887.$$

- The discriminant function can be shown on the scattergram of the data simply by plotting the line

$$0.001948 \times \text{birth weight} - 16.0846 \times \text{factor 68} = 0.$$

- The result is shown in the following diagram:

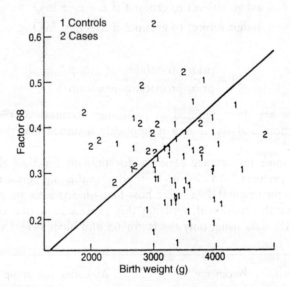

- In terms of the above diagram, a new infant with values of the two variables leading to a position on the plot *above* the line would be allocated to the cases group, and an infant with a position *below* the line would be allocated to the control group.

The **classification matrix** shows that the misclassification rate is approximately 17%. However, estimating this rate by applying the allocation rule to the original data (the training set) is known in general to be optimistic, wildly so in some cases. Consequently, it is generally a poor guide to how the rule will perform in the allocation of a new set of data. A more realistic estimator of the misclassification rate can be obtained by the so-called **leaving one out method**, where the discriminant function is derived on the basis of $n-1$ of the original individuals and then used to classify the individual that is not included. The process is repeated n times, each time omitting a different individual. Such a procedure applied to the SIDS data leads to the following classification matrix.

Actual group	Percentage correct	Allocation rule group	
		Controls	Cases
Controls	81.6	40	9
Cases	81.3	3	13
Total	81.5	43	22

The estimated misclassification rate increases a little to 19%. In many applications the difference between the two estimates will be much greater.

In the derivation of the discriminant function described in Display 12.5 it is assumed that the two groups of interest have the same covariance matrix. If this is not the case, a linear discriminant function is no longer adequate for separating the two groups. The alternative is to use a **quadratic discriminant function** as described by Everitt and Dunn (1991).

The only assumption made by Fisher in the original derivation of his discriminant function was that the two groups had the same covariance matrix. It can be shown that the method is optimal *only* if both groups have multivariate normal distributions (see Appendix A), although Hand (1981) shows that the method is relatively robust against departures from this assumption. However, in cases where some of the variables to be used for discrimination are categorical, Fisher's linear discriminant function may not be the most suitable assignment technique to use. A possible alternative described by Everitt and Dunn (1991) is a method essentially equivalent to logistic regression (see Chapter 7).

Returning to the SIDS data, the linear discriminant function for all four variables can be found by applying the procedure given in Display 12.5 to the mean vectors and within-group covariance matrix shown in Display 12.8. The resulting discriminant function is

$$z = 0.00179 \times \text{birth weight} - 15.533 \times \text{factor } 68 - 0.00178 \times \text{heart rate}$$
$$+ 0.215 \times \text{gestational age}.$$

Display 12.8   Means and pooled covariance matrix for all variables in the SIDS data

- The mean vectors of the two groups on the four variables are as follows:

Variable	Controls	Cases
Birth weight (BW)	3437.86	2964.69
Factor 68 (F68)	0.31	0.40
Heart rate (HR)	129.24	132.95
Gestational age (GA)	40	39.25

- The pooled within-group covariance matrix of the four variables is as follows:

$$S = \begin{array}{c} \\ BW \\ F68 \\ HR \\ GA \end{array} \begin{array}{cccc} BW & F68 & HR & GA \\ \left(278\,612.28 \right. & & & \\ 4.32 & 0.0062 & & \\ 130.94 & 0.24 & 269.40 & \\ 196.29 & -0.01 & 1.26 & \left. 1.09 \right) \end{array}$$

One of the most important questions in practical applictions of the linear discriminant function is often how to select a subset of the original variables which can be used to provide an allocation rule which is simple to use but whose performance remains comparable to a rule which uses *all* the original variables. The answer to this question is to use a stepwise selection procedure which is essentially equivalent to the technique described in Chapter 6 in association with multiple regression. The criteria used for entering variables into, and removing variables from, a discriminant function are the same as those used in multiple regression (this is not suprising once it is realized that it is possible to derive Fisher's linear discriminant function using regression—see Exercise 12.4). Applying such a stepwise approach to all four variables in the SIDS data gives the results shown in Display 12.9. Clearly, birth weight and factor 68 variable are the variables which discriminate most successfully between the cases and controls.

Display 12.9   Results of the stepwise procedure for selecting variables for Fisher's linear discriminant function on SIDS data

Step 0

Variable	F to enter DF = 1 and 63
Birth weight	9.69
Factor 68	16.15
Heart rate	0.62
Gestational age	6.19

Step 1
Variable entered: factor 68

Variable	F to enter DF = 1 and 62
Birth weight	9.88
Heart rate	0.00
Gestational age	3.08

Step 2
Variable entered: birth weight

Variable	F to enter DF = 1 and 61
Heart rate	0.00
Gestational age	0.33

No further variables entered.

When more than two groups are involved, Fisher's linear discriminant function as described in Display 12.5 can be extended relatively simply to provide an allocation rule. The details for three groups are given in Display 12.10 as an example.

Display 12.10   The application of linear discriminant functions in the three-group case

- If $\bar{x}_1$, $\bar{x}_2$ and $\bar{x}_3$ are the mean vectors of the three groups and S is the pooled within-group covariance matrix, the allocation rule is based on the following three functions:

$$h_{12}(x) = (\bar{x}_1 - \bar{x}_2)'S^{-1}[x - (\bar{x}_1 + \bar{x}_2)/2]$$
$$h_{13}(x) = (\bar{x}_1 - \bar{x}_3)'S^{-1}[x - (\bar{x}_1 + \bar{x}_3)/2]$$
$$h_{23}(x) = (\bar{x}_2 - \bar{x}_3)'S^{-1}[x - (\bar{x}_1 + \bar{x}_3)/2].$$

- The classification rule now becomes, to allocate an individual with a vector of observations, x, in the following way:

  group 1 if $h_{12}(x) > 0$ and $h_{13}(x) > 0$
  group 2 if $h_{12}(x) < 0$ and $h_{23}(x) > 0$
  group 3 if $h_{13}(x) < 0$ and $h_{23}(x) < 0$.

12.4   Multidimensional scaling

In the opening section of this chapter, a type of data collected in experiments where subjects are asked to judge the similarity or dissimilarity of objects, stimuli etc. was illustrated. The array of similarity or dissimilarity judgements is often known as a **preference matrix** or, alternatively, as a **proximity matrix**. Such data are often collected in the hope that they can be used to uncover the mechanism behind the similarity judgements, in particular to discover on what 'dimensions' the judgements are made. One class of techniques which often proves extremely useful in this search is **multidimensional scaling**. The underlying purpose that all methods of this class share, despite their apparent diversity, is to represent the structure present in an observed proximity matrix in the form of a simple geometrical model or diagram. What exactly does this mean?

A geometrical model for an observed proximity matrix consists of a set of points specified by coordinate values in a particular number of dimensions. Each point represents one of the objects or stimuli about which subjects make similarity judgements. The object of a multidimensional scaling technique is to determine both the number of dimensions and the position of the points (their coordinate values) so that there is, in some sense, maximum correspondence between the observed similarities and the interpoint distances. In essence, this simply means that the larger the similarity between two objects, the closer together should be those points representing the objects in the geometrical model.

To clarify what multidimensional scaling techniques do, and before describing any particular technique in detail, it will be helpful to show the scaling solution for the similarities between Morse code signals given in Table 12.1. A two-dimensional solution was found to be adequate for these data, and the derived two-dimensional coordinates representing each of the 10 numbers are plotted in Fig. 12.8. At the simplest level this plot indicates which signals were judged to be 'similar' (they are represented by points which are close together), and which to be 'different' (represented by points far apart). The plot should also indicate the general interrelationships between signals. A possible interpretation here is that the horizontal axis corresponds to the increasing number of dots in a signal, whereas the vertical axis is related to the ordering of dots and dashes in the signal.

So how is the geometric representation of an observed proximity matrix arrived at? Many methods have been proposed (see Kruskal and Wish, 1978, and Everitt and Dunn, 1991, for details), but just one method, namely **non-metric multidimensional scaling**, will be briefly described. This method, first suggested by Kruskal (1964), represented a breakthrough in multidimensional scaling, since it allowed a scaling solution to be derived using only the **rank order** of the observed judgements of similarity or dissimilarity. In other words, the actual numerical values of the similarity judgements need not be used. This is important, particularly in psychological experiments where the similarity judgements are collected from human subjects who can only be expected reliably to give *ordinal* judgements. For example, they can specify that one stimulus is 'larger' than another' without being able to attach any reliable value to the exact numerical difference between them. A brief account of non-metric multidimensional scaling is given in Display 12.11.

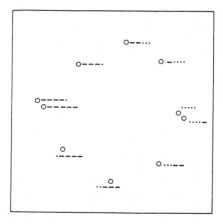

Fig. 12.8 Two-dimensional scaling solution for the data in Table 12.1.

Display 12.11   Non-metric multidimensional scaling

- Suppose the observed similarities are denoted by s_{ij}.
- The aim of multidimensional scaling is to find a set of coordinate values to represent each object or stimuli being judged; suppose that a possible set of coordinate values for the stimulus i are represented by $x_{i1}, x_{i2}, \ldots, x_{id}$, where d is the number of dimensions to be used.
- The Euclidean distance between the points representing stimuli i and j is d_{ij} given by

$$d_{ij} = \left[\sum_{k=1}^{d} (x_{ik} - x_{jk})^2 \right]^{1/2}.$$

- The aim is now to choose the coordinate values so as to make the observed similarity judgements correspond closely to the fitted distances, i.e. if stimuli i and j are judged to be very similar, then they should be represented by points for which d_{ij} is small and vice versa.
- Non-metric multidimensional scaling chooses the coordinate values so that the **ranking** of the pairs of fitted distances corresponds as closely as possible to the **reverse** of the ranking of the observed similarities; i.e. if the observed similarities are ranked from lowest to highest, the corresponding distances should, as far as can be achieved, go from highest to lowest.
- In general, it is not possible to achieve total correspondence between the two rankings, but non-metric multidimensional scaling finds coordinates so that the correspondence is as close as possible by minimizing a numerical function, known as **stress**, which measures the correspondence; for more details see Kruskal and Wish (1978) and Everitt and Dunn (1991).

Table 12.5   Matrix of mean similarity ratings of 18 students from 12 nations

	1	2	3	4	5	6	7	8	9	10	11	12
Brazil	—											
Zaire	4.83	—										
Cuba	5.28	4.26	—									
Egypt	3.44	5.00	5.17	—								
France	4.72	4.00	4.11	4.78	—							
India	4.50	4.83	4.00	5.83	3.44	—						
Israel	3.83	3.33	3.61	4.67	4.00	4.11	—					
Japan	3.50	3.39	2.94	3.84	4.11	4.50	4.83	—				
China	2.39	4.00	5.50	4.39	3.67	4.11	3.00	4.17	—			
USSR	3.06	3.39	5.44	4.39	5.06	4.50	4.17	4.61	5.72	—		
USA	5.39	2.39	3.17	3.33	5.94	4.28	5.94	6.06	2.56	5.00	—	
Yugoslavia	3.17	3.50	5.11	4.28	4.72	4.00	4.44	4.28	5.06	6.67	3.56	—

Adapted, with permission of Sage Publications, Inc., from Kruskal and Wish (1978).

The use of non-metric multidimensional scaling will be illustrated by applying it to the matrix of averaged similarity judgements between nations shown in Table 12.6. (These data were clearly collected before recent radical political changes in particular regions!). The two-dimensional solution given by non-metric scaling is shown in Fig. 12.9. A possible interpretation of the underlying dimensions on which the similarity judgements are made is also given in this figure.

An important question in the application of multidimensional scaling techniques is how to choose the appropriate number of dimensions to display adequately the structure of the observed similarity judgements. In general the questions about the number of coordinates needed for a given set of similarities is as much substantive as statistical. Even if a reasonable statistical method existed for determining the 'correct' or 'true' dimensionality, this would not itself be sufficient to indicate how many coordinates the researcher needs to use. Since multidimensional scaling is almost always used as a descriptive method for representing and understanding particular types of data, other considerations enter into decisions about the appropriate dimensionality. This point is made by Gnanadesikan and Wilk (1969):

> Interpretability and simplicity are important in data analysis and any rigid inference of optimal dimensionality in the light of the observed values of a numerical index of goodness-of-fit, may not be productive.

In the light of this comment, two-dimensional solutions are likely to be of most practical importance because they have the virtue of simplicity, are often readily assimilated by the investigator, and in many cases may provide an easily understood basis for the discussion of observed proximity matrices.

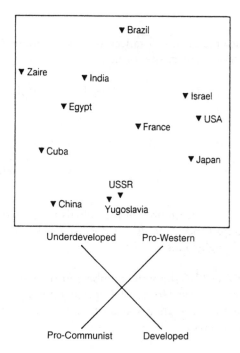

Fig. 12.9 Two-dimensional solution from non-metric multidimensional scaling of the data in Table 12.16.

12.5 Summary

1. Cluster analysis techniques are used to search for clusters in a priori unclassified data.
2. Many methods of cluster analysis have been developed and most studies have shown that no single method is best for all types of data. For this and several other reasons, clustering techniques require care in their application.
3. Discriminant analysis techniques are concerned with deriving rules for allocating unclassified individuals to a priori defined groups using a series of measurements made on each individual.
4. Fisher's linear discriminant function is the most frequently employed method for discriminating between groups. It is optimal (i.e. has the lowest misclassification rate) if the data in each group have multivariate normal distributions with the same covariance matrix.
5. Assessing the performance of a discriminant function by calculating the misclassification rate achieved by applying the derived allocation rule to the training set data is usually hopelessly optimistic.
6. Multidimensional scaling techniques aim to find an informative geometrical representation of a set of observed similarity or dissimilarity judgements of a set of stimuli with a view to uncovering the dimensions on which the judgements are made.

Exercises

12.1 Show that the intergroup distances used by complete linkage clustering and average linkage clustering satisfy the formula

$$d_{k(ij)} = \alpha_i d_{ki} + \alpha_j d_{kj} + \gamma |d_{ki} - d_{kj}|$$

where

$$\alpha_i = \alpha_j = 0.5 \qquad \gamma = 0.5 \qquad \text{(complete linkage)}$$

$$\alpha_i = \frac{n_i}{n_i + n_j} \qquad \alpha_j = \frac{n_j}{n_i + n_j} \qquad \gamma = 0; \qquad \text{(group average).}$$

In the above, n_i and n_j are the number of individuals in the two groups i and j, d_{ij} is the distance between groups i and j, and $d_{k(ij)}$ is the distance between a group k and a group (ij) formed by combining groups i and j.

12.2 The data in Table 12.6 show the numbers of times 15 Congressmen from New Jersey voted differently in the House of Representatives on 19 environmental bills. Apply both multidimensional scaling and cluster analysis to the data to see if any party affiliations can be uncovered.

12.3 The data shown in Table 12.7 were collected in a study designed to investigate whether the outcome of treating enuretic children with an alarm buzzer could be

Table 12.6 Voting in Congress

Name (party)	1	2	3	4	5	6	7	8	9	10	11	12	13	14	15
1. Hunt(R)	0														
2. Sandman(R)	8	0													
3. Howard(D)	15	17	0												
4. Thompson(D)	15	12	9	0											
5. Frelinghuysen(R)	10	13	16	14	0										
6. Forsythe(R)	9	13	12	12	8	0									
7. Widnall(R)	7	12	15	13	9	7	0								
8. Roe(D)	15	16	5	10	13	12	17	0							
9. Heltoski(D)	16	17	5	8	14	11	16	4	0						
10. Rodino(D)	14	15	6	8	12	10	15	5	3	0					
11. Minish(D)	15	16	5	8	12	9	14	5	2	1	0				
12. Rinaldo(D)	16	17	4	6	12	10	15	3	1	2	1	0			
13. Maraziti(R)	7	13	11	15	10	6	10	12	13	11	12	12	0		
14. Daniels(D)	11	12	10	10	11	6	11	7	7	4	5	6	9	0	
15. Patten(D)	13	16	7	7	11	10	13	6	5	6	5	4	13	9	0

R, Republican; D, Democrat.

Table 12.7 Enuresis data

Treatment	x_1	x_2	x_3	x_4	x_5
1	0	0	8.4	1	0
1	1	0	8.7	1	0
1	0	0	8.9	1	1
1	1	0	8.1	1	1
1	1	0	8.6	1	0
1	1	0	8.9	1	0
1	1	0	6.3	1	0
1	0	0	5.3	1	0
1	1	0	8.7	0	0
1	0	0	8.6	1	0
1	1	0	9.0	1	0
1	1	0	8.3	1	0
1	1	0	8.1	1	0
1	1	1	8.5	1	1
1	0	0	7.6	1	1
1	1	0	4.3	1	0
1	1	0	6.8	1	0
1	0	0	5.9	1	0
1	1	0	8.7	1	0
1	1	0	5.9	1	0
1	0	0	9.0	1	0
1	0	0	8.4	1	0
1	0	0	8.2	1	0
1	1	0	8.6	1	1
1	1	0	6.4	0	1
2	0	0	8.1	1	0
2	1	0	8.6	1	0
2	0	0	8.2	1	0
2	0	0	8.8	0	0
2	0	0	8.1	1	0
2	0	0	8.5	1	0
2	1	0	8.9	1	0
2	1	0	8.1	1	0
2	0	0	5.3	1	0
2	0	0	4.8	1	0
2	0	0	5.1	1	0
2	1	0	8.4	1	0
2	0	0	9.0	0	0
2	1	0	8.7	0	0
2	0	0	4.6	1	0
2	0	0	6.7	1	0
2	0	0	8.1	1	1
2	1	0	7.4	1	0
2	1	0	7.1	1	0
2	1	0	6.4	1	0

Table 12.7   Enuresis data – *cont'd*

Treatment	x_1	x_2	x_3	x_4	x_5
2	1	0	7.8	1	0
2	1	0	8.7	1	1
2	0	0	8.4	1	0

Variables: x_1, whether or not there were family background difficulties (1=yes, 0=no); x_2, whether wetting occurred during the day (1=yes, 0=no); x_3, child's age (years); x_4, whether the family had access to an inside WC (1=yes, 0=no); x_5, whether the child shared a room with more than one sibling (1= yes, 0=no).

predicted from certain observations made on the children. The two groups in the data are as follows:

(1) failure or relapse after apparent cure;
(2) long-term cure.

Derive an allocation rule for predicting membership of a group using Fisher's linear discriminant function. Into what group does the derived rule place children with the following observations?

Child	x_1	x_2	x_3	x_4	x_5
1	0	0	9.0	0	1
2	1	1	5.2	1	0
3	0	0	8.4	0	0
4	1	0	6.0	1	0

Is Fisher's method entirely appropriate for these data?

12.4   Apply multiple regression to the SIDS data using as the dependent variable the following coding for group membership:

$$\text{controls} \quad \frac{n_2}{n_1 + n_2}$$
$$\text{cases} \quad \frac{-n_1}{n_1 + n_2}$$

where n_1 is the number of controls and n_2 the number of cases. Compare the results with those obtained by applying Fisher's linear discriminant function (see Display 12.8).

Further reading

Dart, R.P., Lumpkin, J.R., and Bush, R.P. (1990). Private physicians or walkin clinics: do the patients differ? *Journal of Health Care Marketing*, 10, 25–35.

Green, P.E., Carmone, F.J., and Smith, S.M. (1989). *Multidimensional scaling: concepts and applications*. Allyn and Bacon, Boston, MA.

Milligan, G. (1980). An examination of the effect of six types of error perturbation on fifteen clustering algorithms. *Psychometrika*, 45, 325–42.

Morrison, D.G. (1969). On the interpretation of discriminant analysis. *Journal of Marketing Research*, 6, 156–63.

13

The assessment of reliability

13.1 Introduction

The foundation of all psychological investigation consists of the measurements and observations which are made on the subjects or objects of interest. Clearly, such measurements need to be objective, precise and reproducible for reasons nicely summarized by the quotation from Fleiss (1986) given previously in Chapter 1 and repeated here.

> The most elegant design of a study will not overcome the damage caused by unreliable or imprecise measurements. The requirement that one's data be of high quality is at least as important a component of a proper study design as the requirement for randomization, double blinding, controlling where necessary for prognostic factors, and so on. Larger sample sizes than otherwise necessary, biased estimates and even biased samples are some of the untoward consequences of unreliable measurements that can be demonstrated.

Therefore, in all studies it is important to ensure that the data collected are as accurate as possible. In assessing the accuracy of any particular measuring 'instrument' it is usual to distinguish between the **reliability** and the **validity** of the data. Reliability is essentially the extent of the agreement between repeated measurements of the same material, and validity is the extent to which a method of measurement provides a true assessment of that which it purports to measure. This chapter is almost exclusively concerned with issues of reliability. (Two other terms are often used to indicate different aspects of the agreement between repeated measurements: **repeatability**, which is used to describe the variability of measurements made under near-constant conditions e.g. the same observer and the same measuring instrument, and **reproducibility**, the variability of measurements made under different conditions e.g. by different observers possibly using different measuring instruments.)

There are several comprehensive accounts of reliability and the statistical evaluation of measurement errors, for example those given by Fleiss (1986) and Dunn (1989). A relatively concise description of those areas of most relevance to psychologists is given in this chapter. (It might be considered odd or even perverse that a chapter on reliability and measurement error should be the last in the text, rather than making an appearance near the beginning; after all, evaluating the properties and characteristics of the measures to be used is likely to be one of the first tasks undertaken in any psychological investigation. However, the assessment of reliability requires a familiarity with several of the methods described in earlier chapters. Consequently, it does make sense to cover the topic at this late stage rather than earlier.)

The methods appropriate for measuring reliability depend largely on the type of data involved, particularly whether it is the reliability of categorical or continuous variables which is to be assessed. Those methods most relevant for categorical data are discussed in the next section.

13.2 Reliability measures for categorical data

The main concern in this section will be the estimation of the reliability of categorical ratings made by several raters on a sample of subjects. Fleiss (1965) and Landis and Koch (1977) suggest that, when studying such ratings, two components of their possible inaccuracy need to be addressed, namely **inter-observer bias** and **observer disagreement**.

13.2.1 Inter-observer bias

First, consider the data shown in Table 13.1 which were collected in a study comparing the symptomatology of eight schizophrenic patients as judged by five psychiatrists during a psychiatric interview. The specific symptom to which the data in Table 13.1 relate is religious preoccupation, rated 0 if considered absent and 1 if thought present. Inter-observer bias is present if there are differences in the psychiatrists' probabilities of rating that a patient has the symptom. Here the sample estimates of these probabilities, namely the proportions of positive ratings made by each psychiatrist, differ considerably. However, such differences might be simply due to chance effects, and so a formal test of

Table 13.1 Ratings of the 'presence' (1) and 'absence' (0) of religious preoccupations in eight patients by five psychiatrists

Subject	Psychiatrist					Total	Proportion of present ratings
	1	2	3	4	5		
1	0	0	0	0	0	0	0.0
2	0	0	0	0	1	1	0.2
3	0	0	0	0	0	0	0.0
4	0	0	0	0	0	0	0.0
5	0	0	1	0	0	1	0.2
6	0	0	1	1	1	3	0.6
7	0	0	0	0	0	0	0.0
8	1	0	1	1	1	4	0.8
Total	1	0	3	2	3	9	
Proportion of 'present' ratings	0.125	0.000	0.375	0.250	0.375		

the hypothesis of no inter-observer bias is needed. The appropriate procedure, **Cochran's Q test**, is described in Display 13.1. The results of applying the test to the data in Table 13.1 are also shown in Display 13.1. The data give no evidence of inter-observer bias among the five psychiatrists on the particular symptom being assessed.

Display 13.1 Cochran's Q test

- The hypothesis of no inter-observer bias is

$$H_0 : p_1 = p_2 = \ldots = p_r$$

where p_i is the probability that rater i rates the characteristic of interest present (i.e. in the current example that the rater says that religious preoccupations occur in a patient) and r is the number of raters.

- The test statistic is

$$Q = \frac{r(r-1)\sum_{j=1}^{r}(y_{.j} - y_{..}/r)^2}{ry_{..} - \sum_{i=1}^{n} y_{i.}^2}$$

where n is the number of subjects and the remaining terms are defined as follows:

(a) $y_{ij} = 1$ if the ith subject is judged by the jth observer to have the characteristic present and is zero otherwise;

(b) $y_{i.}$ is the total number of raters who judge the ith patient to possess the characteristic;

(c) $y_{.j}$ is the total number of subjects that the jth rater judges as having the characteristic present;

(d) $y_{..}$ is the total number of 'present' judgements made.

- If the hypothesis of no inter-observer bias is true, Q has an approximately chi-squared distribution with $r - 1$ degrees of freedom.

- For the data in Table 13.1, Q is calculated as

$$Q = \frac{5 \times 4 \times [(1 - 1.8)^2 + (0 - 1.8)^2 + (3 - 1.8)^2 + (2 - 1.8)^2 + (3 - 1.8)^2]}{45.0 - 27.0} = 7.55$$

- The associated P-value found from a chi-squared distribution with four degrees of freedom is 0.109.

13.2.2 *Observer agreement: reliability*

Of more importance in most circumstances than inter-observer bias (which itself might be remedied relatively simply) is the degree of inter-observer agreement when rating a categorical variable, since this directly reflects the reliability of the variable. Perhaps the most commonly used index of such agreement for a categorical variable is the **kappa coefficient**, first suggested by Cohen (1960). The data shown in Table 13.2 will be used

Table 13.2 Diagnosis of multiple sclerosis by two neurologists

	A	B	C	D	Total
A	38	5	0	1	44
B	33	11	3	0	47
C	10	14	5	6	35
D	3	7	3	10	23
Total	84	37	11	17	149

to illustrate the use of this index. These data are taken from a study (Westland and Kurland 1953) in which two neurologists independently classified 149 patients into four classes:

(1) A, certainly suffering from multiple sclerosis;
(2) B, probably suffering from multiple sclerosis;
(3) C, possibly suffering from multiple sclerosis;
(4) D, doubtful, unlikely and definitely not suffering from multiple sclerosis.

One intuitively reasonable index of agreement for the two raters is the proportion P_0 of patients that they classify into the same category; for the data in Table 13.2,

$$P_0 = (38 + 11 + 5 + 10)/149 = 0.429. \tag{13.1}$$

Such a measure has the virtue of simplicity and it is readily understood. However, despite such advantages (and intuition), P_0 is not an adequate index of the agreement between the two raters. The problem is that P_0 makes no allowance for agreement between raters that might be attributed to chance. To explain, consider the two sets of data in Table 13.3. In both the two observers are measured as achieving 66% agreement if P_0 is calculated. Suppose, however, that each observer is simply allocating subjects at random to the three categories in accordance with their **marginal rates** for the three categories. For example, observer A in the first data set would simply allocate 10% of subjects to category 1, 80% to category 2 and the remaining 10% to category 3, totally disregarding the suitability of a category for a subject. Observer B proceeds likewise.

Even such a cavalier rating procedure employed by the two observers would lead to some agreement and a corresponding non-zero value of P_0. This **chance agreement** P_c can be calculated simply from the marginal rates of each observer. For example, for the first data set in Table 13.3, P_c is calculated as follows.

1. Category 1: the number of 'chance' agreements to be expected is

$$100 \times \frac{10}{100} \times \frac{10}{100} = 1. \tag{13.2}$$

(Remember how 'expected' values are calculated in contingency tables—see Chapter 7.)

Table 13.3 Two hypothetical data sets each of which shows 66% agreement between two observers

Observer A	Observer B			Total
	1	2	3	
Data set 1				
1	1	8	1	10
2	8	64	8	80
3	1	8	1	10
Total	10	80	10	100
Data set 2				
1	24	13	3	40
2	5	20	5	30
3	1	7	22	30
Total	30	40	30	100

2. Category 2: the number of 'chance' agreements to be expected is

$$100 \times \frac{80}{100} \times \frac{80}{100} = 64. \qquad (13.3)$$

3. Category 3: the number of 'chance' agreements to be expected is

$$100 \times \frac{10}{100} \times \frac{10}{100} = 1. \qquad (13.4)$$

Consequently, P_c is given by

$$P_c = \frac{1}{100}(1 + 64 + 1) = 0.66. \qquad (13.5)$$

Therefore, in this particular table, *all* the observed agreement might simply be due to chance. However, repeating the calculation on the second set of data in Table 13.3 gives $P_c = 0.33$, which is considerably lower than the observed agreement.

A number of authors have expressed opinions on the need to incorporate chance agreement into the assessment of inter-observer reliability. The clearest statement in favour of such a correction has been made by Fleiss (1975), who suggested an index which is the ratio of the difference between observed and chance agreement to the maximum possible excess of observed over chance agreement, i.e. $1 - P_c$. This leads to what has become known as the kappa statistic:

$$\kappa = \frac{P_o - P_c}{1 - P_c}. \qquad (13.6)$$

If there is complete agreement between the two raters so that all the off-diagonal cells of the table are empty, $\kappa = 1$. If observed agreement is greater than chance, $\kappa > 0$. If the observed agreement is equal to chance, $\kappa = 0$. Finally, in the unlikely event of the observed agreement being less than chance, $\kappa < 0$ with its minimum value depending on the marginal distributions of the two raters.

The chance agreement for the multiple sclerosis data is given by

$$P_c = \frac{1}{149}\left(\frac{44}{149} \times 84 + \frac{47}{149} \times 37 + \frac{35}{149} \times 11 + \frac{23}{149} \times 17\right) = 0.2797. \qquad (13.7)$$

Consequently, for the multiple sclerosis data

$$\kappa = \frac{0.429 - 0.280}{1 - 0.280} = 0.208. \qquad (13.8)$$

This calculated value of κ is an estimate of the corresponding population value and, like all such estimates, needs to be accompanied by some measure of its variance so that a confidence interval can be constructed. The variance of an observed value of κ has been derived under a number of different assumptions by several authors, including Everitt (1968) and Fleiss et al. (1969). The formula for the large-sample variance of κ is rather unpleasant, but for those with a strong stomach it is reproduced in Display 13.2. Its value for the multiple sclerosis data is 0.002485, which leads to an approximate 95% confidence interval of (0.108, 0.308). Thus there is some evidence that the agreement between the two raters in this example is greater than chance; otherwise the confidence interval would have included the value zero. However, what constitutes 'good' agreement? Some arbitrary benchmarks for the evaluation of observed κ values have been given by Landis and Koch (1977). They are as follows:

κ	Strength of agreement
0.00	Poor
0.01–0.20	Slight
0.21–0.40	Fair
0.41–0.60	Moderate
0.61–0.80	Substantial
0.81–1.00	Perfect

Of course, any series of standards such as these are necessarily subjective. Nevertheless, they may be helpful in the informal evaluation of a series of κ values, although replacing numerical values with rather poorly defined English phrases may not be to everybody's taste. In fact there is no simple answer to the original question concerning what constitutes good agreement. Suppose, for example, that two examiners rating examination candidates as 'pass' or 'fail' had $\kappa = 0.54$ (in the 'moderate' range according to Landis and Koch). Would the people taking the examination be satisfied by this value? This is unlikely, particularly if future candidates are going to be assessed by one of the examiners but not both. If this were the case, sources of disagreement

should be searched for and rectified; only then might one have sufficient confidence in
the assessment of a lone examiner.

Display 13.2   Large-sample variance of kappa

$$\mathrm{var}(\kappa) = \frac{1}{n(1 - P_c)^4} \left\{ \sum_{i=1}^{r} p_{ii}[(1 - P_c) - (p_{.i} + p_{i.})(1 - P_o)]^2 \right.$$

$$\left. + (1 - P_o)^2 \sum_{\substack{i=1 \\ i \neq j}}^{r} \sum_{j=1}^{r} p_{ij}(p_{.i} + p_{j.})^2 - (P_o P_c - 2P_c + P_o)^2 \right\}$$

where p_{ij} is the proportion of observations in the ijth cell of the table of counts of
agreements and disagreements for the two observers $p_{i.}$ and $p_{.j}$ are the row and column
marginal proportions, and r is the number of rows and columns in the table.

The concept of a chance corrected measure of agreement can be extended to
situations involving more than two observers; for details, see Fleiss and Cuzick (1979)
and Schouten (1985). A weighted version of κ is also possible, with weights reflecting
differences in the seriousness of disagreements. For example, in the multiple sclerosis
data a disagreement involving one rater classifying a patient as A and the other rater
classifying the same patient as D would be very serious and would be given a high
weight. An example of the calculation of weighted κ and some comments about choice
of weights are given by Dunn (1989).

13.3   Measuring reliability for quantitative variables

The concept of the reliability of a quantitative variable can best be introduced via the
use of a series of simple statistical models that relate 'true' measurements or scores to
the corresponding observed values. Examples of such models are shown in Display
13.3; they all lead to the **intraclass correlation coefficient** as a method for indexing
reliability. To illustrate the calculation of this coefficient, the ratings given by a number
of judges to the competitors in a synchronized swimming competition will be used;
these ratings are given in Table 13.4. (Of course, the author realizes that synchronized
swimming may be only a minority interest amongst psychologists.) Before undertaking
the necessary calculations, it might be useful to examine the data graphically in some
way. Consequently, Fig. 13.1 gives the box plots of the scores given by each judge, and
Fig. 13.2 shows the draughtsman's plot of the ratings made by each pair of judges. The
box plots show that the scores given by the first judge vary considerably more than
those given by the other four judges. The scatter plots show that whilst there is, in
general, a pattern of relatively strong relationships between the scores given by each
pair of the five judges, this is not universally so; for example, the relationship between
judges 4 and 5, is far less satisfactory.

Display 13.3 Models for the reliability of quantitative variables

- Let x represent the observed value of some variable of interest for a particular individual. If the observation was made a second time, say some days later, it would almost certainly differ to some degree from the first recording. A possible model for x is

$$x = t + \epsilon$$

where t is the underlying 'true' value of the variable for the individual and ϵ is the measurement error.

- Assume that t has a distribution with mean μ and variance σ_t^2. In addition, assume that ϵ has a distribution with mean zero and variance σ_ϵ^2, and that t and ϵ are independent of each other.
- A consequence of the model is that the variability in the observed scores is a combination of true score variance and error variance.
- The reliability R of the measurements is defined as the ratio of the true score variance to the observed score variance:

$$R = \frac{\sigma_t^2}{\sigma_t^2 + \sigma_\epsilon^2}$$

which can be rewritten as

$$R = \frac{1}{1 + \sigma_\epsilon^2/\sigma_t^2}.$$

- R is usually known as the **intraclass correlation coefficient**. As $\sigma_\epsilon^2/\sigma_t^2$ decreases, so that the error variance forms a decreasing part of the the variability in the observations, R increases and its upper limit of unity is achieved when the error variance is zero. In the reverse case, where σ_ϵ^2 forms an increasing proportion of the observed variance, R decreases to a lower limit of zero which is reached when all the variability in the measurements results from the error component of the model.
- The intraclass correlation coefficient can be directly interpreted as the proportion of variance of an observation due to between-subject variability in the true scores.
- When each of a number of observers rates a qualitative characteristic of interest on each of a number of subjects, the appropriate model becomes

$$x = t + o + \epsilon$$

where o represents the observer effect, which is assumed to be distributed with zero mean and variance σ_o^2.

- The three terms t, o and ϵ are assumed to be independent of one another so that the variance of an observation is given by

$$\sigma^2 = \sigma_t^2 + \sigma_o^2 + \sigma_\epsilon^2.$$

- The intraclass correlation coefficient for this situation is given by

$$R = \frac{\sigma_t^2}{\sigma_t^2 + \sigma_o^2 + \sigma_\epsilon^2}.$$

- A two-way analysis of variance of the raters' scores for each subject leads to the following analysis of variance table:

Source	DF	MS
Patients	$n-1$	PMS
Raters	$r-1$	RMS
Error	$(n-1)(r-1)$	EMS

- It can be shown that the population or **expected** values of the three mean squares are

$$\text{PMS} \quad \sigma_\epsilon^2 + r\sigma_t^2$$
$$\text{RMS} \quad \sigma_\epsilon^2 + n\sigma_o^2$$
$$\text{EMS} \quad \sigma_\epsilon^2.$$

- By equating the observed values of the three mean squares to their expected values, estimators of the three variance terms σ_t^2, σ_o^2 and σ_ϵ^2 can be found as follows:

$$\hat{\sigma}_t^2 = \frac{\text{PMS} - \text{EMS}}{r}$$
$$\hat{\sigma}_o^2 = \frac{\text{RMS} - \text{EMS}}{n}$$
$$\hat{\sigma}_\epsilon^2 = \text{EMS}.$$

- The estimator of R is then simply

$$\hat{R} = \frac{\hat{\sigma}_t^2}{\hat{\sigma}_t^2 + \hat{\sigma}_o^2 + \hat{\sigma}_\epsilon^2}.$$

The relevant analysis of variance table for the sychronized swimming data is shown in Display 13.4 together with the details of calculating the intraclass correlation coefficient. The resulting value of 0.683 is not particularly impressive, and the synchronized swimmers involved in the competition might have some cause for concern over whether their performances were being judged fairly and consistently.

In the case of two raters giving scores on a variable to the same n subjects, the intraclass correlation coefficient is equivalent to Pearson's product moment correlation coefficient between $2n$ pairs of observations, of which the first n are the original values and the second n are the original values in reverse order. When only two raters are involved, the value of the intraclass correlation coefficient depends in part on the corresponding product moment correlation value and in part on the differences between the means and standard deviations of the two sets of ratings. The relationship between the intraclass correlation coefficient and Pearson's coefficient is given explicitly in Display 13.5.

Table 13.4 Judges scores for 40 competitors in a sychronized swimming competition

Competitor	Scores				
	Judge 1	Judge 2	Judge 3	Judge 4	Judge 5
1	33.1	32.0	31.2	31.2	31.4
2	26.2	29.2	28.4	27.3	25.3
3	31.2	30.1	30.1	31.2	29.2
4	27.0	27.9	27.3	24.7	28.1
5	28.4	25.3	25.6	26.7	26.2
6	28.1	28.1	28.1	32.0	28.4
7	27.0	28.1	28.1	28.1	27.0
8	25.1	27.3	26.2	27.5	27.3
9	31.2	29.2	31.2	32.0	30.1
10	30.1	30.1	28.1	28.6	30.1
11	29.0	28.1	29.2	29.0	27.0
12	27.0	27.0	27.3	26.4	25.3
13	31.2	33.1	31.2	30.3	29.2
14	32.3	31.2	32.3	31.2	31.2
15	29.5	28.4	30.3	30.3	28.4
16	29.2	29.2	29.2	30.9	28.1
17	32.3	31.2	29.2	29.5	31.2
18	27.3	30.1	29.2	29.2	29.2
19	26.4	27.3	27.3	28.1	26.4
20	27.3	26.7	26.4	26.4	26.4
21	27.3	28.1	28.4	27.5	26.4
22	29.5	28.1	27.3	28.4	26.4
23	28.4	29.5	28.4	28.6	27.5
24	31.2	29.5	29.2	31.2	27.3
25	30.1	31.2	28.1	31.2	29.2
26	31.2	31.2	31.2	31.2	30.3
27	26.2	28.1	26.2	25.9	26.2
28	27.3	27.3	27.0	28.1	28.1
29	29.2	26.4	27.3	27.3	27.3
30	29.5	27.3	29.2	28.4	28.1
31	28.1	27.3	29.2	28.1	29.2
32	31.2	31.2	31.2	31.2	28.4
33	28.1	27.3	27.3	28.4	28.4
34	24.0	28.1	26.4	25.1	25.3
35	27.0	29.0	27.3	26.4	28.1
36	27.5	27.5	24.5	25.6	25.3
37	27.3	29.5	26.2	27.5	28.1
38	31.2	30.1	27.3	30.1	29.2
39	27.0	27.5	27.3	27.0	27.3
40	31.2	29.5	30.1	28.4	28.4

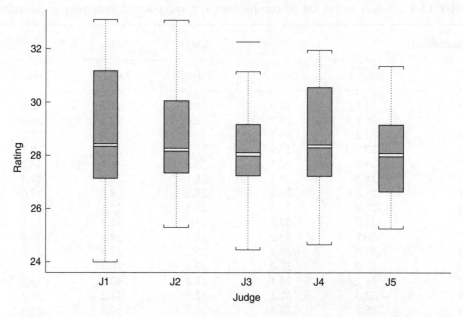

Fig. 13.1 Boxplots of scores given to synchronized swimming competitors by five judges.

Display 13.4 Analysis of variance and calculation of intraclass correlation coefficient for synchronized swimming judgements

• The analysis of variance table is as follows:

Source	SS	DF	MS
Swimmers	521.27	39	13.37
Judges	19.08	4	4.77
Error	163.96	156	1.05

• The required estimates of the three variance terms in the model are

$$\hat{\sigma}^2_t = \frac{13.37 - 1.05}{5} = 2.53$$

$$\hat{\sigma}^2_o = \frac{4.77 - 1.05}{40} = 0.093$$

$$\hat{\sigma}^2_\epsilon = 1.05.$$

• Consequently, the estimate of the intraclass correlation coefficient is

$$\hat{R} = \frac{2.53}{2.53 + 0.093 + 1.05} = 0.69.$$

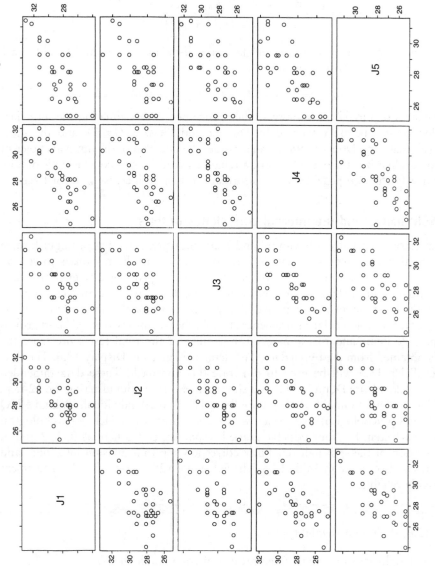

Fig. 13.2 Matrix of scatterplots for scores given by each pair of judges in rating synchronized swimmers.

Display 13.5 Relationship between the intraclass correlation coefficient R and the product moment correlation coefficient R_M in the case of two raters

$$R = \frac{[s_1^2 + s_2^2 - (s_1 - s_2)^2]R_M - (\bar{x}_1 - \bar{x}_2)^2/2}{s_1^2 + s_2^2 + (\bar{x}_1 - \bar{x}_2)^2/2}$$

where $\bar{x}_1$ and $\bar{x}_2$ are the mean values of the scores of the two raters, and s_1 and s_2 are the corresponding standard deviations.

Sample sizes required in reliability studies concerned with estimating the intraclass correlation coefficient are discussed by Donner and Eliasziw (1987), and the same authors (Eliasziw and Donner 1987) also consider the question of the optimal choice of r and n that minimizes the overall cost of a reliability study. Their conclusion is that an increase in r for fixed n provides more information than an increase in n for fixed r.

13.4   Split halves and the internal consistency of tests

One characteristic of many behavioural and social measurements that distinguish them from physical measurements is that they are obtained from the responses to several different questions or test items. The weight of an object is given by a single instrument reading, whereas an intelligence quotient can be calculated from the answers to 50 or 100 individual tests (items) of cognitive ability. One traditional way of obtaining the reliability of a psychological measurement is to split the test into two equal-sized groups of comparable items and to estimate the reliability of the total test score from the subtotals obtained from the two halves. The details are given in Display 13.6. The data shown in Table 13.5 will be used to illustrate this approach. These data (amended slightly) are taken from Dunn (1992) and show the results of administering the 12-item General Health Questionnaire (GHQ) (Goldberg 1972) to 20 individuals. A high GHQ score indicates psychological distress; a low score is indicative of a lack of psychological problems. Each item has four possible graded responses, coded here as 0, 1, 2 and 3. The calculation of the split-half reliability corresponding to a division into 'odd' and 'even' items is also shown in Table 13.5. The value of 0.9201 shows that the instrument is reasonably reliable.

Display 13.6 Split-half reliability

- The test is split into two equal-sized groups of comparable items.
- Let the subtotals obtained by subject i be X_{i1} on the first half and X_{i2} on the second half.
- Assume the following model:

$$X_{i1} = t_{i1} + \epsilon_{i1}$$
$$X_{i2} = t_{i2} + \epsilon_{i2}.$$

- If the error terms are assumed to have zero means, the reliability of the sum of the subtotals is given by

$$R = \frac{\text{var}(t_{i1} + t_{i2})}{\text{var}(X_{i1} + X_{i2})}.$$

- Under certain conditions, Dunn (1989) shows that R can be rewritten as

$$R = 2[1 - \frac{\text{var}(X_{i1}) + \text{var}(X_{i2})}{\text{var}(X_{i1} + X_{i2})}].$$

The major problem with the split-half reliability coefficient as defined in Display 13.6 is that, for a given test, it is not unique. Instead of taking the odd items of the GHQ and comparing them with the even ones, for example, subtotals obtained for a random partition of the items into two equal groups of six might have been compared. A more

Table 13.5   GHQ scores

Odd	Even	GHQ
5	3	8
3	2	5
3	3	6
7	5	12
5	5	10
4	4	8
12	10	22
5	5	10
10	11	21
3	7	10
4	2	6
3	5	8
8	5	13
2	2	4
7	7	14
3	3	6
5	5	10
0	2	2
7	7	14
11	11	22

Var(odd) = 9.7131	Var(even) = 8.2737	Var(sum) = 33.3132

$$R = 2[1 - \frac{\text{Var(odd)} + \text{Var(even)}}{\text{Var(sum)}}]$$

$$= 2[1 - \frac{9.7131 + 8.2737}{33.3132}] = 0.9201$$

appropriate measure of split-half reliability, usually referred to as **Cronbach's** α **coefficient** (Cronbach 1951; Lord and Novick 1968), is described by Dunn (1989); it can be regarded as a measure of the **internal consistency** of a psychometric test.

13.5 How long is a piece of string? The use of confirmatory factor analysis models in the assessment of reliability

Display 13.7 shows the lengths of 15 pieces of string as measured by a ruler (R) and as 'estimated' (in fact guessed) by three different people (G, B and D). Of course, corresponding to each piece of string is a true but unknown length. The true length is actually a somewhat more straightforward example of a latent variable than the examples introduced previously in Chapters 10 and 11 (and, unlike some of those examples, it does not need much imagination to accept its validity!). The four observed measures are clearly all fallible indicators of length, although R is likely to be a far more reliable measure than the others. A simple way to assess reliabilty for these data is to postulate a factor analysis model for the correlations between the observed variables. An obvious model to consider is a single-factor model, where the single factor is simply length. The path diagram of the proposed model is given in Fig. 13.3. If it is assumed that length is in standardized form, i.e. has a variance of unity, the model can be fitted to the correlations between the four measurements (see Display 13.7) to give the results shown in Display 13.8. Both the chi-squared goodness-of-fit statistic and the matrix of residual correlations show that the model fits the data very well. As shown in Display 13.8 the derived results can be used to estimate the reliabilities of the four measurements. As would be expected, the measurement of length using a ruler has the greatest reliability; amongst the 'guessers', B and G appear to have somewhat lower reliability than D. The z test for the hypothesis that the error variance corresponding to measurement by ruler is zero is not significant; consequently, the ruler measurements of length give essentially the true lengths of the pieces of string. Several other interesting examples of this approach to reliability are described by Dunn (1989).

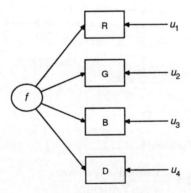

Fig. 13.3 Path diagram for the factor analysis model of string length data.

Display 13.7 How long is a piece of string?

- Measurement by ruler (R) and guesses by three observers (G, B and D) are tabulated below:

Piece	R	G	B	D
1	6.3	5.0	4.8	6.0
2	4.1	3.2	3.1	3.5
3	5.1	3.6	3.8	4.5
4	5.0	4.5	4.1	4.3
5	5.7	4.0	5.2	5.0
6	3.3	2.5	2.8	2.6
7	1.3	1.7	1.4	1.6
8	5.8	4.8	4.2	5.5
9	2.8	2.4	2.0	2.1
10	6.7	5.2	5.3	6.0
11	1.5	1.2	1.1	1.2
12	2.1	1.8	1.6	1.8
13	4.6	3.4	4.1	3.9
14	7.6	6.0	6.3	6.5
15	2.5	2.2	1.6	2.0

- The correlation matrix **R** of the four observed measurements is

$$\mathbf{R} = \begin{array}{c} R \\ G \\ B \\ D \end{array} \begin{pmatrix} 1.0000 & & & \\ 0.9802 & 1.0000 & & \\ 0.9811 & 0.9553 & 1.0000 & \\ 0.9899 & 0.9807 & 0.9684 & 1.0000 \end{pmatrix}$$

$$\begin{array}{cccc} R & G & B & D \end{array}$$

Display 13.8 Results from fitting a one-factor model to the string length data

- The factor analysis model for the string length data is

$$R = \lambda_1 f + u_1$$
$$G = \lambda_2 f + u_2$$
$$B = \lambda_3 f + u_3$$
$$D = \lambda_4 f + u_4$$

where f is the 'true' length of the string.

- The estimates of the parameters in the model and their standard errors are as follows:

Parameter	Estimate	SE	Estimate/SE
λ_1	0.999	0.189	5.279
λ_2	0.982	0.192	5.103
λ_3	0.981	0.192	5.098
λ_4	0.991	0.191	5.199
var(u_1)	0.002	0.005	0.445
var(u_2)	0.036	0.015	2.446
var(u_3)	0.037	0.015	2.454
var(u_4)	0.017	0.008	2.082

- The chi-squared goodness-of-fit statistic takes a value of 2.372 with two degrees of freedom. The associated P-value is 0.305.
- The residual correlation matrix is as follows:

$$
\begin{array}{c}
\begin{array}{cccc} \quad R & \quad G & \quad B & \quad D \end{array} \\
\begin{array}{c} R \\ G \\ B \\ D \end{array}
\left(
\begin{array}{cccc}
0.000 & & & \\
0.000 & 0.000 & & \\
0.001 & -0.008 & 0.000 & \\
0.000 & 0.008 & -0.004 & 0.000
\end{array}
\right)
\end{array}
$$

- Since the model was fitted to the correlation matrix, the variance of each observed variable is unity. The latent variable f is also assumed to be in standardized form with variance unity. Consequently, for each variable,

  observed variance $= 1 = $ (estimated loading)^2 + estimated error variance.

- Thus in this case the ratio of true score variance to observed variance for a variable (i.e. its reliability) is simply the square of the estimated loading of the variable on the common factor f. Consequently the reliabilities of the four observed variables are as follows:

  (a) R: 0.9980
  (b) G: 0.9643
  (c) B: 0.9624
  (d) B: 0.9821.

13.6　Summary

1. The assessment of the reliability of measuring instruments is fundamental in a psychological investigation.
2. Cochran's Q test can be used to assess inter-observer bias for categorical data.
3. The kappa coefficient is useful for assessing agreement between raters on a categorical variable. It is a 'chance-corrected' measure of agreement.

4. The intraclass correlation coefficient can be used to estimate the reliability of quantitative measurements. When only two raters are involved, the intraclass correlation coefficient is related to Pearson's product moment correlation coefficient.
5. Split-half reliabilities are frequently used for psychological measurements composed of a possibly large number of individual items.
6. Confirmatory factor analysis models are often useful in reliability studies.

Exercises

13.1 Lundberg (1940) presented the results of an experiment to answer the question: 'What is the degree of agreement in commonsense judgements of socio-economic status by two persons who are themselves of radically different status'. One set of data collected is shown in Table 13.6. Investigate the level of agreement between the two raters using the κ coefficient.

Table 13.6 Janitor's and banker's ratings of the socioeconomic status of 196 families on a six-point scale

Banker's ratings	Janitor's ratings					
	1	2	3	4	5	6
6	0	0	0	0	0	0
5	0	0	0	6	8	8
4	0	1	0	21	27	0
3	0	1	25	47	13	2
2	0	4	6	4	1	0
1	3	4	11	3	1	0

13.2 Consider the following table of agreement for two raters rating a binary response:

Rater A	Rater B		
	Yes	No	Total
Yes	15	5	20
No	5	35	40
Total	20	40	

Show that the κ statistic for these data is identical to both their intraclass correlation coefficient and their product moment correlation coefficient.

13.3 Calculate the intraclass correlation coefficient for the string length data in Display 13.7. In addition, calculate Pearson's product moment correlation coefficient for raters A and B, and show that it is related to the intraclass correlation coefficient of these two raters by the formula given in Display 13.5.

13.4 Fit a one-factor model to the guesses of string length made by observers G, B and D in Display 13.7 using the procedure described in Chapter 10 for Spearman's data (see Display 10.5).

Further reading

Cronbach, L.J., Glesser, G.L, Nanda, H. and Rajaratnam, N. (1972). *The dependability of behavioural measurements*. Wiley, New York.

Fuller, W.A. (1987). *Measurement error models*. Wiley, New York.

Nichols, P.J.R. and Bailey, N.T.J. (1955). The accuracy of leg-length differences. An 'observer error' experiment. *British Medical Journal*, 11, 1247–8.

Spitzer, R.L., Cohen, J., Fleiss, J.L. and Endicott, J. (1987). Quantification of agreement in psychiatric diagnosis. *Archives of General Psychiatry*, 17, 83–7.

Appendix A
Statistical glossary

This glossary includes terms encountered in introductory statistics courses and terms mentioned in this text with little or no explanation. In addition, some terms of general statistical interest which are not specific to either this text or psychology are defined. Terms which are explained in detail in the text are not included in this glossary. Terms in italics in a definition are themselves defined in the appropriate place in the glossary. Terms are listed alphabetically using the letter-by-letter convention. Readers may find the following two dictionaries of statistics useful:

Everitt, B.S. (1995). *The Cambridge dictionary of statistics in the medical sciences*. Cambridge University Press.
Freund, J.E. and Williams, F.J. (1966). *Dictionary/outline of basic statistics*, Dover Publications, New York.

Acceptance region   The set of values of a *test statistic* for which the *null hypothesis* is accepted.

Additive effect   A term used when the effect of administering two treatments together is the sum of their separate effects. See also **additive model**.

Additive model   A model in which the explanatory variables have an *additive effect* on the response variable. For example, if variable A has an effect of size a on some response measure and variable B has an effect of size b on the same response, then in an assumed additive model for A and B their combined effect would be $a + b$.

Alpha (α)   The probability of a *type I error*. See also **significance level**.

Alternative hypothesis   The hypothesis against which the *null hypothesis* is tested.

A priori comparisons   Synonym for **planned comparisons**.

Asymmetrical distribution   A *probability distribution* or *frequency distribution* which is not symmetrical about some central value.

Attenuation   A term applied to the correlation between two variables, when both are subject to measurement error, to indicate that the value of the correlation between the 'true values' is likely to be underestimated.

Balanced design   A term applied to any experimental design in which the same number of observations is taken for each combination of the experimental factors.

Bartlett's test A test for the equality of the variances of a number of populations. Sometimes used prior to applying analysis of variance techniques to assess the assumption of homogeneity of variance. Of limited practical value because of its known sensitivity to non-normality, so that a significant result might be due to departures from normality rather than to different variances. See also **Box's test** and **Hartley's test**.

Bell-shaped distribution A *probability distribution* having the overall shape of a vertical cross-section of a bell. The *normal distribution* is the most well known example, but *Student's t-distribution* is also this shape.

Beta coefficient A regression coefficient that is standardized so as to allow for a direct comparison between explanatory variables as to their relative explanatory power for the response variable. Calculated from the raw regression coefficients by multiplying them by the standard deviation of the corresponding explanatory variable.

Bias Deviation of results or inferences from the truth, or processes leading to such deviation. More specifically, the extent to which the statistical method used in a study does not estimate the quantity thought to be estimated.

Bimodal distribution A *probability distribution*, or a *frequency distribution*, with two modes.

Binary variable Observations which occur in one of two possible states, these often being labelled 0 and 1. Such data are frequently encountered in medical investigations; commonly occurring examples include 'dead/alive', 'improved/not improved' and 'depressed/not depressed'.

Binomial distribution The *probability distribution* of the number of 'successes' x in a series of n independent trials, each of which can result in either a 'success' or 'failure'. The probability p of a success remains constant from trial to trial. Specifically the distribution of x is given by

$$P(x) = \frac{n!}{x!(n-x)!}p^x(1-p)^{n-x}, \quad x = 0, 1, 2, \ldots, n.$$

The mean of the distribution is np and its variance is $np(1-p)$.

Bipolar factor A factor resulting from the application of factor analysis which has a mixture of positive and negative loadings. Such factors can be difficult to interpret, and attempts are often made to simplify them by the process of factor rotation.

Biserial correlation A measure of the strength of the relationship between two variables, one continuous (y) and the other recorded as a *binary variable* (x), but having underlying continuity and normality. Estimated from the sample values as

$$r_b = \frac{\bar{y}_1 - \bar{y}_0}{s_y}\frac{pq}{u}$$

where $\bar{y}_1$ is the sample mean of the y variable for those individuals for whom $x = 1$, $\bar{y}_0$ is the sample mean of the y variable for those individuals having $x = 0$, s_y is the standard deviation of the y values, p is the proportion of individuals with $x = 1$ and $q = 1 - p$ is the proportion of individuals with $x = 0$. Finally, u is the ordinate (height) of a *normal distribution* with mean zero and standard deviation unity at the point of division between the p and q proportions of the curve. See also **point-biserial correlation**.

Bivariate data   Data in which the subjects each have measurements on two variables.

Box's test   A test for assessing the equality of the variances in a number of populations that is less sensitive than *Bartlett's test* to departures from normality. See also **Hartley's test**.

Ceiling effect   A term used to describe what happens when many subjects in a study have scores on a variable that are at or near the possible upper limit ('ceiling'). Such an effect may cause problems for some types of analysis because it reduces the possible amount of variation in the variable. The converse, or floor effect, causes similar problems.

Central tendency   A property of the distribution of a variable usually measured by statistics such as the mean, median and mode.

Change scores   Scores obtained by subtracting a posttreatment score on some variable from the corresponding pretreatment, baseline value.

Chi-squared distribution   The *probability distribution* of the sum of squares of a number of independent normal variables with means zero and standard deviations one. This distribution arises in many area of statistics; for example, assessing the goodness-of-fit of models, particularly those fitted to contingency tables.

Coefficient of variation   A measure of spread for a set of data defined as

$$100 \times \text{standard deviation/mean.}$$

Originally proposed as a way of comparing the variability in different distributions, but found to be sensitive to errors in the mean.

Commensurate variables   Variables that are on the same scale or expressed in the same units, for example systolic and diastolic blood pressure.

Common factor variance   A term used in factor analysis for that part of the variance of a variable shared with the other observed variables via the relationships of these variable to the common factors. Often known as communality.

Composite hypothesis   A hypothesis that specifies more than a single value for a parameter; for example, the hypothesis that the mean of a population is greater than some value.

Compound symmetry   The property possessed by a covariance matrix of a set of multivariate data when its main diagonal elements are equal to one another, and additionally its off-diagonal elements are also equal. Consequently, the matrix has the general form:

$$\Sigma = \begin{pmatrix} \sigma^2 & \rho\sigma^2 & \cdots & \rho\sigma^2 \\ \rho\sigma^2 & \sigma^2 & \cdots & \rho\sigma^2 \\ \vdots & \vdots & & \vdots \\ \rho\sigma^2 & \rho\sigma^2 & \cdots & \sigma^2 \end{pmatrix}$$

where ρ is the assumed common *correlation coefficient* of the measures.

Confidence interval   A range of values, calculated from the sample observations, that are believed, with a particular probability, to contain the true parameter value. For example, a 95% confidence interval implies that if the estimation process were repeated again and again, then 95% of the calculated intervals would be expected to contain the true parameter value. Note that the stated probability level refers to properties of the interval and not to the parameter itself which is not considered to be a *random variable*.

Conservative and non-conservative tests   Terms usually encountered in discussions of *multiple comparison tests*. Non-conservative tests provide poor control over the *per-experiment error rate*. Conservative tests, in contrast, may limit the *per-comparison error rate* to unecessarily low values, and tend to have low *power* unless the sample size is large.

Contrast   A linear function of parameters or statistics in which the coefficients sum to zero. It is most often encountered in the context of analysis of variance. For example, in an application involving, say, three treatment groups (with means x_{T_1}, x_{T_2} and x_{T_3}) and a control group (with mean x_C), the following is the contrast for comparing the mean of the control group with the average of the treatment groups:

$$x_C - \tfrac{1}{3}x_{T_1} - \tfrac{1}{3}x_{T_2} - \tfrac{1}{3}x_{T_3}.$$

See also **orthogonal contrast**.

Correlation coefficient   An index that quantifies the linear relationship between a pair of variables. A variety of such coefficients have been suggested, for sample observations, of which the most commonly used is Pearson's product moment correlation coefficient defined as

$$r = \frac{\sum_{i=1}^{n}(x_i - \bar{x})(y_i - \bar{y})}{\sqrt{\sum_{i=1}^{n}(x_i - \bar{x})^2(y_i - \bar{y})^2}}$$

where $(x_1, y_1), (x_2, y_2), \ldots, (x_n, y_n)$ are the n sample values of the two variables of interest. The coefficient takes values between -1 and $+1$, with the sign indicating the direction of the relationship and the numerical magnitude its strength. Values of -1 or $+1$ indicate that the sample values fall on a straight line. A value of zero indicates the lack of any linear relationship between the two variables.

Critical region   The values of a *test statistic* that lead to rejection of a *null hypothesis*. The size of the critical region is the probability of obtaining an outcome belonging to this region when the null hypothesis is true, i.e. the probability of a *type I error*. See also **acceptance region**.

Critical value The value with which a statistic calculated from the sample data is compared in order to decide whether a *null hypothesis* should be rejected. The value is related to the particular significance level chosen.

Cronbach's alpha An index of the internal consistency of a psychological test. If the test consists of n items and an individual's score is the total answered correctly, then the coefficient is given specifically by

$$\alpha = \frac{n}{n-1}\left(1 - \frac{1}{\sigma^2}\sum_{i=1}^{n}\sigma_i^2\right)$$

where σ^2 is the variance of the total scores and σ_i^2 is the variance of the set of 0,1 scores representing correct and incorrect answers on item i.

Cross-validation The division of data into two approximately equal-sized subsets, of which one is used to estimate the parameters in some model of interest, and the other is used to assess whether the model with these parameter values fits adequately.

Cumulative frequency distribution A listing of the sample values of a variable together with the proportion of the observations less than or equal to each value.

Data dredging A term used to describe comparisons made within a data set not specifically prescribed prior to the start of the study.

Data reduction The process of summarizing large amounts of data by forming *frequency distributions, histograms, scatter diagrams* etc., and calculating statistics such as means, variances and correlation coefficients. The term is also used when seeking a low-dimensional representation of multivariate data by procedures such as principal components analysis and factor analysis.

Data set A general term for observations and measurements collected during any type of scientific investigation.

Degrees of freedom An elusive concept that occurs throughout statistics. Essentially, the term means the number of independent units of information in a sample relevant to the estimation of a parameter or calculation of a statistic. For example, in a two-by-two contingency table with a given set of marginal totals, only one of the four cell frequencies is free and therefore the table has a single degree of freedom. In many cases the term corresponds to the number of parameters in a model.

Dependent variable See **response variable**.

Descriptive statistics A general term for methods of summarizing and tabulating data that make their main features more transparent; for example, calculating means and variances and plotting histograms. See also **exploratory data analysis** and **initial data analysis**.

DF(df) Abbreviation for **degrees of freedom**.

Diagonal matrix A *square matrix* whose off-diagonal elements are all zero, for example

$$\mathbf{D} = \begin{pmatrix} 10 & 0 & 0 \\ 0 & 5 & 0 \\ 0 & 0 & 3 \end{pmatrix}.$$

Dichotomous variable Synonym for **binary variable**.

Digit preference The personal and often subconscious *bias* that frequently occurs in the recording of observations. Usually most obvious in the final recorded digit of a measurement.

Discrete variables Variables having only integer values; for example, number of trials to learn a particular task.

Doubly multivariate data A term used for the data collected in those longitudinal studies in which more than a single response variable is recorded for each subject on each occasion.

Dummy variables The variables resulting from recoding categorical variables with more than two categories into a series of *binary variables*. For example, marital status, if originally labelled 1 for married, 2 for single and 3 for divorced, widowed or separated, could be redefined in terms of two variables as follows:

Variable 1: 1 if single, 0 otherwise.
Variable 2: 1 if divorced, widowed or separated, 0 otherwise.

Both new variables would be zero for a married person. In general, a categorical variable with k categories would be recoded in terms of $k-1$ dummy variables. Such recoding is used before polychotomous variables are used as explanatory variables in a regression analysis to avoid the unreasonable assumption that the original numerical codes for the categories, i.e. the values $1, 2, \ldots, k$, correspond to an interval scale.

EDA Abbreviation for **exploratory data analysis**.

Effect Generally used for the change in a response variable produced by a change in one or more explanatory or factor variables.

Empirical Based on observation or experiment rather than deduction from basic laws or theory.

Error rate The proportion of subjects misclassified by an allocation rule derived from a discriminant analysis.

Estimation The process of providing a numerical value for a population parameter on the basis of information collected from a sample. If a single figure is calculated for the unknown parameter, the process is called point estimation. If an interval is calculated within which the parameter is likely to fall, the procedure is called interval estimation. See also **least squares estimation** and **confidence interval**.

Estimator A statistic used to provide an estimate for a parameter. For example, the sample mean is an *unbiased* estimator of the population mean.

Experimental design The arrangement and procedures used in an *experimental study*. Some general principles of good design are simplicity, avoidance of *bias*, the use of *random allocation* for forming treatment groups, replication and adequate sample size.

Experimental study A general term for investigations in which the researcher can deliberately influence events and investigate the effects of the intervention.

Experimentwise error rate Synonym for **per-experiment error rate**.

Explanatory variables The variables appearing on the right-hand side of the equations defining, for example, multiple regression or logistic regression, which seek to predict or 'explain' the response variable. They are also commonly known as the independent variables, although this is not to be recommended since they are rarely independent of one another.

Exploratory data analysis An approach to data analysis that emphasizes the use of informal graphical procedures not based on prior assumptions about the structure of the data or on formal models for the data. The essence of this approach is that, broadly speaking, data are assumed to possess the structure

$$\text{data} = \text{smooth} + \text{rough}$$

where the 'smooth' is the underlying regularity or pattern in the data. The objective of the exploratory approach is to separate the 'smooth' from the 'rough' with minimal use of formal mathematics or statistical methods. See also **initial data analysis**.

Eyeball test Informal assessment of data simply by inspection and mental calculation allied with experience of the particular area from which the data arise.

Factor A term used in a variety of ways in statistics, but most commonly to refer to a categorical variable, with a small number of levels, under investigation in an experiment as a possible source of variation. Essentially, simply a categorical explanatory variable.

Familywise error rate The probability of making any error in a given family of inferences. See also **per-comparison error rate** and **per-experiment error rate**.

***F*-distribution** The *probability distribution* of the ratio of two independent *random variables*, each having a *chi-squared distribution*. Divided by their respective degrees of freedom.

Fisher's exact test An alternative procedure to the use of the chi-squared statistic for assessing the independence of two variables forming a two-by-two contingency table, particularly when the expected frequencies are small.

Fisher's z transformation A transformation of Pearson's product moment correlation coefficient r given by

$$z = \frac{1}{2} \ln \frac{1 + r}{1 - r}.$$

The statistic z has mean $\frac{1}{2} \ln[(1 + \rho)/(1 - \rho)]$ where ρ is the population correlation value and variance $1/(n-3)$ where n is the sample size. The transformation can be used to test hypotheses and to construct *confidence intervals* for ρ.

Fishing expedition   Synonym for **data dredging**.

Fitted value   Usually used to refer to the value of the response variable as predicted by some estimated model.

Follow-up   The process of locating research subjects or patients to determine whether or not some outcome of interest has occurred.

Floor effect   See **ceiling effect**.

Frequency distribution   The division of a sample of observations into a number of classes, together with the number of observations in each class. Acts as a useful summary of the main features of the data such as location, shape and spread. An example of such a table is given below:

Class limits	Observed frequency
75–79	1
80–84	2
85–89	5
90–94	9
95–99	10
100–104	7
105–109	4
110–114	2
≥ 115	1

Frequency polygon   A diagram used to display graphically the values in a *frequency distribution*. The frequencies are plotted as ordinate against the class midpoints as abcissa. The points are then joined by a series of straight lines. Particularly useful in displaying a number of frequency distributions on the same diagram.

F-test   A test for the equality of the variances of two populations having *normal distributions* based on the ratio of the variances of a sample of observations taken from each. Most often encountered in the analysis of variance, where testing whether particular variances are the same also tests for the equality of a set of means.

Gambler's fallacy   The belief that if an event has not happened for a long time, it is bound to occur soon.

Goodness-of-fit statistics   Measures of agreement between a set of sample values and the corresponding values predicted from some model of interest.

Grand mean   Mean of all the values in a grouped data set irrespective of groups.

Graphical methods   A generic term for those techniques in which the results are given in the form of a graph, diagram or some other form of visual display.

H_0 Symbol for **null hypothesis**.

H_1 Symbol for **alternative hypothesis**.

Halo effect   The tendency of a subject's performance on some task to be overrated because of the observer's perception of the subject 'doing well' gained in an earlier exercise or when assessed in a different area.

Harmonic mean   The reciprocal of the arithmetic mean of the reciprocals of a set of observations $x_1, x_2, \cdots, x_n$. Specifically obtained from

$$\frac{1}{H} = \frac{1}{n} \sum_{i=1}^{n} \frac{1}{x_i}.$$

Hartley's test   A simple test of the equality of variances of a number of populations. The *test statistic* is the ratio of the largest to the smallest sample variances.

Hawthorne effect   A term used for the effect that might be produced in an experiment simply from the awareness by the subjects that they are participating in some form of scientific investigation. The name comes from a study of industrial efficiency at the Hawthorne Plant in Chicago in the 1920s.

Hello–goodbye effect   A phenomenon originally described in psychotherapy research but which may arise whenever a subject is assessed on two occasions with some intervention between the visits. Before an intervention a person may present himself or herself in as bad a light as possible, thereby hoping to qualify for treatment and impressing staff with the seriousness of his or her problems. At the end of the study the person may want to 'please' the staff with his or her improvement and so may minimize any problems. The result is to make it appear that there has been some improvement when none has occurred, or to magnify the effects that did occur.

Heywood cases   Solutions obtained when using factor analysis in which one or more of the variances of the specific variates become negative.

Histogram   A graphical representation of a set of observations in which class frequencies are represented by the areas of rectangles centred on the class interval. If the latter are all equal, the heights of the rectangles are also proportional to the observed frequencies.

Homogeneous   A term that is used in statistics to indicate the equality of some quantity of interest (most often a variance) in a number of different groups, populations etc.

Hypothesis testing   A general term for the procedure of assessing whether sample data are consistent or otherwise with statements made about the population. See also **null hypothesis, alternative hypothesis, composite hypothesis, significance test, significance level, type I error** and **type II error**.

IDA   Abbreviation for **initial data analysis**.

Identification The degree to which there is sufficient information in the sample observations to estimate the parameters in a proposed model. An unidentified model is one in which there are too many parameters in relation to the number of observations to make estimation possible. A just identified model corresponds to a saturated model. Finally, an overidentified model is one in which parameters can be estimated, and there remain degrees of freedom to allow the fit of the model to be assessed.

Identity matrix A *diagonal matrix* in which all the elements on the leading diagonal are unity and all the other elements are zero.

Independence Essentially, two events are said to be independent if knowing the outcome of one tells us nothing about the other. More formally the concept is defined in terms of the probabilities of the two events. In particular, two events A and B are said to be independent if

$$P(A \text{ and } B) = P(A) \times P(B)$$

where $P(A)$ and $P(B)$ represent the probabilities of A and B.

Independent samples *t*-test See **Student's *t*-test**.

Inference The process of drawing conclusions about a population on the basis of measurements or observations made on a sample of individuals from the population.

Initial data analysis The first phase in the examination of a data set which consists of a number of informal steps including the following:

- checking the quality of the data;
- calculating simple summary statistics and constructing appropriate graphs.

The general aim is to clarify the structure of the data, obtain a simple descriptive summary and perhaps obtain ideas for a more sophisticated analysis.

Interaction A term applied when two (or more) explanatory variables do not act independently on a response variable. See also **additive effect**.

Interval estimate See **estimate**.

Interval estimation See **estimation**.

Interval variable Synonym for **continuous variable**.

Interviewer bias The *bias* that may occur in surveys of human populations because of the direct result of the action of the interviewer. The bias can arise for a variety of reasons, including failure to contact the right persons and systematic errors in recording the answers received from the respondent.

J-shaped distribution An extremely asymmetrical distribution with its maximum frequency in the initial class and a declining frequency elsewhere.

Kruskal–Wallis test A distribution-free method that is the analogue of the analysis of variance of a one-way design. It tests whether the groups to be compared have the same population median. The *test statistic* is derived by ranking all the N observations from 1 to N, regardless of which group they are in, and then calculating

$$H = \frac{12 \sum_{i=1}^{k} n_i (\bar{R}_i - \bar{R})^2}{N(N-1)}$$

where n_i is the number of observations in group i, $\bar{R}_i$ is the mean of their ranks and $\bar{R}$ is the average of all the ranks, given explicitly by $(N+1)/2$. When the *null hypothesis* is true the test statistic has a chi-squared distribution with $k-1$ degrees of freedom.

Kurtosis   The extent to which the peak of a unimodal *frequency distribution* departs from the shape of a *normal distribution* by being either more pointed (leptokurtic) or flatter (platykurtic). Usually measured for a probability distribution as

$$\mu_4 / \mu_2^2 - 3$$

where μ_4 is the fourth central moment of the distribution and μ_2 is its variance. (Corresponding functions of the sample moments are used for frequency distributions.) This index takes the value zero for a normal distribution (other distributions with zero kurtosis are called mesokurtic), it is positive for a leptokurtic distribution and it is negative for a platykurtic curve.

Large-sample method   Any statistical method based on an approximation to a *normal distribution* or other *probability distribution* that becomes more accurate as sample size increases.

Least-squares estimation   A method used for estimating parameters, particularly in regression analysis, by minimizing the difference between the observed response and the value predicted by the model. For example, if the expected value of a response variable y is of the form

$$E(y) = \alpha + \beta x$$

where x is an explanatory variable, then least-squares estimators of the parameters α and β can be obtained from n pairs of sample values $(x_1, y_1), (x_2, y_2), \ldots, (x_n, y_n)$ by minimizing S given by

$$S = \sum_{i=1}^{n} (y_i - \alpha - \beta x_i)^2$$

to give

$$\hat{\alpha} = \bar{y} - \hat{\beta}\bar{x}$$
$$\hat{\beta} = \frac{\sum_{i=1}^{n}(x_i - \bar{x})(y_i - \bar{y})}{\sum_{i=1}^{n}(x_i - \bar{x})^2}.$$

Often referred to as ordinary least squares to differentiate this simple version of the technique from more involved versions such as weighted least squares.

Leverage points   A term used in regression analysis for those observations that have an extreme value on one or more of the explanatory variables. The effect of such points is to force the fitted model close to the observed value of the response, leading to a small residual.

Likert scales Scales often used in studies of attitudes, in which the raw scores are based on graded alternative responses to each of a series of questions. For example, the subject may be asked to indicate his or her degree of agreement with each of a series of statements relevant to the attitude. A number is attached to each possible response (e.g. 1, strongly approve; 2, approve; 3, undecided; 4, disapprove; 5, strongly disapprove) and the sum of these is used as the composite score.

Logarithmic transformation The transformation of a variable x obtained by taking $y = \ln(x)$. Often used to achieve normality when the *frequency distribution* of the variable x shows a moderate to large degree of *skewness*.

Lower triangular matrix A matrix in which all the elements above the main diagonal are zero; for example,

$$L = \begin{pmatrix} 1 & 0 & 0 & 0 \\ 2 & 3 & 0 & 0 \\ 1 & 1 & 3 & 0 \\ 1 & 5 & 6 & 7 \end{pmatrix}.$$

Main effect An estimate of the independent effect of (usually) a factor variable on a response variable in analysis of variance.

Manifest variable A variable that can be measured directly, in contrast to a latent variable.

Marginal totals A term often used for the total number of observations in each row and each column of a contingency table.

MANOVA Acronym for **multivariate analysis of variance**.

Matched pairs A term used for observations arising either from two individuals who are individually matched on a number of variables (e.g. age, sex etc.) or where two observations are taken on the same individual on two separate occasions. Essentially synonymous with **paired samples**.

Matched pairs *t*-test *Student's t-test* for the equality of the means of two populations, when the observations arise as *paired samples*. The test is based on the differences between the observations of the matched pairs. The *test statistic* is given by

$$t = \frac{\bar{d}}{s_\mathrm{d}/\sqrt{n}}$$

where n is the sample size, $\bar{d}$ is the mean of the differences and s_d is their standard deviation. If the null hypothesis of the equality of the population means is true, then t has a *Student t-distribution* with $n - 1$ degrees of freedom.

Matching The process of making a study group and a comparison group comparable with respect to extraneous factors. Often used in retrospective studies when selecting cases and controls to control variation in a response variable caused by sources other than those immediately under investigation. Several kinds of matching can be identified, the most common of which is when each case is individually matched with a control subject on the matching variables, such as age, sex, occupation etc. See also **paired samples**.

Matrix A rectangular arrangement of numbers, algebraic functions etc. Two examples are

$$A = \begin{pmatrix} 1 & 1 & 2 \\ 2 & 1 & 7 \end{pmatrix}$$

$$B = \begin{pmatrix} b_{11} & b_{12} \\ b_{21} & b_{22} \\ b_{31} & b_{32} \\ b_{41} & b_{42} \end{pmatrix}.$$

McNemar's test A test for comparing proportions in data involving *paired samples*. The *test statistic* is given by

$$X^2 = \frac{(b-c)^2}{b+c}$$

where b is the number of pairs for which the individual receiving treatment A has a positive response and the individual receiving treatment B does not, and c is the number of pairs for which the reverse is the case. If the probability of a positive response is the same in each group, then X^2 has a chi-squared distribution with a single degree of freedom.

Mean vector A vector containing the mean values of each variable in a set of *multivariate data*.

Measurement error Errors in reading, calculating or recording a numerical value. The difference between observed values of a variable recorded under similar conditions and some underlying true value.

Measures of association Numerical indices quantifying the strength of the statistical dependence of two or more qualitative variables.

Median The value in a set of ranked observations that divides the data into two parts of equal size. When there is an odd number of observations, the median is the middle value. When there is an even number of observations, the measure is calculated as the average of the two central values. Provides a measure of location of a sample that is suitable for *asymmetric distributions* and is also relatively insensitive to the presence of *outliers*. See also **mean** and **mode**.

Misinterpretation of P-values A *P-value* is commonly interpreted in a variety of ways that are incorrect. The most common are that it is the probability of the null hypothesis and that it is the probability of the data having arisen by chance. For the correct interpretation see the entry for **P-value**.

Mixed data   Data containing a mixture of continuous variables, ordinal variables and categorical variables.

Mode   The most frequently occurring value in a set of observations. Occasionally used as a measure of location. See also **mean** and **median**.

Model   A description of the assumed structure of a set of observations that can range from a fairly imprecise verbal account to, more usually, a formalized mathematical expression of the process assumed to have generated the observed data. The purpose of such a description is to aid in understanding the data.

Model building   A procedure which attempts to find the simplest model for a sample of observations that provides an adequate fit to the data.

Most powerful test   A test of a *null hypothesis* which has greater *power* than any other test for a given *alternative hypothesis*.

Multilevel models   Models for data that are organized hierachically (e.g. children within families) which allow for the possibility that measurements made on children from the same family are likely to be correlated.

Multinomial distribution   A generalization of the *binomial distribution* to situations in which r outcomes can occur on each of n trials, where $r > 2$. Specifically, the distribution is given by

$$P(n_1, n_2, \ldots, n_r) = \frac{n!}{n_1! n_2! \ldots n_r!} p_1^{n_1} p_2^{n_2} \cdots p_r^{n_r}$$

where n_i is the number of trials with outcome i, and p_i is the probability of outcome i occurring on a particular trial.

Multiple comparison tests   Procedures for detailed examination of the differences between a set of means, usually after a general hypothesis that they are all equal has been rejected. No single technique is best in all situations, and a major distinction between techniques is how they control the possible inflation of the *type I error*.

Multivariate analysis   A generic term for the many methods of analysis important in investigating multivariate data.

Multivariate analysis of variance   A procedure for testing the equality of the *mean vectors* of more than two populations. The technique is directly analogous to the analysis of variance of *univariate data* except that the groups are compared on q response variables simultaneously. In the univariate case F-tests are used to assess the hypotheses of interest. In the multivariate case no single *test statistic* can be constructed that is optimal in all situations. The most widely used of the available test statistics is *Wilk's lambda* which is based on three matrices $\mathbf{W}$ (the within-groups matrix of sums of squares and products), $\mathbf{T}$ (the total matrix of sums of squares and cross products) and $\mathbf{B}$ (the between-groups matrix of sums of squares and cross products), defined as follows:

$$T = \sum_{i=1}^{g}\sum_{j=1}^{n_i}(x_{ij} - \bar{x})(x_{ij} - \bar{x})'$$

$$W = \sum_{i=1}^{g}\sum_{j=1}^{n_i}(x_{ij} - \bar{x}_i)(x_{ij} - \bar{x}_i)'$$

$$B = \sum_{i=1}^{g} n_i(\bar{x}_i - \bar{x})(\bar{x}_i - \bar{x})'$$

where $x_{ij}(i = 1, \ldots, g, \quad j = 1, \ldots, n_i)$ represent the jth multivariate observation in the ith group, g is the number of groups and n_i is the number of observations in the ith group. The mean vector of the ith group is represented by $\bar{x}_i$ and the mean vector of all the observations by $\bar{x}$. These matrices satisfy the equation

$$T = W + B.$$

Wilks' lambda is given by the ratio of the determinants of W and T, i.e.

$$\Lambda = \frac{|W|}{|T|} = \frac{|W|}{|W + B|}.$$

The statistic Λ can be transformed to give an F-test to assess the null hypothesis of the equality of the population mean vectors. In addition to Λ, a number of other test statistics are available:

- Roy's largest root criterion: the largest eigenvalue of BW^{-1}.
- The Hotelling–Lawley trace: the sum of the eigenvalues of BW^{-1}.
- The Pillai–Bartlett trace: the sum of the eigenvalues of BT^{-1}.

It has been found that the differences in *power* between the various test statistics are generally quite small and so in most situations the choice will not greatly affect the conclusions.

Multivariate normal distribution The *probability distribution* of a set of variables $x' = [x_1, x_2, \ldots, x_q]$ given by

$$f(x_1, x_2, \ldots, x_q) = (2\pi)^{-q/2}|\Sigma|^{-\frac{1}{2}}\exp -\tfrac{1}{2}(x - \mu)'\Sigma^{-1}(x - \mu)$$

where μ is the *mean vector* of the variables and Σ is their *variance–covariance matrix*. This distribution is assumed by multivariate analysis procedures such as *multivariate analysis of variance*.

Newman–Keuls test A *multiple comparison test* used to investigate in more detail the differences between a set of means, as indicated by a significant *F-test* in an analysis of variance.

Nominal significance level The significance level of a test when its assumptions are valid.

Non-orthogonal designs   Analysis of variance designs with two or more factors in which the numbers of observations in each cell are not equal.

Normal distribution   A *probability distribution* of a *random variable x* that is assumed by many statistical methods. Specifically given by

$$f(x) = \frac{1}{\sigma(2\pi)^{\frac{1}{2}}} \exp[-\frac{1}{2}\frac{(x - \mu)^2}{\sigma^2}]$$

where μ and σ^2 are respectively the mean and variance of x. This distribution is bell-shaped.

Null distribution   The *probability distribution* of a *test statistic* when the *null hypothesis* is true.

Null hypothesis   The 'no difference' or 'no association' hypothesis to be tested (usually by means of a significance test) against an *alternative hypothesis* that postulates non-zero difference or association.

Null matrix   A matrix in which all elements are zero.

Null vector   A *vector* in which all elements are zero.

Oblique factors   A term used in factor analysis for common factors that are allowed to be correlated.

One-sided test   A significance test for which the *alternative hypothesis* is directional for example that one population mean is greater than another. The choice between a one-sided test and *two-sided test* must be made before any *test statistic* is calculated.

Orthogonal   A term that occurs in several areas of statistics with different meanings in each case. Most commonly encountered in relation to two variables or two linear functions of a set of variables to indicate statistical independence. Literally means 'at right angles'.

Orthogonal contrasts   Sets of linear functions of either parameters or statistics in which the defining coefficients satisfy a particular relationship. Specifically, if c_1 and c_2 are two *contrasts* of a set of m parameters such that

$$c_1 = a_{11}\beta_1 + a_{12}\beta_2 + \ldots + a_{1m}\beta_m$$
$$c_2 = a_{21}\beta_1 + a_{22}\beta_2 + \ldots + a_{2m}\beta_m,$$

they are orthogonal if $\sum_{i=1}^{m} a_{1i}a_{2i} = 0$. If, in addition, $\sum_{i=1}^{m} a_{1i}^2 = 1$ and $\sum_{i=1}^{m} a_{2i}^2 = 1$, then the contrasts are said to be orthonormal.

Orthogonal matrix   A *square matrix* that is such that multiplying the matrix by its transpose results in an *identity matrix*.

Outlier   An observation that appears to deviate markedly from the other members of the sample in which it occurs. For example, in the set of systolic blood pressures $\{125, 128, 130, 131, 198\}$ 198 might be considered an outlier. Such extreme observations may be reflecting some abnormality in the measured characteristic of a patient, or they may result from an error in the measurement or recording.

Paired samples   Two samples of observations with the characteristic feature that each observation in one sample has one and only one matching observation in the other sample. There are several ways in which such samples can arise in medical investigations. The first, self-pairing, occurs when each subject serves as his or her own control, as in, for example, therapeutic trials in which each subject receives both treatments, one on each of two separate occasions. Next, natural pairing is particularly likely in, for example, laboratory experiments involving litter-mate controls. Lastly, artificial pairing may be used by an investigator to match the two subjects in a pair on important characteristics likely to be related to the response variable.

Paired samples *t*-test   Synonym for **matched pairs *t*-test**.

Parameter   A numerical characteristic of a population or a model; for example, the probability of a ' success' in a *binomial distribution*.

Partial correlation   The correlation between a pair of variables after adjusting for the effect of a third. Can be calculated from the sample correlation coefficients of each pair of variables involved as

$$r_{12|3} = \frac{r_{12} - r_{13}r_{23}}{[(1 - r_{13}^2)(1 - r_{23}^2)]^{\frac{1}{2}}}.$$

Per-experiment error rate   The probability of incorrectly rejecting at least one null hypothesis in an experiment involving one or more tests or comparisons when the corresponding *null hypothesis* is true in each case. See also **per-comparison error rate**.

Placebo   A treatment designed to appear exactly like a comparison treatment, but which is devoid of the active component.

Planned comparisons   Comparisons between a set of means suggested before data are collected. Usually more powerful than a general test for mean differences.

Point-biserial correlation   A special case of Pearson's product moment correlation coefficient used when one variable is continuous (y) and the other is a *binary variable* (x) representing a natural dichotomy. Given by

$$r_{pb} = \frac{\bar{y}_1 - \bar{y}_0}{s_y}(pq)^{\frac{1}{2}}$$

where $\bar{y}_1$ is the sample mean of the y variable for those individuals with $x = 1$, $\bar{y}_0$ is the sample mean of the y variable for those individuals with $x = 0$, s_y is the standard deviation of the y values, p is the proportion of individuals with $x = 1$ and $q = 1 - p$ is the proportion of individuals with $x = 0$. See also **biserial correlation**.

Poisson distribution   The *probability distribution* of the number of occurrences of some random event x in an interval of time or space. Given by

$$P(x) = \frac{e^{-\lambda}\lambda^x}{x!} \quad x = 0, 1, 2, \cdots.$$

The mean and variance of a variable with such a distribution are both equal to λ.

Population In statistics this term is used for any finite or infinite collection of 'units', which are often people but may be institutions, events etc. See also **sample**.

Power The probability of rejecting the *null hypothesis* when it is false. Power gives a method of discriminating between competing tests of the same hypothesis, with the test with the higher power being preferred. It is also the basis of procedures for estimating the sample size needed to detect an effect of a particular magnitude.

Probability The quantitative expression of the chance that an event will occur. Can be defined in a variety of ways, of which the most common is still that involving long-term relative frequency, i.e.

$$P(A) = \frac{\text{number of times A occurs}}{\text{number of times A could occur}}.$$

For example, if out of 100 000 children born in a region, 51 000 are boys, then the probability of a boy is 0.51.

Probability distribution For a discrete *random variable*, a mathematical formula that gives the probability of each value of the variable. See, for example, *binomial distribution* and *Poisson distribution*. For a continous random variable, a curve described by a mathematical formula which specifies, by way of areas under the curve, the probability that the variable falls within a particular interval. An example is the *normal distribution*. In both cases the term probability density is also used. (A distinction is sometimes made between 'density' and 'distribution', when the latter is reserved for the probability that the random variable fall below some value.)

P-value The probability of the observed data (or data showing a more extreme departure from the *null hypothesis*) when the null hypothesis is true. See also **misinterpretation of P-values**, **significance test** and **significance level**.

Quasi-experiment A term used for studies that resemble experiments but are weak on some of the characteristics, particularly that manipulation of subjects to groups is not under the investigator's control. For example, if interest centred on the health effects of a natural disaster, those who experience the disaster can be compared with those who do not, but subjects cannot be deliberately assigned (randomly or not) to the two groups. See also **experimental design**.

Randomization tests Procedures for determining statistical significance directly from data without recourse to some particular *sampling distribution*. The data are divided (permuted) repeatedly between treatments and for each division (permutation) the relevant *test statistic* (e.g. a t or F), is calculated to determine the proportion of the data permutations that provide as large a test statistic as that associated with the observed data. If that proportion is smaller than some significance level α, the results are significant at the α level.

Random sample Either a set of n independent and identically distributed *random variables*, or a sample of n individuals selected from a population in such a way that each sample of the same size is equally likely.

Random variable   A variable, the values of which occur according to some specified *probability distribution*.

Random variation   The variation in a data set unexplained by identifiable sources.

Range   The difference between the largest and smallest observations in a data set. Often used as an easily calculated measure of the dispersion in a set of observations, but not recommended for this task because of its sensitivity to *outliers*.

Rank correlation coefficients   Correlation coefficients that depend only on the ranks of the variables and not on their observed values. An example is Spearman's rho.

Ranking   The process of sorting a set of variable values into either ascending or descending order.

Rank of a matrix   The number of linearly independent rows or columns of a matrix of numbers.

Ranks   The relative positions of the members of a sample with respect to some characteristic.

Reciprocal transformation   A transformation of the form $y = 1/x$, which is particularly useful for certain types of variables. For example, resistances become conductances, and times become speeds.

Regression to the mean   The process first noted by Sir Francis Galton that 'each peculiarity in man is shared by his kinsmen, but on the average to a less degree'. Hence the tendency, for example, for tall parents to produce offspring who are tall but, on the average, shorter than their parents.

Research hypothesis   Synonym for **alternative hypothesis**.

Response variable   The variable of primary importance in psychological investigations since the major objective is usually to study the effects of treatment and/or other explanatory variables on this variable and to provide suitable models for the relationship between it and the explanatory variables.

Robust statistics   Statistical procedures and tests that still work reasonably well even when the assumptions on which they are based are mildly (or perhaps moderately) violated. For example, *Student's t-test* is robust against departures from normality.

Rounding   The procedure used for reporting numerical information to fewer decimal places than used during analysis. The rule generally adopted is that excess digits are simply discarded if the first of them is less than five; otherwise the last retained digit is increased by one. So rounding 127.249341 to three decimal places gives 127.249.

Sample   A selected subset of a population chosen by some process usually with the objective of investigating particular properties of the parent population.

Sample size   The number of individuals to be included in an investigation. Usually chosen so that the study has a particular *power* of detecting an effect of a particular size. Software is available for calculating sample size for many types of study.

Sampling distribution   The *probability distribution* of a statistic. For example, the sampling distribution of the arithmetic mean of samples of size n taken from a *normal distribution* with mean μ and standard deviation σ is a normal distribution, also with mean μ but with standard deviation $\sigma/\sqrt{n}$.

Sampling error   The difference between the sample result and the population characteristic being estimated. In practice, the sampling error can rarely be determined because the population characteristic is not usually known. However, with appropriate sampling procedures it can be kept small and the investigator can determine its probable limits of magnitude. See also **standard error**.

Sampling variation   The variation shown by different samples of the same size from the same population.

Saturated model   A model that contains all *main effects* and all possible *interactions* between factors. Since such a model contains the same number of parameters as observations, it results in a perfect fit for a data set.

Scatter diagram   A two-dimensional plot of a sample of bivariate observations. The diagram is an important aid in assessing what type of relationship links the two variables.

SE   Abbreviation for **standard error**.

Semi-interquartile range   Half the difference between the upper and lower quartiles.

Sequential sums of squares   A term encountered primarily in regression analysis for the contributions of variables as they are added to the model in a particular sequence. Essentially, the difference in the residual sum of squares before and after adding a variable.

Significance level   The level of probability at which it is agreed that the *null hypothesis* will be rejected. Conventionally set at 0.05.

Significance test   A statistical procedure that, when applied to a set of observations, results in a *P-value* relative to some hypothesis. Examples include *Student's t-test, the z-test* and *Wilcoxon's signed rank test*.

Singular matrix   A *square matrix* whose determinant is equal to zero; a matrix whose inverse is not defined.

Skewness   The lack of symmetry in a *probability distribution*. Usually quantified by the index s given by

$$s = \frac{\mu_3}{\mu_2^{3/2}}$$

where μ_2 and μ_3 are the second and third moments about the mean. The index takes the value of zero for a symmetrical distribution. A distribution is said to have positive skewness when it has a long thin tail at the right, and to have negative skewness when it has a long thin tail to the left.

Spearman's rho   A *rank correlation coefficient*. If the ranked values of the two variables for a set of n individuals are a_i and b_i, with $d_i = a_i - b_i$, then the coefficient is defined explicitly as

$$r = 1 - \frac{6 \sum_{i=1}^{n} d_i^2}{n^3 - n}.$$

In essence, r is simply Pearson's product moment correlation coefficient between the rankings a and b.

Split-half method   A procedure used primarily in psychology to estimate the reliability of a test. Two scores are obtained from the same test, either from alternative items, the so-called odd–even technique, or from parallel sections of items. The correlation of these scores, or some transformation of them, gives the required reliability. See also **Cronbach's alpha**.

Square contingency table   A contingency table with the same number of rows as columns.

Square matrix   A matrix with the same number of rows as columns. Variance–covariance matrices and correlation matrices are statistical examples.

Square root transformation   A transformation of the form $y = \sqrt{x}$ often used to make *random variables* suspected to have a *Poisson distribution* more suitable for techniques such as analysis of variance by making their variances independent of their means. See also **variance stabilizing transformations**.

Standard deviation   The most commonly used measure of the spread of a set of observations. Equal to the square root of the variance.

Standard error   The *standard deviation* of the *sampling distribution* of a statistic. For example, the standard error of the sample mean of n observations is $\sigma/\sqrt{n}$, where σ^2 is the variance of the original observations.

Standardization   A term used in a variety of ways in psychological research. The most common usage is in the context of transforming a variable by dividing by its *standard deviation* to give a new variable with standard deviation unity.

Standard normal variable   A variable having a *normal distribution* with mean zero and variance unity.

Standard scores   Variable values transformed to zero mean and unit variance.

Statistic   A numerical characteristic of a sample, for example the sample mean and sample variance. See also **parameter**.

Student's *t*-distribution   The *probability distribution* of the ratio of a normal variable with mean zero and standard deviation unity, to the square root of a chi-squared variable. In particular the distribution of the variable

$$t = \frac{\bar{x} - \mu}{s/\sqrt{n}}$$

where $\bar{x}$ is the arithmetic mean of n observations from a *normal distribution* with mean μ and s is the sample standard deviation. The shape of the distribution varies with n, and as n becomes larger it approaches a standard normal distribution.

Student's *t*-tests   Significance tests for assessing hypotheses about population means. One version is used in situations where it is required to test whether the mean of a population takes a particular value. This is generally known as a single sample *t*-test. Another version is designed to test the equality of the means of two populations. When independent sample are available from each population, the procedure is often known as the independent samples *t*-test and the *test statistic* is

$$t = \frac{\bar{x}_1 - \bar{x}_2}{s(1/n_1 + 1/n_2)^{\frac{1}{2}}}$$

where $\bar{x}_1$ and $\bar{x}_2$ are the means of samples of size n_1 and n_2 taken from each population, and s^2 is an estimate of the assumed common variance given by

$$s^2 = \frac{(n_1 - 1)s_1^2 + (n_2 - 1)s_2^2}{n_1 + n_2 - 2}.$$

If the *null hypothesis* of the equality of the two population means is true, t has a *Student's t-distribution* with $n_1 + n_2 - 2$ degrees of freedom allowing *P-values* to be calculated. In addition to homogeneity, the test assumes that each population has a *normal distribution* but is known to be relatively insensitive to departures from this assumption. See also **matched pairs *t*-test**.

Symmetric matrix   A *square matrix* that is symmetrical about its leading diagonal, i.e. a matrix with elements a_{ij} such that $a_{ij} = a_{ji}$. In statistics, correlation matrices and covariance matrices are of this form.

Test statistic   A statistic used to assess a particular hypothesis in relation to some population. The essential requirement of such a statistic is a known distribution when the *null hypothesis* is true.

Tolerance   A term used in stepwise regression for the proportion of the sum of squares about the mean of an explanatory variable not accounted for by other variables already included in the regression equation. Small values indicate possible multicollinearity problems.

Trace of a matrix   The sum of the elements on the main diagonal of a *square matrix*; usually denoted as tr($\mathbf{A}$). So, for example, if $\mathbf{A} = \begin{pmatrix} 3 & 2 \\ 4 & 1 \end{pmatrix}$ then tr($\mathbf{A}$)=4.

Transformation   A change in the scale of measurement for some variable(s). Examples are the *square root transformation* and *the logarithmic transformation*.

Two-sided test   A test where the *alternative hypothesis* is not directional, for example that one population mean is either above or below the other. See also **one-sided test**.

Type I error   The error that results when the *null hypothesis* is falsely rejected.

Type II error   The error that results when the *null hypothesis* is falsely accepted.

Univariate data   Data involving a single measurement on each subject or patient.

U-shaped distribution   A *probability distribution* or *frequency distribution* shaped more or less like a letter U, although not necessarily symmetrical. Such a distribution has its greatest frequencies at the two extremes of the range of the variable.

Variance   In a population, the second moment about the mean. An *unbiased* estimator of the population value is provided by s^2 given by

$$s^2 = \frac{1}{n-1} \sum_{i=1}^{n} (x_i - \bar{x})^2$$

where $x_1, x_2, \ldots, x_n$ are the n sample observations and $\bar{x}$ is the sample mean.

Vector   A matrix having only one row or column.

Wilcoxon's signed rank test   A *distribution-free method* for testing the difference between two populations using matched samples. The test is based on the absolute differences of the pairs of observations in the two samples, ranked according to size, with each rank being given the sign of the original difference. The test statistic is the sum of the positive ranks.

Yates' correction   When testing for independence in a contingency table, a continuous *probability distribution*, namely the *chi-squared distribution*, is used as an approximation to the discrete probability of observed frequencies, namely the *multinomial distribution*. To improve this approximation Yates suggested a correction that involves subtracting 0.5 from the positive discrepancies (observed–expected) and adding 0.5 to the negative discrepancies before these values are squared in the calculation of the usual *chi-squared statistic*. If the sample size is large, the correction will have little effect on the value of the test statistic.

Z-scores   Synonym for **standard scores**.

z-test   A test for assessing hypotheses about population means when their variances are known. For example, the *test statistic* for testing that the means of two populations are equal, i.e. $H_0: \mu_1 = \mu_2$, when the variance of each population is known to be σ^2, is

$$z = \frac{\bar{x}_1 - \bar{x}_2}{\sigma(1/n_1 + 1/n_2)^{\frac{1}{2}}}$$

where $\bar{x}_1$ and $\bar{x}_2$ are the means of samples of size n_1 and n_2 from the two populations. If H_0 is true, z has a *standard normal distribution*. See also **Student's t-tests**.

Appendix B
Answers to selected exercises

Chapter 1

1.2 One alternative explanation is the systematic bias that may be produced by always using the letter Q for Coke and the letter M for Pepsi. In fact, when the Coca-Cola Company conducted another study where Coke was put into *both* glasses, one labelled M and the other Q, the results showed that a majority of people chose the glass labelled M in preference to the glass labelled Q.

1.4 The quotations are by the following:

1. Florence Nightingale
2. Lloyd George
3. Joseph Stalin
4. W.H. Auden
5. Mr Justice Streatfield
6. Logan Pearsall Smith.

Chapter 2

2.2 The graph in Fig. 2.28 commits the cardinal sin of quoting data out of context; remember that graphics often lie by omission, leaving out data sufficient for comparisons. Here a few more data points for other years in the area would be helpful, as would similar data for other areas where stricter enforcement of speeding had not been implemented.

Chapter 3

3.2 Here the simple plot of the data shown in Fig. B1 indicates that the 90° group appears to contain two outliers, and that the observations in the 50° group seem to split into two relatively distinct classes. Such features of the data would, in general, need to be investigated further before performing any formal analysis.

The analysis of variance table for the data is as follows:

Source	SS	DF	MS	F	P
Between angles	90.56	2	45.28	11.52	0.002
Within angles	106.16	27	3.93		

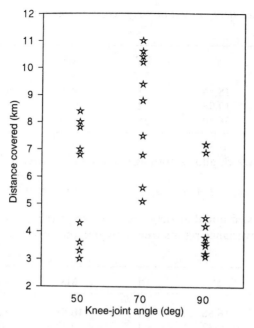

Fig. B1 Simple plot of data from ergocycle study.

Since the groups have a clear ordering, the between-groups variation might be split into components with one degree of freedom representing variation due to linear and quadratic trends.

3.3 The term μ in the one-way analysis of variance model is estimated by the grand mean of all the observations. The terms $\alpha_i, i = 1, 2, \ldots, k$, are estimated by the deviation of the appropriate group mean from the grand mean.

3.5 The three analyses of variance tables are as follows:

Analysis of variance of the anxiety scores on discharge

Source	SS	DF	MS	F	P
Between groups	8.53	2	4.27	2.11	0.14
Within groups	54.66	27	2.02		

Analysis of variance of the difference of the two anxiety scores

Source	SS	DF	MS	F	P
Between groups	48.29	2	24.14	13.20	0.0001
Within groups	49.40	27	1.83		

Analysis of covariance using initial anxiety score as covariate

Source	SS	DF	MS	F	P
Initial anxiety	18.26	1	18.26	13.04	0.0013
Between groups	19.98	2	9.99	7.13	0.0034
Within groups	36.40	26	1.40		

A suitable model which allows both age and initial anxiety to be covariates is

$$y_{ij} = \mu + \alpha_i + \beta_1(x_{ij} - \bar{x}) + \beta_2(z_{ij} - \bar{z}) + \epsilon_{ij}$$

where x and z represent initial anxiety and age respectively.
The analysis of covariance results from applying this model are as follows.

Source	SS	DF	MS	F	P
Initial anxiety	16.68	1	16.68	11.55	0.0023
Age	0.32	1	0.32	0.22	0.64
Between groups	19.51	2	9.75	6.76	0.0045
Within groups	36.08	25	1.44		

Chapter 4

4.1 Survival times are generally positively skewed and so a logarithmic transformation might be helpful.

4.3 The 95% confidence interval is given by

$$(\bar{x}_1 - \bar{x}_2) \pm t_{12}\, s \left(\frac{1}{n_1} + \frac{1}{n_2}\right)^{1/2}$$

where $\bar{x}_1$ and $\bar{x}_2$ are the mean weight losses for novice and experienced slimmmers both using a manual, s is the square root of the error mean square from the analysis of variance of the data, t_{12} is the appropriate value of Student's t with 12 degrees of freedom and n_1 and n_2 are the sample sizes in the two groups. Applying this formula leads to

$$[-6.36 - (-1.55)] \pm 2.18(3.10)^{1/2}\left(\frac{1}{4} + \frac{1}{4}\right)^{1/2}$$

giving the required interval as $(-7.52, -2.10)$.

4.6 The separate analyses of variance for the three drugs give the following results:

Drug X

Source	SS	DF	MS	F	P
Diet (D)	294.00	1	294.00	2.32	0.1436
Biofeed (B)	864.00	1	864.00	6.81	0.0168
D×B	384.00	1	384.00	3.03	0.0973
Error	2538.00	20	126.90		

Drug Y

Source	SS	DF	MS	F	P
Diet	3037.50	1	3037.50	21.01	0.0002
Biofeed	181.50	1	181.50	1.26	0.2758
D×B	541.50	1	541.50	3.74	0.0672
Error	2892.00	20	144.60		

Drug Z

Source	SS	DF	MS	F	P
Diet	2773.50	1	2773.50	13.97	0.0013
Biofeed	1261.50	1	1261.50	6.36	0.0203
D×B	181.50	1	181.50	0.91	0.3504
Error	3970.00	20	198.50		

The separate analyses give non-significant results for the diet × biofeed interaction, although for drugs X and Y the interaction terms approach significance at the 5% level. The three-way analysis given in the text demonstrates that the nature of this interaction is *different* for each drug.

4.9. The main effect parameters are estimated by the difference between a row (column) mean and the grand mean. The interaction parameter corresponding to a particular cell is estimated as (cell mean − row mean − column mean + grand mean).

4.10 An analysis of covariance of the data gives the following results:

Source	SS	DF	MS	F	P
Pre-treatment 1	19.34	1	19.34	1.48	0.2409
Pre-treatment 2	12.79	1	12.79	0.98	0.3369
Between treatments	27.57	1	27.57	2.10	0.1650
Error	222.66	17	13.10		

The estimated regression coefficients are

$$\text{pre-treatment } 1 = 0.4436$$
$$\text{pre-treatment } 2 = -6.2892.$$

The adjusted cell means are

$$\text{placebo} = 10.04$$
$$\text{active} = 7.56.$$

Chapter 5

5.2   The multivariate analysis of variance of the reverse stroop data gives the following results:

Source	T^2	F	DF	P
Cue	44.67	21.32	2.21	< 0.0001
Cue × group	3.18	1.52	2.21	0.24
Type × cue	10.41	4.97	2.21	0.02
Group × type × cue	1.49	0.71	2.21	0.50

In the univariate analysis given in Table 5.13 the type × cue interaction is non-significant at the 5% level. To investigate why there is a difference between the univariate and multivariate results in this case construct a plot of the following pair of type × cue interaction effects calculated for each subject in the study:

$$\text{interaction effect } 1 = b_1c_1 - b_1c_2 - b_2c_1 + b_2c_2$$
$$\text{interaction effect } 2 = b_1c_1 - b_1c_3 - b_2c_2 + b_2c_3.$$

5.7   A repeated measures analysis of variance of the data gives the following results:

Source	SS	DF	MS	F	P
Between subjects	1 399 155.00	15	93 277.00		
Between electrodes	281 575.43	4	70 393.86	3.15	0.02
Error	1 342 723.37	60	22 378.72		

This analysis suggests that there is a difference between the electrodes. However, if the Greenhouse and Geisser or Huynh and Feldt correction factors are calculated (GG = 0.5358, HF = 0.6279) and applied, the between-electrode P-value becomes considerably less significant (GG-corrected P-value = 0.0534; HF-corrected P-value = 0.0440).

A further complication with these data is the two extreme readings on subject 15. The reason for these readings was, in fact, that this subject had very hairy arms! Repeating the analysis of variance after removing this subject gives the following result:

Source	SS	DF	MS	F	P
Between subjects	852 509.55	14	60 893.54		
Between electrodes	120 224.61	4	30 056.15	2.63	0.0436
Error	639 109.39	56	11 412.67		

In this case the correction factors are GG = 0.5923 and HF = 0.7209, and the corrected P-values for between electrodes are GG = 0.0783 and HF = 0.0649. Therefore, after removal of the outlier, the evidence for a difference between the five electrodes is not particularly convincing.

Chapter 6

6.1 The estimated coefficients for the quadratic and cubic models are as follows:

Model	Intercept	Age	Age^2	Age^3
Quadratic	2.30	488.07	10.77	
Cubic	8.04	−458.64	318.08	−29.17

The residuals from the quadratic model (Fig. B2) show an unsatisfactory pattern; those from the cubic model are far more satisfactory (Fig. B3). The fitted cubic curve is shown in Fig. B4.

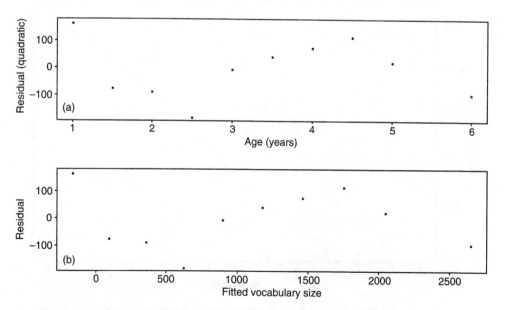

Fig. B2   Residuals from the quadratic model fitted to vocabulary data: (a) age; (b) vocabulary size.

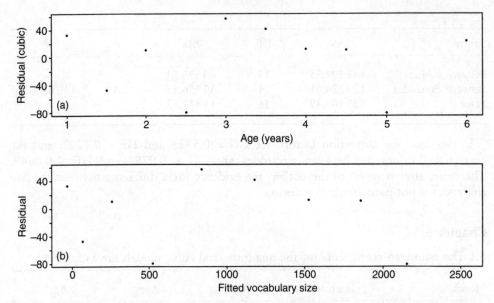

Fig. B3   Residuals from the cubic model fitted to vocabulary data: (a) age; (b) fitted vocabulary size.

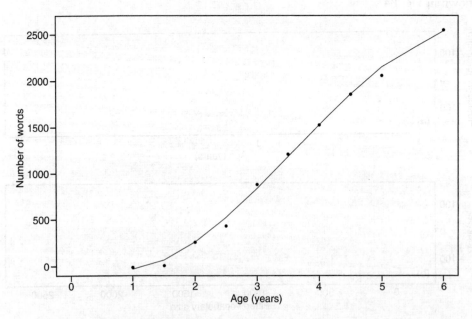

Fig. B4   Fitted cubic curve for vocabulary size versus age.

6.4 The estimated regression coefficient in this case is simply the difference in percentage fat between men and women.

6.8 A possible model is $p = \exp(-\beta t)$, suggesting geometric loss of memory. Such a model could be fitted by a linear regression of $\log p$ on t. Unfortunately, a scatter plot of $\log t$ against t still gives a pronounced curve. A model giving a better fit, but one less easy to explain, results from plotting p against $\log t$.

Chapter 7

7.1 Investigation of a number of logistic regression models, including ones containing interactions between the three explanatory variables, shows that a model including each of the explanatory variables provides an adequate fit to the data. The fitted model is

$$\ln(\text{odds of being severely hurt}) = -0.9401 + 0.3367(\text{weight}) + 1.030(\text{ejection})$$
$$+ 1.639(\text{type})$$

where weight is 0 for small and 1 for standard, ejection is 0 for driver not ejected and 1 for driver ejected, and type is 0 for collision and 1 for rollover. The 95% confidence intervals for the conditional odds ratios of each explanatory variable are:

$$\text{weight } (1.18, 1.66)$$
$$\text{ejection } (2.31, 3.40)$$
$$\text{type } (4.38, 6.06).$$

Thus, for example, the odds of being severely hurt in a rollover accident are between 4.38 and 6.06 those that for a collision.

7.2 The estimated odds ratio for the suicidal feelings data is

$$\hat{\alpha} = \frac{2 \times 14}{6 \times 18} = 0.2592 \ .$$

The approximate 95% confidence interval found from the results given in Display 7.5 is (0.0438, 1.5334). Since this includes the value 1, which would correspond to the independence of the two variables forming the table, the data provide no evidence that the incidence of suicidal feelings differs in the two diagnostic groups.

7.3 With four variables there are a host of models that can be examined. A good way to begin is to compare the following three models:

(A) main effects model, i.e. Brand + Prev + Soft + Temp;
(B) all first-order interactions, i.e. model (A) above + Brand.Prev + Brand.Soft + Brand.Temp + Prev.Soft + Prev.Temp + Soft.Temp;
(C) all second-order interactions, i.e. model (C) above + Brand.Prev.Soft + Brand.Prev.Temp + Brand.Soft.Temp + Prev.Soft.Temp.

The likelihood ratio goodness-of-fit statistics for these models are as follows:

Model	LR statistic	DF
A	42.93	18
B	9.85	9
C	0.74	2

Model A does not describe the data adequately, but models B and C do. Clearly, a model more complex than A but possibly simpler than B is needed. Consequently progress might be made by either forward selection of interaction terms to add to A or backwards selection of terms from B to search for the 'best' model.

Chapter 8

8.2. Introduce four variables x_1, x_2, x_3 and x_4 defined as follows:

		Group			
	1	2	3	4	5
x_1	1	0	0	0	0
x_2	0	1	0	0	0
x_3	0	0	1	0	0
x_4	0	0	0	1	0

A multiple regression using these four variables gives the same analysis of variance table as that in Display 8.3, but the regression coefficients are now the differences between a group mean and the mean of group 5.

Chapter 9

9.3 The results for various numbers of bootstrap samples are as follows:

N	95% confidence interval
200	1.039, 7.887
400	1.012, 9.415
800	1.012, 8.790
1000	1.091, 9.980

Chapter 10

10.1 Multiply the coefficients as given by the square root of the corresponding variance. The results are as follows:

PC1	PC2	PC3	PC4
0.96	0.03	−0.13	0.24
0.13	−0.98	−0.17	−0.04
0.89	−0.21	0.39	−0.05
0.89	0.33	0.23	−0.19

10.4   When the approach detailed in Display 10.5 is used, the parameters in the model satisfy the relationships

$$\hat{\lambda}_1\hat{\lambda}_2 = 0.84$$
$$\hat{\lambda}_1\hat{\lambda}_3 = 0.60$$
$$\hat{\lambda}_2\hat{\lambda}_3 = 0.35$$
$$\hat{\lambda}_1^2 + \hat{\psi}_1 = 1.00$$
$$\hat{\lambda}_2^2 + \hat{\psi}_2 = 1.00$$
$$\hat{\lambda}_3^2 + \hat{\psi}_3 = 1.00$$

leading to the following solution:

$$\hat{\lambda}_1 = 1.2$$
$$\hat{\lambda}_2 = 0.7$$
$$\hat{\lambda}_3 = 0.5$$
$$\hat{\psi}_1 = -0.44$$
$$\hat{\psi}_2 = 0.51$$
$$\hat{\psi}_3 = 0.75.$$

Clearly, this solution is unacceptable because of the negative variance estimate.

Chapter 11

11.1   Suppose the matrix of estimated loadings is Λ given by

$$\Lambda = \begin{pmatrix} \lambda_{11} & 0 & 0 \\ \lambda_{21} & 0 & 0 \\ 0 & \lambda_{32} & 0 \\ 0 & \lambda_{42} & 0 \\ 0 & \lambda_{52} & 0 \\ 0 & \lambda_{62} & 0 \\ 0 & 0 & \lambda_{73} \\ 0 & 0 & \lambda_{83} \end{pmatrix}$$

The estimated correlation matrix $\boldsymbol{\Phi}$ of the three factors, is given by

$$\boldsymbol{\Phi} = \begin{pmatrix} 1.0 & & \\ 0.0 & 1.0 & \\ 0.0 & \phi & 1.0 \end{pmatrix}$$

Let the specific variances be $\psi_1, \psi_2, \cdots, \psi_8$. Then the predicted correlation matrix $\hat{\mathbf{R}}$ is given by

$$\hat{\mathbf{R}} = \begin{pmatrix} \lambda_{11}^2 + \psi_1 \\ \lambda_{21}\lambda_{11} & \lambda_{21}^2 + \psi_2 \\ 0 & 0 & \lambda_{32}^2 + \psi_3 \\ 0 & 0 & \lambda_{42}\lambda_{32} & \lambda_{42}^2 + \psi_4 \\ 0 & 0 & \lambda_{52}\lambda_{32} & \lambda_{52}\lambda_{42} & \lambda_{52}^2 + \psi_5 \\ 0 & 0 & \lambda_{62}\lambda_{32} & \lambda_{62}\lambda_{42} & \lambda_{62}\lambda_{52} & \lambda_{62}^2 + \psi_6 \\ 0 & 0 & \lambda_{73}\phi\lambda_{32} & \lambda_{73}\phi\lambda_{42} & \lambda_{73}\phi\lambda_{52} & \lambda_{73}\phi\lambda_{62} & \lambda_{73}^2 + \psi_7 \\ 0 & 0 & \lambda_{83}\phi\lambda_{32} & \lambda_{83}\phi\lambda_{42} & \lambda_{83}\phi\lambda_{52} & \lambda_{83}\phi\lambda_{62} & \lambda_{83}\lambda_{73} & \lambda_{83}^2 + \psi_8 \end{pmatrix}$$

Such a model would be *unidentified*. Why?

11.3 The estimated 95% confidence interval for the correlation between ability and aspiration is $(0.60, 0.72)$. This does not include the value of 1.0, which would be the correlation if a model with a single common factor was adequate.

Chapter 12

12.1 In complete linkage clustering the distance between a group k and a group (ij) formed by the fusion of groups i and j is defined to be the maximum interindividual distance between an individual in group k and one in groups i or j. According to the formula given, the distance is

$$d_{k(ij)} = 0.5d_{ki} + 0.5d_{kj} + 0.5|d_{ki} - d_{kj}|.$$

Now, if $d_{ki} > d_{kj}$ then $|d_{ki} - d_{kj}| = d_{ki} - d_{kj}$, and if $d_{ki} < d_{kj}$ then $|d_{ki} - d_{kj}| = d_{kj} - d_{ki}$. Consequently, if $d_{ki} > d_{kj}$ then

$$d_{k(ij)} = d_{ki},$$

and if $d_{ki} < d_{kj}$ then

$$d_{k(ij)} = d_{kj}.$$

In other words $d_{k(ij)} = \max[d_{ki}, d_{kj}]$, which is what is required.

12.3 The allocation rule derived by applying Fisher's linear discriminant function is to allocate a child to group 1 if

$$1.073x_1 - 0.445x_2 + 0.034x_3 + 0.338x_4 + 0.989x_5 - 1.235 > 0.$$

Calculation of the discriminant score from the variable values given for child 1 results in the value of 1.295; consequently the prediction is that such a child will relapse after treatment.

Chapter 13

13.4 The observed correlation matrix for observers G, B and D is

$$R = \begin{pmatrix} 1.0000 & & \\ 0.9553 & 1.0000 & \\ 0.9807 & 0.9684 & 1.0000 \end{pmatrix}.$$

Therefore the parameters in a one-factor model are estimated from the following series of equations (see Display 10.5):

$$\hat{\lambda}_1 \hat{\lambda}_2 = 0.9553$$
$$\hat{\lambda}_1 \hat{\lambda}_3 = 0.9807$$
$$\hat{\lambda}_2 \hat{\lambda}_3 = 0.9684$$
$$\hat{\lambda}_1^2 + \hat{\psi}_1 = 1.0000$$
$$\hat{\lambda}_2^2 + \hat{\psi}_2 = 1.0000$$
$$\hat{\lambda}_3^2 + \hat{\psi}_3 = 1.0000.$$

Solving the equation leads to the following set of parameter estimates:

$$\hat{\lambda}_1 = 0.9835$$
$$\hat{\lambda}_2 = 0.9713$$
$$\hat{\lambda}_3 = 0.9941$$
$$\hat{\psi}_1 = 0.0327$$
$$\hat{\psi}_2 = 0.0566$$
$$\hat{\psi}_3 = 0.0118.$$

Appendix C
About the diskette

Many of the data sets in the book are available on the disk in ASCII format. Data sets are stored on a directory, \DATASETS\ and are identified by the table or display number in which they appear in the text; for example, TAB21.TXT contains the data in Table 2.1. Most data sets appear in exactly the form given in the text; in a few cases, however, the format has been changed to make them more suitable for the main statistical packages.

References

Aitkin, M. (1978). The analysis of unbalanced cross-classification. *Journal of the Royal Statistical Society, Series A*, **141**, 195–223.

Andersen, B. (1990). *Methodological errors in medical research*. Blackwell Scientific, Oxford.

Anderson, N.H. (1963). Comparisons of different populations: resistance to extinction and transfer. *Psychological Review*, **70**, 162–79.

Bartlett, M.S. (1950). Test of significance in factor analysis. *British Journal of Psychology (Statistical Section)*, **3**, 77–85.

Bentler, P.M. (1980). Multivariate analysis with latent variables: causal modelling. *Annual Review of Psychology*, **31**, 419–56.

Bertin, J. (1981). *Semiology of graphics*. University of Wisconsin Press, Madison, WI.

Bickel, P.J., Hammel, E.A. and O'Connell, J.W. (1975). Sex bias in graduate admissions. Data from Berkeley. *Science*, **187**, 398–404.

Boniface, D.R. (1995). *Experiment design and statistical methods for behavioural and social research*. Chapman and Hall, London.

Box, G.E.P. (1954). Some theorems on quadratic forms applied in the study of analysis of variance problems. II Effects of inequality of variance and of correlations between errors in the two-way classification. *Annals of Mathematical Statistics*, **25**, 484–98.

Calsyn, J.R. and Kenney, D.A. (1977). Self-concept of ability and perceived evaluation of others. Cause or effect of academic achievement? *Journal of Educational Psychology*, **69**, 136–45.

Chambers, J.M, Cleveland, W.S., Kleiner, B. and Tukey, P.A. (1983). *Graphical methods for data analysis*. Chapman and Hall, London.

Chatfield, C. (1985). The initial examination of data. *Journal of the Royal Statistical Society, Series A*, **148**, 214–53.

Chatterjee, S. and Price, B. (1991). *Regression analysis by example* (2nd edn). Wiley, New York.

Chernoff, H. (1973). The use of faces to represent points in k-dimensional space graphically. *Journal of the American Statistical Association*, **68**, 361–8.

Cleveland, W.S. (1994). *The elements of graphing data*. Hobart Press, Murray Hill, NJ.

Cliff, N. (1983). Some cautions concerning the application of causal modelling methods. *Multivariate Behavioural Research*, **18**, 115–26.

Cohen, J. (1960). A coefficient of agreement for nominal scales. *Educational and Psychological Measurement*, **20**, 37–46.

Collett, D. (1991). *Modelling binary data*. Chapman and Hall, London.

Colman, A.M. (ed.) (1994). *The Companion encyclopedia of psychology*. Routledge, London.

Cronbach, L. (1951). Coefficient alpha and the internal structure of tests. *Psychometrika*, **16**, 297–334.

Cronbach, L. (1957). The two disciplines of scientific psychology. *American Psychologist*, **12**, 671–84.

Crowder, M.J. and Hand, D.J. (1990). *Analysis of repeated measures*. Chapman and Hall, London.

Crutchfield, R.S. (1938). Efficient factorial design and analysis of variance illustrated in psychological experimentation. *Journal of Psychology*, **5**, 339–46.

Crutchfield, R.S. and Tolman, E.C. (1940). Multiple variable design for experiments involving interaction of behaviour. *Psychological Review*, **47**, 38–42.

Daly, F., Hand, D.J., Jones, M.C., Lunn, A.D. and McConway, K.J. (1995). *Elements of statistics*. Addison-Wesley, Wokingham.

Davidson, M.L. (1972). Univariate versus multivariate tests in repeated measures experiments. *Psychological Bulletin*, 77, 446–52.

Davis, C. (1991). Semi-parametric and non–parametric methods for the analysis of repetaed measurements with applications to clinical trials. *Statistics in Medicine*, 10, 1959–80

Diggle, P.J., Liang, K. and Zeger, S.L. (1994). *Analysis of longitudinal data*. Oxford University Press.

Dizney, H. and Gromen, L. (1967). Predictive validity and differential achievement on three MLA comparative Foreign Language Tests. *Educational and Psychological Measurement*, 27, 1127–1130.

Donner, A. and Eliasziw, M. (1987). Sample size requirements for reliability studies. *Statistics in Medicine*, 6, 441–8.

Dunn, G. (1989). *Design and analysis of reliability studies: statistical evaluation of measurement errors*. Edward Arnold, London.

Dunn, G. (1992). Design and analysis of reliability studies. *Statistical Methods in Medical Research*, 1, 123–57.

Dunn, G., Everitt, B. and Pickles, A. (1993). *Modelling covariances and latent variables using EQS*. Chapman and Hall, London.

Eliasziw, M. and Donner, A. (1987). A cost-function approach to the design of reliability studies. *Statistics in Medicine*, 6, 647–56.

Efron, B. and Tibshirani, R.J. (1993). *An introduction to the bootstrap*. Chapman and Hall, London.

Everitt, B.S. (1968). Moments of the statistics kappa and weighted kappa. *British Journal of Mathematical and Statistical Psychology*, 21, 97–103.

Everitt, B.S. (1979). Cluster analysis: a discussion of some unresolved problems and possible future developments. *Biometrics*, 35, 169–81.

Everitt, B.S. (1984). *An introduction to latent variable models*. Chapman and Hall, London.

Everitt, B.S. (1992). *The analysis of contingency tables*. Chapman and Hall, London.

Everitt, B.S. (1993). *Cluster analysis* (3rd edn). Edward Arnold, London.

Everitt, B.S. (1994). *A handbook of statistical analyses using S-Plus*. Chapman and Hall, London.

Everitt, B.S. (1995). The analysis of repeated measures: a practical review with examples. *Statistician*, 44, 113–35.

Everitt, B.S. and Dunn, G. (1991). *Applied multivariate data analysis*. Edward Arnold, London.

Fergusson, D.M. and Horwood, L.J. (1986). The use and limitations of structural equation models of longitudinal data. Personal communication.

Fisher, R.A. (1936). The use of multiple measurements in taxonomic problems. *Annals of Eugenics*, 7, 179–88.

Fleiss, J.L. (1965). Estimating the accuracy of dichotomous judgements. *Psychometrika*, 30, 469–79.

Fleiss, J.L. (1975). Measuring agreement between judges on the presence or absence of a trait. *Biometrics*, 31, 651–9.

Fleiss, J.L. (1986). *The design and analysis of clinical experiments*. Wiley, New York.

Fleiss, J.L. and Cuzick, J. (1979). The reliability of dichotomous judgements: unequal numbers of judgements per subject. *Applied Psychological Measurement*, 3, 537–542.

Fleiss, J.L. and Tanur, J.M. (1972). The analysis of covariance in psychopathology. In *Psychopathology* (ed. M. Hammer, K. Salzinger and S. Sutton), pp. 509–27. Wiley, New York.

Fleiss, J.L., Cohen, J. and Everitt, B.S. (1969). Large sample standard errors of kappa and weighted kappa. *Psychological Bulletin*, 72, 323–7.

Frison, L. and Pocock, S.J. (1992). Repeated measures in clinical trials: analysis using means summary statistics and its implication for design. *Statistics in Medicine*, 11, 1685–704.

Gardner, M.J. and Altman, D.G. (1986). Confidence intervals rather than P-values: estimation rather than hypothesis testing. *British Medical Journal*, 292, 746–50.

Garrett, H.E. and Zubin, J. (1943). The analysis of variance in psychological research. *Psychological Review*, 40, 233–67.

Gaskill, H.V. and Cox, G.M. (1937). Patterns in emotional reactions: I. Respiration; the use of analysis of variance and covariance in psychological data. *Journal of General Psychology*, 16, 21–38.

Gnanadesikan, R. and Wilk, M.B. (1969). Data analytic methods in multivariate statistical analysis. pp. 593–638 In *Multivariate analysis*, Vol. II (ed. P.R. Krishnaiah). Academic Press, New York.

Goldberg, B.P. (1972). *The detection of psychiatric illness by questionnaire*. Oxford University Press.

Goldstein, H. (1995). *Multilevel statistical models* (2nd edn.). Edward Arnold, London.

Good, P. (1994). *Permutation tests: a practical guide to resampling methods for testing hypotheses*. Springer-Verlag, New York.

Gorbein, J.A., Lazaro, G.G. and Little, R.J.A. (1992). Incomplete data in repeated measures analysis. *Statistical Methods in Medical Research*, 1, 275–95.

Greenhouse, S.W. and Geisser, S. (1959). On the methods in the analysis of profile data. *Psychometrika*, 24, 95–112.

Hand, D.J. (1981). *Discrimination and classification*. Wiley, Chichester.

Hand, D.J. and Taylor, C.C. (1987). *Multivariate analysis of variance and repeated measures*. Chapman and Hall, London.

Hansen, K.M. and Tukey, J.W. (1992). Tuning a major part of a clustering algorithm. *International Statistical Review*, 60, 21–44.

Howell, D.C. (1992). *Statistical methods for psychology*. Duxbury Press, Belmont, CA.

Huba, G.J., Wingard, J.A. and Bentler, P.M. (1981). A comparison of two latent variable causal models for adolescent drug use. *Journal of Personality and Social Psychology*, 40, 180–93.

Huck, S.W. and Sandler, H.M. (1979). *Rival hypotheses: alternative interpretations of data based conclusions*. Harper and Row, New York.

Huynh, H. and Feldt, L.S. (1976). Estimates of the correction for degrees of freedom for sample data in randomised block and split-plot designs. *Journal of Educational Statistics*, 1, 69–82.

Jackson, J.E. (1991). *A user's guide to principal components*. Wiley, New York.

Jain, A.K. and Dubes, R.C. (1988). *Algorithms for clustering data*. Prentice Hall, Englewood Cliffs, NJ.

Jolliffe, I.T. (1989). Rotation of ill-defined principal components. *Applied Statistics*, 38, 139–48.

Jöreskog, K. and Sörborm, D. (1993). Lisrel 8 structural equation modelling with the simplis command language. Erlbaum, Hillsdale, NJ.

Kapor, M. (1981). Efficiency on ergocycle in relation to knee-joint angle and drag. Unpublished Master's dissertation, University of Delhi.

Keselman, H.J., Keselman, J.C. and Lix, L.M. (1995). The analysis of repeated measurements: univariate tests, multivariate tests or both? *British Journal of Mathematical and Statistical Psychology*, 48, 319–38.

Kruskal, J.B. (1964). Multidimensional scaling by optimizing goodness-of-fit to non-metric hypotheses. *Psychometrika*, 29, 1–27.

Kruskal, J.B. and Wish, M. (1978). *Multidimensional scaling*. Sage, London.

Labovitz, S. (1970). The assignment of numbers to rank order categories. *American Sociological Review*, 35 512–24.

Landis, J.R. and Koch, G.C. (1977). The measurement of observer agreement for categorical data. *Biometrics*, **33**, 1089–91.

Lenk, P.J. (1986). Review of 'An introduction to latent variable models', by B. S. Everitt. *Journal of the American Statistical Association*, **81**, 1123–4.

Lindmann, H.R. (1974). *Analysis of variance in complex experimental designs*. Freeman, San Francisco, California.

Lord, F.M and Novick, M.R. (1968). *Statistical theories of mental test scores*. Addison-Wesley, Reading, MA.

Lovie, A.D. (1979). The analysis of variance in experimental psychology: 1934–1945. *British Journal of Mathematical and Statistical Psychology*, **32**, 151–78.

Lovie, P. (1991). Regression diagnostics. In *New developments in statistics for psychology and the social sciences* (ed. P. Lovie and A.D. Lovie), pp. 95–134. BPS Books and Routledge, London.

Lundberg, G.A. (1940). The measurement of socioeconomic status. *American Sociological Review*, **5**, 29–39.

McCullagh, P. and Nelder, J.A. (1989). *Generalized linear models* (2nd edn). Chapman and Hall, London.

McDonald, G.G. and Ayers, J.A. (1978). Some applications of the Chernoff faces. A technique for graphically representing multivariate data. In *Graphical representation of multivariate data* (ed. T.C.C. Wang). Academic Press, New York.

McKay, R.J. and Campbell, N.A. (1982*a*). Variable selection techniques in discriminant analysis. I. Description. *British Journal of Mathematical and Statistical Psychology*, **35**, 1–29.

McKay, R.J. and Cambell, N.A. (1982*b*). Variable selection techniques in discriminant analysis II Allocation. *British Journal of Mathematical and Statistical Psychology*, **35**, 30–41.

McNemar, Q. (1962). *Statistical methods for research workers* (4th edn). Oliver and Boyd, Edinburgh.

Mann, H.B. and Whitney, D.R. (1947). On a test of whether one of two random variables is stochastically larger than the other. *Annals of Mathematical Statistics*, **18**, 50–60.

Marriot, F.H.C. (1974). *The interpretation of multiple observations*. Academic Press, London.

Marsh, C. (1988). *Exploring data*. Cambridge University Press, Cambridge.

Matthews, J.N.S. (1993). A refinement to the analysis of serial measures using summary measures. *Statistics in Medicine*, **12**, 27–37.

Matthews, J.N.S., Altman, D.G., Campbell, M.J. and Royston, P. (1990). Analysis of serial measurements in medical research. *British Medical Journal*, **300**, 230–5.

Maxwell, S.E. and Delaney, H.D. (1990). *Designing experiments and analysing data*. Wadsworth, Belmont, California.

Meddis, R. (1984). *Statistics using ranks*. Blackwell Scientific, Oxford.

Mehta, C.R. and Patel, N.R. (1983). A network algorithm for performing Fisher's exact test in $r \times c$ contingency tables. *Journal of the American Statistical Association*, **78**, 427–34.

Milligan, G.W. and Cooper, M.C. (1985). An examination of procedures for determining the number of clusters in a data set. *Psychometrika*, **50**, 159–79.

Nelder, J.A. (1977). A reformulation of linear models. *Journal of the Royal Statistical Society, Series A*, **140**, 48–63.

Nelder, J.A. and Wedderburn, R.W.M. (1972). Generalized linear models. *Journal of the Royal Statistical Society, Series A*, **155**, 370–84.

Novince, L. (1977). The contribution of cognitive restructuring to the effectiveness of behavior rehearsal in modifying social inhibition in females. Unpublished doctoral dissertation, University of Cincinatti.

Oakes, M. (1986). *Statistical inference: A commentary for the social and behavioural sciences*. Wiley, Chichester.

Paykel, E.S. and Rassaby, E. (1978). Classification of suicide attempters by cluster analysis. *British Journal of Psychiatry*, **133**, 45–52.

Pike, J. (1974). Craters on Earth, Moon and Mars. Multivariate classification and mode of origin. *Earth and Planetary Science Letters*, **22**, 245.

Rawlings, J.O. (1988). *Applied regression analysis*, Wadsworth and Brooks, Pacific Grove, CA.

Robertson, C. (1991). Computationally intensive statistics. In *New developments in statistics for psychology and the social sciences* (ed. P. Lovie and A.D. Lovie), pp. 49–80. BPS Books and Routledge, London.

Rosenthal, R. and Rosnow, R.L. (1985). *Contrast analysis*. Cambridge University Press, Cambridge.

Rothkopf, E.Z. (1957). A measure of stimulus similarity and errors in some paired associate learning tasks. *Journal of Experimental Psychology*, **53**, 94–101.

Schmid, C.F. (1954). *Handbook of graphic presentation*. Ronald Press, New York.

Schouten, H.J.A. (1985). Statistical measurement of interobserver agreement. Unpublished Doctoral Dissertation, Erasmus University, Rotterdam.

Schuman, H. and Kalton, G. (1985). Survey methods. In *Handbook of social psychology* (ed. G. Lindzey and E. Aronson) (3rd edn), Vol. 1, p. 635. Addison-Wesley, Reading, MA.

Shapiro, S.S. and Wilk, M.B. (1965). An analysis of variance test for normality (complete samples). *Biometrika*, **52**, 591–611.

Singer, B. (1979). Distribution-free methods for non-parametric problems: a classified and selected bibliography. *British Journal of Mathematical and Statistical Psychology*, **32**, 1–60.

Spearman, C. (1904). General intelligence, objectively determined and measured. *American Journal of Psychology*, **15**, 201–93.

Spicer, C.C., Lawrence, G.J. and Southall, D.P. (1987). Statistical analysis of heart rates in subsequent victims of sudden infant death syndrome. *Statistics in Medicine*, **6**, 159–66.

Sprent, P. (1993) *Quick statistics*. Penguin, Harmondsworth.

Stevens, J. (1992). *Applied multivariate statistics for the social sciences*. Lawrence Erlbaum, Hillsdale, NJ.

Thurstone, L.L. (1947). *Multiple factor analysis*. University of Chicago Press.

Tufte, E.R. (1983). *The visual display of quantitative information*. Graphics Press, Cheshire, CT.

Venables, W.N. and Ripley, B.D. (1994). *Modern applied statistics with S-Plus*. Springer-Verlag, New York.

Vetter, B.M. (1980). Working women scientists and engineers. *Science*, **207**, 28–34.

Wang, P.C. and Lake, G.E. (1978). Application of graphical multivariate techniques in policy sciences. In *Graphical representation of multivariate data* (ed. P.C. Wang). Academic Press, New York.

Westland, K.B. and Kurland, L.T. (1953). Studies on multiple sclerosis in Winnipeg, Manitoba and New Orleans, Louisiana. *American Journal of Hygiene*, **57**, 380–96.

Wetherill, G.B. (1982). *Elementary statistical methods* (3rd edn). Chapman and Hall, London.

Wheaton, B. Muthen, B., Alwin, D. and Dummes, G. (1977). Assessing reliability and stability in panel models. In *Sociological methodology* (ed. D.R. Hase) pp. 84–136. Jossey Bass, San Francisco, CA.

Wilcoxon, F. (1945). Individual comparisons by ranking methods. *Biometrics*, **1**, 80–3.

Williams, K. (1976). The failure of Pearson's goodness of fit statistic. *Statistician*, **25**, 49.

Wilkinson, L. (1992). Graphical displays. *Statistical Methods in Medical Research*, **1**, 3–25.

Winer, B.J. (1971). *Statistical principles in experimental design* (2nd edn). McGraw-Hill, New York.

Wright, S. (1934). The method of path coefficients. *Annals of Mathematical Statistics*, **5**, 161–215.

Zeeman, E.C. (1976). Catastrophe theory. *Scientific American*, **234**, 67.

Index